Social Capital

Social Capital

Critical Perspectives

EDITED BY

Stephen Baron

John Field

and

Tom Schuller

OXFORD
UNIVERSITY PRESS

OXFORD
UNIVERSITY PRESS

Great Clarendon Street, Oxford OX2 6DP

Oxford University Press is a department of the University of Oxford.
It furthers the University's objective of excellence in research, scholarship,
and education by publishing worldwide in

Oxford New York

Athens Auckland Bangkok Bogotá Buenos Aires Calcutta
Cape Town Chennai Dar es Salaam Delhi Florence Hong Kong Istanbul
Karachi Kuala Lumpur Madrid Melbourne Mexico City Mumbai
Nairobi Paris São Paulo Shanghai Singapore Taipei Tokyo Toronto Warsaw

and associated companies in Berlin Ibadan

Oxford is a registered trade mark of Oxford University Press
in the UK and in certain other countries

Published in the United States
by Oxford University Press Inc., New York

© the various contributors 2000

The moral rights of the author have been asserted

Database right Oxford University Press (maker)

First published 2000

British Library Cataloguing in Publication Data
Data available

Library of Congress Cataloging in Publication Data
Data available

ISBN 0–19–829713–0
ISBN 0–19–924367–0 (pbk)

1 3 5 7 9 10 8 6 4 2

Typeset by Hope Services (Abingdon) Ltd.
Printed in Great Britain
on acid-free paper by
T.J. International
Padstow, Cornwall

PREFACE

This volume has its origins in 1998 in research carried out as part of the Economic and Social Council's *Learning Society Programme* which ran from 1995 to 2000. Field and Schuller were jointly running one project on comparative patterns of participation in continuing education, Baron another on the meaning of the Learning Society for adults with learning difficulties; Field was in Northern Ireland at the time, and Baron and Schuller in Scotland. During the course of the research both research teams became aware of the purchase which the concept of social capital offered for their work despite its not being part of the original design. These origins explain both the leaning towards educational issues and the distinctive geographical balance of the UK contributions.

This original focus was widened, and the book formed, by a systematic search of the literature and of the editors' networks to identify authors who were using the concept of social capital in innovative ways across a variety of disciplinary and institutional settings. The volume gained momentum from a seminar organised through the good offices of Simon Szreter at St John's College, Cambridge, in May 1999, which was attended by some 60 people from similarly wide backgrounds. This enabled most of the contributors to meet face to face—and build social capital—and the seminar benefited from the stimulating, self-effacing, presence of Robert Putnam.

The wide range of research reported in this book reflects the attraction of the concept of social capital to authors with very differing concerns and theoretical perspectives: from the history of Scottish civil society to AIDS prevention programmes in South Africa; from seeing social capital as providing the ideological coherence for the 'third way' to seeing it as a Trojan horse by which neoclassical economics can subsume all social life into the equations of utility maximization. Two consequences for the book flow from the meteoric rise of the concept in recent years: it is subtitled *Critical Perspectives* out of a sense that the initial wave of enthusiasm now needs to be tempered by a sympathetic but critical moment of reflection; and each contribution is structured by a common set of questions, specified in the first chapter, about the value of the concept.

Our contributors have been uncomplaining in their responses to our repeated requests for revisions. We would like to thank them, along with others who provided secretarial and other assistance: Anne Currie, Mary Cheesewright and Elaine Kitteringham. The production of the book has benefited immensely from the patience and support of Dominic Byatt and the attention to detail of Michael James of Oxford University Press.

Stephen Baron
John Field
Tom Schuller

June 2000

CONTENTS

Contents

LIST OF FIGURES

LIST OF TABLES

LIST OF CONTRIBUTORS

Stephen Baron	Senior Lecturer in Education, University of Glasgow, Scotland
Phillip Brown	Professor of Social Research, University of Cardiff, Wales
Catherine Campbell	Associate Director, The Gender Institute, London School of Economics, University of London, England
Ralph Fevre	Professor of Social Research, University of Cardiff, Wales
John Field	Professor of Lifelong Learning, University of Warwick, England
Ben Fine	Professor of Economics, School of African and Oriental Studies, University of London, England
Francis Green	Professor of Economics, University of Kent, England
Hugh Lauder	Professor of Education and Political Economy, University of Bath, England
Jon Lauglo	Senior Education Expert, Sub-Saharan Department, World Bank, Washington, USA
Peter Loizos	Professor of Anthropology, London School of Economics, University of London, England
Alex MacGillivray	Deputy Director, New Economics Foundation, London, England
William Maloney	Reader in Politics and International Relations, University of Aberdeen, Scotland
Peter Maskell	Professor of Economics, Copenhagen Business School, Denmark
Pamela Munn	Professor of Curriculum Research, University of Edinburgh, Scotland
Lindsay Paterson	Professor of Educational Policy, University of Edinburgh, Scotland
Tom Schuller	Professor of Lifelong Learning, Birkbeck College, University of London
Graham Smith	Lecturer in Politics, University of Strathclyde, Scotland
Gerry Stoker	Professor of Government, University of Strathclyde, Scotland
Simon Szreter	Fellow of St. John's College and Lecturer in History, University of Cambridge
Perry Walker	Co-ordinator of the Centre for Participation, New Economics Foundation, London

1

Social Capital: A Review and Critique

TOM SCHULLER, STEPHEN BARON, AND JOHN FIELD

Introduction

SOCIAL capital—broadly, social networks, the reciprocities that arise from them, and the value of these for achieving mutual goals—has become an influential concept in debating and understanding the modern world. It features in much scholarly discourse, across a variety of disciplines; it also reverberates through the politics of the centre-left, as well as in new thinking about international economic development and social renewal. An idea that draws attention to the importance of social relationships and values such as trust in shaping broader attitudes and behaviour is clearly highly attractive to many people. It has also attracted its critics. Much of the current debate about social capital has been partial and mono-disciplinary. This collection offers a sympathetic, critical approach to the analysis of social capital. It is made up of contributions from a range of different contexts—though with a primary focus on education—written by an international group of authors from a variety of disciplinary and policy backgrounds.

The concept has an immediate intuitive appeal, but where did it spring from? There are three kinds of conceptual genealogy by which the origins of social capital might be mapped. The first limits itself to those writings which use the term explicitly; its scope is then defined by what emerges when 'social capital' is entered into the search engines available to us. The second takes the key elements, such as trust or networks, and reviews the literature relating to these. The third, most extensive, kind would include all the theories which seem to be related in some way to social capital, even though they make no explicit reference to the concept itself.

We adopt a mix of all three strategies in this introductory chapter. In the 'Seminal Perspectives', we present an analysis of the way the concept of social capital has been developed in its explicit form, focusing primarily on three authors who have generally been credited with introducing it to the theoretical debate: Pierre Bourdieu, James Coleman, and Robert Putnam. We offer an interpretation of why the concept has come so rapidly to the fore in recent

Thanks for comments on an earlier draft go to Jon Lauglo, Peter Loizos, and Lindsay Paterson.

years: primarily, we suggest, because of a growing concern to revalorize social relationships in political discourse; to reintroduce a normative dimension into sociological analysis; to develop concepts which reflect the complexity and inter-relatedness of the real world. Second, in 'Trust and Networks', we select texts addressing the two terms which have, overwhelmingly, been taken as central to definitions of social capital. We use these to illustrate how the concept has been used implicitly as well as explicitly in a range of contexts and disciplines. We conclude this section with a brief overview of key points from three extensive accounts of the intellectual origins of social capital

Next, in 'The Resistible Rise of Social Capital?', we review critical responses elicited by the use of social capital in a variety of analyses. We deal here with its definitional diversity and suggested over-versatility; the problems it poses for rigorous measurement; the charge of circularity; and lastly with the criticism that it opens the way for dangerous forms of normative control. In the final section, 'Conspectus', we provide the common framework for the chapters that follow. In these, our contributors, leading writers from academic, policy and practitioner backgrounds, assess the importance of social capital both for their particular area of concern and more generally. We ask about the analytical productivity of the concept; how far it can be applied empirically; whether it can deal with issues of conflict, social exclusion and power; and what its social and political implications might be. Our goal has been to offer not a synthesis of all the different strands in the social capital debate, but a platform for further debate. The contributions offer a wide range of responses, from the sceptical to the enthusiastic. In our view the answers are generally positive to most of the questions, but we conclude by giving pride of place to the heuristic potential of social capital—its capacity to open up issues rather than to provide definitive answers—and that is the tenor of the introduction as a whole.

Seminal Perspectives: Bourdieu, Coleman, and Putnam

There have been various attempts to pinpoint the first use of 'social capital' (see MacGillivray and Walker, this volume). A little known work titled *Housing and Social Capital*, published in 1957 by the Royal Commission on Canada's Economic Prospects, predates most of the more cited œuvres. The authors define social capital in terms of 'schools and universities, churches and related buildings, hospitals, roads and streets, airports, sewer and water systems, and other buildings and installations appertaining to public institutions and departments of government' (Dube, Howes, and McQueen 1957: 1–2). Social capital, in this formulation, is the public physical infrastructure of a nation and is marginal to current concerns, but Dube and colleagues foreshadow some aspects of more recent debates:

One might argue that it is the industrial component of capital which is ancillary to the social, rather than the other way around. Industry and industrial organization are, after all, primarily a means to an end. But social capital and its associated institutions are both this and more. They relate, in part, to what is meant by civilization in the highest sense; they are worth having in themselves; they justify industry even as they facilitate it. (Dube, Howes, and McQueen 1957: 3)

Sewer systems may not be everyone's idea of the highest form of civilization, but this has the seeds of something very fruitful. Means-ends relations remain a central but under-explored issue in the social capital debate. However, having laid out its terms the report then quite reasonably turned its attention to the practical matter of housing policy; we now turn to the theorizing which has launched the current interest in social capital.

Pierre Bourdieu

The recent interest in the concept of social capital can in part be traced to the early work of Pierre Bourdieu. Throughout the late 1960s and early 1970s Bourdieu produced a series of studies seeking to establish culture as a dynamic and creative, but also a structured, phenomenon. The concept of 'social capital' only gradually emerged from Bourdieu's interest in the social space, initially as a metaphor linked with a galaxy of other forms of 'capital'. Only latterly did Bourdieu develop the metaphor into a defined concept with a specified relationship with other defined concepts. However, we need first to trace something of its pre-history.

In 1968 Bourdieu introduced the concept of the 'habitus', 'a system of more or less well assimilated and more or less transposable schemes of thought' (Bourdieu 1991a: 5) as a means of linking subjectivity with structure without reducing either to the other. In 1970 the highly influential *Reproduction* (Bourdieu and Passeron 1977) developed this by offering a theory of how cultural reproduction fosters the social reproduction of the relations between groups and classes. The central but curiously ill-defined explanatory gambit of this text is the use of the concept of 'capital'. Different forms of capital appear through the book, each without proper definition: economic capital (implicitly), cultural capital, linguistic capital, scholastic capital, social capital. Cultural capital is the most developed of these, being used to explain how the cultural 'judgement' of the dominant group is presented as universal and selectively endowed, allowing it to legitimize its domination.

Despite the apparently marginal appearance of social capital in *Reproduction*, this text established the framework within which Bourdieu's concept was to develop. It also displayed some of the theoretical and operational difficulties that his concept of social capital was to inherit. The use of the 'capital' signals the intention of addressing differential resources of power, and of linking an analysis of the cultural to that of the economic. Although titled a theory of 'symbolic violence', *Reproduction* strangely lacks a sense of struggle: the various forms of dominant capital are presented as simply dominant without account of the subordinated forms of capital, how they resist dominant capitals and how they come actively to be subordinated. The practical import of Bourdieu's early work is to present the cultural judgement of the dominant as *the* cultural capital, subordinated groups as lacunae. This tends to reproduce, in the theory, the power relation which it is itself criticizing.

In *Reproduction* the use of the 'capital'—across its proliferation of forms—varies between the realist and the metaphorical: for most of the text the concept seems to refer to claims about real, stored quantities of money, language, cultural knowledge, credentials, and so on, while in other parts of the text it acts more as a general metaphor for power or social advantage. The contrast between sophisticated theoretical claims and weak empirical data is stark. Mechanisms of cultural reproduction and social reproduction are operationalized through the simple crosstabulation of percentages of, for example, working/middle/upper class students by male/female by above/below twelve out of 20 in a particular test (Bourdieu and Passeron 1977: 81, Table 5). While statistical analysis later became more complex, the problem of operationalizing non-tangible 'capitals' has remained significant.

In *Distinction*, forms of capital are presented as real entities: 'the overall volume of capital, understood as the set of actually useable resources and powers—economic capital, cultural capital and also social capital' (Bourdieu 1984: 114). In this formulation 'also' is the key word as social capital effectively drops from Bourdieu's vision, being subsumed under economic and cultural capital. In *Language and Symbolic Power*, a series of essays written between 1977 and 1982 (Bourdieu 1991*b*), social capital appears along with economic capital, cultural capital, and symbolic capital as the principal fields which combine to constitute the social position of any particular person, but the inter-relation of these concepts is not explored. The elaboration of forms of capital continues in *Homo Academicus* (Bourdieu 1988), with social capital now appearing alongside yet new forms of capital such as academic capital or the capital of services rendered. Social capital, however, is also highlighted in the text in that it constitutes half of the domain from which the highly orthodox, explanatory quantitative variables are drawn (Bourdieu 1988: Table 1, Appendix 1).

The evocative use of the concept 'capital', with its promiscuous proliferation of varieties, was reined in by Bourdieu in 1983 in an essay on 'The Forms of Capital' (Bourdieu 1997). While acknowledging the primacy of economic capital in his previous work, Bourdieu had tended to stress cultural capital, with social capital a very distant third. In a subtle shift of position Bourdieu posits a unitary capital which 'can present itself in three fundamental guises' (1997: 47), economic, cultural, and social. The key theoretical question thus becomes not how different, and relatively independent, forms of capital inter-relate but how these different appearances of capital transform themselves into each other in order to maximize accumulation. Social capital—at last—is defined as 'the aggregate of the actual or potential resources which are linked to possession of a durable network of more or less institutionalized relationships of mutual acquaintance and recognition . . . which provides each of its members with the backing of collectively-owned capital' (Bourdieu 1997: 51).

For Bourdieu, social capital is not reducible to economic or cultural capital, nor is it independent of them, acting as a multiplier for the other two forms, while being created and maintained by the conversion of economic and cultural capital in the 'unceasing effort of sociability'. Primacy is reserved for economic capital 'at the root of all other types of capital . . . in the last analysis' (1997: 54) and as the home to which all accumulation eventually returns, but despite the primacy of the economic Bourdieu dwells heavily in his empirical and theoretical work on 'symbolic' capital.

In this sustained attempt to theorize the reproduction of class relations through cultural mechanisms Bourdieu repeatedly places social capital close to the heart of his analysis as one of the three fundamental species of capital, yet it remains curiously undeveloped. This corpus of work, however, was crucial in establishing social capital as a field of study. The use of the concept 'capital' foreshadows a non-reductionist, materialist reading of culture, while the study of the transformation of the different forms of capital promises a dynamic, holistic analysis. Much is delivered on both counts, yet the use of the concept of capital is often metaphorical rather than analytically disciplined. When applied by Bourdieu to empirical research the substantial problems of operationalizing the concept make this important theoretical corpus appear ill-founded.

In 1989 Bourdieu and James Coleman co-organized a conference on *Social Theory for a Changing Society* (Bourdieu and Coleman 1991) which, despite their both having published seminal work on social capital, scarcely addressed the issue. This surprising omission becomes more understandable once the difference of Coleman's conception is analysed. It is to this that we now turn.

James Coleman

James Coleman's work on social capital has been particularly influential in the English-speaking world. Coleman's studies of social capital derived from his interest in drawing together the insights of two separate disciplines, sociology and economics. An exponent of rational choice theory, as well as author of a number of robustly empirical studies of adolescence and schooling, by the time of his death Coleman was one of the most highly regarded of North American social theorists.

For Coleman, social capital was significant primarily as a way of understanding the relationship between educational achievement and social inequality. His empirical contribution concentrates on studies of this issue, though some of his examples refer to other arenas. Coleman's empirical work on social capital included a series of longitudinal studies of sophomores in US high schools in 1980 and 1982, designed to compare outcomes in state schools with those in Catholic schools. Finding markedly higher levels of attainment in most subjects among pupils at the Catholic high schools, Coleman also noted the higher expectations of teachers in the schools, suggesting that this was particularly beneficial for pupils coming from the least-advantaged backgrounds (Hoffer, Greeley, and Coleman 1985). Although these findings attracted controversy, Coleman's work had considerable influence over policy makers, and helped shift the terms of the schools performance debate—which risked focusing on school characteristics to the exclusion of other influences. It also inspired a series of replication studies, some of which confirmed Coleman's findings, while others drew more nuanced conclusions (for example, Stanton-Salazar and Dornbusch 1995: 130).

Coleman's use of social capital provided a *post hoc* explanation for his findings.[1] His chief contribution to the social capital debate, however, lay in his relatively straightforward sketch of the concept, which attracted widespread attention among social researchers. In what rapidly became a seminal contribution, still widely cited, Coleman drew on his earlier writings to explore relations between social capital and human capital (Coleman 1988a; reprinted in Halsey *et al.* 1997).

Coleman's starting point was a mild critique of the dominance of human capital theory over contemporary policy thinking, arguing instead that social capital had a profoundly beneficial effect on the acquisition of educational credentials. In this paper, he defined social capital as 'a particular kind of resource available to an actor', comprising a 'variety of entities' which contained two elements: 'they all consist of some aspect of social structures, and they facilitate certain actions of actors—whether persons or corporate actors— within the structure' (Coleman 1988a: 98).

Placed more clearly in the educational context, where he had developed his notion of social capital, Coleman offered the following, necessary, refinement: 'social capital is the set of resources that inhere in family relations and in community social organization and that are useful for the cognitive or social development of a child or young person' (Coleman 1994: 300).

In positing a clear causal linkage between social capital and access to resources, Coleman went somewhat beyond earlier conceptions, which tended to be circular in nature: the powerful remained powerful by virtue of their contacts with other powerful people. However, he also went further in seeking to refine the concept and locate it within a broadly neo-functionalist theoretical framework. Social relations, Coleman argued, constituted useful capital resources for actors through processes such as establishing obligations, expectations and trustworthiness, creating channels for information, and setting norms backed by efficient sanctions (Coleman 1988a: 103–4).

Coleman accepted that the resources endowed by social capital might be shaped by such matters as:

The general level of trustworthiness that leads obligations to be repaid, the actual needs that persons have for help, the existence of other sources of aid (such as government welfare services), the degree of affluence (which reduces the amount of aid needed from

---

[1] We owe this observation to Jon Lauglo.

others), cultural differences in the tendency to lend aid and ask for aid, the degree of closure of social networks, the logistics of social contracts and other factors. (1994: 306)

Moreover, Coleman believed that any given form of social capital might be
limited in its scope of application: 'like physical capital and human capital,
social capital is not completely fungible, but is fungible with respect to specific
activities. A given form of social capital that is valuable in facilitating certain
actions may be useless or even harmful in others' (1994: 302). Nevertheless, as
a general proposition Coleman claimed that social capital possessed common
features, and in particular he believed that 'social capital and human capital
are often complementary' (1994: 304).

In much of this analysis, Coleman shares marked similarities with Bourdieu,
including, strikingly, a concern for social capital as a source of educational
advantage. Coleman and Bourdieu did not acknowledge each other; while
Coleman identified a number of earlier explorations of the concept, he did not
refer to Bourdieu, even though the two collaborated with one another towards
the end of Coleman's career, as already noted. Unlike Bourdieu, however,
Coleman saw the creation of social capital as a largely unintentional process,
which he defined mainly in functional terms. For Coleman, social capital
functions precisely because it arises mainly from activities intended for other
purposes. Yet if a 'major use of the concept of social capital depends on its
being a by-product of activities engaged in for other purposes', it followed that
'there is often little or no direct investment in social capital' (Coleman 1994:
312).

Coleman's work has strongly shaped the contemporary debate. He has also
been widely criticized. In his detailed survey of recent treatments of social capital, Portes identified a number of weaknesses in Coleman's work, accusing
him of using a 'rather vague definition' that subsequently 'opened the way for
re-labelling a number of different and even contradictory processes as social
capital' (Portes 1998: 5). In particular, Portes wished to draw a clear line
between membership of social structures on the one hand—which might be
defined as social capital—and the resources acquired through such membership on the other (1998: 4). However, Portes also argued that Coleman had
overemphasized close or dense ties, to the neglect of weaker ties which might
prove more effective than dense ties in providing access to new knowledge and
resources (1998: 5).

Certainly it is the case that Coleman focused largely on such matters as kinship and neighbourhood. This arose partly from his primary interest in schooling, which meant that his empirical evidence was drawn largely from studies
of the social networks, attitudes and influences of schools on pupils rather
than on the networks of adults. Although Coleman also referred to the
strength of social capital among New York diamond traders, this was more in
the nature of an exemplar than a rigorous case study (Coleman 1994). One
result of this empirical focus was that, as well as overstating the importance of
closure and dense ties, Coleman generally treated social capital in a somewhat

unproblematic manner. Yet as Kolankiewicz and others have shown, while closure and dense ties may provide an effective defensive or coping resource, they tend to be associated with an amoral familism and clientelism that are certainly not invariably positive in their consequences (Kolankiewicz 1996).

Furthermore, Coleman's functionalism appears to be associated with a somewhat conservative and organicist concept of social capital. In one paper, Coleman has distinguished between 'primordial' forms of social organization, which are rooted in the relations established by childbirth, above all family, and 'constructed' forms of social organization, which tend to focus around a defined purpose. Locating social capital mainly within the 'primordial domain', Coleman speculates that the decline of family may entail the erosion of the 'social capital on which societal functioning has depended' (Coleman 1991: 9). This is clearly vulnerable to feminist critique, among others, not least on the ground that it takes a somewhat undifferentiated view of relationships within the family. Nor does Coleman consider how 'primordial' and 'constructed' forms of social organization can be clearly distinguished from one another; in a formulation which echoes Ferdinand Tönnies' earlier separation of *Gemeinschaft* from *Gesellschaft*, Coleman appears to be appealing to a common-sensical, and nostalgic, division which cannot withstand close scrutiny. We explore these issues in more detail in Chapter 14.

Despite these reservations, Coleman's contribution has been both influential and significant. By subjecting the concept of social capital to empirical scrutiny, he was able to develop ways of operationalizing it for research purposes. By exploring how the resources of social capital might counterbalance low levels of human and cultural capital, he was able to demonstrate tangible ways in which social capital appeared to interact with other aspects of stratification. By contrast with Bourdieu, who used social capital to denote the ways in which elite groups used their contacts to reproduce their privilege, Coleman extended the scope of the concept to encompass the social relationships of non-elite groups. Perhaps it was for these reasons that Robert Putnam, in his study of civic engagement in Italy, cited Coleman's *Foundations of Social Theory* as a central source (Putnam 1993*a*: 241). Although now overshadowed by Putnam in the wider public policy debate, Coleman has arguably still had greater influence over scholarship in the debate so far, at least in the domain of education, which primarily interests us.

Robert Putnam

As we have said, social capital is now deployed as a concept in many different fields; but currently the author whose work is cited across a wider range than any other is Robert Putnam. Above all, Putnam has popularized the concept, and can claim responsibility for its entry into mainstream political discourse.

Putnam's work to date can be divided into three parts. The seminal study was on the rather unlikely topic of regional government in Italy, titled *Making Democracy Work* (Putnam 1993*a*), in which Putnam with two colleagues set out to explore differences between regional administrations in the north and south of the country. The core of the study concentrates on 'institutional performance', the institution being regional government, with a familiar political science focus on policy processes. The study then moves on to the notion of civic community as an explanatory variable. Putnam draws explicitly on de Tocqueville for two of his four key measures, vibrancy of associational life and newspaper readership; the other two are electoral turnout and preference voting. However, it is worth pointing out, in the light of the semi-canonical status that the work has attained, that it is only very late in the book that the notion of social capital is explicitly brought in. Even then the discussion refers mainly to rotating credit associations, from Java to Nicaragua.

Putnam then transferred his attention to his native United States, and the perceived decline in civic engagement there. The title of a short piece, 'Bowling Alone' caught the imagination of many, and has become almost emblematic; it is the title of his latest, wide-ranging book (Putnam 2000). The piece boils the argument down to the example of bowling as an activity which used to be highly associational, with bowling clubs serving not just as recreational channels but as sustainers of the wider social fabric. In analyses of attitudes and behaviour, ranging from drinking coffee with neighbours to active political participation, Putnam identifies a general secular decline in levels of social capital. This trend, moreover, is depicted as occurring in spite of the contemporary rise in educational levels, which are generally positively associated with civic participation. Controversially, Putnam unambiguously identifies television as the 'villain', with Americans spending such time in front of the screen that they are not free to sustain networks of sociability. Thus, a piece in *Prospect* (1996) is titled 'Who Killed Civic America?', and the title question receives a very direct affirmative answer (see Norris 1996 for a critique).

In that piece, Putnam offers a succinct definition of social capital: 'by "social capital" I mean features of social life—networks, norms, and trust—that enable participants to act together more effectively to pursue shared objectives' (Putnam 1996: 56).

These three 'features'—networks, norms and trust—are the triad which dominates conceptual discussion. We explore in some detail in this introduction whether or not the two central terms, networks and trust, are new, or not so new, labels for notions which have long intellectual antecedence—and we explain why we do not give the same treatment to norms. It is worth pausing to examine three of the other significant terms in this compact phrase.

'Participants' suggests activity, and this is at the heart of the notion of civic life and is therefore central to social capital. We turn below to the forms of participation, and how these are to be brought together for analysis. Both the definition of what counts as civic participation and the extent to which the various forms of participation can be aggregated to allow statistical analysis to take place are major issues, for Putnam and for many others.

Second, 'more effectively' suggests an instrumental role for social capital. Building and sustaining networks, norms and trust are the means by which

common objectives are achieved; they are not the goals themselves. One criticism of Putnam is that he conflates means and ends, so that it is unclear
whether high levels of social capital constitute a desirable end-state where
people interact trustfully and morally, or a way of achieving a good society
which may be characterized in a different way. Putnam has robustly rejected
the criticism; we address the issue later when we come to consider the complexities of methodology and epistemology.

Third, Putnam refers to 'shared objectives'. This follows closely the previous
point about instrumentalism, but it has also prompted accusations of strong
communitarianism, or, more mildly, fears that this approach might lead to
reduced tolerance of deviant behaviour. There are two points at issue here. The
first is the extent of the sharing: just how far do participants all have to be
singing from the same hymn-sheet? For example, in the classic case of
Coleman's school achievements, is it necessary for parents to subscribe to the
church's beliefs, or can they, as unbelievers, nevertheless join with the church
to promote educational aspirations? The second is the question of whether it
is actually necessary for objectives to be shared, or whether it may be enough
for there to be a degree of mutual acknowledgement by participants of each
others' objectives as valid. For example, schools and employers may not actually share objectives, even in their understandings of employability, but if they
can acknowledge the validity of each others' systems and values, this may be
enough to allow social capital to develop (Schuller and Field 1999). This links
to broader debates, notably within political philosophy, on liberalism and
rational choice theory.

Putnam, like Coleman, has been criticized for functionalism and for failing to
address issues of power and conflict. He rejects this, and in recent times has
made strong claims for an intrinsic and universal link between social capital and
egalitarian policies. He is not advocating a compassionate conservatism, with
hierarchical classes peacefully bound to each other by mutual obligation.
Instead, he sees social capital as incompatible with high levels of inequality; it
is a complement, not an alternative, to egalitarian policies. He traces out extensive correlations between measures of inequality and levels of social capital
across the individual States of America (Putnam 2000; World Bank 2000: Ch. 4).

In support of this, Putnam now gives considerable emphasis to the tension
between 'bridging' and 'bonding' forms of social capital (see also Narayan
1999). Bonding social capital refers to the links between like-minded people,
or the reinforcement of homogeneity. It builds strong ties, but can also result
in higher walls excluding those who do not qualify, American college frater-
nities being a prominent example of such bonding. Bridging social capital, by
contrast, refers to the building of connections between heterogeneous groups;
these are likely to be more fragile, but more likely also to foster social inclusion. Putnam argues that there may well be trade-offs, or tensions, between
the two forms.

Putnam's definition of social capital, given above, is concise enough. More
recently, in the Alfred Marshall lectures delivered in Cambridge in 1999,

Putnam has applied Occam's razor with even greater rigour, identifying social capital directly with networks alone. This definitional parsimony, however, leaves many questions unanswered, and has opened the way for other criticisms which have been levelled at him, notably to do with the all-purpose nature of the concept (Portes 1998). However, in jettisoning 'norms', as it were, Putnam has significantly shifted his position. He now acknowledges the 'dark side' of social capital, accepting that it may have negative consequences, both externally—for society at large—and internally—for the members of the network.[2]

Putnam's latest work shifts the emphasis from trust to reciprocity.[3] Thus, he acknowledges that people may have high trust levels and yet be socially inactive or even antisocial. Conversely, people may have good reasons to be untrusting and yet make a major contribution to building social capital, for example through civic projects in areas of high criminality: 'social trust can easily generate vicious spirals (or virtuous circles), as my expectations of others' trustworthiness influences my trustworthiness, which in turn influences others' behavior.' (Putnam 2000: Ch. 1). But overall, trustworthiness 'lubricates social life'. It promotes the kinds of interaction which reinforce norms of generalized reciprocity. This generalized reciprocity is the touchstone of social capital. It is, Putnam observes, 'so fundamental to civilized life that all prominent moral codes contain some equivalent of the Golden Rule' (Putnam 2000: Ch. 1).

'Bowling Alone' is confined to the experience of the United States, but it offers an impressive historical sweep and breadth of detailed observation. Putnam traces a massive decline in social capital over the last quarter century, but the rejects the 'declensionist' label: in other words, he does not align himself with pessimistic and conservative nostalgia for better days of strong social networks. Rather, he suggests that the coming decades may—could, he challenges us to accept—see a contemporary construction of forms of association and mutuality adapted to meet the demands of the coming century, to parallel the remarkable efflorescence of the turn of the last century.

The empirical core of the book lies in the State-level analysis of social capital across the United States. Putnam remorselessly traces the correlations between high levels of social capital and all kinds of relatively desirable social conditions: lower crime rates, higher levels of economic prosperity, better levels of health and happiness, and more successful educational outcomes. The analysis turns on a central composite index of social capital, made up of 14 indicators of formal and informal community networks and social trust which are 'sufficiently inter-correlated that they appear to tap a single underlying dimension' (Putnam 2000: Ch. 16). It is worth listing these, as they typify the operational form of the concept of social capital which dominate the debate. They are:

---

[2] The most pointed criticism took the form, 'Wouldn't it have been better if Timothy McVeigh had gone bowling alone?', since McVeigh, whose bomb in Oklahoma killed 168 people, and his associates used to go bowling together.

[3] We are grateful to the author for trusting us with a pre-publication copy of the book.

(1) measures of community organizational life:
    (a) percentage served on committee of some local organization in last year;
    (b) percentage served as officer of some club or organization in last year;
    (c) civic and social organizations per 1000 population ;
    (d) mean number of club meetings attended in last year; and
    (e) mean number of group memberships;
(2) measures of engagement in public affairs:
    (a) turnout in presidential elections, 1988 and 1992; and
    (b) percentage attended public meeting on town or school affairs in last year;
(3) measures of community voluntarism:
    (a) number of non-profit organizations per 1000 population;
    (b) mean number of times worked on community project last year; and
    (c) mean number of times did volunteer work last year;
(4) measures of informal sociability:
    (a) agree that 'I spend a lot of time visiting friends'; and
    (b) mean number of times entertained at home last year;
(5) measures of social trust:
    (a) agree that 'Most people can be trusted'; and
    (b) agree that 'Most people are honest'.

Putnam's theoretical and empirical arguments have attracted criticism from within the ranks of his own discipline of political science, in part for straying from the canons of the discipline, and from other disciplines, perhaps for trespassing. Examples of both are to be found in this volume (see for example Chapters 4, 5, and 12). This may be the inevitable fate of academics who make broad claims, and who engage publicly and prominently in debates around them.

Why Now?

Bourdieu, Coleman, and Putnam approach the notion of social capital from quite different perspectives. In the case of the first two scholars, their standing does not derive directly from their discussion of social capital but from wider theoretical contributions. In the case of Bourdieu, as we have shown, his place in the debate derives more from his generation of the parallel, and perhaps competing, notion of cultural capital, and his treatment of social capital is decidedly sketchy. Coleman's was more fleshed out, but not fully so. Putnam has now taken over the baton. He has played a leading part in making the concept globally accessible and policy relevant. But whatever the allocation of conceptual paternity, the impetus provided by these scholars has been powerful; we conclude this section with some remarks on why the concept may have come so powerfully to the fore at this juncture.

A first explanation is offered by Lemann (1996), in what might semi-jokingly be called a politico-psycho-anthropological vein. He suggests that certain segments of the population, small but with significant influence because of their location in the heartland of political debate, have been subconsciously attracted to the concept of social capital because it chimes with their personal circumstances. Members of elite professional households in Boston and Washington—one the centre of intellectual, the other of political—debate in America, read about the decline of social capital in the US and have found that it resonates with their own inability to find enough time for family and non-professional social activity. From their dinner tables is the tenor of the debate fashioned (see Lasch 1991, on the narcissism of elites, for a fuller treatment of this point).

If this is speculation, there is, secondly, a more generally observable concern with the excesses of individualism. This is hardly a new concern; it is discernible over a long period in widely contrasting ideological homes: conservative, populist, religious, and even as part of radical critiques of capitalism (see for example Sennett 1998). But the economic implosion of eastern Europe and the difficulty of re-establishing civic society in most parts of the former Soviet empire, together with an increased sensitivity to perceived globalization, may have played a part in bringing it to the fore in recent times.

Entirely different, thirdly, is the notion that ideas live in cycles, and that what we are seeing is another turn of the wheel, bringing back notions from time to time in some recurrent pattern. Thus the precursor theories to which we have referred above scatter their seeds which flower periodically, though not of course with seasonal regularity, and we are seeing now some kind of recrudescence of familiar themes. This has a number of variants. One is that this cyclicity is just an abstract intellectual pattern, occurring irrespective of material circumstances. The second is that this simply is a re-branding of ideas which have never really gone away; what fluctuates is the attention paid to them.

A fourth explanation is more meaty. In this version, we are witnessing a revalorization of social relationships in political discourse, after a period of harsh dismissal of them in the face of globalized market relationships. On this reading, social capital is to be taken quite simply at face value: an attempt—though not necessarily one consciously planned by any set of individuals—to reintroduce the social dimension into capitalism. Perceptions of a rapid erosion of trust in daily relationships in multiple spheres, but notably in employment and marriage, have generated a wish to refocus attention on the quality of these relationships, and social capital has proved an attractive vehicle for bringing this about. If this explanation is accurate then it is richly ironic that Francis Fukuyama, with his 'end of history' pedigree of celebrating an assumed global victory of capitalism, should be one of social capital's most prominent exponents (1992; 1995) and, later in this volume, Ben Fine and Francis Green develop a critique such neo-liberal attempt—once more—to reduce the social to the individual.

Another explanation is the methodological equivalent of what has just been said, and is reflected in the attention paid to the inherently value-laden notion of trust. It suggests that social analysts wish to reintroduce a normative dimension into a debate dominated by bloodless technical discussions, epitomized by hyper-mathematical econometrics. If this has any plausibility there is a certain irony here too, as the regressionists are hard at work on social capital, and the World Bank may be as demanding of a tangible, quantified and relatively immediate return on social capital as it is of return on any other investment. The centrality of networks to social capital indeed poses a challenge to the dominance of linear models of social analysis (Abbott 1988). In short, social capital opens up the way for different approaches to modelling social relations, which address some of the moral and technical complexities of their protean character.

Finally, it may be that the world of policy analysis is catching up with the inter-relatedness of the world. It has been commonplace to call for better policy coordination, and for inter-sectoral approaches. But 'coordination' implies the kind of top-down and mechanistic approach which is at odds with the dynamic fluidity of social and economic life. Interaction and complexity are the hallmarks of the world as we experience it, even if it does not appear so on the charts of bureaucrats or in the models of analysts. Social capital offers a purchase on such interaction, but not an unrealistic promise of holding it still. This is why in our conclusion we stress the heuristic value as its strongest merit.

Having analysed the seminal contributions of Bourdieu, Coleman, and Putnam and asked some questions about why their seeds should have sprouted so prolifically in recent years, we turn now to an analysis of work on the two key terms definitive of social capital, trust and networks.

Trust and Networks

Across the diverse social capital literature, trust and networks are taken to be two key component terms of the concept. Other terms, such a norms or obligations, are mentioned almost as frequently; but these concepts are so general, and their use so often rhetorical, that their development and application in social theory and research cannot properly be encompassed, even in summary form. Even for the two terms which we have chosen, our analysis is necessarily highly selective, with the aim of providing insights into the reach of the terms rather than a comprehensive survey and critique.

In reviewing each of these terms we will focus mainly on the work of two writers, one of whom makes the connection between the particular term and the concept of social capital explicit, whilst the other provides a major statement of position on the particular term before the concept of social capital became popular. For trust we will review the work of Francis Fukuyama on the social virtues, the link between trust, social capital and national economic success (Fukuyama 1995); we will also review the 1970s work on institutionalized trust by the industrial sociologist Alan Fox (1974). For networks we will review the work of Ronald Burt which differentiates types of network in terms of their social capital value derived from their structural locations (Burt 1992; 1997; 1998); we will also review the classic work of Elizabeth Bott (1957) on social networks which was seminal in establishing the concept in Britain.

Trust

The notion of trust lends itself to all kinds of philosophical and political debate, with a puzzling interaction between institutions and individuals. As Gambetta observes, in his Foreword to a collection of essays by major scholars from a range of social sciences:

The importance of trust pervades the most diverse situations where co-operation is at one and the same time a vital and a fragile commodity: from marriage to economic development, from buying a second-hand car to international affairs, from the minutiae of social life to the continuation of life on earth. But this very pervasiveness seems to have generated less analysis than paralysis: in the social sciences the importance of trust is often acknowledged but seldom examined, and scholars tend to mention it in passing, to allude to it as a fundamental ingredient or lubricant, an unavoidable dimension of social interaction, only to move on to deal with less intractable matters. (Gambetta 1988: ii)

And in his contribution Luhman endorses this: 'trust has never been a topic of mainstream sociology. Neither classical authors nor modern sociologists use the term in a theoretical context. For this reason the elaboration of theoretical frameworks, one of the main sources of conceptual clarification, has been relatively neglected' (Luhman 1988: 94).

Dasgupta (2000: 329) picks up on Luhman's distinctions. He confirms the neglect in his own field of economics, argues that 'trust is riddled with external economies' and goes on: 'It is not easy to model the link between personal, group and institutional reputation. However, the link needs to be studied if we are to understand the idea of social capital' (Dasgupta 2000: 333). He concludes his discussion by observing that 'trust and a reputation for trustworthiness are rather like knowledge; they are valuable both intrinsically and instrumentally' (2000: 334). The overlap between intrinsic and instrumental is a key characteristic of social capital, as we discuss below, but it is time to turn to one of the most extended treatments of trust in relation to social capital.

Trust as the End of History: Fukuyama   It is perhaps in the work of Francis Fukuyama that trust is assigned the greatest status in terms of understanding, and forming, economic and social order. The roots of this lie in Fukuyama's best-seller, *The End of History and the Last Man* (1992). In the aftermath of the collapse of eastern bloc regimes, and with Reaganomics and Thatcherism apparently triumphantly dismantling the postwar welfare states, this perspective celebrated the arrival of humankind at its final form of society: 'liberal democracy is the only legitimate ideology left in the world', 'an "end of history" in the Marxist-Hegelian sense of History as a broad evolution of human societies towards a final goal' (Fukuyama 1995: 3). With no competing macro-economic systems to market capitalism, and with the competitive advantages of location or technological innovation being rapidly diminished through globalization, Fukuyama seeks to explain the relative success of national economies in terms of culture. Circumstances favouring success, he suggests, are found among communities 'formed not on the basis of explicit rules and regulation but out of a set of ethical habits and reciprocal moral obligations internalized by each of the community's members' (1995: 9).

Fukuyama takes this 'end of history' as not only having arrived but as having found its Hegel: himself. The postwar visions of social engineering 'the great society', are assumed no longer to be realistic or desirable goals and 'virtually all serious observers understand that liberal political and economic institutions depend on a healthy and dynamic civil society for their vitality' (1995: 4). The field of social capital is thus elevated to being *the* crucial factor, forging the only viable forms of economy and polity.

Fukuyama claims that 'a nation's well-being, as well as its ability to compete, is conditioned by a single, pervasive, cultural characteristic: the level of trust inherent in the society' and this depends on 'the crucible of trust', social capital (1995: 7, 33). He goes on to distinguish between societies characterized by high trust or low trust and, consequently, between forms of solidaristic organization which are 'older, economically harmful or inefficient' and those which are 'wealth creating' (1995: 159). Trust is defined as 'the expectation that arises within a community of regular, honest, and co-operative behaviour, based on commonly shared norms, on the part of other members of the community . . . these communities do not require extensive contractual and legal regulation of their relations because prior moral consensus gives members of the group a basis for mutual trust' (1995: 26). Examples of high-trust societies for Fukuyama are Japan, Germany and the United States characterized by the development of large-scale corporations out of family firms through the medium of 'rich and complex civil society' (1995: 130). Low-trust societies are those of China, Italy and France, the first two characterized by the restriction of trust, and thus enterprise, to the 'family'; the latter by the destruction of a rich civil society by a centralizing state. The test criterion for distinguishing between high- and low-trust, and between inefficient and efficient, forms of solidarity is in each case 'economic progress', necessarily unanalysed as it is assumed to be the universal of human societies.

Japan is hailed as the contemporary nation with the most appropriate form of 'spontaneous sociability' (1995: 159). The lean manufacturing of Mr Ono of Toyota Corporation, where 'each worker has a cord at his workstation by which he can bring the entire assembly line to a halt if he sees a problem', is presented as the model of 'high trust workplace' where the role of the worker is 'not to manipulate a simple operation on a complex machine, as in Adam Smith's pin factory, but to contribute their judgement to help run the production line as a whole' (1995: 258–9). As capitalism moves towards more flexible forms of accumulation, so the protocol based forms of labour discipline appropriate to Fordist organized capitalism become inhibitive (Lash and Urry 1993). Worker discretion becomes increasingly central to the smooth running of production and a new form of discipline is required, a form which is internalized and self-maintaining. 'Trust' between workers and managers, with the shared goal of efficient production, replaces the 'rule book'.

With only one economic and political system thought viable, Fukuyama is thus enabled to restrict his conceptual field to fine-tuning heaven: the basic structures of—a certain self-image of—the United States of America are taken as universal, with the only problems remaining being to ensure maximum conformity of human factors to this inevitable moral and economic order. Fukuyama thus envisages an untrammelled capitalism seeking 'friction-free economies' (1995: 149) in which the primacy of profit is not questioned by a trusted and trusting workforce, dedicated to the enterprise.

Trust in Industrial Sociology: Alan Fox   The work of Fukuyama on 'trust' has been covered in much of the literature on social capital. One author whose work is highly germane but who has to our knowledge not previously figured in the debate is the British industrial sociologist Alan Fox. His work, *Beyond Contract: Work, Power and Trust Relations* (1974), does not seem to have been picked up, in spite of the fact that it offers a far-reaching application of trust to the central sphere of employment in capitalist societies. We give him space here partly because of this, but also because his critical analysis encapsulates many of the issues raised in the social capital debate.

Fox's work offers three major perspectives. First, he concentrates on what he calls 'institutionalized trust'. He acknowledges that trust can be thought of in purely personal terms, but focuses on the notion that trust and distrust 'are embodied in the rules, roles and relations which some men impose on, or seek to get accepted by, others' (Fox 1974: 67). Rules include both formal and informal understandings, whilst relations are construed in terms of interdependence, communication, supervision and authority. He is concerned not with personal feelings between people as individuals, but with relationships which are structured and institutionalized.

Second, central to Fox's analysis is a sense of the way high- and low-trust situations are dynamic, and usually self-reinforcing. 'The essential feature of all trust relations is their reciprocal nature. Trust tends to evoke trust, distrust to evoke distrust' (Fox 1974: 66). This reciprocation, he suggests, can be measured along two dimensions: long-term to short-term, and specific to diffuse. The point of lowest trust is characterized by short-term specific reciprocation, the point of highest trust by long-term and diffuse (Fox 1974: 72). This matrix can be applied, he suggests, directly to the analysis of employment relations at different levels.

Third, Fox distinguishes between vertical and lateral trust. These may be in tension with each other, for example where high levels of lateral trust take the form of worker solidarity in opposition to management. High vertical and low lateral trust comes with ideologies of competitive individualism, with highly differentiated levels of individual reward. Fox's view of employment relations is one of inherent conflict; as a result he observes that 'those who enjoy high-trust relations both vertically and laterally are exceptionally favoured' (Fox 1974: 79).

Fox applies this to industrial contexts, but the general relevance of his ana-lytical framework to the discussion of social capital is striking. The focus on institutionalized relations challenges those analyses which rely on individual level data, most prominently in the form of personal responses to questions about trust. He reminds us of the need to build in awareness of underlying structures of power and inequality as major factors in shaping trust relations, foreshadowing the critiques of social capital offered by such commentators as Edwards and Foley (1998). The stress on the dynamics of the relationships is fundamental. In particular, it should help us avoid reliance on static cross-sectional approaches which purport to measure stocks of social capital with-out accompanying these with a sense of trajectory. The temporal dimension is essential, as Putnam's historical perspective on Italian governance makes clear. Finally, the lateral-vertical matrix addresses exactly the issues raised by the debate over whether social capital inheres in horizontal associations, or is to be found also in hierarchical relationships.

This account is enough to demonstrate both the relevance of Fox's approach to the social capital debate and, conversely, the relevance of social capital—even though the term is not used explicitly by Fox—to employment rela-tions—even though Fox concentrates on the diminishing world of large-scale male industrial employment. The applicability is such that it is worth quoting at length his concluding remarks about a perceived lack of commitment to the exercise of discretion in work organizations:

Lack of ambition, fear of responsibility, and the absence of talent are usually offered as possible reasons but these beg questions rather than answer them. Within a society and a culture where ambition is apt to be an individualistic thrust towards personal achieve-ment, recognition, and success; where 'acceptance of responsibility' is often no more than the upward reach of the confident man who knows that his particular abilities can supply a particular demand, and where 'talent' refers to whatever abilities and aptitudes happen to be marketable within the currently prevailing economic arrangements, there need be no surprise that many fail to clear these definitional and practical hurdles, espe-cially when to them is added the inequalities of life chances which so patently inhibit or frustrate aspirations. Social structures and work arrangements are, however, theoreti-cally conceivable which would invite and promote high-discretion contributions in a setting where no premium was placed on individualistic ambition and self-assertion; where men ready to offer their involvement, judgement and discretion were not deterred from doing so by the prospect of being drawn out to a fine point of 'success or 'failure'. (Fox 1974: 365)

In the contrasting work of Fukuyama and Fox 'trust' is seen as a central dynamic of the workplace and, in the case of the former, of the whole of civil society. Both focus on trust not as a personal attribute but as a characteristic of systems. Where they diverge, dramatically, is over power and inequality.

Fukuyama, with only one socioeconomic system possible, offers a straightforward, and tautological, functionalism: differentials of power, status and reward are those 'necessary' for the system, and trust is the mechanism by which such unequal individuals unite around the shared objective of economic progress. For Fox, such inequalities militate against trust. This contrast foreshadows something of the contemporary debates about whether social capital is an essentially conservative notion built around an assumption of consensus and social unity.

Networks

Manuel Castells titles the first volume of his monumental trilogy on 'The Information Age' *The Rise of the Network Society* (Castells 1996). Towards the end of the book, he for the first time defines the concept of network as 'a set of interconnected nodes', but gives this somewhat sparse definition illustrative flesh. Nodes are, for example, stock exchange markets in financial networks; national councils of ministers in European political networks; secret landing strips, street gangs and laundering institutions in drug trafficking networks; and television systems, computers and entertainment studios in the global media networks. Networks are 'open structures, able to expand without limits, integrating new nodes as long as they share the same communication codes (for example, values or performance goals)' (Castells 1996: 470).

Across various social science literatures there is widespread agreement on the significance of networks at all levels, from corporate success on the global scale to individuals struggling to cope with daily life. Norms and information flows are seen as essential features of functioning networks, but it has proved to be hard to give a definition which is less abstract than Castells' yet which retains general application. Analyses of networks range from the anthropological and highly socially contextual to the technological and highly formal.

Social network analysis is a field with an established history and set of techniques whose central terms and concepts overlap extensively with the concerns of social capital. In an excellent account Scott (1991) traces the history of the field, starting from the founding of sociometrics, taking us through the Harvard research on cliques to the Manchester anthropologists of families and kinships built up in the mid-twentieth century. Social network analysis stresses the relationships among social entities and the patterns and implications of these relationships. Its key assumptions are that actors and actions are to be viewed as interdependent rather than dependent, and that the relational ties between actors are channels for the transfer or flow of material and non-material resources. The relational types to be investigated include transactions, communications, instrumental relations, sentiment, authority/power, and kinship (Knoke and Kuklinski 1991: 177). Social network analysis therefore deals in what Scott calls relational data, 'the contacts, ties and connections, the group attachments which relate one agent to another and so cannot be reduced to the properties of the individual agents themselves' (1991: 3).

Relational data, Scott argues, are handled by network analysis, in contrast to attribute data for which discrete variable analysis is appropriate. This line of argument is clearly congruent with the position that social capital is not an attribute of individuals but a function of relationships between agents and between social institutions.

Social network analysts have debated measurement issues in terms that are highly relevant to our own concerns. Marsden (1990) provides a useful item-ization of the conceptual questions and of the measurement issues involved. Under the first, he lists: whether we address actual social relations, or those perceived by the actors involved; how to reconcile the tensions between dif-ferent timescales, between micro-level episodes and persistent patterns; how to understand the dynamics of changing relationships; how to differentiate description from analysis. On indicators, he lists as the current dimensions measured size, density, tie strength, and network range. Both of these lists could be transposed to the social capital debate almost wholesale. Social net-work analysis therefore occupies a significant place in the conceptual geneal-ogy of social capital.

Families and Social Networks: Elizabeth Bott   *Family and Social Network* by Elizabeth Bott (1957) reports on research conducted from the late 1940s until the mid-1950s with 20 families in London. The research, based at the Tavistock Institute, was conducted within a psychoanalytic frame but the work has had a lasting impact of wider intellectual debates internationally. In part, this impact is due to the commitment of the researchers to linking psy-choanalytic perspectives with theories about social systems: the family itself is conceptualized as a social system rather than as an aggregation of individuals each with their own psyches, and this social system is itself understood in terms of its place in external social systems.

Having classified families according to the dominance of segregated conju-gal roles or joint conjugal roles, Bott attempts, unsuccessfully, to explain the observed distribution of roles in terms of classic ecological variables: phase of family cycles, social class, and neighbourhood. Not only do these variables not correlate but they cannot 'uncover the mechanisms by which social class and conjugal segregation are related to each other' (Bott 1957: 58). Bott adapts the anthropological idea of 'network' to address these shortcomings: 'in a network the component external units do not make up a larger social whole; they are not surrounded by a common boundary' (1957: 58–9).

The crucial variable feature of networks for Bott is their connectedness—'the extent to which people known by a family know and meet one another independently of the family' (1957: 59)—precisely Coleman's notion of clo-sure. This generates the major interpretation: 'The more connected the net-work, the greater degree of segregation between the roles of husband and wife. The less connected the network, the smaller the degree of segregation between the roles of husband and wife' (1957: 60). For Bott this is counter-intuitive but she explains the pattern in terms of the power of a connected network to formulate and impose norms on individuals so that both husband and wife continue to depend on their network(s) for emotional satisfaction, thereby placing less emphasis on joint activities of the marriage. Conversely, the less connected a network the more husband and wife will seek satisfaction within the marriage through joint enterprises and shared conjugal roles. Bott then proceeds to explain variations in the connectedness of networks in terms of: the economic ties between members; the nature of neighbourhood; the opportunity—through male employment—to make relationships outside existing networks; physical and social mobility; personality characteristics. These she sees as more important than social class in determining the segregation of conjugal roles.

The significance of Bott's work for our current concerns lies in its translating the term 'network' from its largely descriptive use in British anthropology into an independent explanatory field in its own right. Networks, for Bott, mediate between the personal and the structural and are to be understood in their own right. In seeing the key characteristic of networks as their connectedness, and the implicitly positive consequences of loose connections, Bott foreshadows the later work of Granovetter (1985) on weak and strong ties, and Putnam's notions of bonding and bridging social capital.

Networks and Structural Holes: Ronald Burt   Probably the most prominent scholar to have made an explicit bridge between networks and social capital is Ronald Burt, stemming from his work on 'structural holes' (Burt 1997). 'The structural hole argument defines social capital in terms of the information and control advantages of being the broker in relations between people otherwise disconnected in the social structure' (Burt 1997: 340). Burt's key insight, notably in his empirical work on managers in large organizations, is that people gain advantages by exploiting informational gaps in the formal organizational structure. In particular, managers with few peers find social capital all the more valuable because it enables them to mobilize the information contained within informal networks. One of the merits of Burt's work is the way it explores the differential values of networks, and relates these to social variables such as gender. He observes from his empirical data that, for women, smaller networks are more effective than large ones, and he seeks to explain this. He concludes that the explanation lies not in the density of their networks, but in their hierarchical location. It is women with networks that connect them to senior levels in the hierarchy, as distinct from those with networks that are close but horizontal, who benefit from higher rates of promotion (Burt 1998). Clearly this kind of analysis deals with the instrumental type of relationship, and focuses on individual benefits in a way that does not sit easily with the wider civic benefits claimed for other forms of social capital; social capital as merely a career asset would have less general appeal than the wider conception. Burt's approach exemplifies a linear methodology of the kind challenged by Abbott (1988). Nevertheless, it constitutes an informative example of empirical work which distinguishes between different network types, showing that they do not function to the same ends, and vary in their impacts on different social units.

Coda: Genealogical Syntheses   In this section we have focused on two key components of social capital, of rather different kinds. In each case we have given a brief general introduction, and followed this with a very limited set of arguments presented by individual scholars who have deployed the term. We have selected these to include both uses of the terms which have been explicitly related to social capital, and cases where social capital has not formed part of the vocabulary but can be discerned as lurking within it. The aim has been to show both how social science has already embedded the main components of social capital and how by making these explicit further insights can be generated.

We conclude the section by drawing attention to three extensive and authoritative general accounts of the intellectual origins of the social capital as a concept. We offer indicative highlights rather than summaries, since it would be impossible to compress the detail coherently; readers are referred to the texts themselves for detail. Those by Alejandro Portes and Michael Woolcock are already thoroughly embedded in the debate; that by Gary Sturgess is less well-known.

Sturgess's critique of social capital sheds substantial further light on the roots which lie in political and economic thinking. It serves to highlight two important features: first, he counters the tendency to view social capital as primarily a local and economic phenomenon by pointing to its importance for the restructuring of the state. As globalization proceeds 'Leviathan' forms of hierarchical state organization are increasingly ineffective and social capital has an important role in providing 'order for free' (Sturgess 1997: 60). Second, he rejects the neo-classical vision of the market as the analytically given to which all other concepts have to be related. Markets for Sturgess are socially constructed through, in part, social capital, and thus networks and trust are analytically prior to markets.

Portes's (1998) review of the literature comes from a more directly sociological tradition. He adds two important points: first, he suggests that the distinctions between the possessors of social capital, the sources of social capital and the resources that are being claimed through the deployment of social capital are necessary to avoid tautology. Second, he develops the possible negative consequences of social capital as being the exclusion of outsiders; excessive claims of group membership; the restriction of individual autonomy; self-perpetuating opposition to the social mainstream.

Woolcock's (1998) work on social capital and economic development is important for its critique of the binary nature of much of the debate. Rather than seeing social capital as either an intrinsically negative or intrinsically positive social phenomenon, he argues that any particular form of social capital will have simultaneously benefits and disadvantages and that the balance between these will vary from context to context. He traces different patterns of social development to different formations of social capital and, particularly, to the dynamic tension between these. Following his seminal 1998 piece, Woolcock has further developed his thinking in a number of publications (for example Woolcock 2000).

These specific points are significant in themselves; but the chief rationale for listing them is to endorse the texts in which they are embedded as impressive genealogies which amply display the range of intellectual wells from which social capital is watered.

The Resistible Rise of Social Capital?

In this section we review some of the critical responses generated by the use of social capital as a conceptual tool. These cover a wide range, from the methodological to the political; but since the issues raised overlap extensively it is often inappropriate to distinguish sharply between the different types. This is inherent in the breadth and protean character of the concept, and the reader should therefore bear in mind the ways in which these categories interact with one another. For the most part our account is synthetic. We do not evaluate each of the points made under each heading and come to conclusions about their strength or validity. We do, however, offer two general conclusions.

First, in most instances the criticisms are serious ones and carry weight—for obvious reasons, we do not include arguments that seem to us trivial or simply wrong-headed. Yet the fact that they may at one level be 'valid' does not necessarily undermine the case for using the concept. This is not a matter of acknowledging that the concept has weaknesses that can be eradicated by more rigorous application, though this may of course be true in specific cases. It reflects the fact that a concept that has such breadth is bound not to be a perfect fit for all, or even many, of the cases where it is applied. This raises some quite basic epistemological questions about the nature of critical discourse and the outcomes envisaged by its participants. Is the aim to subject the concept to such rigorous examination that it either becomes discredited or else survives in fitter shape—what might be called the Darwinian view of academic debate? Or is it to make the case that it should be reserved for a more limited range of applications, or for a more narrowly defined type of analysis?

Our view is that there is scope for genuine disagreement over the nature of the concept, without the need to come to a consensus. In other words, it is perfectly possible to acknowledge the weight of certain criticisms, and yet to argue that the concept remains one that is on balance valuable. Indeed, as we explain later, our conclusion is that despite, or even because of, its problematic nature, social capital has, at this juncture, enormous potential for opening up new issues and providing fresh perspectives. This makes it important to distinguish critiques which seek to explore and develop its potential from those which imply a rejection of the concept's utility.

The second general conclusion is that many of the problems inhere not so much in social capital but in the complex and multi-faceted nature of social reality. This may appear to be a mere banality. But one of the most striking characteristics of social capital is the way that some of its weaknesses are also its strengths.

Definitional Diversity

There is a set of terms that are commonly used in the literature's definition of social capital but these are operationalized in such very different ways as to bring into question the notion of social capital as a single conceptual entity. Whilst there may be considerable debate over the precise definition and oper-ationalization of other general social science concepts, such as social class, the range of debate is in most of these cases much narrower. Ethnicity may be closer to the case of social capital than are class or gender due to its possible heterogeneity; but these variables are in any case of a different order from social capital. In the case of the other 'capitals', physical, financial and human, they appear to command a far higher degree of consensus than social capital in the way they are deployed. Human capital, in itself the most 'qualitative' of the three, is almost universally defined in terms of skills, qualifications or length of schooling. The question for social capital is whether a term that can be defined so variably has failed to attain a proper status of accepted intelligibility.

We make two points in this connection. First, the fact that other terms are not usually considered to be as definitionally problematic does not mean that they are immune to similar criticisms. Arguably, the way in which human cap-ital has been defined is partial and unsatisfactory, a result more of the data which are available to operationalize it than of its 'natural' sense (see OECD 1998), and one very significant outcome is the almost universal exclusion from human capital analyses of more informal ways of learning (see Chapter 14).

Second, we need to recognize the relative immaturity of social capital as a concept. Its very rapid proliferation has allowed a diversity of approach which may simply indicate an early stage of conceptual development, and it may well be that a few more years will see a consensus emerge that gives a more tightly stated definition—although, as the logic of our point above on human capital indicates, this consensus may not itself be unproblematic. As Mondak observes:

We face a risk that the meaning of social capital will become muddled, and I agree with the criticism that some discussions of social capital have mixed together multiple con-cepts. But the solution to these problems is for individual analysts to be as precise as pos-sible in their use of language, not for others to rule some viewpoints to be off limits. We are too early in the game for some paths of inquiry to be excluded from our sights. (Mondak 1998: 434)

Over-versatility

Social capital has aroused suspicion because of the huge range of social issues on which it has been deployed. As Portes (1998: 3) observes: 'the point is approaching at which social capital comes to be applied to so many events and in so many different contexts as to lose any distinct meaning'. In his exhaustive theoretical overview Woolcock (1998: 193–6) sorts the literature into seven substantive fields: social theory and economic development; families and youth behaviour problems; schooling and education; community life; work and organizations; democracy and governance; and general cases of problems of collective action. Similarly, the World Bank website on social capital and poverty suggests the following string of issues which 'interact with and are affected by social capital': Crime and Violence; Economics and Trade; Education; Environment; Finance; Health, Nutrition and Population; Information Technology; Poverty and Economic Development; Rural Development; Urban Development; and Water Supply and Sanitation. Fieldwork sponsored by the Bank includes studies of water management in Java and genocidal conflict in Rwanda.

Other specific examples of empirical studies include the economic performance of immigrant communities (Portes 1987); managerial incomes (Meyerson 1994; Boxman, de Graaf, and Flap 1991); health profiles at community and international levels (Kawachi *et al.* 1997; Wilkinson 1996, especially Ch. 11, 'Social Capital: Putting Humpty back together again'); and intergenerational transmission of cultural capital (Nauck 2000). To this selective and rather indigestible list can be added the contributions in this volume, which present specific applications of social capital to: the pattern of civic society over 200 years in Scotland; the historical development of the British political economy; the imperialism of economics as a discipline; sociology as a discipline; the formation of industrial districts; the maintenance of cultures by Mediterranean refugees; Norwegian immigrant educational achievement; exclusion from school in Scotland; AIDS programmes in South Africa; local regeneration in urban England; engagement in voluntary associations in Birmingham, England; the notion of collective intelligence; and informal learning and learning disability.

Can such versatility be justified, or must a concept that can be deployed in so many different contexts and at so many different levels be inherently incoherent, or alternatively trivial, as an analytical device? There are apparent parallels in the basic social variables of class, gender and ethnicity, but social capital is not defined in terms of the characteristic of individuals which enable them to be located in social structure. The more pervasive a concept is, the greater the centrifugal pressure appears to be. Can the centre hold?

Part of the diffusion inherent in current usages of social capital can be traced to an uncertainty about the status, real or metaphorical, being claimed for the 'capital'. As Arrow (2000: 4) observes:

I would urge abandonment of the metaphor of capital and the term 'social capital'. The term 'capital' implies three aspects: a) extension in time; b) deliberate sacrifice in the present for future benefit; and c) alienability. . . . It is especially b) that fails. The essence of social networks is that they are built up for reasons other than their economic value to the participants.

Similarly, in the same volume Solow (2000: 6) asks: 'Why social capital? I think it is an attempt to gain conviction from a bad analogy . . . just what is social capital a stock of?' Solow does go on to be more positive about the importance of looking at the mechanisms by which societies and groups instil norms, and therefore at the ways in which patterns of behaviour come to be entrenched. We thus have two Nobel Laureates advocating dropping the term in order to defend economists' monopoly of the concept 'capital'. On the other hand, an economist of equal distinction argues as follows:

It is premature to regard social capital in the same way as we do physical capital and the measurable forms of environmental capital. This is not a pessimistic conclusion. Before we try to measure anything, we ought to ask why we wish to measure it. I do not believe we lose anything of significance in not being able to arrive at an estimate of social capital in a country, a region, a city or wherever. The concept of social capital is useful insofar as it draws our attention to those particular institutions serving economic life that might otherwise go unnoticed. (Dasgupta 2000: 398)

As Fine and Green argue later in this volume, economists either approach social capital in an attempt to draw all areas of social life into the conceptual framework of utility maximization or reject the concept as imprecise and confounding of equations. We return to the value of social capital as a metaphor at the end of this introduction; in the meantime we maintain that the criticism of over-versatility relates more to the ways the concept has been applied than to its intrinsic quality.

Measurement Challenges

Questions of measurement take a number of forms. First, where such diversity of definition exists it is inevitable that an equivalent heterogeneity of measures is used, so the same question about coherence is posed: can the centre, even defined operationally, hold? Second is an elementary issue of validity: do the variables or factors used measure what they are supposed to measure? Within this is the question of the relative strengths of the different measures: can they be ordered in any sense, such that some are established as having stronger validity than others? To what extent are combinations of measures required, as opposed to single factors? We concentrate here on three central issues: the methodological challenges of measuring social capital; the problems of explanation across time; and the problem of aggregation of data from individual levels to social structural levels.

Appropriate Technomethodologies   This neologism (from Schuller 2000) is an analogy with the notion of appropriate technology which was developed in response to concerns about the application of First World technologies to Third World contexts. Tractors rusting in African fields because spare parts were beyond the means of indigenous farmers symbolized the application of inappropriately elaborate or expensive technologies to infrastructures which could not support them. Arguably, social capital is a prime example where social scientists deploy techniques that the quality or quantity of the data available cannot sustain.

This applies particularly to quantitative exercises that build towers of elaborate statistics on shaky foundations. We must stress that this is not a generalized attack on quantitative analyses—see Lauglo in this volume for an excellent example of such analysis. Our point is that work of this kind requires careful acknowledgement—and not only in preliminary discussion or footnotes—of limitations to the validity of the data. One particularly poor example is the use of international attitudinal survey data: single questions about trust levels are used as indices of social capital, and then linked through sophisticated regressions to very broad measures of national economic performance (Knack and Keefer 1997), with conclusions drawn to several decimal points.

We need a 'methodological deflator' which will present readers with assessments of the relationship between the precision of the results and the validity of the measures. More generally, we make the conventional, but nonetheless crucial, plea for an appropriate mixture of quantitative and qualitative approaches. A particular example is the measurement of associational life. Grossing up the numbers of organizations to which people belong tells us very little about the strength of social capital if it is not accompanied by information on two scores: what people actually do as members of an association, and how far this relates to public as well as private goods. Similarly, including petition-signing as an index of political participation (P. Hall 1999) sets such a low threshold for civic activity that it becomes virtually vacuous.

We suggest that the value of social capital as a concept is not best served by pinning it tightly to the latest quantitative modelling techniques. We are at a stage in the development of the term where on balance more work needs to be done on the *validity* of the measures to be used than on putatively precise analysis. Both are necessary but we stress the question of balance and self-awareness.

Temporal Issues   If, as Putnam argues, social capital is a phenomenon of long duration, how can it be so quickly eroded? It should first be said that there is no logical requirement of temporal symmetry. In other words, it is not impossible for something which has developed incrementally over a long period to be summarily destroyed, as politicians have found to their cost in relation to their personal trustworthiness. But inherent in the analysis of such factors as trust is the difficulty of discerning movement over time, and isolating it from the range of other factors which in a long timescale is bound to be present. Putnam's work in Italy derived much of its strength from the happy timing of a major country-wide innovation, the introduction in 1970 of identical governmental structures in 20 regions. This allowed extremely neat comparisons to be made against a longer historical background, holding institutional design constant. Yet even this brings measurement problems: as Boix and Posner (1996) observe, in most cases we need to understand exactly the relative power of social capital and institutional design to make government more effective, and this is excluded when the latter is held constant.

At one level this issue comprises no more than an instance of the general difficulty of securing a long enough timescale for measuring change, combined with the problem of matching cross-sectional with longitudinal analysis. On this Braudel's distinction between different *durées* is the *locus classicus* for most disciplines. In his studies of the Mediterranean world, the French historian distinguished between short-term events (*évènements*), medium-term groupings of different forces and relationships (*conjonctures*) and the longer-term influence of great civilizations (*la longue durée*) (Braudel 1973). Yet the issue is given extra edge by the notion of social capital as something which, at least at societal level, has a particular temporal quality and this is addressed in this volume by Paterson's analysis of Scottish social capital formation and Szreter's account of the development of the British political economy

Associated with this is the difficulty of disentangling generational, lifecycle and period effects (P. Hall 1999). Again, this is an issue which applies more widely than just to social capital. Generational effects refer to differences between age cohorts that do not change over time; cohort differences are between younger and older people which tend to disappear over time; and period effects impinge on all age cohorts but only for specific periods. Coping with the interacting dynamics of these sets of effects compounds the measurement problem.

Aggregation   The sections above have sketched out the range of activities and fields to which social capital has and can be applied. These cover, evidently, a range of levels of social unit, from the individual—although the application of social capital at this level is contested—through the household, community, organization or sector, to the nation, and beyond to the global system. This is not necessarily problematic. What is difficult is the assumption sometimes made that social capital can simply be aggregated up across these levels. As Dasgupta observes of Putnam's general characterization: 'it encourages us to amalgamate incommensurable objects, namely (and in that order), beliefs, behavioural rules and such forms of capital assets as informal networks—without offering a hint as to how they are to be amalgamated' (Dasgupta 2000: 327).

This alerts us to the danger of bundling up. It looks clear that the validity of social capital depends critically on its contextualization, and it takes significantly different colours according to these different contexts (see, for example, Sandefur and Lauman 1998). Some measures may appear universal—for example, individual attitudinal responses to questions on trust (Brehm and Rahm 1997); but even here the context is crucial, since people will give different answers according to whether they take the question to refer to their immediate social surroundings or to be pitched at a much wider level. Generally, social capital will be operationalized very differently according to the focal issue. Such qualitative differences make it very hard, perhaps impossible, to aggregate up results from enquiries made at the different levels.

Contrast this with human capital. The levels of skill or qualification of any given population can in principle be standardized, across communities and, with greater difficulty, across countries, so that the stocks and flows of human capital in the north and south of the country, or in France and Taiwan (for example, Ashton and Green 1996), can be compared using something like the same yardstick. Similarly, stocks of physical capital can be estimated using measures which remain constant across levels.

This line of argument seems to reinforce the fissile nature of social capital—indeed, it does. On the other hand, reflection of this kind may prompt reflection on just how open to aggegation other capitals are. Arguably, the dynamic of differential distribution of human capital, between levels in the occupational hierarchy for example, deserves to be given greater attention for the way it affects collective working relationships. In other words, it is not only the overall amount of human capital which affects productivity or other measures of performance, but the way this is distributed and the degrees of inequality which prevail in this distribution. Posing this kind of issue is akin to the approach used by Wilkinson (1996) in his seminal cross-national epidemiological research, showing that health levels are related to material inequalities within the populations studied more than to absolute levels of material well-being. P. Hall (1999) and Edwards and Foley (1998) are amongst those who make a strong case for paying more attention to the distribution of social capital as a key aspect in the understanding of it.

In short, aggregation is a problem, especially at this stage in the concept's evolution. But that is not a reason for denying its validity at different levels.

Circularity   Is social capital itself a characteristic of a flourishing society, or a means of achieving it? Is it an instrument, an outcome or a desideratum? Social capital is criticized for its circularity, being used both as the explanatory variable, for example in relation to social cohesion, and as a descriptor for that same phenomenon:

As a property of communities and nations rather than individuals, social capital is simultaneously a cause and an effect. It leads to positive outcomes, such as economic development and less crime, and its existence is inferred from the same outcomes. Cities that are well governed and moving ahead economically do so because they have high social capital; poorer cities lack in this civic virtue. (Portes 1998: 16)

If accurate, this seems to be a fairly damning criticism of a logical kind. But one can well argue, from a different perspective, that a social capital approach is relational, and requires us to look at social phenomena from different angles simultaneously in ways that at least attempt to capture the changing nature of relationships (for example, see Somers 1994). Such relationships cannot be captured in any single line of analysis, just as physics tells us that we cannot measure speed and location at the same time. This is, emphatically, to be distinguished from a post-modernist position of unqualified relativism, and

should not be taken as a defence of each and every application of social capital. Applications which adopt a single-lensed and orthodox methodology
should be treated on that basis. But in our view several criticisms of social capital ignore crucial epistemological issues which social capital can, we repeat
can, address.

The issue is addressed by Boix and Posner, who see Putnam's account as
embodying an equilibrium concept of social capital, with virtuous and vicious
circles characterizing respectively the north and the south of Italy. They argue
that an equilibrium approach avoids the charge of circularity, whilst laying
itself open to the criticism that it skirts the issue of how these circles come into
being. Their defence in respect of circularity is to stress the complexity dimension—which, incidentally, also illustrates our point above concerning
timescales: 'to think purely in terms of linear causation is to do injustice to the
interconnectedness of these two variables [actual present cooperation and the
likelihood of future collaboration] and to fail to capture the stability of social
capital stocks over the long term' (Boix and Posner 1998: 687).

'Complexity' here is not merely a synonym for complicatedness, but refers
to the field of scientific debate which addresses the interconnectedness of systems and the problems of modelling their interaction. In either sense, social
capital engages with issues in ways which more tidy linearly-oriented concepts
tend to exclude.

Normative Control   The relationship between normative and descriptive is
one of the oldest issues in philosophical and sociological thought. 'Norms' is
a central and explicit term in both early Putnam's and Coleman's conceptualizations of social capital, but this has not pre-empted the criticism that discussion of social capital blurs the distinction between analysis and
prescription. The criticism is most clearly articulated in relation to fears about
strong forms of communitarianism being imposed in the name of fostering
social capital (see, for example, Sennett 1998: 142). Coleman's work on educational achievement implicitly stresses the benefits of robust links between
family, school and church, but whilst most of us would accept the positive
value of success in schooling, some might at the same time harbour reservations about the central involvement of organized religion in shaping the values and content of school life.

Whether or not the use of 'social capital' encourages authoritarian forms of
government or oppressively normative forms of communitarianism is a contingent matter demanding empirical observation and, where necessary, political action. As Paterson makes clear in his contribution to this volume, the
strength of Scottish civil society over the past 200 years has created and
defended a 'public life' independent, and often critical, of the state.
Oppressive communitarianism or authoritarian government does not seem to
us to be inherent in the notion, but to depend on the perspective and values
of individual commentators, which they may or may not choose to make
explicit. On the other hand, there has been a significant debate over whether

social capital is to be reserved for exclusively positive aspects of social life, such that there is a direct relationship between high levels of social capital and the quality of life. In Putnam's original formulations this was the case, and this has persisted in implicit form in much subsequent writing. However, there have been many instances of 'negative social capital', where trust levels are high within efficiently functioning networks which would nevertheless be generally regarded as socially undesirable. The usual examples given are the Mafia or racist organizations, the most pointed case being Timothy McVeigh, the Oklahoma bomber who did indeed go bowling with his associates and apparently used these occasions to develop the knowledge which led to the deaths of 168 innocent people. Putnam now acknowledges that social capital can have its 'dark side'. But as Loizos observes in his contribution to this volume, the existence of a Dr Crippen or Dr Mengele is not enough to invalidate the medical profession.

Does this mean that social capital is, as it were, unambiguously neutral? Our view is that the choice is not a binary one, between normative and analytical. The term predisposes one to the view that social capital is a social asset, but this does not rule out its potential for evil. In this, as in other respects, social capital is asymmetrical. Whether social capital can adequately address issues of conflict and exclusion is one of the questions which the authors of the chapters in this volume address, as we outline below.

Conspectus

In setting out to put this collection together, we were already very aware of the spread of intellectual, disciplinary and political interest in social capital. We had no intention of claiming a definitive account of the notion, still less of its applications. Instead, in order to achieve a measure of coherence without attempting to constrain our contributors unduly, we asked them to address a number of common questions. We left them free to decide how explicitly they would address these.[4]

The questions were:

1. Is the concept genuinely new and how does it relate to contiguous concepts in existing theoretical frameworks?
2. Is the concept analytically productive?
3. Is the concept empirically operationalizable and useful?
4. Can the concept deal adequately with issues of conflict and social exclusion and what are its political and social implications?

The first question has been extensively dealt with above. In this section we draw directly on the contributors' responses to address the other three questions. However, we do so somewhat obliquely, not trying to summarize the

---

[4] The questions were revised and confirmed at a day-long seminar in Cambridge, attended by most, though not all, of the contributors and animated by the presence of Robert Putnam.

totality of the responses under each heading, but to draw out key themes and messages. For the detail, we are happy to let the contributions speak for themselves; moreover, these have fed into the arguments presented elsewhere in this introduction, and not only into this section.

The first question prompted reflections on the intellectual origins of the term, and we have dealt with this directly above. The historical chapters, from Lindsay Paterson and Simon Szreter, are naturally the ones which offer the broadest sweeps, but it is impressive how wide is the collective range of intellectual pedigrees adduced to social capital. Many of the classic figures of social science appear—Ferguson, Smith, Marx, Durkheim, and Douglas, to name only some. Sometimes the lineage identified is surprising: for instance, the inspiration provided by John Dewey to Phillip Brown and Hugh Lauder in their presentation of the notion of collective intelligence. At other times the lineage adduced acts as a corrective to the dominant debate over social capital: Peter Maskell sees the Hegelian view of the state as more helpful for understanding a small country than the Tocquevillean view prevalent in the USA. Alex MacGillivray and Perry Walker write from a non-academic standpoint, but nevertheless describe themselves as standing on the shoulders of giant historical intellectual figures. One merit of the current debate is the way it refreshes debates with long lineages, and encourages us to return to sources which may have become rather sedimented. Paterson's piece is particularly illuminating in that he argues very strongly for the continuing relevance of social capital to our understanding of historical processes and of contemporary politics, but also points out how, like other more familiar concepts such as social class, social capital may change its colour over time in response to the current intellectual climate.

The central questions relate to the analytical status of social capital. In what senses, if any, does social capital strengthen the investigative capacity of the social sciences and their capacity to illuminate significant social issues? Our first answer to this is prevaricatory: namely, it depends on the discipline or area of research, and on the stance of the researcher. Catherine Campbell, for example, reviews some of the critiques made of social capital in its application to public health issues. In particular, she reminds us that the dynamics of community in Luton, England, are very different from those in the USA and that the conceptions of social capital necessary to apprehend them are different. Her judgement on the value of social capital is positive, specifically in the way it enables links to be made between macro and micro levels; but she reaches this judgement as a function of the deficient state of our current understanding of public health. The implication is that in areas where research has a stronger record, the judgement might be different.

Alex MacGillivray and Perry Walker not only find social capital a useful analytic tool for understanding urban regeneration at the grassroots but also find the act of researching social capital an opportunity for its reflexive creation. Several authors—for example, Phillip Brown and Hugh Lauder and Simon Szreter—pursue such a line by appealing, implicitly or explicitly, to concepts of equality such as that of Habermas (1984) as a necessary condition for the formation of social capital. Szreter (1999) argues that social capital can provide a political economy of the 'third way'.

On a very different tack, Ben Fine and Francis Green reach a clear-cut negative verdict on social capital. This derives explicitly from their fundamental disagreement with the tenets of mainstream economics, and the inability of social capital to challenge these. The key for Fine and Green is the struggle for the soul of the discipline; social capital is a palliative rather than a cure, and therefore disguises the real problem. Their piece can be contrasted with Ralph Fevre's defence of sociology, in which he sees social capital, especially in conjunction with a concept of identity, as potentially a bulwark against the imperialism of economics. Fine and Green are disciplinary dissidents; Fevre is a worried loyalist. Both see social capital as a possible Trojan horse, but looking up from different ends of the beast—and therefore with potentially different consequences. The book is multi- rather than inter- disciplinary, which means, in this instance, that there is variation rather than integration between disciplinary approaches. However, we should of course note that disciplines themselves can rarely be represented by a single position.

These positions illustrate the impossibility of separating out analytical from political significance—perhaps generally, but almost certainly in the case of social capital. Campbell makes the 'pragmatic' point that social capital is a particularly suitable instrument for pooling energies to achieve consensual definitions of what constitutes health-enhancing community resources. Peter Maskell's discussion of the role of social capital in regional and sectoral economic development is similarly grounded in pragmatism. He does not offer a judgement on the wider effects of globalization—nor was he asked to—whereas the Fine/Green position is clearly critical of these. Szreter's stance is equally broad, but differs radically in the conclusion he reaches as to the potential for social capital as an instrument of political economy; he argues that it has the potential to address fundamental issues of power and inequality.

A related theme that cuts across several of the contributions is the relationship between social capital and state institutions. The disciplinary context remains important: as one would expect, political scientists are particularly concerned with this, and William Maloney, Graham Smith and Gerry Stoker follow other disciplinary colleagues in criticizing Putnam for failing to explore this relationship adequately. Following current arguments about the nature of 'governance', they argue that the state has a substantial role in creating the conditions for social capital. Paterson's exploration of Scotland's tradition of civic society shows, conversely, how an autonomous public sphere acts as a brake on the state. Pamela Munn makes state intervention against poverty a central theme in her chapter dealing with schooling and exclusion, arguing that it is only in conjunction with such interventions that inclusive policies which rely on social capital can operate.

Social capital can thus be seen to focus attention on the dynamics of state institutions along three dimensions. First is the presumption that there should be devolution downwards of power and responsibility within the state—in European terms, subsidiarity. Second is the acknowledgement of the need to consider and foster linkages between different sectors, for instance between health and education. This is recognisable as another contemporary political motif, that of 'joined-up thinking' across policy fields. Third is the dispersion of decision-making from state organs to community and voluntary bodies. To present it in these terms, however, gives this theme a rather top-down complexion, whereas the central issue is both how the dynamics operate and what the consequences are. This is not straightforward, practically or ideologically. Thus whilst there is a presumption that low-level and participatory decision-making are to be encouraged, one criticism of social capital has been that it offers the state the opportunity to divest itself of key responsibilities, notably in the provision of welfare; Munn's chapter ends with this warning. On the other hand, Maloney and his colleagues join other commentators in pointing out that the state can play a positive role in fostering voluntary and community activity by providing decent levels of resource but also by giving a political lead in valuing such work (see also P. Hall 1999).

We have already referred to the fuzziness of the boundaries between the analytical and the normative. If we pursue this theme there is an interesting divergence of position amongst our contributors. Paterson, for example, presents social capital as a neutral vehicle: 'It can absorb ideological challenges because it itself is empty. It describes structures not content'. Peter Loizos' chapter points similarly to the way on which morally dubious groupings may be powerful creators of social capital, and warns against some of the more utopian enthusiasm for the term. But whilst none of the contributions are naïve in their support—we trust—there is an unmistakable tendency to attribute value to the creation of social capital, except where this is specifically challenged. One way of putting this is to say that the default position is for social capital to be assumed to be beneficial, but this does not prevent critical analyses of its potential for inequitable or even corrupt application.

Several contributors express anxieties about the application of the term when it comes to practical measurement. Jon Lauglo gives a sophisticated but sensitive quantitative application of the concept to explain relative scholastic achievement amongst different ethnic groups in Norway. Not all measurement is so appropriately constructed. Thus Fine and Green refer trenchantly to the arrogance of economics in assuming the superiority of its own methodologies over those of other disciplines; they go on to expose the impossibility of capturing the complexities of the circuits of social capital through the formalized mathematical models of conventional econometrics. MacGillivray and Walker argue for bottom-up approaches to measurement, so that the act of measurement does not itself have the paradoxical effect of depleting social capital. Loizos effectively makes the anthropologist's case for qualitative case-by-case analysis to ensure that content is not overpowered by form.

We posed the question whether social capital can encompass issues of conflict and power. It is easy to see why such doubts might emerge. If notions such as trust, value-sharing and common objectives lie at the heart of social capital, surely this signals a consensual or unitary view of the world, where conflict is either denied or suppressed. Fine and Green pursue such a line, arguing that the concept cannot deal with issues of class conflict. To our mind, there is little doubt that social capital can address issues of conflict at all levels, from fundamental/structural to incidental, but it is of course an empirical question as to how far this actually occurs. Conflict is not built in to the concept, and it is doubtful whether anyone could plausibly construct a kind of updated Marxist theory of social capital with over-accumulation leading to collapse—although its potential for re-invigorating debates about the nature of collective labour and fetishism should not be ignored, as Brown and Lauder remind us. But it is very clear that issues of equality and distribution are integrally linked to social capital. This has become especially evident in the more recent emphasis placed by Putnam on the tension between bridging and bonding capital, with the latter's potential for exacerbating inequalities and social division.

Conclusion: The Promise of Social Capital

We can sum up our position as follows. Social capital has several adolescent characteristics: it is neither tidy nor mature; it can be abused, analytically and politically; its future is unpredictable; but it offers much promise.

   1. One of the key merits of social capital is the way it *shifts the focus of analysis from the behaviour of individual agents to the pattern of relations between agents, social units and institutions*. This stress on relations seems to us to offer generally greater encouragement to explanations which not only go beyond the particularized individual but are more capable of dealing with the ambiguous complexities of friction, where relationships exhibit both cooperation and conflict, than approaches which assume that relations are either inherently conflictual or unitary. In short, social capital can be used in a blandly functionalist way, as with other community-linked concepts; but there is nothing inherent in the concept which promotes this perspective.

   2. Closely linked with this is the merit of social capital developing out of empirical research of diverse kinds to act as *a link between micro-, meso-, and macro-levels of analysis*. Social theory has long struggled with the problem of the relationship between individual/ small group events and social structural events. Often this has been resolved by the simple celebration of one to the exclusion, or spectacular reduction, of the other. Increasingly from the 1970s, explicit attempts to theorize the relationship, for example between 'micro to macro' or 'agency to structure', have been accompanied with quasi-Kuhnian claims of instituting a paradigm shift, if not implicit claims to being the new Durkheim. This seems to us to misunderstand the Kuhnian vision of scientific revolutions as emerging from anomalies in the routine of normal science rather than from the triumph of will of individual theorists. The rather messy origins of social capital in empirical research on schooling and inequality and

on regional government, some of the negative consequences of which we have
traced in this introduction, offer, we suspect, a better base for long-term theoretical development than self-conscious claims to establishing a new paradigm.

3. An analogous argument applies about *multi-disciplinarity and inter-
disciplinarity*. The segmentation of the social sciences into separate disciplines,
let alone their division from other sciences, is one which is frequently
deplored but rarely addressed at a level where a sustained conversation
between disciplines can be initiated. Again, self-conscious attempts at formal
synthesis seem either to strike thin air or to celebrate one version of one discipline at the cost of all others. The profusion of research on social capital
across disciplines, some of the dangers of which we have outlined above,
seems to us to offer the ground for such sustained dialogue and theoretical
development.

4. A further key merit of social capital as a concept is that it *reinserts issues
of value into the heart of social scientific discourse*. Terms such as trust, sharing
and community are central to it; these may make technicists uncomfortable,
but they directly generate questions about the assumptions concerning
human behaviour on which analysis and policy are based. In the economic
sphere, they directly challenge analyses which rely on individualized notions
of maximizing self-interest as underpinning all behaviour. They do not allow
grossly unequal rewards to be justified solely on the grounds that the market—
local or global—requires it. They raise questions about the quality of relationships in different contexts, home, workplace, locality, but also—notably in an
environmental perspective—global, which cannot be measured by conventional indicators of income or productivity. Precisely because they are value-
laden they call into question relationships between professionals and the
public; between decision-makers and other citizens; between the more and the
less powerful. The effect of this is uncertain. But the point is that a widespread
and vigorous debate about the meaning and application of social capital takes
us beyond heartfelt pleas for a stronger morality, and builds value questions
into the way debates about society are framed. This is uncomfortable for analysts and ideologues, but holds out promise for re-invigorating rather tired
debates about the place of values in social science.

5. This leads us to what we see as the key feature *social capital's heuristic
quality*. We can think of a simple triangle, with the points labelled applied
analysis, prescription, and heuristic. The first point—analysis—represents,
perhaps too simply, the positions which seek to explain a dependent variable
such as economic performance or health, though not necessarily statistically
so. Social capital, however it is conceived and operationalized, acts as some
kind of independent variable or intermediary factor. Higher levels of social
capital mean better health, less crime, and so on. The outcomes of the analyses are answers, stated with varying degrees of conviction or precision. The second point of the triangle—prescription—deals with recommendations for
action, again at different levels and with a variety of potential audiences, as to

how trust might be fostered and networks built. The third point of the triangle refers to the capacity of social capital to open up avenues for exploration, to shed new insights into the way we might conceive of issues, at whatever level of generality, and to strengthen the case for complex and multidimensional investigation.

Orthodox empirical studies, notably those sponsored by the World Bank, fall mainly in the first category. They come in two shapes (Dasgupta and Serageldin 2000: xi): case studies of particular institutions, and statistical analyses connecting key socioeconomic variables. They play an essential role in developing our understanding of the applicability and limitations of the concept; without such efforts, it would lose anchorage. Most of these are open to critique, on the intrinsic validity of their data and/or on the appropriateness of the methodology to the robustness of the information to hand. Some are so weak that they will rapidly disappear without trace; but others will at least contribute to the sedimented foundations of scientific progress, and may well offer valuable insights, practically and politically. We can acknowledge their value but still recognize that we have not yet achieved the conceptual consensus or data quality which would give them enduring status.

We are only beginning to see worked-through policy prescription, our second category, based on the notion of social capital. Much of this remains implicit—for example, in the putative benefits of enhanced levels of trust. If high levels of social capital improve economic competitiveness or social cohesion, what does this actually mean in policy terms? Clustering of innovative companies can be encouraged, to be sure, but if the success of Silicon Valley derived in part from the informal exchange in the Valley's bars and cafes is this to be replicated by sponsoring more social refreshment in other regions? If bottom-up community development generates social capital and therefore social cohesion, how should policy-makers up at the top intervene without infringing the very principle that this represents? The response might be that this is too narrow a conception of policy relevance, and to some extent we concur; we argue in our later contribution to this volume that in switching the focus from individual skills and qualifications to relationships a social capital approach requires a reorientation of policy and a greater emphasis on social infrastructure to complement individual human capital accumulation. There is no evident consensus—matching, for example, the need for investment in human capital—on the kinds of policies which flow across the board from adopting a social capital perspective, although the World Bank is exploring these actively in various corners of the world, and Putnam himself is directly addressing practical issues in a number of American cities through the Sagauro initiative.

Policy stasis is not an option. On the other hand, the sheer unpredictability generated by the pace of change destabilizes conventional policy frameworks. One of the most important aspects of this is the way in which relationships between generations are conceived of and managed. In both environmental and welfare spheres, the costs and benefits of one generation's activities impinge heavily on those of its successors—and to a more limited extent its predecessors. Even making such issues explicit runs risks, for example of increased intergenerational conflict over public expenditure, but the risks are unavoidable. If social cohesion is to be maintained and improved, we need more sophisticated and flexible instruments for assessing and evaluating the implications of our actions, and these instruments will have to accommodate widely differing timescales. Social capital brings this to the fore. This is why we believe that social capital's strongest claims are in challenging existing modes of thinking and opening up fresh paths. We concur with Edwards and Foley when they say:

The heuristic value of the social capital concept in recent debate has lain in its calling attention to crucial aspects of social relations that impinge on economic and political life and that are neither easily nor convincingly incorporated into an explanatory model based on the rational pursuit of individual self-interest. (Edwards and Foley 1998: 126)

To applaud social capital purely for its heuristic value has its dangers because it opens the way for loose thinking in the name of openness. Yet at this stage we stress this aspect in order precisely to keep the debate open, and to avoid premature forcing into binary oppositions of valid/invalid, conservative/progressive, and so on. Social capital is not something that is to be accepted or rejected on a yes/no basis. All we argue is that, on the one hand, we should avoid overblown claims for the concept as one which can override conflicts of perspective or interest and address all social issues within one framework; and, on the other hand, we should avoid premature dismissal of it as an empty vessel, or a shiny new bottle filled with non-vintage wine. Social capital perhaps matches the spirit of an uncertain, questing age.

2

Civil Society and Democratic Renewal

LINDSAY PATERSON

Introduction

IN his *Theory of Moral Sentiments* of 1759, Adam Smith wrote: 'Kindness is the parent of kindness; and if to be beloved by our brethren be the great object of our ambition, the surest way of obtaining it is by our conduct to show that we really love them' (Smith 1984 [1759]: VI, ii, 1, 19).

The argument of the present chapter is that the Scottish philosophers of the Enlightenment had a well-developed sense of mutual human obligation that is quite close to the ideas on social capital that have become popular again in academic circles recently. The purpose of making this argument is not to add a footnote to the history of the concept. It is to ask what, in fact, may happen to a political order that is founded on the principles of social capital. It is suggested, in conclusion, that the outcome of a politics based on social capital is most likely to be a tension between two versions of public—civic or state—and that a good testing ground over the next couple of decades for observing that tension will be in the conflicts and accommodations between Scottish civil society and the new Scottish parliament which was inaugurated in 1999.

Putnam most prominently and explicitly, but several others implicitly as well (Almond and Verba 1963; Gellner 1995; Habermas 1984; J. Hall 1995; S. Hall and Held 1989; Hirst 1984; Marquand 1988; Parry, Moyser, and Day 1992; Ranson and Stewart 1994; Schuller 1997), have proposed that social capital can be the basis for a renewal of democratic state institutions: 'the performance of representative government is facilitated by the social infrastructure of civic communities and by the democratic values of both officials and citizens' (Putnam 1993*a*: 182). Faced with a widespread popular suspicion of politics and the state, such enthusiasts for social capital believe that democracy can be renewed by the networks of civic morality.[1] The history of the analogous concepts from the Scottish Enlightenment, and of their application in actual political practice in Scotland, however, suggests that matters are not so simple.

This chapter has benefited from the advice of Jonathan Hearn, David McCrone, Graeme Morton, and the editors.

[1] Such propositions are discussed more fully in the introductory chapter to this volume.

Strengthened social capital is as likely to induce civic scepticism of the state as a refounding of the state in civic ideals.

This chapter is in three main parts. First, it examines some of the social thinking of the Enlightenment Scots. Second, it traces what happened to that thought in the practice of Scottish politics in the ensuing two centuries. The argument in that part is that the Enlightenment left a dual legacy. On the one hand, there was a thoroughly moral public sphere in the institutions of an autonomous civil society. On the other, there was a deep suspicion of the state which was, nevertheless, not a matter of privatism: the public civic life ensured that. Then, third, the implications of this Scottish experience are examined: commitment to a moral public sphere need not endorse a renewal of specifically state institutions at all.

In short, this chapter asks what happened to developing democracy during a sustained attempt to found a society on principles closely akin to social capital: sustained, that is, over two centuries. Of course, the nature of the state, of civil society and of social capital itself changed profoundly in this period. We return to this dilemma of interpretation at the end, because it is in fact a further, methodological, conclusion of the chapter: the problem of changing interpretations is unavoidable if the long-term implications of a social philosophy are to be investigated, and yet the long term is the only reasonable timescale in which this kind of exercise yields valid conclusions about the social impact of an entire system of thought.

Scottish Philosophy

It is not unreasonable to claim that sociology was born in Scotland, notably through the writings of Adam Ferguson (Brewer 1989a; MacRae 1969). In some respects, the inspiration for this Enlightenment thinking was in what appeared to be the political void which the Scottish philosophers faced in their own country. The central institutions of the Scottish state had been removed to London: the monarchy in 1603 and the parliament in 1707. Most of the Scottish writers were enthusiastic about this union, but they were left with a puzzle: how could a society continue to exist when it did not have the validation of its own state? That question was becoming urgent as the first pangs of industrialism began to disrupt the old social order: how could an apparently leaderless society avoid falling apart when its conventional basis was being destroyed (Davie 1991; Forbes 1966)? The danger, as writers such as Ferguson saw it, was of political apathy and privatism. The luxury which accompanies commercialism, he wrote, induces people to 'practic[e] apart, and each for himself, the several arts of personal advancement, or profit.' (Ferguson 1966 [1767]: I, viii). According to Smith, the accompanying division of society into ranks had a similar effect: admiring the rich and despising the poor is 'the great and most universal cause of the corruption of our moral sentiments' (Smith 1984 [1759]: I, iii, 3, 1).

The core of the response from these thinkers was a searching discussion of an idea that went variously under such headings as 'moral sense', 'sense of duty', 'moral faculty' and—the one on which they had settled by the early nineteenth century—'common sense' (Chastaing 1954; Grave 1960; Madden 1998; Manns 1994). The content of this varied with the names, of course, most notably depending on the extent to which it was religious; but there was a core that was continuous, based on the belief that society depends on human beings' mutual dependence. The history of that goes back through Grotius and Aquinas to Aristotle (Coplestone 1955), but it entered the Scots' discussions from English writers such as the third Earl of Shaftesbury, and principally to start with from the Irish philosopher Francis Hutcheson who was professor of moral philosophy at Glasgow University in the first half of the eighteenth century (Allan 1993; Darling 1989). His rather undeveloped notion of instinctive 'benevolence' became much more rigorous in the hands of Adam Smith, who suggested that we regulate our actions by means of an imaginary 'equitable judge', the internalization of society's norms: 'we can never survey our own sentiments and motives . . . from our own natural station. . . . We endeavour to examine our own conduct as we imagine any other fair and impartial spectator would examine it' (Smith 1984 [1759]: VI, 1, 3).

This moral sense arises from a variety of sources: instinct (Allan 1993: 223), kin and friendship (Hume 1978 [1739]: II, ii, 4; Smith 1984 [1759]: VI, ii, 1, 20), an aesthetic preference for a well-regulated social realm (Hume 1978 [1739]: III, iii, 1; Manns 1994), but, above all, a sense of mutual obligation. The most systematic development of that idea comes from David Hume, and his is also the interpretation that survives best into the much more secular world of twentieth-century politics. He is concerned to understand how we can feel under any obligation to people whom we do not hold in any particular affection, if we cannot rely on a deity to command such duty: 'I learn to do a service to another, without bearing him any real kindness, because I forsee that he will return my service, in expectation of another of the same kind, and in order to maintain the same correspondence of good offices with me or with others' (Hume 1978 [1739]: III, ii, 5).

Hume offers a parable which fixes these idea in his characteristically graphic style: 'Your corn is ripe today; mine is tomorrow. 'Tis profitable for us both, that I should labour with you today, and that you should aid me tomorrow' (Hume 1978 [1739]: III, ii, 5). Hume thus found social capital growing in bonds of obligation that owe nothing to religion, but that also counter the destructive individualism of Hobbes (Berry 1997: 160).

These bonds may be enforced by government, as a last resort. Smith argued that the ideal society was one where mutual assistance is 'reciprocally afforded from love' (Smith 1984 [1759]: II, ii, 3, 1)—a society infused with the 'public spirit' which these writers took from the ancient Greeks (Allan 1993). Society could survive in the absence of that affection if all its members saw it as being in their separate private interests to sustain a society (Smith 1984 [1759]: II, ii, 3, 2); Hume, less sanguine about human affection, believed that this instrumentality was the normal mode of social stability (Hume 1978 [1739]: III, ii, 5, 7). But society would fall apart, according to Smith, if there was not a common sense of justice (Smith 1984 [1759]: II, ii, 3, 6-9), and there was a role for government in upholding that. Hume believed this role to be the very origin of 'civil government and allegiance' (Hume 1978 [1739]: III, ii, 7).

It was also believed that public spirit could be actively created—in our terms, that social capital could be built. Both Smith and Hume argued that a sense of justice required educating (Smith 1984 [1759]: V, 2, 3; Hume 1978 [1739], III, ii, 1). Their successors, as Phillipson (1983) put it, turned this whole tradition of thought into a form of education for moral responsibility, in the so-called Common Sense School. Common sense, in turn, underpinned legitimate government. Thus Thomas Reid, regarded as the founder of the school, believed that 'there is a certain degree of [common sense] which is necessary to our being subjects of law and government, capable of managing our own affairs, and answerable for our conduct towards others' (Reid 1969 [1785], VI, ii).

He called this 'common sense' because it was about the bonds of trust and obligation that subsist among citizens: 'it is common to all men with whom we can transact business, or call to account for their conduct' (Reid 1969 [1785]: VI, ii). On the other hand, despite this connection between these social bonds and good government, the Scots also had a deep suspicion of the state. This is, in fact, their best-known legacy, the reason why Smith, especially, could have come to be so admired by New Right thinkers in the past 30 years. Coleman himself describes Smith's philosophy as straightforwardly 'individualist' (Coleman 1990a: 40–1, 300–1). Ferguson feared that luxury and stable government would induce the same apathy which commercialism threatened. Division of labour in the state, the specialization of bureaucracy, was necessary as states became larger—such as in the Union between Scotland and England. But that also threatened to empty citizenship of meaning (Ferguson 1966 [1767]: VI, v), which is why Ferguson, like many of his fellow philosophers, enthusiastically supported a continuing distinctiveness for Scottish civil society within the Union (Sher 1985). Ultimately, good government rested on vigilant citizens (Ferguson 1966 [1767]: III, vi). The institutions of the state depend for their health on a 'sense of mutual dependence' among the people (Ferguson 1966 [1767]: IV, iii).

The Enlightenment ideas are related to social capital in four ways. They are, first, quite clearly about moral obligation, a theme which is pervasive in the writing of Coleman, Putnam, and others. Portes's warning that these authors do not adequately distinguish between social capital and 'the resources acquired through it' merely reinforces the point (Portes 1998: 5): the Enlightenment Scots would not have recognized such a distinction, practically minded as they were, and responsible as they were for teaching morality to university students who could be as young as 14 (Darling 1989; Phillipson 1983). They would have seen no point in studying networks without also simultaneously studying what networks generate, and on what they are based.

The analytical confusion noted by Portes in most of the writers on social capital probably stems from the same concern with social reform.

Second, the Enlightenment ideas are about creating and maintaining a common culture. The Scottish philosophers' principle of 'common sense' is analogous to Putnam's notion that social capital enables citizens 'to act together more effectively to pursue shared objectives' (Putnam 1996: 66). Third, the idea of a common social ethics can be found both in the writing of the Scottish philosophers, for example Smith's 'equitable judge', and the social capital writers, with their interest in norms and trust. Indeed, Coleman has used almost the same parable as Hume, of farmers' helping each other to bring in the harvest (Coleman 1990a: 93–4, 307), although it has to be said that Coleman is apparently as oblivious to the precedents in Hume as he seems to have been to those in Bourdieu. And, fourth, both the Scottish philosophers and the social capital writers are interested in the active creation of the principles of social organization. In Coleman's words, 'social relationships die out if not maintained; expectations and obligations wither over time; and norms depend on regular communication' (Coleman 1990a: 321). These echo, although again unconsciously, the admiration for vigorous social virtue by Ferguson and others (Ferguson 1966 [1767]: IV, iii).

Two Legacies

The similarity of their theories to ideas of social capital suggests that the interpretation of the Scots as straightforwardly opposed to government is simplistic (Robertson 1990). The Scots philosophers' attachment to mutual obligation and other recognisable features of social capital laid the basis for a highly distinctive form of civil government in the nineteenth century, with a further legacy that persisted well into the twentieth. It was, at once, anti-statist and yet public, private and yet moral, depoliticized—in one sense of politics—and yet civic. It is to this peculiar national history that we now turn.

The key point about the Union with England was that it did not interfere with the institutional autonomy of Scottish civil society. The details of this have been fully rehearsed elsewhere (Fry 1987; Harvie 1977; Lenman 1981; McCrone 1992; Morris 1990; Morton 1999; Paterson 1994; Phillipson 1969). What matters for present purposes is the implicit theory of government which Scotland thus evolved.

On the one hand, and most important through later nineteenth-century eyes, was a highly moral public sphere. As Seligman (1992) argues, this was the main intellectual legacy which the eighteenth century Scottish thinkers gave to European thought. It became the basis of Hegel's reaction against Kant's assigning of morality to private interactions among autonomous individuals, and so also became a source of both Hegel's and Marx's reattempt to solve the tension between private and public by subsuming the whole of the public into the state as the only agency capable of generalizing morality to society as a whole (Cohen and Arato 1992: 91–116). Scottish thought on a moral public space also became the basis of Durkheim's notion of social citizenship (Seligman 1992: 123).

In practice in Scotland itself, however, the Scots' belief in a public sphere of mutual obligation paid little attention to the state. It was founded on voluntarism (Allan 1993; Berry 1997; Morton 1996; 1998*a*). It was emphatically not the state: Smith's *Wealth of Nations* became the 'foundation of Victorian liberalism', in Scotland as throughout the developed world (Robertson 1990; see also Chitnis 1986). But it was also highly moral and, despite Hume's atheism, religious, drawing from the eighteenth-century thinkers a sense of the duty of good Protestants to aid those who had fallen victim to the ravages of capitalism (Withrington 1988). The most notable and influential writer and activist along these lines was the theologian Thomas Chalmers (Harvie 1990), who in 1820 justified his evangelical campaign to develop elementary schools in urban areas on the grounds that they would re-create the social bonds which the industrial revolution had broken: 'the ties of kindliness will be multiplied between the wealthy and the labouring classes, . . . the wide and melancholy gulf of suspicion will come at length to be filled up by the attention of a soft and pleasing fellowship' (quoted by Withrington 1988: 48).

Religion, indeed, gave ideological coherence to civil society in nineteenth-century Scotland and popularized these ideas of mutual human responsibility. The key defining moment was in 1843, when about half the ministers and congregations of the dominant Church of Scotland left it (C. Brown 1987; S. Brown and Fry 1993). The issue was the autonomy of the church from state interference, a principle that had been re-asserted a year earlier in a Claim of Right—the title of which echoed a similar appeal in the late seventeenth century. The seceders then set up their own Free Church, with ministers, local churches, and local schools in around 500 of the 900 parishes; the resulting voluntary activity was seen then, and subsequently, as a nation renewing itself (Morton and Morris forthcoming), and helped to stimulate voluntary activity from the other churches as well—from older, smaller secessionist groups as well as from the Church of Scotland.

Like Adam Ferguson, these people believed that public morality could be maintained only by the vigilance of active citizens (Morton 1998*a*: 356–7). They thus developed a network of civic institutions which carried forward a sense of the public national interest even in the absence of a Scottish state. Their practice in this regard illustrates social capital in formation in response to economic change and acute social need, a process which critics of Coleman and Putnam—such as Portes (1998)—have noted as being absent from most accounts. There were straightforwardly philanthropic organizations to administer to the poor (Checkland 1980). There was elected local government, open to middle-class influence after the democratic reforms of the 1830s, which saw itself as a guardian of voluntarism against the state, and which gradually came to assume the responsibilities of a nascent welfare state, but locally not centrally (Morton 1999; Whetstone 1981). Most significant of all, there were the public boards that proliferated from the 1840s onwards, committees of bourgeois notables who administered public legislation and even public money in the same spirit as the voluntary organizations (Paterson 1994). Morton (1998*a*) has argued that these networks structured civil society by creating a space of public communication, through the professional associations, the modernizing intellectual traditions (Kidd 1993) and, from mid-century, a vigorous local press (Donaldson 1986). The role of communication was strengthened by the sheer eminence and popularity of such literary luminaries as Walter Scott, James Hogg, John Galt, and above all Robert Burns, who read Adam Smith and the common sense philosophers with enthusiasm, and embodied their notions of natural sympathy in several of his poems (Kinsley 1968: 1030, 1172).

The view of the state which came from this practice was eloquently summed up by one of its functionaries, W. L. MacKenzie, who was statutory medical adviser to the board that oversaw local government. Writing in 1914, he said:

Usually we think of the state as an organization compelling as from above, not as an organization created by ourselves from below. [But] the state is simply the name for all the institutions and mechanisms necessary to enable the citizen to realize the life of the family. If we keep steadily to that view, the State can never become an opponent of the family; it will become rather the higher plane of organization on which the inner purposes of the family can alone be realized. (quoted by Levitt 1988: xl)

The essence of the nation, in other words, lay in the individual acting locally through civic institutions (Morton 1996). The state, if it existed at all, was on sufferance. This created a most unusual style of politics. On the surface it was thoroughly and typically liberal (Fry 1987), based on liberalism's support for this separation of state from civil society. But it was also nationalistic, because the underlying philosophy, bequeathed from the previous century, equated the public and the national with the civic. Nairn has characterized this politics as aberrant, and in a historical sense it certainly was (Nairn 1977; 1997: 194–209; Morton 1998*b*). The Scots felt no need to assert a unifying or centralizing nationalism to express the nation's sense of its public self. They were happy to leave imperial matters to the distant central state in London. But, odd though it may have been, this civic politics was firmly public. It was also a genuine politics: long before late-twentieth-century feminism, Scots bourgeois men and women had discovered that power was open to negotiation in public and private spaces far removed from the state.

In thus separating the public from the state, Scotland in the nineteenth century resembled a much more famous instance, the USA. Indeed, the link is more than merely one of similarity, because the dominant political philosophy of the new American Union came from those very roots we have been examining, the Scots philosophers of the eighteenth century. At the most basic level, that was simply because Scots doctors, lawyers, ministers, teachers and other professionals emigrated to America in large numbers in the nineteenth century (Aspinwall 1984: 43; Sloan 1971). They had imbibed the ideas of the Common

Sense School of philosophy during their attendance at Scottish Universities. But the influence on American politics was more explicit than that. Several of the early leaders of American universities were Scots themselves, such as John Witherspoon, a signatory of the Declaration of Independence, who was president of Princeton University from 1768 to 1794, and 'reorganized its curriculum on Scottish lines' (Phillipson 1983: 82; Sloan 1971). Others were strongly influenced by Scottish philosophy. A prominent example is Frances Wayland, principal of Oberlin college (Madden 1968; Blau 1963). The citizen, Wayland learnt from his Scottish teachers, should 'observe the law of reciprocity in all his intercourse with others' (Wayland 1963 [1835]: 334). Echoing Hume's parable of the harvest—although also the dominant Scottish religious feeling—he argued that 'as we are all equally liable to be in need of assistance, it must be the design of our Creator that we should . . . help each other' (Wayland 1963 [1835]: 339). Consequently, like the Scots at the same time, he posited a public sphere that was prior to the state, and from which the state derived its authority: 'a government derives its authority from society, of which it is the agent; . . . society derives its authority from the compact formed by individuals' (Wayland 1963 [1835]: 329). As with the Scots, then, being sceptical about the state did not, for Wayland and his contemporaries, mean being sceptical about society (Bender 1978; Kaestle 1983; Hall and Lindblom 1999).

Wayland influenced a line of American thinkers: Asa Mahan, Emerson, Thoreau. The same dominant spirit of voluntarism can be found in the nineteenth-century USA as in Scotland, both influenced by the Scottish Enlightenment: 'if the "theory" of civil society received its fullest articulation in the Scottish Enlightenment, the historical model of this theory was seen to reside across the Atlantic' (Seligman 1992: 61).

All of this character of the nineteenth-century USA is well-known, ultimately because de Tocqueville made it the defining feature of American democracy (de Tocqueville 1835). It is well-known recently because a sort of return to de Tocqueville provides an important source for the thinking of Putnam, Coleman and others, such as Almond and Verba (1963), who have attributed the decay of American government to the decay of voluntary association and civic vigilance. For such thinkers, as we noted, apathy has to be overcome if the democratic state is to be renewed: the enemy of public democracy is privatism (Sehr 1997). In the Putnam tradition, especially as it applies further to Europe, reforming the state and reinvigorating civil society are mutually supportive.

The American case seems to make this argument persuasive. If the state is an expression of social bonds, and if the state has declined because these bonds have weakened, then one apparently obvious route to renewing the state is to strengthen the bonds. That may seem obvious provided that one rather crucial step in the philosophy which we have traced is glossed over, the step from, say, Ferguson to Hegel in which the public sphere that social capital underpins can be equated, at least in aspiration, with the state (Cohen and Arato 1992: 92). That step has become part of the taken-for-granted apparatus of modern politics, in particular of nationalist politics and also, through that, of most versions of socialism (Sassoon 1996). It is a step which Ferguson himself would not have disowned in his own time: his definition of the state tolerates it so long as it grows out of social bonds among individuals (Ferguson 1966 [1767]: I, ix; III, vi; IV, iii). But as the state began to take on a distant and centralizing form, partly aided on its way by Hegel's own advocacy, Ferguson's Scottish heirs came to believe that civil society was defined in opposition to it. It is because of this that Scottish politics in the nineteenth century can seem so odd: Scots kept the public part of Ferguson's legacy, but did not follow the route which led to the state.

But what if a public sphere does not entail a state? What if strengthened social capital may actually still be in tension with the state? What if, even, a public sphere at the beginning of the twenty-first century may increasingly require not to have a state? Further examination of the later trajectory of Scottish politics may help to give some answers.

Re-Moralizing the Scottish Public Sphere

Like most European nations in the early twentieth century, Scotland acquired a much more interventionist state as democracy expanded. Its system of welfare was increasingly distinctive administratively, despite there being no separate Scottish parliament, because it was run by an autonomous branch of the welfare bureaucracy, the Scottish Office. Founded in 1885, and achieving substantial significance in policy development from the 1930s onwards, this department grew by the 1970s to administer most areas of domestic social policy; the main exception was social security. But because there was no elected parliament until the very end of the twentieth century, the politics which surrounded the welfare bureaucracy continued to draw heavily on the civic culture of the age of liberalism.

Part of the reason for this was that many aspects of welfare actually lay in civic hands, not in the state at all. The early versions of municipal socialism grew directly out of Presbyterian philanthropy, retaining well into the twentieth century a strong current of moralizing Protestantism, and also, from the 1920s, an even stronger attachment to social Catholicism. As the influence of the Labour party grew in the 1920s, segments of so-called middle opinion detached themselves from Victorian liberalism to favour state intervention (Marwick 1964). They genuinely changed their positions: their networks, inherited from the previous era of civic autonomy, adapted to the ideas of social democracy and thereby achieved reforms that largely satisfied the social democrats themselves. The re-orientation of the networks of civil society in response to social change was another instance of social capital in formation, just as in the early years of the nineteenth century.

This was a feature of the UK welfare state in general (Addison 1975; Johnson 1972; Pierson 1991). It became normal to trust committees of professionals to run large segments of welfare. Doctors ran the health service, social workers ran the social services, teachers controlled the schools, and professors continued to be autonomous in their universities (Harvie 1981; Paterson 1994). Their socialization and qualifications may have been modernized, but their primary allegiances in civil society were no weaker than had been that of their predecessors on civic boards in the nineteenth century. The allegiance was to a profession and to a particular locality before it was to the politicians who ostensibly granted them their licence to operate. If they were close to the state, it was in order to extract resources and legislation that would benefit their own professional area: not cynically, but because they genuinely held to an ethic of the professional as the custodian of the public good. As in the nineteenth century, too, the character of the Scottish nation itself continued to be felt to lie in these professions. They and their professional associations became the embodiment of Scottish national identity, the holding of the nation in trust despite the absence of a national parliament.

The other reason why the politics of welfare drew on the legacy of a civic culture is the character of policy making in the welfare state generally. The state in the liberal democracies has rarely been able to impose its will. It has had to negotiate with representatives of civil society by bargaining that could be characterized as pluralist, corporatist, or various nuanced shades of these (Hill 1993). It has had to trust professionals to implement policies that have been agreed nationally (Hogwood and Gunn 1984). And state politicians have depended on a professional bureaucracy to tell it what society is thinking and what to do about it. In Scotland, all these ways in which the state has been forced to talk to civil society have tended to embed the state in a civic culture with autonomous roots in the distinctive history we have discussed.

No less than in the nineteenth century, moreover, did this civic culture have a moral tone. Until the middle of the century it continued to be imbued with a sense of Protestant responsibility (Maxwell 1982). It drew enthusiastically on T. H. Marshall's interpretation of Durkheim's concept of social citizenship (Marshall 1950). And, during the formative years of the welfare state up to the middle of the twentieth century, it drew from its still distinctive traditions of philosophy a continuing sense of common moral purpose (Davie 1986).

Scotland also, however, shared sufficiently in the common experience of liberal democracies to have faced something of a crisis of democracy by the 1970s. To the reforming left and to nationalists, the problem seemed obviously to be the lack of a national parliament. If, as elsewhere, the bureaucracy of the welfare state seemed to be getting out of hand in Scotland, the answer seemed to be to place it under an elected public body (for example, Dewar 1988; Mackintosh 1968). If, as in the USA, the roots of voluntarism and philanthropy seemed to be shrivelling, then the answer seemed to be a reinvigorated civic culture (for example, Church of Scotland 1989; McMillan 1997). If, as in many small nations, the integrity of Scotland's public culture seemed to be threatened, then the solution surely must be that standard embodiment of public culture, an elected parliament (Scott 1989). Above all, if the credibility of politicians in the state parliament was declining, again as in all democracies, then the solution was to create a breed that would be home-grown.

These remained minority political tendencies until the 1980s, with probably majority sympathy but no really enthusiastic support in the general population. What changed then was the character of the UK state under the New Right government of Margaret Thatcher. Reversing a century of Conservative friendliness to civil society, she undermined its authority, and, despite her rhetorical allegiance to a grossly simplified version of the individualist element in the ideas of Adam Smith, she increased the powers of the central state. This pushed majority political opinion in Scotland into favouring the setting up of a Scottish parliament. That was emphatically endorsed by referendum in 1997 shortly after the Labour Party won the 1997 UK general election. The new parliament was elected in May 1999 and in July took over full legislative responsibility for most domestic policy, in other words took over the running and direction of the former Scottish Office (Brown, McCrone, and Paterson 1998).

The campaign for this parliament acquired a highly moral tone from its roots in civil society, and so in one sense seems to draw strongly on social capital. A popular line of argument proposes that the new democratic body can re-moralize politics (Cohen 1996; Hearn 1998; Morris 1992). It thus links with a wider current of thought and practice, to which Putnam belongs, that sees civil society as a moral realm that can counter the potential amorality of excessive individualism and of a dominant state (Hearn forthcoming), in the words of Seligman (1992: 10) 'an ethical vision of social life'. In the Scottish debate, there are four identifiable strands to this.

The first comes directly from the opposition to the Thatcher Government. It was argued that Scottish civil society was maintaining a public realm, or social capital, in the face of aggressive privatization, and that a Scottish parliament could ensure that this would become permanent. This strand is the most explicit statement that the parliament is an expression of civil society.

The second is the familiar theme of making the bureaucracy of the state accountable. It is claimed that reducing political debate to technical analysis is to empty it of its moral purpose. The Scottish bureaucracy has been out of control precisely because its political rulers have come mostly from another nation—England—and have been based for most of the time 400 miles away—in London. In this analysis, part of the problem with the Scottish public realm is that it has not in fact been autonomous enough of the state bureaucracy, not sufficiently rooted in the networks of social capital. The professionals in schools, say, have paid too much attention to schools inspectors and not enough to the communities they are supposed to serve. As a result, it is claimed, there is a peculiarly Scottish angle to people's alienation from bureaucracy: the closeness of Scottish professionals to the bureaucracy has induced precisely the kind of popular alienation against which Adam Ferguson warned.

The third moral strand comes from the women's movement (Brown and Galligan 1993). Since the proportion of women among Scottish elected politicians was very low before 1997, there was an obvious equal-opportunities argument to start from. The first elections to the new parliament in fact yielded a sharp rise to 37 per cent women. But the argument has also been that having more women in politics would create a different kind of politics, less confrontational, more caring, and so forth. If the daily relationships of normal life are political, then, it is argued, we can draw lessons from these about how to reform the most supremely political of all institutions, the state: there is a personal ethic of care which can be generalized (Gilligan 1982; Mackay 1996). There have been other sources of these hopes for a 'new politics'—mostly coming from new social movements (Crowther, Martin, and Shaw 1999)—but the women's movement has been the strongest. The most visible embodiment of this in the new era will probably be the new Civic Forum, an organization which is intended to channel the debates of civil society into the proceedings of the parliament. It contains representatives of civil society, and brings together their expertise into constructive critique of legislative proposals.

The fourth and final strand of moralism comes from the immediate origins of the campaign which led to the new parliament. These are in the Constitutional Convention, dominated by the then opposition Labour Party between 1989 and 1995, in which an agreed scheme for a parliament was put together by them, other smaller parties and representatives of many institutions in civil society. The presence of these civic leaders helped create a consensus for the scheme (Paterson and Wyn Jones 1999), and helped ground the whole project in the autonomous civil society that Scotland had maintained throughout the Union. The philosophy of the Convention was laid out in a Claim of Right published in 1988 by a group of civic notables established by the cross-party Campaign for a Scottish Assembly (Edwards 1989; Morris 1992). The title, and much of the rhetoric, of that document draws from the same Presbyterian heritage that underlay Scotland's civic autonomy, the same lineage as the Claim of Right of 1842. In this tradition, secular sovereignty is divided, because only God has supreme authority. In particular, the state has literally no jurisdiction over the church, and attempts by the state to intrude on ecclesiastical autonomy is not merely an affront to civil liberties, but also a spiritual transgression (Church of Scotland 1989). The secularization of this principle, it can be argued, was another of the legacies of the Enlightenment Scots (Seligman 1992: 29): their ideas that became those of 'civil society' recognized the right to autonomy of social spaces outside state control.

That sense of civic virtue coming from an ancient civil society was reinforced in the parliament's opening ceremony on 1 July 1999. The Scottish Labour leader and First Minister in the new parliament, Donald Dewar, invoked an age-old Scottish moralism, and pointed to the inscription on the parliament's mace: 'wisdom, justice, compassion, integrity'. The whole event was a potent illustration of Durkheim's idea that ritual can forge the bonds of community—can itself both celebrate social capital and help to renew it: 'there can be no society which does not feel the need of upholding and reaffirming at regular intervals the collective sentiments and the collective ideas which make its unity and its personality' (Durkheim 1976 [1915]: 427).

So the parliament appears to have its origins firmly in the morality of the public sphere of civil society. A new branch of the state has been built up from the networks of civic life, once again, as in the early nineteenth century and in the 1930s, renewing social capital in order to respond to social and political change. The networks resisted Thatcher, felt alienated by state bureaucracy, found moral inspiration in the ideas of new social movements, and combined these in a civic campaign that eventually won clear majority support in the 1997 referendum. These immediate origins of the parliament allow us to trace its roots right back through the civic autonomy of Scotland in the Union to the thinking of the Enlightenment. If the aspirations of the reformers are realized, then it would appear that they will have found a way of overcoming Adam Ferguson's fears that large states such as the UK could alienate popular support.

Told like that, the story leading to the new parliament seems to be a straightforward version of the renewing-democracy thesis of Putnam. A new democracy is being born out of a renewed public sphere of civic engagement. For Putnam and others emerging from the American tradition, privatism is related to, even synonymous with, scepticism about politicians and the state. Anti-statism cannot be democratic or moral or public. The same is true, it would have to be said, for most theorists of the Scottish situation, such as Nairn, but now embracing most influential segments of Scottish public opinion. According to these Scottish writers, only a full return to a democratized version of state politics could rescue the Scottish public realm from the torpor to which it has been consigned, not only for the half century that Putnam would identify in most liberal democracies, but for the full three centuries of stateless absorption in the Union.

But it cannot be simply like that, because of the complex legacy which we have looked at. Scotland never lost a public space which was, moreover, highly moral. Indeed, Scotland was that public space, in stark distinction from the remote politics of the central state in London. In Scotland it has been possible to be opposed to the state and in favour of a public democracy; it has been possible to be sceptical about the state and yet not private—or, rather, to interpret 'private' as including the individual's relations with others. The current legacy of all that is an abiding deep trust in the civic institutions, a sense that it was they that maintained Scotland and that, most recently, refused to let Scotland be consumed by the alien government of Thatcher. The civic institutions may have led the process which brought the parliament into being, but they will not now wither away and let the parliament have a monopoly of public authority.

Scottish civil society is now as likely to be in tension with the actual practice of the parliament as enthusiastic supporters of it. Part of the reason for that is immediate and short term. Popular expectations of the parliament are so high that they are bound to be disappointed (Brown, McCrone, Paterson, and Surridge 1999). Now that the parliament is a reality, not a utopian dream, the reality of its being filled with yet another bunch of politicians will detract from its lustre. The first year of its operations, when it was inevitably concerned with details of working practices and financing its own operations, saw just this kind of cynicism abundantly in evidence.[2]

These problems are ephemeral, and will wane. But the other part of the reason why civil society is likely to be in tension with the parliament is deeper, and brings us back to our main theme. Civil society is autonomous, and the networks of social capital which it embodies are first of all the autonomous activities of citizens, not the state. Because these networks inherit the Enlightenment philosophy which we discussed earlier, they inherit the firm belief that a shared public and moral space is necessary to the very existence of a society but also, and quite consistently, sceptical of the state and of state-directed politics. In the absence of a separate Scottish state, the very existence of Scotland as a society has seemed to depend on the forging and maintaining of social bonds by people working through civic institutions, such as schools, universities, community centres, youth clubs, hospitals, churches, elected local government, and organizations for lobbying central government. These social forums depend on and actively recreate the sense of mutual obligation which Ferguson and Hume talked about two centuries ago and which writers from de Tocqueville to Putnam recognize as underpinning democracy. Scotland resides in these civic spaces; it does not lie, at least not yet, in the parliament. In Scotland, there would be widespread assent to Gellner's proposition that civil society can 'prevent the state from dominating and atomizing the rest of society' (Gellner 1995: 32).

Conclusions

What does this story tell us about the concept of social capital? The most obvious, but least important, point is that it suggests the concept is not new at all. Something like it was a commonplace of Scottish thinking in the eighteenth century, and underpinned the specific public life which the country constructed for itself in the Union. Scottish thought also influenced the character of civil society in the nascent USA, and so is part of the Tocquevillean golden age to which writers such as Putnam seek a return.

It is true that there is an obvious danger of anachronism in tracing a current concept to such old roots—of forgetting that social thinkers exist in a particular time, and that their ideas are shaped by their own concerns, in particular by the distinctive forms of the state and civil society which they encountered. If anything, indeed, the eighteenth-century Scots tended to be more practically involved than Enlightenment thinkers elsewhere, and therefore even more inclined to be shaped by their social context. The main point in defence

---

[2] An illustration of this tone—by no means the most strident—is found in *New Statesman*, 5 July 1999.

of the approach to intellectual origins that has been taken in this chapter is to point out that we have not simply been applying eighteenth-century ideas to the twentieth century. These ideas are used here to help explain the character of the civil society which Scotland created in the early phases of industrialization, and to help also to understand the ways in which that civil society was reformed repeatedly as the state and the economy changed over the ensuing two centuries. In the course of these various changes, the Scots also modified the dominant ideas into forms that go far beyond anything which Ferguson, Smith or Hume would recognize. That is in the nature of political philosophies. They are themselves historically specific, and eventually, through history, may be modified profoundly. There is an historical sociology of ideas as well as of social structures.

We can go further, however, in justifying the approach taken here. The mere fact of intellectual change does not tell us that drawing parallels between ideas is worthless, at least over the couple of centuries of modern industrialism which have concerned us: doing this makes at least as much sense as, say, applying our theories of social class to understanding early-nineteenth century social transformations. Hume's notion of moral obligations can be recognized around us, just as Putnam's social capital can be found in de Tocqueville's idea of early American democracy. Concepts such as moral obligation, a common culture, a unifying social ethic, and the active creation of social trust are at the core of what recent writers have meant by social capital, and can be found, it has been argued here, in thinkers such as Ferguson, Hume, Smith and Reid. Indeed, a direct line of intellectual evolution could be traced from then to now, through the development of the discipline of sociology—although a full treatment of that would require much greater space than has been available here. More to the point, there is also a direct line in popular understanding of human beings' relationship to each other. When Smith says, for example, that 'we must view ourselves not so much according to the light in which we may naturally appear to ourselves, as according to that in which we naturally appear to others' (Smith 1984 [1759]: II, ii, 2,2) he provided a template for Burns's rather more elegant desire 'to see ourselves as others see us'. The poetry of that version has then given Smith's thought a popular life in Scotland—and elsewhere—that lasts to this day.

More important than this point about precedent is the suggestion from the present analysis that these ideas not only can be readily operationalized, but also can be productive analytically. The Scots went far beyond operationalizing the concept of social capital in a theoretical sense; they actually used it as the basis of a constitution for their nation: not a written document, but the guiding philosophy of their civic institutions and their relationship to the state. The concept of social capital is productive analytically because it provides a way of understanding the Scottish history we have been surveying. We could say the same for 'social capital' as Morton says for 'civil society': 'the value of this concept . . . is that it better allows us to make sense of local political structures as well as cross-class associational activity'(Morton 1998a: 349).

Social capital working in civil society provides a theoretically well-developed counter to the classic nationalist and socialist positions that the public life of a nation requires a state.

Because the Scots had their own variegated public space, they also contained within it the usual conflicts over power which have pervaded civil society for at least two centuries. Thus the Labour movement could emerge from civil society in the 1930s with a strong inheritance from the dominant Presbyterian ethos, challenge the old structures of civic Scotland, and yet build a new Scotland that was in recognisable continuity with the old. Similar kinds of stories about civic institutions adapting to absorb conflict can be told of, for example, the period of democratic reform in the 1830s. Probably much the same is happening now with the new parliament: the civic networks will adapt to the new era, and will thus have contained a potentially more radical break with the Union. If we ask, with Portes (1998), how and when social capital is created, perhaps the answer lies in moments of sharp social conflict, where power relations are shifting, and where the outcome is not determined in advance because there is a myriad of possible new networks to be formed. Each segment of civil society is forced to choose new allies—the churches and the rising middle class in the 1830s, middle opinion and the Labour Party in the 1930s, the professional classes and the forces of Scottish nationalism in the 1980s—and thereby to create new bonds of social capital.

The heterogeneity and conflicts in civil society have been a source of significant social and political change. In recent years, some segments of civil society, notably business, have remained quite sceptical of the new parliament, while others are likely to press it to go further in the direction of social reform than the cautious Labour Party will favour. But, despite this diversity, and despite the resulting changes in the content of what civil society does as different segments gain or lose access to power, its structural foundation remains intact. Social capital is a sufficiently malleable idea to be able to fit most prevailing conditions. It can absorb ideological challenges because it itself is empty. It describes structures, not content. That is why Portes's distinction between social capital and the resources acquired through it is indeed useful (Portes 1998: 5). It is analogous to the distinction drawn by theorists of civil society between its institutions as a morally neutral network of exchange and their role as a morally respectable bulwark against amoral state power and amoral free markets (Hearn forthcoming; Keane 1998: 36–7). The moral conclusions drawn from civic networks by late-twentieth century feminists, say, might be quite different from those drawn by mid-nineteenth century bourgeois men, but the role of social networks in making morality practical is common. The word 'capital' is, then, well chosen: like money, social capital can be spent on anything—including on things that are quite revolutionary—but is a real guarantor of human exchange nonetheless.

For similar reasons, social capital is neither good nor bad in itself. It can be excluding of those who are not in the relevant networks, as Portes (1998) notes. In nineteenth-century Scotland, despite the strong moral ethos,

Catholics were barely part of accepted civil society, even middle-class women managed only a tenuous role in public life by the end of the century, and the working class had to wait until the 1940s for any undisputed access at all. In the 1980s and 1990s, as during any period of nationalist activism, the social capital of the civic networks always risked keeping some people out. But because all this has taken place in a highly pluralist society, homogeneity has never been able to last for long in Scotland. Its social capital has always been segmented. Thus the recent nationalism has insisted that it is civic not ethnic (Brown, McCrone, and Paterson 1998: Ch. 9).

Our main conclusion about the concept of social capital concerns its political implications. The histories of theory and practice which we have sketched here are intended to illustrate the working out of social capital in action. Scotland invented for itself in the eighteenth century a society based on what we can now call social capital. It was public but also opposed to the state; it identified the nation with the civic, not the political defined in a conventional, state-dominated way. Scottish thinkers' influence on the USA ensured that Scotland would resemble de Tocqueville's idea of democracy, but, unlike the USA, Scotland has been able to maintain the distinction between the public and the state because of its peculiar status as an autonomous nation within a larger Union. Being opposed to the state in the USA has recently meant being opposed to politics, and sometimes, though not always (Hall and Lindblom 1999), to the public realm itself, and countering that cynicism lies behind the political campaigning of writers such as Putnam. Being opposed to the state in Scotland has meant nothing of the sort.

So Scotland, with its new parliament, will remain a crucial test of whether social capital really does invigorate the state or simply induces greater scepticism of it. The civil society that was ultimately founded on eighteenth-century ideas of social capital, and which repeatedly renewed these ideas at crucial moments of conflict during the intervening period, has now brought into being a national public forum of a traditional sort. If that forum draws its authority from civil society, then the reforming thesis of Putnam and others will be sustained. The state really will have been renewed by founding itself in social capital. But the Scottish case is worth continuing to study because that is not inevitable. Civil society is likely to continue to command the legitimacy which it has enjoyed during the three centuries of Union. It may interpret that as being the guarantor of the ideal of the parliament, the conscience which holds the parliament's actual members to account. But civil society will do this from a position of historical and conceptual self-confidence, and will cede nothing to the new body of its own central role in the nation's public life.

3

Social Capital, the Economy, and Education in Historical Perspective

SIMON SZRETER

Introduction

SOCIAL capital is an important new concept which, when added to the established, analytical categories already used by mainstream liberal economists, holds out the promise of a much superior understanding of the way in which real, rather than theoretical, market economies, businesses, and competition function today and for the foreseeable future. It does this by explicitly incorporating, instead of excluding, the complex social, institutional and political contexts in which economic transactions actually occur. As with most important ideas in the social sciences, once recognised many precursors can be traced, such as the notion of 'social capability' in development economics, or the idea of 'civic virtue', which Machiavelli derived from the Greeks (Woolcock 1998). In the last decade or so social capital has been increasingly appearing in the work of a wide range of thinkers and investigators, an expansion in its usage across the social sciences which has almost become exponential in the last two years. At the same time there remains genuine debate and further work to be done over the meaning and validity of the concept: compare the sceptical contributions by Arrow and Solow with the positive evaluations by Krishna, Ostrom, and Dasgupta in Dasgupta and Serageldin (2000). It is clear from some of the most important contributions to this developing debate (Tarrow 1996; Woolcock 1998; Portes 1998; Foley and Edwards 1999) that part of the reason for this lies in the significant conceptual deficiencies within the work of the two most influential early disseminators of the term, the late James Coleman (1988*a*; 1990*a*), professor of sociology at the

I am grateful to the editors of this volume and to a large number of individuals for numerous improving comments on earlier drafts and presentations given at the State University of Michigan, East Lansing, Southampton University, the London Nexus conference at KCL, Oxford, and Cambridge. I can only offer apologies to those many whom the following short list omits: John Ashton, Flavio Comim, Hilary Cooper, Julian Cooper, Partha Dasgupta, David Halpern, Peter John, Robert Hinde, Tristram Hunt, Crystal Lane, Melissa Lane, Peter Robinson, Allan Schmid, Bernard Trafford, Stuart White, Peter Wilby, David Winkley, Michael Woolcock.

University of Chicago, and Robert Putnam (1993; 1995*a*; 1998*a*; Gamm and Putnam 1999), the current Dillon Professor of International Affairs at Harvard University. It therefore remains incumbent on users to commence their work by specifying their understanding of the term's meaning.

So What Is Social Capital?

It is simultaneously an economic, sociological and political concept. 'Social' and 'capital' brings together the key terms in the disciplines of sociology and political economy. A satisfactory definition therefore involves the language of both of these disciplines. Social capital flows from the endowment of mutually respecting and trusting relationships which enable a group to pursue its shared goals more effectively than would otherwise be possible. Social capital therefore depends on the *quality* of the set of *relationships* of a social group. It can never be reduced to the mere possession or attribute of an individual. It results from the communicative capacities of a group: something shared in common and in which all participate. The relationships among the participants must be uncoerced and set on a basis of formal equality and mutual respect—though they may freely choose to organize themselves with leaders and representatives and endow themselves with some form of communication or authority structure. Thus, James Coleman wrote that 'social capital . . . is embodied in the relations among persons . . . a group whose members manifest trustworthiness and place extensive trust in one another will be able to accomplish more than a comparable group lacking that trustworthiness and trust' (1990*a*: 304).

As a set of relationships of a certain quality, social capital is an intrinsically social and political phenomenon: an emergent property, in sociological terms, of institutions and group practices. It simultaneously has an economic character—explored in more detail in the next section. This can be summarily defined here, in the terms of positive economics, as the additional productive benefits to the society or economy as a whole that result from the synergy of a set of mutually trusting social relationships. It is, by definition, something that cannot be produced without these relationships. An elementary example occurs every time a citizen, instead of persevering with the independent process of trial and error, asks another citizen for directions in the street and receives time-saving help.[1]

A social group or institution which is potentially capable of generating social capital may be composed in almost any conceivable way: a neighbourhood, those in a business company, a set of companies doing business with each other, an occupational or employment association, a choral meeting, a group

---

[1] This is an example whose proverbial gender bias in its incidence raises the interesting and complex issue, not pursued here, of the gendered propensity to engage in trusting communication, on which see, for instance, the accessible Deborah Tannen (1990).

of bird watchers, the crew of a boat, a football club, a political party or its local branches, an academic institution or a school, a 'social class'—in the Marxist or Weberian senses—an ethnic group, a nation, a congregation, a religion. But it is not simply the fact of the existence of these civic institutions or voluntary associations or networks of personal contact in society which generates social capital, but their functioning in certain ways, including important 'details' of the way in which their participants communicate with each other. In Britain, certain clubs are endemically exclusionist, in terms of class, race, gender or all three; and many are also internally authoritarian and hierarchical, notoriously so with the one of the most famous of all, the Marylebone Cricket Club (MCC). Britain, the society of clubs and voluntary associations par excellence, might at first sight appear to have a claim to be the utopia of social capital; and there is certainly much potential to build upon. But it is the quality of the relationships that these associations engender among their members and in their relations with the wider society which is critical in determining whether or not they truly promote extensive social capital, carrying productive benefits to the whole of society, as opposed to sectional advantages for the favoured few who are the members. The capacity of associations not only to draw from, but also to promulgate, mutual respect and trust is of fundamental importance in assessing whether they are net generators of social capital.

Studying empirically and measuring social capital is not quickly or easily done (Woolcock 1998; Halpern 1999; Maloney, Smith, and Stoker, this volume). Social capital is an abstract property of relationships and is multidimensional. It is manifest through certain kinds of attitudes and dispositions towards fellow-citizens and civic institutions, through networks of contact and association and through participation in civic and public institutions. Empirical work which aims to measure and quantify can observe social capital, indirectly and inferentially, through examining the character and incidence of these phenomena. But ideally considerable contextual knowledge is required for unambiguous interpretation: see below where 'strong' and 'weak' ties are discussed. This has not deterred some of the leading proponents of social capital from utilizing and analyzing a range of more readily available sources of social data for many communities and for different countries. Robert Putnam's research, initially on Italy and latterly on USA, has been consistently the most impressive and innovative in this vein, though certainly not without its critics (Tarrow 1996; *Politics and Society* 1996). Putnam has, for instance, measured the density and membership of voluntary associations of different types— sports clubs, choral societies, hiking clubs—along with newspaper readership and electoral turnout of voters to assess the varying strength of 'civic participation', or social capital, in each of the different regional government areas of Italy (Putnam 1993: Ch. 4).

The intrinsic difficulty involved in developing direct measures of social capital has inevitably resulted in some confusion over its true meaning and, especially, its political implications. Two sets of misconceptions in particular need to be corrected. The first is the spurious right-wing, libertarian attempt crudely to hijack the idea of social capital to buttress undiscriminating hostility to 'the state', by arguing that the activities of the state are intrinsically inimical to the vitality of social capital because it 'crowds out' voluntary associations (Green 1994, 1995). This is a naïve simplification. As the above example of the MCC illustrates, voluntary associations are as capable of damaging as of contributing to social capital. The analysis and historical review presented below will demonstrate that in Britain the activity and the inactivity of the state have been equally capable of building or of depleting social capital.

A second important confusion is the idea that all that is required for social capital is tight-knit, 'traditional' communities. However, such communities are likely to produce only sectional, not extensive, social capital, if, indeed, any at all. Whether or not such insular face-to-face relations lead to effective interpersonal negotiation and respectful collaboration is an entirely contingent matter: the feuding and distrust of tight-knit 'hillbilly' Appalachian hamlets or the quiet, claustrophobic 'tyranny of village vexation'—Edmund Burke's aphorism on pre-industrial rural England—being equally possible alternative outcomes. Hence, Putnam's study confirmed previous research in finding that the 'traditional' village and town communities of southern Italy were mostly characterized by hierarchical and authoritarian social and political relations and an 'amoral individualism' among mutually distrustful citizens, whereas in the 'modernized' cities of the north, social and political relations were more egalitarian and associated with much more voluntary civic participation on a basis of personal freedom. Only under these latter circumstances did community foster liberty and genuine social capital in Italy (Putnam 1993a: 109–15).

The set of relationships which generate genuine, extensive social capital should therefore have two key qualities relating, respectively, to the internal and to the external relations of the institution or group in question: that they entail active participation on a basis of formal equality; and that they do not contribute to forms of social exclusionism and closure of lines of communication and fellow-feeling with other citizens (Cox 1995). On the contrary, true and extensive social capital is built from practical lessons and experience in dialogue with as wide a variety of others as possible. It follows from this that there is an important general principle of maximizing 'communicative equality', upon which such extensive social capital is premised. Thus Putnam has always emphasized that it is horizontal contacts of association between equals, rather than vertical networks which imply inequalities of power or authority—he uses the example of the Mafia in his studies of Italy—that produce true social capital in human institutions.

In recognition of these considerations Putnam follows Granovetter (1973; 1985) in emphasizing the importance of 'weak', rather than 'strong' ties, as formative of social capital. Michael Woolcock (1998) has developed this further, arguing that social capital requires a balance to be struck between 'embeddedness' and 'autonomy' in social relations. Hence, research on social capital and social exclusion in USA has found that, among the very poor living in inner city ghettos, those who have a relatively small number of intense family and neighbourhood gang ties and loyalties are too embedded and effectively locked into their poverty and lack of opportunities, whereas those with a wider pool of weaker contacts outside their immediate environment fare better (Putnam 1998a). It has long been known that the relatively mobile—socially and geographically—middle classes typically benefit from their participation in a relative abundance of networks of such weak ties. An extensive and dense range of relatively weak ties, establishing multilateral lines of communication between the maximum number of citizens, gives individuals an optimum balance between embeddedness and autonomy. This is the key sign of well-developed, extensive social capital, rather than a set of strong, intensive and binding ties, which simply divide sections of the population from each other. Another negative example would be the caste system of India, persistently one of the poorest and most unequal societies in the world. The institution of caste tends to restrain the sphere of choice and the range of 'play' that is available in communication between diverse individuals in the population. Conversely, the extent to which there are wide bridges of understanding and contact between all the various associations and institutions in civil society is now coming to be seen as an important indicator of their capacity to sponsor social capital and counter the forces of social exclusion.

Networks of association can therefore be double-edged swords. The kinds of groupings and voluntary associations which can generate social capital always also carry the potential to exclude others. As with everything in the world of human affairs, voluntary association can have either beneficial or negative effects, from the perspective of the whole society or economy. Voluntary associations exist in relative profusion wherever liberal market societies and economies function, whether we like it or not. The only question is: what kind shall there be? To recognize that such groupings, like everything else, have potential for generating both gains and losses directs our attention to the most important conclusion for politicians and economists. It is a society and economy which seeks to minimize social exclusion and which maximizes its endowment of weak ties, allied to a plethora of bridges between its different institutions, voluntary associations, businesses, and local communities, which will benefit to the greatest degree from the phenomenon of extensive social capital.

Social Capital and a New Political Economy

The issue of information is now generally recognized in economics to be a central one for understanding the way in which markets, businesses, and economies work. The concept of social capital has strong affinities with this. Its modern intellectual roots can be traced to a seminal work within the liberal economics tradition. This was Ronald Coase's extraordinary article of 1937 which asked the astoundingly obvious question, 'Why do firms exist?'. By providing a revolutionary and innovative answer Coase founded the modern field of transaction costs, the study of the critical importance of information in the functioning of economic systems (Coase 1937).

By enabling us to focus on the crucial issue of how individuals' capacities to process information are distributed across an economy, social capital makes its vital contribution to a new political economy. In particular it can show how the politics of a society and its particular mix of institutions critically influence the distribution of information-processing capacities among its citizens and so, ultimately, affect the efficiency and growth potential of the economy. Thus, James Coleman (1990a) has argued that a proper understanding of the workings of a market-oriented economy requires the recognition of four analytical categories: (1) bio-physical capital: land and the environment, more widely conceived; (2) financial capital, including appropriately valued industrial plant; (3) human capital; and (4) social capital.

From a normative economics viewpoint, social capital can be briefly defined as that general set of relationships which minimizes the transaction costs of information across the whole economy. Given the fundamental economic importance of transaction costs, social capital has equivalent productive significance to the other recognized forms of capital. Sustainable, optimal economic growth and development require giving approximately equal weight and attention to the deployment and reproduction of all four forms of capital together.

Why should information-processing be so central to the economy? It is only by interpreting relevant information that we can make a judgement of the value of anything in a market economy: information both about what the thing in question can do for us and, especially, information about what alternatives are available currently or in the near future. Anybody who has tried to buy a car knows that it is important to invest considerable time compiling information on the range of prices from different sources for all the models which satisfy your requirements of size, age, and so on before you are in a position to judge whether you are getting a reasonable deal or not. The sellers in the market do not guarantee to offer you that fair deal. This example relates to the importance of information processing in the exchange, or 'consumption', side of the economy; but it is equally, if not more, important in the production side of the economy, the focus of Coase's work.

Coase pointed out that in fact the only economic reason why such a thing as a 'firm', the most basic element in the production side of the economy, exists at all is the need to minimize the transaction costs of the information needed to make anything. By employing everybody within a firm, the owners routinize and reduce all these information costs by creating a set of 'experts'— the workers—who, in return for the security and recompense of their regular wages and salaries, all share continuously, and without having to be hired each time their input is needed, all their specialized knowledge of how best to find and process the raw materials and then sell the products at the best prices.

Thus, the problem of how to manage the costs of information lies at the very heart of the reason for an economy's organisation into firms in a market system. Those companies which can maximize their access to and control over the relevant, high-quality information for the minimum economic outlay will triumph over their competitors. Most truly successful companies, those that have become household names, have found over the years that the most effective strategy for achieving this *and for maintaining it over the long term* includes ensuring the commitment and goodwill of an experienced and trusted workforce, by offering them a good deal (Collins and Porras 1994; Kay 1993).

This insight has led a number of studies to explore the reasons for economic success and failure in these terms. In particular, one phenomenon that had always puzzled economists was the existence of what Alfred Marshall called 'industrial districts', such as, in his own time around the turn of the twentieth century, the North Staffordshire Potteries earthenware industry or the South Staffordshire Black Country making nuts, bolts, chains and springs, or Sheffield's cutlery workshops. In each case a large number of small, medium-sized and even large firms clustered together, all manufacturing similar products for decades on end without apparently driving each other out of business but, rather, prospering or declining all together. A similar phenomenon has been noted in the 1980s and 1990s with Silicon Valley in California, and with the computing and biotech 'Cambridge phenomenon' in England, and other such districts in south Germany and north-central Italy, for instance (Putnam 1993*a*: 160; Granovetter 1994; see also Maskell in this volume). It has been found that in these cases the companies exist in clusters, enjoying the benefits of 'competitive cooperation' by flexibly sharing and subcontracting with each other a pool of specialist knowledge of the state of the market and the technologies, a pool of workers and their skills, and a local environmental infrastructure of communications and social services that their industry and workforces require to work and live efficiently, but which any one firm or small number of firms could not provide on their own.

In the 1980s and 1990s it has often been the state, typically in the form of the local government administration, which has helped to organize the environment and provided the facilities and services required by these industrial clusters—and of course, the central state also provides further facilitating support of a more general kind in terms of the wider infrastructure supporting the locality in its relations with the rest of society and in maintaining confidence in the rules of the market. This is an example of what is called 'coproduction' in the social capital literature, a partnership across the public-private divide, showing that success in the global market often depends on the state nurturing its industries and companies and *vice versa*, in that the productivity of the companies then nourishes the state and society (Evans 1995). In addition to their embeddedness in a long-term mutually beneficial relationship with state agencies, the long-term interdependence of all the companies means that there is little sense in naked commercial opportunism on the part of any one company trying to profit unduly at the expense of the others, because it thereby risks consequent ostracism and breakdown of high-quality communications with the other companies in the industrial community. There are, instead, many incentives to cooperation, and there is also often a rich shared associational life among the employers and among the employees outside work in these industrial districts. Together the firms in the industrial district with their joint resources and high-quality, shared information can compete on price and quality against anything else in the rest of the world.

This is an example of the socially and economically beneficial effects flowing from social capital, and the central importance for both firms and their workers of access to high-quality information in order to make effective choices and decisions in a productive context. But information can also, of course, be used and controlled by restricted sections of the population so as to have less generally beneficial, more socially and economically divisive effects. Thus, it is the principle of the transaction costs of valuable information which explains why young traders not long out of Oxbridge or, occasionally, the famed 'barrow boys' from London's East End, are paid such enormous salaries and bonuses in the City, apparently in defiance of the conventional laws of supply and demand. There is no problem with labour supply, as many of the best graduates—and many others—are not surprisingly queuing up for these high-paying jobs. According to conventional economic theory this should exert strong downward pressure on levels of remuneration. The point is that the extremely high value of the informal information that is the primary commodity which individuals working in this market deal in makes it vital for companies to command the loyalty of the workers in whose heads the precious information-processing capacity resides. The only tool they have to discourage defection of workers with their valuable commercial expertise is to pay them sufficiently handsomely to make it too expensive to run off with their precious knowledge of how to interpret information. There is a nice irony in all this: that the conditions governing the labour market of the City itself, supposedly the paradigm 'free market', is a leading example of the fact that economic relationships in a free market are *not* determined primarily by the competitive pricing laws of supply and demand but by the more complex implications of the transaction costs of managing, deploying, and interpreting high quality, informal information.

This example of the city trader in financial services illustrates a highly significant implication of one of the most important general properties of information-processing in the market context: its fundamental asymmetry. Not all information is equally valuable. Therefore having access to and the capacity to interpret the more valuable information can be of great personal advantage to certain sections of society. The conventional wisdom of economic liberalism is that the great virtue of markets is that they obey the price laws of supply and demand and therefore there is always automatic pressure to reduce any temporary imbalances, so that no seller or buyer can establish a self-perpetuating advantage in the market leading to gross imbalances of power. But the information theory of the free market predicts, to the contrary, that its operation is actually conducive to the opposite tendencies. This follows from the combination of the two truisms, 'Time is money' and 'Knowledge is power', when applied to the asymmetry of information and its processing. As Coase realized, in order to acquire high quality information about anything of value it is necessary to invest time in the process of finding out. The quintessential virtue of social capital should be that it facilitates this, ideally, for everyone, thereby reducing all the transaction costs across the economy. In the absence of well-distributed social capital, however, it is principally the rich who benefit, differentially, from being able to reduce their transaction costs. Typically they pay others to do the information-processing for them. As a moment's reflection will confirm, in a competitive market economy the most commercially valuable individual item of information—that which can put an individual in a position to gain substantial money and power from knowing it—must be of an informal nature, rather than public or published information or formal knowledge. The firm is one example of the way in which the wealthy—the share-owners of the firm—systematically harness the value of this informal, esoteric information, by giving employment contracts to a group of specialists in a particular field of activity on the understanding that they use their several information processing powers to increase the value of the firm.

The more we create markets in everything important in our lives, the more the phenomenon of the transaction costs of information-processing can compound differences between the wealthy and the poor, if there is no attempt to equalize their communicative competence. The rich can create an ever greater distance between themselves and the rest of society through superior access to the processing of the most privileged information, which enables them to play these markets better. The wealthier you are in a market society, the better position you are in to harvest the commercial value of specialist, informal information in various fields of activity. This can be both through employing more and better-informed agents to promote your interests, because by paying them you establish quasi-property rights over their knowledge and expertise; but an equally important method is by 'swapping' informal information with others in a similar privileged position to yourself. This, of course, is why the rich and powerful place such emphasis on the importance of exclusive informal social interactions with their peers. It is at the clubs, parties, charity events, public-school functions, and holiday visits of the wealthy and the super-wealthy that they do some of their most important business. They know that establishing friendship and relations of trust with a network of others who are in a position to share and exchange their interpretations of the most valuable informal information is one of the most efficient and reliable ways to make spectacular gains in a market economy.

Information-processing and the coordination of its interpretation are crucially important for all economic activity, and especially the production side relating to the way in which firms treat their workers. This means that we really need to think through what it is that influences access to and interpretation of relevant information if we want to understand how economies work best and how people can perform most effectively in the economy. Ironically, this is a truth about maximizing economic opportunities that the wealthy elite instinctively understand and practice. Hence the old adage, 'It's not what you know, it's who you know'.

Social Capital, Communicative Competence, and the Education System

In advanced economies, such as Britain's today, services already account for almost two-thirds of the value produced. The economy is increasingly knowledge- and information-driven, including much manufacturing: much of what you're paying for when buying a car is the salaries of the research teams who perfected its design, not the metal, glass and plastic from which it is made. Creative ideas, cultural diversity, and path-breaking science matter ever more directly to the productivity of the economy—even more than 'technology', that great buzz word of the 1960s. It has become uncontentious among economists that a key issue for the future success of advanced economies will be developing and nurturing human capital, whether funded by the state, by the employing, private companies, or by some combination of the two.

However, there is also the critical question of how human capital, skills and expertise, once 'produced' through available education and training systems—a process which, in principle, can continue throughout life—is most effectively combined in the market economy into creative and productive commercial partnerships and teams. This is where social capital is of crucial significance. Social capital facilitates the maximum diversity and density of positive social relationships between individuals in the marketplace of work and production. This, in turn, permits human capital to achieve its most productive combinations and outcome, both for the individuals concerned and for the economy. As efficiency in the simple physical processing of the material content of products becomes less central to the productivity of our advanced economies, while the commercial value of the creative content of goods and services steadily grows, we must develop an economic analysis which gives correct weighting to this new economic fact of life: the ever-increasing importance of information sharing and manipulation. That means not only highly educated and trained individuals but also a political economy focused around the promotion of effective social relationships as the critical accelerator of appropriately interpreted information around the economy, thereby enhancing the value of human capital investment.

It follows from this that it is a crucial goal to maximize the social and cultural scope of information exchange among the economy's workers. In generating the capacity to process information most effectively on the part of the greatest proportion and diversity of citizen-workers, social capital will provide the most dynamic primary driving force for a knowledge-processing, creative economy of the future, just as the cheap and accessible supply of coal, oil, and electricity have each successively driven, at a basic level, the material-processing economies of the recent past.

This capacity on the part of individuals to converse with each other to a high degree of intelligibility and informality and to process cultural and economic information effectively, both face to face and through printed and electronic media, we might call their 'communicative competence'. This concept has a close affinity with Habermasian political theory concerning 'communicative action'. In particular, Habermas has insisted that 'the social'—forms of life—profoundly influences the 'rationality' of communication. (Habermas 1987*a* [1968]; 1984 [1981]; for an excellent introduction to this aspect of Habermas's thinking, see Bernstein 1985, and for further discussion see Calhoun 1997). Thus, Habermas has been important in equating the emergence of such 'rational' forms of communication in the 'public sphere' of discourse with the post-Enlightenment bourgeoisie of eighteenth-century and early nineteenth-century European society, thereby emphasizing that this 'democratic' political model of communication has an intimate historical relationship with the functioning of liberal market economies and civic societies (Habermas 1989). Habermas draws our attention to something that intellectuals in particular may take too much for granted. To enjoy communicative competence in a relationship with any other individuals depends on a high level of prior trust and 'sympathy', which might be termed a disposition to engage in understanding. This, in turn, presupposes relationships of roughly equal status and mutual respect. Social capital only flourishes where there is shared communicative competence among the parties involved. It follows, therefore, that in order to maximize the terrain over which extensive social capital can flourish, the political and cultural conditions must obtain in a society or economy which promote to the maximum a widely diffused communicative competence among the greatest diversity of individuals or citizens.

Thus, integration of the concept of social capital within a liberal economics framework leads to the normative conclusion that, in order to promote the optimal efficiency of agents within the market, a society should strive to promote to the maximum the communicative competence of *all* its citizens. This is because only in doing this can the same citizens, who are the workers, optimize their personal information processing capacities to interact with others and so promote economic productivity and competitiveness across the greatest extent of the economy.

Liberal economists, since at least John Stuart Mill, have recognized that 'imperfect' information radically distorts the practical workings of exchange in a market economy and that this is a regrettable feature of the real world. They are consequently in favour of the maximum of 'transparency' of all relevant economic information to the agents in a market, since otherwise, by definition, agents cannot exchange on the basis of knowing what their true economic options and opportunity costs are. This in turn would make a mockery of both the moral legitimacy of the operation of a market and its practical claim to provide the most effective allocation mechanism. There is a corollary here with the issue of production. The process by which information is passed and received between individuals in the productive side of the economy is neither simple nor neutral. The social capital perspective emphasizes that it is only mutually trusting human relationships which permit the most efficient and transparent communication of the most relevant and valuable informal information to occur between workers engaged in production: Coase's insight. This implies that a firm, an industrial cluster, or a whole society must be so arranged as to maximize the likelihood of mutually trusting relationships existing between the individual workers who comprise it, in order to maximize its productive efficiency. This can only be achieved to the maximum extent on a national basis if there is a state of relative equality of communicative competence prevailing, in order that everyone, or at least the greatest possible proportion of the citizen-workers in society, may converse with each other on a basis of trust and mutual respect.

This normative conclusion leads to two far-reaching policy implications relating to economic inequality and to education. First, the social capital perspective alerts us to sound reasons, internal to the liberal economics view of the market as an optimal allocative and competitive mechanism, to favour policies which reduce, to the minimum acceptable, degrees of inequality of income and wealth among the freely interacting, information-processing citizens who comprise the productive workers. This is because the more unequal the distribution of wealth and income is, the more this presents a hindrance to relations of mutual respect and trust, and equality of communicative competence among citizens.

This leads to the radical and highly distinctive policy implication that, in order to promote the efficiency and productivity of its market economy, governments should act systematically to correct the tendency towards income, wealth, and power inequality which the free market's functioning otherwise produces. Previously it has typically been argued, under the dispensation of the 'Washington consensus', that liberal economic theory offers a primary presumption broadly in favour of the economic benefits of a relatively high degree of inequality, invoking issues of incentives and rewards for risk-taking enterprise and competitiveness. According to this viewpoint, separate, off-setting social justice arguments might be admissible to justify the moderation of economic inequality in a market-oriented society but arguments for economic dynamism and efficiency were supposed to point strongly the other way. The inclusion of social capital in our liberal economics introduces further considerations. It indicates that a polity which permits too much accumulation of capital in the hands of too few of its citizens in order to stimulate their individual enterprise may well be paying a very high price if its social capital is being systematically compromised by the same policy. While it may be perfectly possible to point to the dynamism of individual wealth-creators, this does not prove that the economy in general could not have been more productive with more economic equality, if that enhanced social capital.

The importance of widely-dispersed social capital, rather than concentrated financial capital, might be especially relevant if the production of creative, knowledge-based and information-sharing commodities and highly customized services is becoming an ever more important part of a modern economy's productivity. Competition between companies and national economies to produce more and more of these sorts of products is of an entirely different nature to the kind of competition required to succeed in mass manufacturing of enormous volumes of relatively standardized material commodities. This is an important point, deriving from an historical perspective on the changing nature of the productive economy. At any time there is always a balance in the economy between one set of companies that are mainly trying to deliver already-established commodities and services at the cheapest possible price, and another set of enterprises that are innovating new kinds of products and services. There is not, in fact, just one single kind of 'market competition' but at least two quite distinct forms. It is only the former kind of company which is competing with its rivals in the classic 'law of the jungle' sense, where ruthless managers must drive down the costs of the factors of production, including labour, to the minimum in order to survive against competition. A completely different kind of market competition obtains where companies are innovating new kinds of product; and similarly where they are competing on quality to produce the most stylish or effective product or service. In both these latter cases the creativity of the company, and therefore its competitiveness, will critically depend on the careful nurturing of its most creative human resources and social capital, quite the opposite of a cost-cutting approach towards the labour force. It seems *a priori* plausible that as developed economies such as Britain's become ever more focused on the production of services, it is this form of competition which will become ever more significant.

Second, in addition to the question of income and wealth distribution the social capital perspective also indicates that the overall characteristics of the national education system will be extremely influential upon the possibilities for equality of communicative competence among the citizenry. The new view of political economy which social capital makes possible indicates that the nation's education system plays a critical role because it is simultaneously producing not just one economic product, human capital, as previously understood by economists, but two: both human capital *and* social capital. Ideally, these two should be simultaneous, joint products of the education system. But unfortunately this is not necessarily so. Individual good schools and good teachers can produce individuals with well-developed human capital characteristics, which they and the economy will both benefit from, *ceteris paribus*. But only a good overall education *system*, free from gross disparities of provision and status, in which all can have pride in their schools and from which all can derive a sense of personal achievement and worth, can lay the necessary foundations for the proliferation of extensive social capital all across the economy, by providing its basis in common communicative competence and mutual respect among all citizens. This argument from social capital also holds in principle for a range of other important social policies and public goods, all of which affect the equality of citizens' communicative capacities, such as health, housing, and social security.

Social Capital and Human Resources in Britain's History

How long has social capital been important? Although a newly-coined term, the phenomenon it describes has probably been significant to some extent in the health and efficiency of all market societies. This can be illustrated with a brief sketch of the history of social capital in one of the world's first major market economies, Britain.

Following the English Civil Wars and the Glorious Revolution of the seventeenth century, British economy and society reconstituted itself as a relatively advanced civic society with a constitutional monarchy, a comparatively effective central state and a dynamic market-oriented economy, experiencing full-scale industrialization during the second half of the eighteenth century and on into the first half of the nineteenth century, before any other country in the world (Wrigley 1988; Brewer 1989; Langford 1989; Floud and McCloskey 1994: vol. I). It subsequently relinquished its economic lead, first to the USA, and then also to a number of other European states during the period 1870–1950 (Floud and McCloskey 1994: vol. II; Clarke and Trebilcock 1997). British economy and society then rallied during the postwar golden age, 1950–73, in that it no longer continued to slip significantly down the world rankings in terms of economic performance while it also held its own as one of the leading liberal and democratic polities with a relatively vigorous civic society in the context of a reforming, progressive, and liberalizing state (Floud and McCloskey 1994: vol. III). More recently the British state has shown signs of becoming more autocratic and centralist, markedly so during the important Thatcher administration, while the economy has offered an increasingly mixed performance, especially between the prospering metropolitan southeast and the struggling, former industrial heartlands of the north. State policy has acquiesced in the growth of income and wealth inequality to a more marked extent than in almost any other developed society (Floud and McCloskey 1994: vol. III; Hutton 1996; Marr 1995). How then can we relate this course of events to a putative history of social capital in Britain?

During the century or more in which the world's first industrial revolution was incubating, c.1660–1760, Britain's social infrastructure and quality of human capital were extremely advanced by the standards of the day, thanks to a relatively interventionist state and a well-dispersed distribution of wealth supporting an unusually large propertied class of both land-owning gentry

and yeoman families and urban merchants, professionals and traders. There was
a notably efficient welfare state, the Elizabethan Poor Laws, which kept the
British people free from lethal dearth and subsistence crises, quite unlike, for
instance the subjects of the French monarchy, the other principal European case
where sufficient historical evidence exists to study the incidence of 'crisis mortality' in the early modern period (Appleby 1978; Schofield 1972; Slack 1988).
Furthermore, we can be quite certain of Britain's global advantage over even
Holland in respect of the density and efficiency of her populace's commercial
information and communications systems by the last quarter of the eighteenth
century, simply because of the enormous size of her principal entrepot, London
(Wrigley 1987, Part II). Before the advent of modern telecommunications, large
city agglomerations have always represented the most efficient possible information exchange systems. The fact that the island of Britain, not the continent
of Europe, sustained clearly the largest city of the time signals that it had the
most developed information concentration and exchange system of the period,
the sign of its advanced civic society and social capital.

   This is also confirmed in that the highly communicative 'polite and commercial people' of mid-eighteenth century Britain provided a buoyant market
for the cheap printed word. The first provincial weekly, the Norwich *Post-Boy*,
was founded in the first year of the eighteenth century and there were over a
hundred such weeklies in existence by the beginning of the next century
(Read 1961: 59). Not surprisingly, then, the British were already a highly liter-
ate populace on the eve of the industrial revolution, recording just over 60 per
cent male literacy and about 40 per cent female literacy in England by the
1740s and 1750s and even higher levels in Scotland (Schofield 1981: 207).
Indeed, late eighteenth-century Anglo-Saxon society and culture, including
the American colonies, has been considered a paradigm case of the creation of
the Habermasian 'bourgeois public sphere', meaning a communicative space
or network of non-noble persons perceiving themselves to be representative of
the interests of 'the public' (Breen 1993: 257). The British were avid consumers
of 'print capitalism', a term which usefully encapsulates the essential social
capital point that there was an intimate connection between a relatively diffuse revolution in information availability and its consumption and that of
the market for mass production of material goods and industrial capitalism.
(Anderson 1991: Ch. 3).

   This, then, was the society which gave birth to the world's first sustained
episode of rapid per capita economic growth, driven forward by risk-taking
entrepreneurs, often supported by the many and proliferating nonconformist
religious congregations and sects to which they belonged (Hagen 1964:
303–8). These, along with the proliferating attorneys who brokered local loans
from landowners to industrialists (Rule 1992: 165–6), were classic examples of
the kind of trusting networks which represent small-scale social capital and
which have also been documented contemporaneously among immigrant
Mexican entrepreneurs in USA in an important recent social capital study
(Portes 1995).

But Britain's industrial revolution was also one which was had 'on the cheap' (Williamson 1994). Renewal and replenishment of all aspects of the supporting social capital and physical infrastructure were, unfortunately, not priorities for this society undergoing such unprecedented economic growth. First, the British state allowed itself to become semi-detached from the supervision of the market economy, ceasing to take such a close interest in the nation's human resources. In the name of free markets in labour as a factor of production, expenditure on the Poor Law was abruptly halved in the 1830s as it was turned into a system of deterrence; and in the 1840s a catastrophic famine in Ireland was supinely witnessed by the British central state. By these decades the nation's voluntary hospitals, a classic product of social capital as the proud creation of networks of private subscribers in provincial towns all around the country in the previous century, had become submerged under the weight of local demand in the fast-growing cities, without any continuation of the previous century's building programme (Cherry 1980). Apart from the mortality disaster in Ireland, death rates in the industrial towns in the second and third quarters of the nineteenth century were higher than they had been at the start of the century and there was also a measurable decline in urban children's height attainments at this time (Szreter and Mooney 1998; Floud, Wachter, and Gregory 1990). Finally, contrary to the subsequent experiences of Germany and Japan during their initial periods of industrial expansion, literacy rates in England and Wales registered only a slight improvement from the 1770s to the 1850s, despite the enormous urbanization of the population that occurred across those eight decades; indeed by the middle of the nineteenth century the literacy rates of the new industrial cities were actually well below the national average (Sanderson 1972; Schofield 1981: 209, 213; Cressy 1993: 318).

Thus, there is substantial evidence of decline and deterioration in social infrastructure and in measurable dimensions of human and social capital in the urban heart of the mid-Victorian industrial economy of mainland Britain. The proximate reason for this was a chronic failure of adequate public health and other social infrastructure investment in Britain's industrial cities throughout the first three quarters of the nineteenth century. The underlying reason was the rise to prominence of the 'dismal science' of classical, *laissez faire* political economy as the dominant ideology of the age. For it was this radically individualist mode of thought among the governing and business classes which legitimized the curious process whereby they withdrew from effective collective action in their towns and cities for half a century or more, dedicating themselves instead to the accumulation of private wealth (Dyos and Reeder 1973; Szreter 1997a). While income and wealth inequality widened across this period (Perkin 1969: 135–6, 419; Phelps Brown 1988: Chs 11.1, 14.3–4), social infrastructure, health, and educational investment was permitted to lapse into increasing abeyance. The multiplicity of congregational networks which had provided the local, small-scale social capital for early industrial enterprise to prosper now became something of a barrier to the wider alliances which were required to find the political will to invest in the heavily stressed urban environment.

Small-scale, localized networks and social capital had been sufficient to empower Britain's home-made early industrialization of the eighteenth century; but there was a failure in the first half of the nineteenth century to 'scale-up' and to promote extensive social capital on a cross-class, national basis. The elementary condition for this would have been the early granting by the state of the conditions for full and active citizenship, as defined in the classic article by T. H. Marshall (1950). But, having finally conceded the vote to the propertied middle classes in 1832, the nation's reconstituted governing class then dug in their heels, using the police powers of the state to face down the Chartist movement's demands for universal manhood suffrage over the ensuing two decades. Similarly, the municipal corporations were reformed in 1835 but this resulted only in a narrow, petty bourgeois electorate, a 'shopocracy' whose principal goal was to ensure that their council practised 'economy': avoidance of all unnecessary expenditure out of the rates. In social capital terms, this symbolized a class-divided turning away for a generation or more from the project of creating a wider Habermasian public sphere on the part of the Victorian bourgeoisie.

Only with the gradual weakening and popular questioning of classical liberal political economy over two to three decades from the late 1860s onwards were there the beginnings of a serious attempt to repair the neglect and damage to the social infrastructure of several decades of relatively unplanned intensive urban growth. Central government provided important general stimuli. There was some financial encouragement, in the form of grants in aid; but also, crucially, in the late 1860s, after a decade of further pressure from below, there was franchise extension, especially the municipal franchise which now included a substantial section of propertyless working-class men. Apart from this, it was largely left to municipal councils to determine their own pace in reviving their towns. The vital driving force was the diffuse social movement, known as the civic gospel, after the nonconformist, Unitarian and Congregationalist ministers who began preaching this home-grown urban crusade against the inequity, filth, and poverty of their own cities in the mid-century decades (Hennock 1973). The movement gained momentum throughout most of the second half of the century, transmuting into what its detractors called 'gas and water municipal socialism'.

Eventually large municipalities, including even London itself with the formation of the London County Council (LCC) in 1889, came to endorse ambitious spending programmes, often involving large-scale loans on the rates, much demolition and building activity, and the running of local utilities and transport services for profits, used as revenue which was then reinvested into the city. Leaders of the movement often included local magnates such as the paradigm case, Joseph Chamberlain, the Liberal Mayor and largest screw-manufacturer in Birmingham. This was a new breed of urban patricians who had themselves been born into wealth and whose privileged upbringing and education was conducive to high moral principles and aspirations, seeking to emulate in their own cities the cultivated ideals of civic society of classical and Italian city states (Briggs 1968). Even the more hard-nosed local businessmen found that the flow of associated public building and service contracts was good for trade; and this muted opposition from that quarter. The influx of non-rate-paying working-class voters were an important part of the electoral arithmetic which made it possible to sell this progressive programme.

Thus, Britain's new urban patriciate, inspired by a mix of religious and political, high-minded and venal motives, launched in this period, c.1865–1914, what amounted to a classic social movement of social capital building in Britain's new industrial towns, spending increasingly on their environments and local social and health services by devising various financial mechanisms for mobilizing the funds of the wealthy towards these purposes (Szreter 1997a; Bell and Millward 1998). Following this provincial activism the last decade before World War I witnessed something of a revolution in central government's social policy as these locally pioneered policies finally fed through into national government. The year 1902 saw the belated establishment, long after most European competitors, of a coherent, secular national education system from elementary through to university levels. After this came the creation of insurance-based national social security schemes for health, unemployment, and old age, something Germany had famously had since the 1880s—albeit incomplete in their coverage of the populace's needs: women not in employment were a major category of omission, for instance (Hennock 1987; Thane 1982). However, in a pre-Keynesian era, this revolution in the activism of the central state and its willingness to tax the propertied class directly for social purposes remained a partial and incomplete revolution. It failed to lift dramatically or permanently the living conditions and opportunities of the working poor: the subsequent inter-war decades of international economic difficulties brought heavy unemployment and deprivation to areas of traditional industry accompanied by an orthodox, Treasury-led government reaction of retrenchment (Laybourn 1990).

It was not until the needs of the home front in World War II once again brought a unanimity of purpose in public opinion, while concentrating the minds of politicians, administrators, and local government on the health, morale and efficiency of the civilian side of the war economy, that many of the problems of access and local disparity of provision which had plagued the inter-war period were addressed (Titmuss 1950). As a result, it was not until the 1940s that the long, slow process of raising the level of investment in human resources from the slough of despond into which it had fallen in the early and mid-nineteenth century had finally been formally completed. As T. H. Marshall pointed out in his essay, the conditions he identified for a full participatory citizenship were not in fact formally fulfilled until after 1945, reflecting a history of extremely sporadic and halting development of extensive social capital in Britain. By the end of the 1940s this had finally produced a set of facilities, in terms of health, social security, and education—if not training—which could realistically be seen as laying the minimal basis for promoting extensive social capital and shared communicative competence throughout society, comparable to those of the other most advanced economies and societies of the age, principally those of continental northern Europe.

Hence, the period from the beginning of the twentieth century until the 1970s witnessed a long, slow process of socioeconomic 'equalling upwards' in modern Britain. This was encouraged by the gradual acceptance of a progressive, strongly redistributive fiscal regime funding a widening range of social and health services, which was extended to a formal welfare state and a full-employment policy from the 1940s onwards under the first full Labour administration subscribing to a 'Keynesian' demand-management macroeconomic policy. Whereas 1 per cent of the populace still owned almost 60 per cent of the nation's wealth in the 1920s, this had been cut in half, to under 30 per cent, by the beginning of the 1970s. Conversely, the poorest 80 per cent of the population had seen their share in the nation's wealth almost triple over the same period, from just 6.4 per cent in the 1920s to almost 20 per cent by 1970 (Rubinstein 1986: 95). This capped a gradual but protracted rise in investment by the state in the full range of the nation's human resources across the first two-thirds of the twentieth century which dated back to the New Liberal legislation of Asquith and Lloyd George in the Edwardian period.

Furthermore, after 1945 there was a much improved context for the functioning of social capital within the production side of the economy because of the postwar sense on the part of the working class that a fair national settlement had been delivered by 'their own' government, in the form of Attlee's Labour administration and its implementation of the Beveridge plan. This facilitated a temporary class rapprochement between bosses and workers, following the more turbulent and confrontational decades of the first half of the century, which had witnessed the great unrest of 1908–13, the General Strike of 1926 and the Jarrow March of 1936. In this postwar context, with extensive social capital at last being given some chance to benefit the economy, there was a return, for almost a quarter of a century from the beginning of the 1950s, to the highest economic growth rates yet seen in British history, consistently in excess even of those experienced during the mid-Victorian decades (Crafts 1995: 435–6, 441–2).

Yet, as we know, over the long term, despite the initial success of the postwar settlement, the peace between bosses and workers did not last and British economic performance suffered accordingly during the again turbulent 1970s and 1980s. The contention here is that this was partly due to a continuing chronic failure of British public opinion and government policy to perceive the true significance of continuing investment in social capital and the necessity of nurturing its reproduction in each generation, something which could only ultimately be reflected in a polity continuing to give the highest collective priority to matters of income, health, housing, social services, and, above

all, education and training for its citizenry. In effect, Britain had 'got lucky' in
1945, on the back of a national catharsis, a society brought together by the bitter experience of the depressed 1930s and the collective battle for survival in
World War II. But it was not a society that had truly learned the lessons of the
importance of continually replenishing social capital through a healthy 'public sphere' as being a fundamental and essential condition for the promotion
of national economic growth. There was a portentous shift away from local
democracy towards heavily centralized planning during the war. Furthermore,
Britain remained a society content to reproduce its infamous class system. The
1944 'Butler' Act granted a new lease of life to a divisive set of educational
institutions. The Beveridge plan and the postwar Labour government in fact
saw their revolution in social provision of the 1940s as a matter of securing the
defensive rights of citizens, negative freedoms from wants, in Isaiah Berlin's
(1969) terminology rather then the promotion of positive freedoms, including
economic ones. This was really conceived as humane and advanced state charity, not as the essential basis for raising national economic productivity
through nurturing social capital with a highly informed, healthy, educated citizenry capable of forming multiplex networks for the communication of ideas
and information.

   Thus, the most recent and thorough attempt to provide an empirical analysis for an overview of trends in social capital in Britain since World War II has
concluded that 'governments can and do affect the levels of social capital in
their nation. . . . Through both their educational policies and social policies, it
seems that governments can have a significant effect on levels of social capital
and . . . on the distribution of that capital through the populace' (P. Hall 1999:
458). Hall has argued that the detailed findings in the evidence he has assembled demonstrate that the course and character of the state's educational policy has a clear impact on the reported patterns of both cohort and period social
capital. He finds that the most marked effects in the data are due to increased
access to post-secondary education during the postwar era (P. Hall 1999:
435–7). Hall's overall interpretation is, however, highly questionable due to
his rather over-optimistic evaluation of the significance of the principal consistent finding of the sequence of major social mobility studies undertaken
since the late 1950s (Goldthorpe *et al.* 1968–9; Goldthorpe, Llewellyn, and
Payne 1980; Marshall *et al.* 1989). These have consistently shown the effectiveness of the postwar British education system in excluding those with working-class parents from access to both the higher education system and,
therefore, the elite service sector jobs. The original 'affluent worker' studies
drew the direct connection between the workers' correct perception of their
exclusion from the privileged world of the middle-class service sector and the
boss class on the one hand, and their increasing militancy in the workplace
and instrumental, cynical and opportunist attitudes towards national politics
and collective bargaining on the other. This is a classic example of social capital failure and its consequences for industrial relations. Hall, by contrast,
seems to believe that the fact that 4 per cent of the working-class achieved a

post-secondary education in 1990 is a positive achievement! (P. Hall 1999: 436). When this interacts with another of his main findings, that since 1945 the principal gainers in social capital have been post-secondary educated women, it adds a further social capital dimension to the widening income and cultural inequality since the 1970s between the ill-educated, employment-short, working-class north and the highly educated, two-earner households of the south. What Hall's evidence confirms is the original 'affluent worker' analysis that Britain has been plagued with the industrial relations she deserved, in consequence of her neglect of the vital importance of an equitable national education policy, delivering real opportunity to all the population and providing a basis for mutual respect and communication between labour and capital.

Unfortunately the Thatcher years only compounded this social capital problem. Deliberate dis-investment, certainly relatively and by some measures even absolutely, in the public sector's social services and in state education exacerbated this deficit in social capital among the working-classes (Rowthorn 1992: Table 12.4). Britain's state schools lost 50,000 teachers, one in ten of the workforce, during the 1980s, to help fund a short-termist electoral strategy of populist tax-cuts (Szreter 1997b: 98–9). These teachers have not been replaced nor has the associated decline in their relative pay levels been restored by the Blair administration. Yet private schools, in sharp contrast, have continued throughout the last two decades to focus on resources and to take on additional teachers. Consequently the private sector now boasts almost exactly twice as many teachers per pupil as the public sector, the greatest discrepancy between the two since the relevant records began. This situation contributes directly to the greatest systematic disparity in the educational opportunities available to different citizens since before World War II. Thus, Adonis and Pollard have described Britain's school system in the late 1990s as the 'English apartheid' (Adonis and Pollard 1997: Ch. 2).

Conclusions

The social capital perspective reveals that the current neo-liberal economic orthodoxy of 'mainstream' economics is premised on a defective and incomplete understanding of the workings of the market economy. Social capital offers the prospect of a superior understanding of market economics and competition and of how to promote a nation's economic efficiency in the world's markets through the promotion of its citizens' communicative competence. The brief historical review offered here confirms that government policy, both in what it does and what it does not do, has strongly influenced the extent to which Britain has replenished or depleted its social capital from one generation to the next.

In order to promote extensive social capital for rising generations, government will have to redefine the relationship between private and public, in the light of the importance of coproduction—partnership—and investment in widespread citizen participation. This means, first, more transparency in central government activities and the use of public resources. Second, much more authority and power will need to be devolved to properly open and participatory organs of local government to enable them to energize local economies and clusters of companies by being sensitive and responsive to the requirements and needs of citizens, businesses, and the full range of civic associations in their local contexts.

There is also a fundamental role for the state to play in equipping each generation of citizens with their shared communicative competence and the basis for mutual respect. In Britain at the beginning of the twenty-first century, this will require a radical reappraisal of the sheer scale of resources which the state is prepared to ask its citizenry to devote to this goal. Private schools lead the way in demonstrating the high quality of education to which citizens in fact aspire for their children. To emulate this level of provision for the great majority of the populace implies a dramatically enhanced and entirely transformed, comprehensive range of publicly-funded educational facilities and associated key social services. This would be necessary to avoid the reproduction of further generations of a class-divided citizenry and produce, instead, a mutually respectful population of communicative equals. In the longer term only this can create the quality of relationships generally throughout society which can generate the maximum extensive social capital, enabling human capital to flourish all across the British economy.

4

Economics, Social Capital, and the Colonization of the Social Sciences

BEN FINE AND FRANCIS GREEN

Introduction

ONE reason for the rise of 'social capital' in social discourse is that the concept appears to constitute a new weapon to deploy at the perennial skirmishes on the borders between economics and other social sciences. Although only a minority of economists will yet have heard of it, social capital appears to be both quantifiable and related to traditional economic variables like Gross Domestic Product growth rates, thus potentially trumping economists at their own game. Or, to be less confrontational, social capital may be viewed as a way for other social sciences to engage with economists, to introduce a social element into the analysis of economic phenomena and thus achieve a unified theory. If social capital can be set alongside the other pillars of physical, financial and human capital, it is suggested, the result will be a more integral understanding of both the economic and the non-economic worlds (Fukuyama 1995). Just as ambitious, social capital is even heralded as a scientific basis for the new politics of the 'Third Way' (Szreter 1999).

We argue in this chapter that the prospect of changing economics through the concept of social capital has little hope of success. It is, of course, correct that neo-classical economics, besides being excessively formalistic at its core, is fundamentally asocial. Because it is constructed on a foundation of methodological individualism, its concepts are timeless, universal and not infused with real history: these are criticisms familiar to students of political economy. Those economists who have emphasized the social character of economic phenomena—for example, neo-marxist economists, certain types of institutionalists and post-Keynesians—have generally been relegated to the periphery of the discipline. Nevertheless, social capital is unlikely to make substantive

We thank Euclid Tsakalatos for his helpful comments on an earlier version of this article, which was completed whilst Ben Fine was in receipt of a Research Fellowship from the UK Economic and Social Research Council (ESRC) under award number R000271046 to study 'The New Revolution in Economics and Its Impact upon Social Sciences'. For his broader appraisal of social capital, see Fine (2001).

inroads on economic theory, even though increasing numbers of studies are beginning to demonstrate the salience of quantitative social or institutional indicators as explanands of economic variables.

We base this prognosis only in part on the looseness of the empirical operationalization of the concept: on which, see the section 'Quantifying the Social' below. More importantly, the internal strength of economics' core theories, with their axiomatic and mathematical rigour, combined with the overwhelming dominance of methodological individualism, means that social capital, if it is to gain acceptance, will be incorporated within economics' individualistic tradition. Thus social capital, rather than agent for socializing economics, could become turncoat in the colonial conflict in which more and more areas of the social sciences are claimed for economics' own methods. We suggest that this development is already taking place. Thus, Gary Becker explicitly subsumes his version of social capital theory within the theory of the utility-maximizing individual (Becker 1996; Fine 1999a). Less extreme, the not-so-new developments of information-theoretic economics, allied to game-theoretic modelling of social interactions, allow many social or non-market phenomena a part to play in economic behaviour. In several cases, social capital writers draw on the findings of this literature to underpin the hypothesized effects of social capital.

We set out this main argument in 'Bringing the Social Back In', and follow, in 'Human and Social Capital', with an illustration through a discussion of the relationship between social capital and the earlier concept of human capital. In 'Quantifying the Social' we examine the significance of attempts to quantify social capital, and comment on the contribution of standard econometric methods in this burgeoning literature. We conclude in 'Social Capital as a Trojan Horse' by locating the policy implications of social capital theory alongside those of standard economics.

Bringing the Social Back In

Social capital has achieved most prominence in economic circles in the context of research within the World Bank (Fine1999b). An extensive programme of research and popularization has been inaugurated, in which its leading economists have participated, including Joe Stiglitz, Senior Vice-President and Head of Research. Social capital is understood as the 'missing link' in understanding economic development.[1] It is a telling metaphor, implying that the notion completes the chain of explanation, filling out what has otherwise been absent. Since 'capital' is not absent from economics, incorporation of social capital has the effect of addressing the 'social'. In its own way, an explicit recognition is being made that mainstream economics has previously excluded the social and now it is time to bring it back in again. For, from the

---

[1] See Grootaert (1997), for example; the term is frequently to be found reproduced in the latest World Bank publications.

perspective of other social sciences, economics is infamous for its methodological individualism, by which society is to be understood merely by aggre-
gating the behaviour of its constituent quasi-autonomous individuals.
Moreover, economics has for the most part proceeded with a particular version
of methodological individualism, one in which preferences are given 'exogenously'—that is, taken as given and neither explained nor situated historically
and socially—and motivation is confined to 'utility maximization', whereby
behaviour is explained in terms of attainment of the highest feasible level of
satisfaction of the exogenous preferences.

However, in the hands of Gary Becker, leading mainstream neo-classical
economist and Nobel prize-winner, neither exogenous preferences nor utility
maximization is sacrificed in addressing the social. It is of considerable
significance that Becker and sociologist James Coleman, generally acknowledged as one of the founding fathers of social capital, should both have been
situated at the University of Chicago.[2] For this is more than a symbolic coincid-
ence, with the duo having run a seminar together on the application of rational
choice to social sciences from 1983 when Becker took up a joint appointment
in the Department of Sociology. Not surprisingly, Becker has himself taken up
the notion of social capital in his later writing. His work provides a most
instructive initial focus for assessing the position of social capital within economics. Although Becker is often perceived as a mainstream economist who
takes the application of rational choice theory too far,[3] he presents in particularly undiluted form the analytical content that is readily deployed by others
with reservations and qualifications. Indeed, paradoxically, social capital is
used by Becker in order to retain the assumptions of utility maximization and
exogenous preferences, whilst widening the explanatory scope of the rational
choice approach. Let us see how this feat of explaining the social on the basis
of the individual, rather than the other way around, is achieved.

Becker continues to take underlying preferences, which he calls 'extended'
preferences, as exogenously given. These extended preferences are a function
of the goods and services currently consumed and also 'personal capital' and
'social capital'. The personal and social capital, however, evolve over the individual's lifetime according to his or her individual and social experiences, giving rise to changing 'subutility functions'—as explained below. Most
explicitly, Becker writes that 'the influence of childhood and other experiences
on choice can explain why rich and poor, whites and blacks, less and more
educated persons, and persons who live in countries with totally different traditions have subutility functions that are radically different' (Becker 1996: 6).

Such a view, if taken as part of an explanation, might be considered
uncontroversial, even tautological. Yet it is turned into a complete explana-

---

[2] For an account of Coleman's and Becker's positions on the new economic sociology, see
Swedberg (1990), Coleman (1990b), and Becker (1990) themselves.

[3] George Akerlof (1990: 73), who is acknowledged as having initiated a less extreme marriage
between economics and sociology, refers to Becker's use of utility maximisation by analogy with
Samuelson's comment on Friedman: like someone who had learnt to spell banana but did not know
how to stop!

tion in terms of rational choice by being wedded to the notion that the evolution of subutility out of extended preferences is a matter of choice, subject to parental and other influence and to random fluctuation. From the moment of birth our representatives or we ourselves, it is suggested, chart out an optimal path for our lives' activities and simultaneously for our evolving preferences, both creating our preferences and indulging them. We choose both to become skilled in art criticism and to spend time at art galleries or, in a more sinister vein, to become a drug addict, fully aware of the future pain and material costs which are discounted in view of the heavier weight of present pleasure. In short, the only reason why preferences or utility functions appear to change is that biologically given preferences alter with experience which is itself either optimally chosen or results from accidental events. Subutility functions reflect the apparent changes in the underlying but unchanging extended utility function as individuals evolve over time from such experiences and choices.

In this light, let us examine the notion of capital more closely. For mainstream, neo-classical economics, the starting point for a definition of capital is a physical object that is able to contribute to output for the purposes of consumption in a future period. Thus, a squirrel's store of nuts is an investment of capital for future consumption, at the expense of present consumption. More generally, such a 'store', if embodied in machinery of some sort, provides for an even greater consumption in the future than would be possible in the present. In short, capital is, in the first instance, to be understood as a physical object which directly or indirectly contributes to future well-being. Nevertheless, the physicality of capital is conceptually unnecessary. For something to be capital, all that is needed is that it promises a future flow of utility. Hence, financial capital and human capital need not be visible in any tangible form in order to be capital.

Just as human capital can be obtained from on-the-job-learning, so current consumption and experiences are said to change one's future capacity to derive utility from goods and services. Becker defines this as 'personal capital', the capacity for enjoyment that has been built up through personal experience. Personal capital is capital because it is a result of past accumulation of experiences and promises a future stream of utility. Whilst all individuals might have the same underlying extended preferences, differences in their personal capital suffice to explain why they might appear not to do so, since their subutilities correspondingly differ.

At this stage, it is important to note how personal capital represents the fullest possible logical progression for rational choice based on isolated individuals. Such individuals are said to engage with an externally given society which provides them with resources and experiences, whether via the market or other mechanisms. Their optimizing choices lead to their own 'personal' evolution as well as that of society as an aggregated outcome. Having demarcated this analytical territory, all other factors that affect an individual's utility are then designated as social capital, summed up in the phrase 'the influence of past actions by peers and others in an individual's social network or central system' (Becker 1996: 4).

Now, as with personal capital, social capital becomes in part a matter of choice. Becker supposes that people choose social networks in ways that will maximize their utility. That network once decided, however, choice is constrained since one individual can normally have little impact on social capital. Nevertheless, social interactions could be modelled in game theory and, indeed, economics has not shied away from analysing public choices in a framework of methodological individualism.

To summarize the results of Becker's conceptual endeavours: his claim is to have re-confirmed the autonomous individual as the central determinant of economic and social life, even though tastes change across time and space. Becker writes: 'the utility function is itself independent of time, so that it is a stable function over time of the goods consumed and also of the [personal and social] capital goods . . . The extended utility function . . . is stable only because it includes measures of past experiences and social forces' (Becker 1996: 5). By this means the notion of a utility function, for all time and place, has acquired universal applicability in explaining human behaviour. Further, it is the filter through which the influence of the social forces is incorporated. The analytical horizons for rational choice become more or less unlimited: 'personal and social capital are crucial not only for understanding addictions . . . but also for most other behavior in the modern world, and probably in the distant past as well' (Becker 1996: 6).

It seems that no idle boast is involved in Becker's claim to be able to explain addiction and 'most other behavior'. Even in this one work, under the umbrella of the economic approach come churchgoing, playing tennis, child abuse, divorce, unemployment, advertizing, jogging, violence, lying, sexual abuse, psychotherapy, patriotism, and government propaganda.

Economics as Colonizing Social Science

Even though Becker may be regarded by some economists as unduly ambitious in his attempts to extend the economic approach to all domains of human behaviour, this movement is not confined just to the margins of mainstream economics. Extensions to Becker's theory of addiction would normally be considered important enough developments to warrant publication in high ranking mainstream journals (for example Orphanides and Zervos 1998). Previously, it has been conventional to restrict the domain of the economic approach to the market, or to areas of resource allocation where there may be 'market failures'. Rationality, conceived as utility maximization, was confined to the world of the price system. Preferences, technology and endowments, and guaranteed and well-defined property relations were taken as given. The analyses of these exogenous factors were the subject matter of the other social sciences. However, over the past decade or so, this situation has begun to change quite rapidly.

Economics has considerably extended its scope of analysis beyond the long-standing imperialistic ventures associated with Becker. New theoretical developments within economics have allowed it to explain why social structures, institutions, and customs might arise even on the basis of individual optimization. The analytical squaring of the circle, by deriving the social from the individual rather than *vice versa*, has been crucial in allowing economics to address the non-economic and to straddle the boundaries between disciplines.

The new theory began with the discovery that markets functioned differently when buyers and sellers had imperfect information about either the commodities being exchanged or each other's behaviour. Introducing assumptions about incomplete product information, especially information that is asymmetric between buyers and sellers, proved initially productive in understanding particular markets; two of many are those for second-hand cars (Akerlof 1970) and for education (Spence 1973). The extension of this perspective to institutions and attitudes is what enables economics to sally forth beyond its traditional boundaries.

Just as the theory acknowledges that the market's function is modified by lack of perfect information, traditionally non-economic phenomena can be rationalized in this framework as the individually entered relations for handling situations with imperfect information. The formation of associations, for example, for non-economic purposes or on non-economic criteria, can be an indirect way of gaining information about uncertain market transactions and for disciplining transgressors. In other words, non-market relations are a way of compensating for informational imperfections within the market. By the same token, apparently non-optimal forms of behaviour, such as trust, reciprocity, custom, and norms are an individually optimal way of responding to market imperfections. A favoured illustration of these points is given by the trust and obligations engendered in ethnic communities or families, although these can also be sources of inefficiency when obligation unduly overrides economic calculation (for example Fukuyama 1995).

These new developments within economics have broadened the latter's scope beyond the market by making endogenous what was previously exogenous, and by addressing the interaction between market and non-market. This has given rise to a range of 'new' sub-disciplines—the new institutional economics, the new household economics, the new political economy, the new financial economics, and so on—in which information asymmetries and imperfections are the basis on which different kinds of non-economic phenomena are analysed. But perhaps the most broad-based area in which economics is assaulting previously non-economic terrain is through new or endogenous growth theory, which is little more than a decade old (Fine 2000). In this theory, factors such as technological change or politics, previously taken as exogenously given to economics, become endogenous. Such factors, now explained on the basis of the individualistic methodology, with an appeal to informational and market imperfections, are used to account for why growth rates differ across nations.

Thus, in the new sub-disciplines mainstream economics makes no method-ological concessions. Whilst Becker always applied the economic approach to all social phenomena and has simply added different types of capital to aug-ment explanatory power and scope, initially less aggressive colonizers of the other social sciences have expanded outwards from more modest explanations of the traditionally economic phenomena along the information-theoretic road to non-economic phenomena, using the same individualistic tools that they use at home. The effect is to reduce historical and sociological phenom-ena merely to means of overriding informational deficiencies.

This excursion now allows us to situate the potential of the idea of social capital within the trajectory of economics. Thus, the non-market forms of individual interactions, especially if they are beneficial in correcting market imperfections, can constitute social capital for those economists who may care to employ the term. It encapsulates the full range of social mechanisms or institutions which might be seen as rationally induced in response to infor-mational imperfections.

Both the generality and, in a sense, the corresponding emptiness of this framework is illustrated by Collier's (1998) attempted synthesis of the notion of social capital from the perspective of a mainstream economist.[4] Collier maintains that social capital is 'capital' if it has the economic effect of sus-taining a stream of income. In addition, it is 'social' because it involves 'some non-market interaction of agents which nevertheless has economic effects. The economic effects are consequently not "internalized" into the decision calculus of each agent by the prices faced in markets. In the language of eco-nomics, they are "externalities"' (Collier 1998: 8).

On this basis, the notion of social capital is further refined according to 'the forms of social interaction, the particular type of externality which is being generated, and the mechanisms which induce it to be generated' (Collier 1998:12). More specifically 'the building blocks of the analysis are thus the three externalities, the four types of social interaction, and the six mecha-nisms of internalization' (Collier 1998: 18).

The three externalities are said to be knowledge of others' behaviour, know-ledge of the non-behavioural environment, and collective action. The types of social interaction are hierarchies, clubs, networks, and observation. The mech-anisms of internalization are: the internalization of knowledge externalities through pooling and through copying the knowledge, the internalization of opportunism through the trust engendered by repeat transactions or by reputation-building, and the avoidance of free-riding through the formation of norms and rules.

In principle, this list could be extended to incorporate any of the behav-ioural or organizational variables to be found across the social sciences. Corresponding institutions and mechanisms can be perceived to be varied and complex in origin and content, depending on the market concerned, the

---

[4] For other attempts by economists to tie down the notion of social capital, see Dasgupta and Serageldin (2000) and Schiff (1992) for example. For empirical application, see section 4 below.

nature of the imperfection and the historically given conditions. As a result, economists are capable of conducting an imagined dialogue with other social scientists: 'Tell us what non-economic factors you think are important to the economy and how they reflect or create market imperfections. We will then model them on the basis of our own methodology and return them to you as a contribution to your own discipline'.

From this perspective social capital seems to present considerable scope for economic theorists. Nevertheless, we judge it unlikely that, even if this scope is embraced fully, it will have much of an impact on the core of economics itself. As a discipline, economics depends upon highly formalized mathematical models. These become intractable once more than a few variables, of which those derived from the social are more or less indefinite in number, are included under the rubric of social capital. Yet once social forces are introduced, the number of variables that need to be modelled in a formal model becomes potentially very large. We therefore think it unlikely that social capital will enter the core of mainstream economic theorizing under any simple and consistent definition.

Is It Social, Is It Capital?

Yet, even if mathematical economics were to be successful in exploiting the scope of social capital in the manner suggested, it follows from our characterization of this potential that social capital would not introduce an adequate new social element into core economic theory. Nor would social capital enrich the concept of capital in any fundamental way.

For mainstream economics social relations, customs, and structures as such do not exist independently of the individuals that constitute them. It is as if marriage, for example, is simply the set of couples who are married and who agree to abide by the associated customs. Marriage as a social relation does not prevail other than as such an agglomeration. By the same token, the market is merely the outcome of a historically evolved set of exchanges with the intervention of money. Crucial to mainstream economics and its methodological individualism is the notion that the social cannot be identified independently of individual interactions except in the form of some historically inherited constraint. Such an approach continues to isolate economics from other social sciences, except where the latter adopt rational choice.

In Becker's economic worldview, individuals spring *ab initio* with biologically given extended preferences. For him, social capital is something that individuals possess, and may rise or fall like physical and human capital, although they do share and create social capital with other individuals.[5] Only

[5] Non-economists, typically retaining a distaste for exclusive reliance upon methodological individualism as a result of the traditions of their disciplines, tend to see social capital as separate from and independent of interpersonal relations alone. This does, however, lead to an unresolved tension between the micro and macro approach to the social. For an excellent discussion of this in the context of sociology and the theory of social exchange which predates that of social capital, see Ekeh (1974).

in this limited sense has social capital been rendered social. By the same token, social capital is ahistorical in a number of senses. First, it draws upon concepts that are universal across time and place without specificity to particular countries or periods of history. In this respect, the domain of social capital is no different from the narrower terrain of economics with its exclusive dependence upon abstract, general and universally applied notions such as utility and preferences, inputs, outputs, production, consumption, and so on. Traditionally, economics has seen market exchange between individuals as forging outcomes between these variables in an unexamined social setting. Now, it allows the non-economic to be involved as well, with social capital standing for the universe of individual interactions which comprise trust, associations, networks, and so on. By doing so, these are no longer taken as the given context within which the market works, but there is little or no advance in understanding the social. Indeed, such analysis adds nothing to these universals in constructing social capital even if it does endogenize some of them a little more than previously.

Second, reflecting much of what has gone before, economics remains remarkably untouched by postmodernism and its insistence that there be critical reflection upon the meaning of the objects of analysis. Precisely because economics is asocial and deploys universal categories, including that of the individual, it is incapable of addressing the social construction of the meaning of items of consumption, for example, which are perceived exclusively in terms of given physical properties. Social capital will not enable mainstream economics to evade this critique.

Third, history is not absent from economics and it can be important in its effects, but the analysis remains shallow. Economists are ultimately unduly dependent for their history upon path dependence—the momentum inherited from the past—random shocks—accidents of history—or unexplained initial conditions—the given starting point of our models. The history has to be incorporated in this way since it has otherwise been precluded at the outset by the understanding of the social in terms of universal—and individualistic—categories. Such a limited role for history reflects the absence of social relations other than as the interpersonal so that the dependence of historical contingency upon the outcomes of struggle over the continuing exercise of power, or its transformation, are necessarily absent. It is hard to see how the proposed integration of social capital will enrich the historical element in political-economic analysis.

If social capital for economists is social in only a limited sense, does it nevertheless enrich the understanding of capital? As we have seen, capital, in the hands of conventional economics, is simply anything that can contribute directly or indirectly to a future stream of utility. In that framework capital is asocial and ahistorical in the senses already covered, being incapable of recognizing capitalism as a specific formation based on definite economic and social relations which incorporate and generate conflict, power, and change. Since social capital is a set of non-economic exchanges amongst individuals with continuing effects, it qualifies for the title of capital in the economic sense, but also, by the same token, for a similar critique of the associated analytical limitations. The idea of seeing social capital alongside physical capital and human capital as inputs in the production of goods or utility is merely to extend the fetishism of commodities beyond its traditional realm. Thus, mainstream economics treats labour as a physical input like any other. By the same token, social capital is essentially reduced to a thing that can enhance production or economic performance even though it is conceptually designed explicitly to deal with the social. So just as commodity fetishism defines how real production relationships appear as relations between things, so the individualistic conceptions of human and social capital obscure the nature of the social relations through which learning takes place and through which society impinges upon individuals' experiences of life.

In sum, we are not optimistic that the idea of social capital will engender a progressive response from mainstream economists to long-standing criticisms of mainstream economic theory; and our best judgement is that social capital will not greatly affect the core of mainstream economics. One way to develop this argument is to examine further the links between social capital and human capital. We may usefully consider the proposition as to whether an integration of social and human capital theory is a helpful objective. In fact, the conceptual and empirical links between human and social capital are instructive for illustrating the role of social capital in economics, as we now demonstrate.

Human Capital and Social Capital

As is well-known, since the work of Schulz (1961a) and of Becker (1964) human capital theory has come to occupy a dominant, though not exclusive, position in economics' understanding of skill formation. The notion of autonomous individuals and firms investing in skill acquisition through education or training is pivotal. Because of the idiosyncratic nature of certain skills or knowledge, the analysis of investment seeking the highest return is nuanced: whether the employee or the employer pays depends on the type of skills being created and the competitive structure of the capital and goods markets.

The dominance of human capital theory, including its extensions to the domains of educational sociologists, has seemed by some to be a mixed blessing. Schuller and Field (1998), for example, note the productiveness of the idea of human capital, but berate the narrowness of the notion of education that human capital theory evokes, and the problems surrounding the measurement of human capital. The role of social capital might be seen to counterbalance the hegemony of the human capital approach to education, emphasizing the non-economic objectives of learning and the social norms that may deliver a learning culture and motivate individual participation in education. Unfortunately, the investment-like character of education—

something for the future—has often come to be equated with human capital theory. Yet the essence of the theory is the individualistic conception of skill formation, and it is largely around this individualism that a full critique needs to be constructed. While the operationalization of human capital theory in empirical work may raise questions about measurement and simplistic notions of payback, or about the consumption aspects of education, these criticisms could always be countered in neo-classical economics and are superficial in comparison with the issue of individualism. If, for example, it is agreed that the enjoyment of higher learning is a prime function of education, this can simply be seen as one of the individual's main objectives, reflected in utility functions. That education for economic purposes has been greatly emphasized in recent years is a consequence of a perceived increased importance attached to skills and knowledge in determining economic performance, not of human capital theory as such.

The critique of individualism in human capital theory refers to the assumption that autonomous individuals decide on how much skill to acquire in their lifetime, depending only on the costs and benefits as determined by prices and by their ability to learn. The social function of education within an unequal economy, the social conflicts over the definition of, and access to, skill, and indeed the social character of the prevailing technology and methods of work organization which determine skill demands, are all precluded by an individualistic analysis (Ashton and Green 1996:14–21). These are enduring problems with human capital theory, which pre-date and exist independently of the concept of social capital.

Another reason why it might seem that social capital takes us beyond human capital theory is that one of the seminal articles in the social capital lexicon used the acquisition of human capital as the focus of an empirical test. Coleman (1988a) argues that pupils attending religiously-based schools enjoyed greater social capital than other pupils by virtue of the associated community networks. Their social capital advantage, rather than their religion as such, accounted for superior performance at school, measured in terms of lower drop-out rates. Now, however robust and generalisable this finding turns out to be,[6] it is not hard to see how links between social capital and human capital could be explained by Becker's individualistic methodology. Autonomous individuals could be seen as optimally investing in more education because this would raise their taste for learning, part of their personal capital. Since 'learning skills' are said to be at a premium in this era of rapidly changing production processes, this might in itself raise educational participation. The impact of social capital is but one step further: people might choose a social network—for example, enrol in a religiously-based school— with a view to the potential impact on the taste for learning, in order to maximize their extended utility functions.

[6] Neal (1997), revisiting the empirical evidence on the superior performance of Catholic schools in the United States, finds that much of the advantage can be ascribed to the inferior quality of the public schools in urban neighbourhoods.

More generally, the impact of asymmetric information about workers' skills has generated a formal literature on the forms of contractual relationships that foster—or hinder—skill acquisition (for example, Katz and Ziderman 1990). The role of education as a potential signal of ability, rather than as a creator of new skills, has been an issue for a long time (Spence 1973). Industrial politics and the efficiency of teamworking are just two examples of issues that have been tackled within the information-theoretic framework (Lazear 1998: Chs 10 and 12). Although such developments undoubtedly advance the understanding of human capital acquisition in the market sphere beyond simple notions of rate of return, the analysis of the non-market sphere remains limited in the human capital information-theoretic approach. In particular, it fails adequately to conceptualize the role of the state. The economic approach advocates and explains the state's role as intervening to redress market failures and to promote less inequality. However, the state's role is potentially much broader, including the control of both skills demand and skills supply through its manipulation of markets in certain contexts (Green *et al.* 1999). Whether or not the state performs such a role depends on, amongst other things, the historical conjuncture of social forces—which, of course, is precisely the point: the individualistic approach cannot cope with this.

Quantifying the Social

Part of the attraction of the concept of social capital derives from the aspiration that it may be quantified and applied to statistical analyses of economic performance to rival and surpass more conventional analyses. A successful quantitative application of social capital could, it is hoped, provide the 'missing link' to conventional empirical studies by accounting for the 'residual' economic growth beyond that explained by physical and human capital. This prospect of quantification is enhanced by the modern-day proliferation of cross-national and micro data sets, covering many social and economic variables.

The willingness to deploy quantitative social data in defence of simple hypotheses has no doubt helped to interest a growing band of researchers in the project. Allied to the adoption of statistical and econometric techniques, several researchers have begun to explore the empirical productiveness of various definitions of social capital.

The result is an expanding list of studies that show, in some way or other, a non-economic factor having a substantive impact on economic performance, whether economic growth, inequality, or some microeconomic indicator such as personal income. Part of the project has been to re-interpret and appropriate results from studies that pre-dated social capital as a popular concept. Knack (1999) provides an excellent summary of those factors interpretable as social capital that, according to his survey, have been investigated for their impact on economic growth.[7] They include political instability, the density of local associations, measures of civil liberties and freedom, property rights indicators—including political violence as an adverse index—political risk ratings, measures of contract enforceability and of bureaucratic integrity, measures of the performance of civic communities including local governments, indices of generalized trust—especially trust in strangers—inequality and ethnic polarization, and measures of cultural attitudes. There are also many micro-level studies that deploy various indices of social capital: see, for example, the World Bank Social Capital web page at http://www.worldbank.org/poverty/capital.

Empirical studies in this vein may vary in their quality: for example, an important dimension is the extent to which studies are able to distinguish cause and effect. Use of econometric methods is a distinct advantage in this respect, since the procedures for picking out causal factors are most sophisticated in this field. However, the most notable aspect of these studies is the sheer breadth of phenomena that are being potentially claimed for social capital. This entails problems if social capital is to acquire both worth and respectability as an identifiable concept in empirical work. The search is now on for the holy grail: a consistent measurement instrument that can be applied without major adaptation across a range of situations, for both research and for policy purposes.

Undoubtedly many of the quantitative studies cited as part of the argument for this social capital project are useful in their own right. They serve to remind us, if that were necessary, of the salience of the social within the economic sphere; they each throw light on particular aspects of economic performance. Nevertheless, the empirical studies operate in a middle ground, in which it would seem virtually impossible to test the relevance of social capital as a concept.[8] The very breadth of the empirical measures would seem to preclude such a test. It is conceivable that some measurement instruments may be devised that will achieve a degree of regularity in diverse findings.[9] It is unlikely that such an instrument would have any simple correspondence with social capital theories, let alone any core economic theories.

There are, in any case, some obvious dangers in narrowing down the list of what is empirically deemed social capital. Any agreed consistent measure may limit the extent to which empirical researchers can allow for social and political factors to impinge on the economy. As an illustration, there is a small literature, normally shunned by mainstream economics, that investigates the links between macroeconomic performance and class conflict (for example, Weisskopf 1987). Though this is a prime example of the economic being

---

[7] For other empirical applications of social capital by economists, see Knack and Keefer (1997) and Temple (1999).

[8] In one recent empirical study of the role of social factors in influencing unemployment exit rates, Hannan (1999) explicitly rejects the concept of social capital, arguing that confusion over its conceptualization hindered an understanding of the effect of social context in this instance.

[9] Though it could hardly match the regularity with which wage equations based on human capital theory have been replicated many hundreds of times in varied settings.

infused with the social, it is hard to see how the impact of class conflict could be interpreted in terms of social capital, since that concept allows no genuine space for class conflict.

Social Capital as Trojan Horse

In terms of themes addressed throughout this book, social capital, as a renewed attempt to push out the subject's boundaries, is new within economics. However, it has been attached to the not quite so new theory of informational market imperfections. As such it is only a productive concept for those mainstream economists working on the margins of the discipline and seeking to occupy or contribute to analytical terrain that has previously been the preserve of other social sciences.

In our judgement, the extension of economics' boundaries in this way has nothing to recommend it. When meeting around social capital, the posture of economics in relation to the other social sciences involves a mixture of arrogance, contempt and ignorance. Respectively: the arrogance comes from 'discovering' what has long been known as a matter of course in other social sciences, that institutions matter, for example, as do customs, norm and social structures; the contempt for the perceived failure of previous analyses to base themselves on 'rigorous' mathematical models and individual optimization; the ignorance from the lack of knowledge of what has been achieved within other social sciences; and the disregard for anything that involves a substantive social and historical content. In short, economics' treatment of social capital is reductionist across a number of dimensions: to the individual, to utility maximization, and to universal categories.

Nonetheless, it might be argued that social capital provides for a civilizing flow of ideas from the other social sciences to economics rather than colonization proceeding in the opposite direction. Despite, and even accepting, our critical commentary, at least there is surely some prospect of economics incorporating social factors and taking them seriously?[10] Whilst accepting this as a logical possibility, we are doubtful of its significance in practice. The cutting edge of research within economics has been and is becoming more mathematically and conceptually esoteric. As such, economics has not only become more intolerant of heterodox approaches that depart from an ever-narrowing orthodoxy,[11] it has sought to appropriate them on the same basis of methodological individualism by which it has included the non-market in general and social capital in particular. We have not here considered the scope for social capital for non-mainstream economics. Although the notion is clearly compatible with a number of heterodox approaches emphasizing collective action, institutions, and so on, it is unclear what social capital offers them other than

[10] Such appears to be the view of social theorists within the World Bank.
[11] See especially Coats (1996), Hodgson and Rothman (1999), and Lee and Harley (1998) for the 'Americanisation' and 'mainstreaming' of economics.

an umbrella term with an imprecise meaning. Traditionally, heterodox economic schools of thought have always emphasized the dependence of economics on other social sciences, and have for the most part shunned
methodological individualism. Recent developments have made substantive
progress in understanding many of the interdisciplinary links, including
mechanisms through which institutions impact on economic behaviour
through norms, habits and so on (for example Hodgson 1988), and the social
and psychological mechanisms through which preferences are influenced
(Bowles 1998). Such developments do not have to acknowledge the idea of
social capital for their origins.

These observations are also important for assessing the social and political
implications of social capital within and through the hands of economists. For
some, social capital represents a breath of fresh air in rationalizing economic
intervention in the wake of the ideological supremacy of neo-liberalism associated with Reaganism and Thatcherism. However, such interventionism is
justified in mainstream economics only if market imperfections can be
identified, and if the state has the capacity—including low corruption levels—
and the detailed knowledge to counterbalance the imperfections.
Corresponding to economic engineering to handle traditional market imperfections, social capital has its counterpart in social engineering to address non-
market imperfections and the capacity of the non-market to compensate for
the market. In this perspective, social exclusion derives from insufficient levels of physical, personal, and social capital which should be targeted and aug-
mented accordingly. Previously, the postwar boom was based, at least in
principle, on a commitment to Keynesianism, welfarism, and modernization.
Essentially these philosophies incorporated policy goals in terms of employment, well-being, and economic and social development as well as an understanding of capitalism as being fraught with both systemic problems and a
healthy dynamic. Irrespective of the verities of these perspectives, the world to
which social capital belongs involves stripping out these earlier systemic goals
and substituting a paler vision. If neo-liberalism took two steps back, social
capital is at most a short stumble forward even if representing itself as incorporating and advancing upon all that has gone before.

The notion of social capital may or may not be a passing fad, but its emergence and popularity do reflect in part the declining influence of postmodernism and the wish across the social sciences to incorporate a greater material
content of which the economic is a part. It would appear to be inescapable
that social capital address the economic. The crucial issue is how and by
whom. We suspect that the influence of economics across social sciences is
going to increase, and that the concept of social capital may be an explicit
channel for this influence. However, within economics itself, social capital is
set to experience a more marginal existence. At most, highly heterogeneous
and esoteric models of social capital will be developed, most probably around
theories of growth, and large data sets of social capital variables will be used to
estimate such models statistically. Otherwise, social capital will be used as part

of mainstream economics' assault on development studies, putatively explaining successes or failures in development by the extent to which market imperfections have prevailed and how they have been handled outside the market. A more promising outcome would be that critical realization of the limitations of the notion of social capital would lead to a serious examination of both the 'social' and the 'capital', a genuine political economy, as the basis for future interdisciplinary work across the social sciences.

5

Socializing Social Capital: Identity, the Transition to Work, and Economic Development

RALPH FEVRE

Introduction

THE critical role of social capital in the colonization of the social sciences by economics is discussed by Fine and Green in their contribution to this volume. Their chapter follows a brilliant series of articles in which Fine has charted the imperialist inroads of economics (Fine 1997; 1999*a*, *c*). Fine argues that when non-economists adopt ideas of social—or human—capital as part of the process whereby economics colonizes their disciplines, this does little or nothing to improve understanding in these other disciplines unless they already happen to favour rational choice explanations.

The present chapter accepts all of this as its starting premise, and briefly considers why the tide has been flowing so strongly in favour of economics. It then moves on to discuss the possibility that the other social sciences can resist colonization while still making something genuinely useful out of the idea of social capital. While Fine points out that social capital is taking over explanations of economic development, growth, and prosperity, he also suggests that social capital had other possibilities before being turned against the other social sciences by economics. It might therefore be feasible to reverse the process and put the idea of social capital to more productive use.

This chapter argues that paying attention to social identities proves a very effective way of reintroducing social content in a more sociological application of the idea of social capital. Careful attention to social identity helps us to avoid an oversocialized theory; and the manner in which identities facilitate the transition to work in many different societies adds much to our understanding of economic development. The relationship between social capital and economic development is central to Fine's (1999*c*: 416–17) argument and, in the final section of the present chapter, the contribution of an appropriately socialized theory of social capital to our understanding of this relationship is compared with the sort of reductionist account that accompanies colonization by economics. This section argues the gains to be made by reclaiming the idea of social capital for the other social sciences.

A Cultural Explanation of Economic Imperialism

In Fine's seminal thesis other social scientists adopt the key concepts of the new economics, like human and social capital, in ignorance of their origins and associated assumptions. They are uncritical of these concepts and too readily assume that their empirical demonstration is not required. Non-economists also succumb to the inherent reductionism, and risks of determinism, in the economists' approach and often fail to realize that their own disciplines may have long-established and more sophisticated alternative explanations (Fine 1999c: 413).

Fine argues that the colonizing potential of human capital has run its course, because economists have become less enthusiastic about what it can explain, and that Gary Becker and his followers have turned to the more promising field of social capital to continue the endeavour of making economics *the* science of human behaviour. Fine argues that the new economics of optimizing individuals gives economists unprecedented opportunities to explain the social rather than treating it as a given. They can now adopt 'a more reasonable position in which the social is both incorporated and explained, often with a healthy dose of historical contingency' (1999c: 414–15).[1] Because these economists are actually interested in explaining the social, other social scientists, perhaps flattered by this 'social turn' in economics, embrace their ideas willingly. Yet there must be more to say about the way in which other social scientists succumb with so little attempt at resistance.

After all, if Fine is correct in his portrayal of human and social capital as Trojan horses which export flawed methodological assumptions, reductionism, and determinism to other social sciences, then it is as if non-economists are throwing away their solid, intellectual capital because they have been enticed into some conceptual version of pyramid selling. One way to make this behaviour seem more plausible is to introduce a cultural explanation. I wish to argue that the colonization of the other social sciences with ideas like social and human capital is occurring because we are experiencing one of those periodic upswings when economic rationality comes to the fore in all aspects of our lives (Bauman 1998; Fevre 1998).

---

[1] Much of this writing on social capital is open to the criticisms made by Goldthorpe (1996; also see Fevre 1990) when considering the various illegitimate uses of history of which sociologists had been guilty. One of his targets was Skocpol, who has subsequently contributed to the literature on social capital but Fukuyama—see below—could also be criticized for his inappropriate and selective use of history. Such writing frequently has the character of 'just-so stories' (Elster 1989) which stretch the ingenuity of their authors to breaking point (see Fukuyama 1995: 251 on the economic performance of the UK for example).

This colonization is simply a special case of the more general process of submission to this limited form of rationality (Hollis 1988). This much might be gleaned simply from the 'plethora of capitals' (Baron and Hannan 1994) our societies generate. Consider, for example the recent theorization of biodiversity and other environmental 'goods' as 'natural capital' (Hawken, Lovins, and Lovins 1999). Why should we choose the term 'capital' to describe such varied phenomena as undergraduate degrees, church coffee mornings, business networks, and rain forests?[2] Such usage seems eccentric unless we admit the moral power which economic rationality has now assumed (Fevre 1998).

In the current climate, arguments for the disposition of resources, or even the reallocation of intellectual interest, have to be grounded in an explicit appeal to economic rationality. The re-labelling of the various phenomena which are central to those arguments as 'capital' is meant to do the trick where terms like 'neighbourhood', 'club', and 'network' do not carry the same charge because they do not fit the desiderata of economic rationality. The term 'capital' has all the right connotations for a culture in which economic rationality is hegemonic (Schuller 1997). If economic rationality is acknowledged as the legitimate yardstick against which all 'goods' are measured, it is no surprise that social scientists apply the same yardstick in their efforts to generate explanations of human behaviour. Yet, although social scientists are not immune to cultural pressure, they have not been deprived of their powers of resistance.

We should conclude from this that there is hope somewhere for an anti-colonial resistance movement, a hope that Fine shares, as otherwise there would be no point in his plea for a 'genuine political economy' (1999c: 420). At this point in our history the concepts of economics are clearly seductive, and there are cultural reasons why they are so attractive to non-economists; but the cultural explanation confirms that economic imperialism can indeed be resisted. Indeed, once we are aware of the source of the seductive power of ideas like social capital we can be inoculated against the effects of economic imperialism and retain social capital as a useful concept.

Social Identities and the Transition to Work

This section argues that social capital can be reclaimed for the other social sciences without fear of undersocialization—as exemplified by neo-classical economics or rational choice theory—or oversocialization—where actors are simply slaves to society's norms. The revitalized idea of social capital is then deployed in the final section where we can compare a sociologically informed account with the somewhat brutalized reductionism which accompanies the imperialism of economics.

---

[2] See Fine and Green (this volume) for the much more diverse range of phenomena Gary Becker and others claim to be able to explain and for the list of phenomena which have been described as social capital derived from Knack.

The way in which social capital serves to distribute job-seekers into employment has long been of interest to sociologists (Granovetter 1974; Portes 1995; 1998) who have consistently tried to show that it is a mistake to theorize job seeking simply in terms of the rational choices of optimizing individuals (Portes 1998: 14). The twin problems of oversocialization and undersocialization have been discussed in the sociological literature for a long time (see for example Granovetter 1985; Portes 1995; 1998). The classical solution to this problem has entailed the networks solution to the problem of oversocialization as recommended by Granovetter (1985) and revised by Burt (1992).

According to Granovetter, both undersocialized and oversocialized arguments have atomized actors at their core and ignore the fact that actors' behaviour is embedded in social relations. For Granovetter the way to re-establish the embedded nature of action is networks. Therefore, by focusing on networks we move away form the conception of individuals as slavish followers of society's norms: that is just as reliant on atomized actors as is the theory of 'economic man'. In a more recent example of this strand, Woolcock (1998: 162–5) theorizes networks in terms of combinations of levels of embeddedness and autonomy while also trying to systematize theories about the negative as well as the positive effects of social capital (also see Fevre 1989; Portes 1995: 18; 1998: 12–15).

To the extent that it invites the conception of social capital as minimizing the transaction costs of relations, this classic treatment of the importance of 'weak ties', or of 'structural holes', perhaps over-corrects in the direction of bounded rationality and the undersocialized version of social capital. With complex labour markets with bewildering arrays of career trajectories, the idea of bounded rationality might be superficially attractive. Yet there is more to the role of social capital in the transition to work than norms and networks, and there is another way to develop a theory which successfully steers between oversocialization and undersocialization.

Let us remind ourselves of what we know of the transition to work, and of the part played by norms and networks within it, in industrial societies. Empirical enquiry has revealed a world which had little to do with the sort of behaviour explained by game theoretic approaches (Fevre 1989; 1992). While many people made the transition to work equipped only with the knowledge of how one other person got a job—this could be empirical knowledge derived from direct observation or theoretical knowledge derived from an interview with a careers adviser or from a public information programme—even this much was superfluous in many cases.

There is little you need to know when your passage into paid work is arranged for you. This much applies to working-class practices and the old school tie, which constitute a range of complete and sufficient career channels (Antikainen *et al.* 1996; Hodkinson, Sparkes, and Hodkinson 1996).[3] Thus a

---

[3] Hodkinson *et al.* (1996) explicitly acknowledge the work of Bourdieu as they try to make sense of their empirical information. Indeed this sort of sociology, including Fevre (1989), shares a great deal with Bourdieu—even if it does not always acknowledge him—on the way social and cultural

recent study of patterns of participation in post-compulsory education and training in south Wales shows how in the long postwar boom the transition to work was frequently arranged for school leavers (Gorard, Rees, and Fevre 1999*a*). For many people entering the labour market for the first time, the most that they have required to find work was some sketchy knowledge of the career and labour market experience of one or two other family members or members of a peer group. For many others such knowledge was superfluous because their family or wider social network simply channelled them into their first—and perhaps only—job. This system was underpinned by norms of trust and reciprocity: the job 'seeker' trusted his/her future to those who arranged employment for him/her and all concerned expected that, once in employment, this individual would become part of the network that arranged jobs for others coming into the labour market.

Thus far we have social capital in the form of norms and networks contributing to the economy by filling vacancies in employment; but the account remains both unsatisfactory and incomplete. In particular, why should individuals leave the decisions which have such important effects on their life chances to others? At best, why should they make such decisions simply by copying the behaviour of their mother or uncle? As it stands, our account depends on a grossly oversocialized conception of human behaviour because it neglects the importance of identity. Identity has been a central component in the effort to develop a sociological theory on participation in education and training and there is every reason to think that identity is crucial in all other aspects of the transition to work (Rees *et al.* 1997; Gorard, Rees, and Fevre 1999*b*).

The importance of identity in the transition to adulthood has already been recognized by Fernandez Kelly (1995) who uses social capital and the economic sociology of the transition to work to develop a sophisticated account of high teenage pregnancy rates in a population with poor employment prospects. She castigates others, for example the proponents of the optimizing individual, for failing to explain 'the sequences that lead to behavioural outcomes' (1995: 227). In her view girls get pregnant because of their truncated networks and their norms; but for present purposes the key contribution Fernandez Kelly makes is the inclusion of identities in her conception of social capital which 'depends on processes of identity formation through *norms of exclusion and inclusion*' (1995: 217, emphasis in original).

In her ethnography Fernandez Kelly finds girls who 'present motherhood as a desirable condition, not as a calamity. In the light of expert judgements to the contrary, this is perplexing' (1995: 233). She concludes that:

poor adults occupy with their children a similar position *vis-à-vis* labor market alternatives. In this context, motherhood represents the extension of responsibilities assumed at an early age and expresses a specific relationship with the labor market. That partly

capital closes off options. This Weberian-Durkheimian strand is much stronger in Bourdieu than in Coleman or Putnam (Woolcock 1998: 155–7).

explains why, at seventeen, Latanya Williams can state with conviction 'I waited for a long time before I had my baby'. That's why she can ask, 'What's there to wait for?' (1995: 234)

Here an oversocialized conception of teenage pregnancy rates in terms of norms is avoided by introducing a new argument about aspirations to adult identity.

Putnam (1995a) notes the importance of identity and Portes (1998: 8) makes a link between the idea of a common fate informing behaviour and the Marxist method of understanding of that behaviour. He then goes on to use the vocabulary of 'bounded solidarity' to discuss what amount to social identities (1998: 8). Because an identity tells you what behaviour is right for you, identities are able to carry norms into the hearts of those that aspire to them.

Elsewhere in this volume, Catherine Campbell refers to identity in the context of health promotion; and the idea that the effect of networks on feelings of identity is one of the ways in which social capital works—for economic good, for instance—is not a new one in the social capital literature. Clearly people would not care about identities at all if they had no prior norms; but I contend that identities are a third, neglected component of social capital, neither norms nor networks but intimately tied to both. Indeed it is doubtful whether either norms or networks can work properly, or perhaps at all, without identities. In fact, identities solve the problem of finding a reliable mechanism by which social capital can take effect through individuals (cf. Elster, cited in Woolcock 1998: 205).

Identities provide an alternative to the apparently oversocialized willingness of individuals to give way to the direction of others, or simply ape the behaviour of others, that lies at the heart of the sociological conception of the transition to work. Once we introduce identity we can see, for example, why some sketchy knowledge of the career and labour market experience of one or two other family members or members of a peer group is apparently all that is needed to make the transition to work. In this case men and women recognize their own adult identity in the models that are close at hand. To assume one of these identities, they must follow in the footsteps of someone they know to be very like themselves. Making the idea of identity central to our account of the transition to work reminds us that for most of the history of industrial societies the great majority of people have not grown up thinking that they could choose to be anyone they wanted to be. No less than in the idea of a 'learning identity' (Weil 1986) the identity that guides individuals making the transition to work is associated with assumptions about one's ability and aptitude. When identity matters, people are not thought of as clean slates but as individuals with set capabilities—which education simply reveals—from the start, or at least from very early in their lives. This is one reason why Portes (1998: 8) is quite right to emphasize the element of fatality inherent in the notion of identity. However there are others, such as the way the fatality of birth into an occupational community confirms for the individual that his or her transition to that particular occupation is somehow natural and irresistible (cf. Anderson 1991).

Emerging data from the south Wales study mentioned above (see, for example, Gorard *et al*. 1997) shows people explaining that progress through education, labour market, and occupational career reveals only what has already been determined by birth or very early educational experience. A change in fate is readily accommodated in this model by taking recourse to the idea of— usually early—mis-recognition of fate: I was *wrongly* labelled as having low ability at school. Thus the individual case is accounted for but the general explanation of natal fatality is preserved.

The one or two other family members, or members of a peer group, who figure so centrally in the individual's transition to work are the people who are believed to share that individual's aptitudes and level of ability, and hence their correct adult fate. When the individual looks to them for help and advice he or she is modelling the experience of another individual who is believed to merit the same fate. In this way the introduction of identity provides an empirically grounded alternative to the slavish following of norms entailed in an oversocialized theory and makes real progress in the socialization of social capital. The benefits of this progress can be seen in the way that a theory which makes much of identity also introduces the possibility of the transition to work becoming dependent on self-transformation.

If we apply the idea of identity within the south Wales study, we can see how social capital both furnishes identity and, on occasion, also provides the means to transform this identity into another. At the end of the nineteenth century, the region was dominated by the coal mining industry. Most boys born in the coalfield were simply taken to the pit at the appropriate age by their fathers or other older male relatives; and indeed it was often family members who would train them to mine coal and keep themselves safe down the pit (Rees 1997). Both productivity and safe working depended on the simple reproduction of identity: in these families and villages all the boys were born to be coal miners and this meant they would be made to acquire particular skills and knowledge (Fevre, Gorard, and Rees 2000).

Questions of identity and aspirations amongst those making the transition to work in the south Wales coalfield became more complex in the early twentieth century. Evening classes were organized at which individuals could acquire the technical qualifications that were now needed for career advancement in the industry, and which were consolidated during the period after nationalization in 1947. But with unionization and, subsequently, the intensification of conflict between miners and owners during the inter-war years, the nature of participation was transformed through the rise of 'workers' education' aimed at raising political awareness and feeding the labour movement with activists, a pattern which was not replicated even in other coalfield areas (Rees 1997; Rees *et al*. 1997)

This movement was both a reaction to, and an internal insurrection within, the existing pattern of education and training in the region; but it also drew on existing social capital because philosophy and social science had already become topics of informal discussion amongst the miners when their shifts finished (Fevre, Gorard, and Rees 2000). These men—and indeed they were *all* men (Gorard *et al.* 1998)—were not engaged in reproducing what their parents had been capable of. The new identity to which they aspired necessarily entailed self-transformation and in fact led them to shun the mere reproduction of occupational identity and the more mundane ideas of career advancement through vocational education and training. Their new belief was that people like themselves were capable of much more, capable perhaps of running the country, but needed to educate themselves to make this potential a reality. But this was not to be a transformation fuelled by self-interested individualism since it was done in the name of, and for the good of, class, community, and family (Fevre, Rees, and Gorard 1999). Here the traditional sources of identity provided the rationale, in fact the imperative, for self-transformation.

The idea of linking identity to self-transformation is clearly derived from the sociology of Mead (1967) but the traditional sociology that attempted to use this sort of theory in what were, in fact, the first sociological contributions to this field did not appreciate the subtlety of Mead's approach. Commitment to self-transformation obviously means a commitment to more education and training for longer periods, because education and training are in principle the essence of transformative activity; but the sort of education and training that will be chosen will also be affected with a strong preference being shown for more transformative activities.

As the next section of this chapter focuses on the relationship between social capital and economic development, this section closes by discussing identity, self-transformation and economic development. The starting point of this discussion is Streeck's (1989) classic explanation of why the norms and networks that determined the behaviour of labour market entrants had such a spectacular effect on the skill levels of German manufacturing workers. Streeck's is an oversocialized account of the relationship between social capital and economic development. This problem can be corrected if we introduce the notion of identities and when we do so we begin to uncover a process of self-transformation that has some parallels to the example from south Wales.

Streeck argues that it is much harder for market societies like the US and Britain than for countries like Germany and Japan, with their 'heritage of community bonds', to create such high skill levels. These skills are not created as a product of the rational behaviour of optimizing individuals but out of a sense of obligation which is much more likely to arise in Germany and Japan than it does in the US and Britain (Streeck 1989: 91–3). According to Streeck, 'moral obligations and close communitarian bonds' lead to higher skills through much more positive attitudes to training (1989:100). In Streeck's account networks and norms are therefore made to do the work of identities.

With a variety of colleagues, A. J. Brown has been involved in longitudinal research on international patterns of skill formation for over a decade. After documenting recent threats to the German system, Brown explains how in

Germany people learn as part of their 'entry into a community of practice' and 'becoming skilled . . . within a wider process of identity formation' where 'recognition of significant achievement (and attainment of the status of experienced practitioner) is itself a socially mediated (or contested) process, dependent on others and a sense of self-worth' (A. J. Brown 1997: 7). Social identities constructed by and for an occupational community are what make those who participate in the German system want to take part in education and training—and we might speculate that this also occurs in the academic track of the 'dual system'.

German workers have to undergo some degree of self-transformation in order to be able legitimately to assume these identities and it was this transformation that was responsible for the acquisition of the skills discussed by Streeck. The suggestion that self-transformation is central to the efficacy of social capital in the German system follows from the idea that one must become a different person to be admitted to the occupational community and be worthy of the rewards accorded to members. People who have been educated and trained in the German system have done this in order to become someone different at the end of the process, someone with an identity which can be achieved only by undergoing the process of transformation. Where self-transformation lies at the heart of identity acquisition, people are more likely to find themselves in possession of the sort of skills that have the most dramatic effect on productive potential in high-skilled manufacturing. In contrast, the natural base level for all British training is accurately described as 'mimetic' rather than transformative. Employers and employees alike share the same distaste for training and do not regard it as transformative (Rees, Fielder, and Rees 1992: 9; see also Fevre, Rees, and Gorard 1999).

This brief discussion of the differences in skill formation between Germany and other countries is simply meant to illustrate the potential of an appropriately socialized version of social capital in which norms and networks are complemented by social identities. Earlier in this section we saw how socialized social capital might play a part in the politicization of individuals and societies but here we have seen some of its potential for explaining different patterns of economic development. The next section of this chapter will consider the explanatory possibilities of social capital when conceived in this way alongside the more familiar, undersocialized, version derived from economics. It is to the latter that we turn first.

Social Capital and Economic Development

This section uses the work of Francis Fukuyama to provide a clear example of the dangers of colonization by economics which Fine describes. If many writers are no longer be prepared to take Fukuyama seriously, this could well be because they have begun to share some suspicions of the imperialism of economics. Fukuyama's work is only the most obvious example of this process, but the violence done to history[4] and the sort of distorted view of the relationship between social capital and economic development that we find there, especially in his most recent work (Fukuyama 1999), are immanent in all economic colonialism and are not peculiar to Fukuyama. After summarizing Fukuyama's approach I will then use the socialized concept of social capital, in which identities are of central importance, to take an approach that does not diminish the importance of history to explanations of economic development, growth and prosperity.

Francis Fukuyama: Social Capital is Disposable and Renewable

Fukuyama has now published two full-length treatments of social capital (1995; 1999). In *Trust* Fukuyama, referencing Coleman, claims that 'the role of culture, and particularly spontaneous sociability, has been greatly underestimated by conventional economic analysis in explaining the large variations among societies that are otherwise at a similar level of development'. Therefore 'a society's endowment of social capital is critical to understanding its industrial structure, and hence its place in the global capitalist division of labour' (1995: 325) but 'the causal relationship between social capital and economic performance is indirect and attenuated' (1995: 321). In *Trust* Fukuyama thinks social capital can be renewed but finds the process mysterious (1995: 11). If self-organizing fails the state can step in but this is almost always at the cost of market efficiency.

The Great Disruption is an even more ambitious project and it is in this, most recent, work that the economic imperialist version of social capital is fully present in its most thoroughly reductionist form. Fukuyama is no longer interested in mere self-organizing but in social order and the moral rules that make it possible. In the manner of Schumpeter's 'gales of creative destruction' (1934), the basis of social order has been broken and remade throughout history and now the remaking is happening again. Just as the industrial revolution had the effect of creative destruction on social capital so the information society of the second half of the twentieth century, with its accompanying technological innovations, has had the same disruptive effect. We have only to look around to see that people are coming to terms with this disruption and to begin to discern the benign effects of the reconstitution of social order: for example, crime is falling again, just as it did at a similar stage in the nineteenth century.

The painful process of destruction and reconstruction is absolutely necessary for prosperity:

In economic life, group co-ordination is necessary for one form of production, but when technology and markets change, a different type of co-ordination with perhaps a different set of group members becomes necessary. The bonds of social reciprocity that

---

[4] In fact much of the time Fukuyama is engaged in writing real history out of the picture altogether and replacing it with something more neutral and amenable to the new economics like 'change' or 'evolution'.

facilitated production in the earlier time period become obstacles to production in the later one . . . To continue the economic metaphor, social capital can be said to be obsolete and needs to be depreciated in the country's capital accounts. (Fukuyama, 1999: 18–19)

Now the process of renewal is no longer mysterious, as it was in *Trust*: it will be founded in our 'very powerful innate human capacities for reconstituting social order' (1999: 282). The certainty that social capital will be renewed, in the form required by the new times, lies in the human nature that biological science is now discovering—while game theory shows how this plays out in terms of norms. The policy prescription that Fukuyama draws from this is even stronger than before: the state interferes in the spontaneous production of order at its peril.

Fukuyama's work provides an instructive example because it offers a disturbingly ahistorical and distorted view of the relation between social capital and economic development. We now see that this distortion has become so extreme in Fukuyama's most recent work that social capital has become both disposable and *infinitely renewable*. Fukuyama tells us we must simply leave people alone and social capital will be created, particularly where people are making money.[5] Social capital and capitalism have something of a mutually beneficial, reciprocal relationship. There are obstacles to re-norming such as moral individualism, and relativism—and the associated 'miniaturization of community'—but market relations and capitalism are never the problem: they only cause good, albeit that the unavoidable side-effects are sometimes, temporarily, inconvenient.

The Great Disruption may be one more instance of the increasing power of re-launched sociobiology to persuade us of the inadequacies of social science (Tiryakin 1998; Runciman 1998) but the underlying reason that history has been demoted in Fukuyama's argument lies in the hegemony of economic rationality and the imperialism of economics. Indeed *The Great Disruption* should be cited as one of the most notorious examples of the excesses of this form of rationality. Here Fukuyama proposes that not only all policy action has to be justified in these terms, but so even does our continued existence in families and communities with moral commitments: Fukuyama's 'ethical habits'. It is as though we have to plead with governments and corporations to let us hold onto our lives: 'if only you let us, we will make you prosperous'.

Such consequences may be inherent in current usages of social capital but they are not, happily, inevitable. If we turn to an appropriately socialized conception of social capital, for example, we find ourselves in a better position to fully understand the relationship between various forms of social capital and capitalism. The section that follows illustrates what inter-disciplinary work risks losing if the application of social capital turns society into a means to an

---

[5] For example, 'market exchange promotes habits of reciprocity that carry on from economic life into moral life' (Fukuyama 1999: 261). For examples of economists short-circuiting the problem of social order in an analogous way, see Granovetter (1985: 484).

end. It does so by returning to the discussion of identities, the transition to work and economic development.

The Implications of a Socialized Concept of Social Capital

We have already seen that the addition of social content—networks, families, and identities—to social capital makes it possible to restore real history in our accounts. It has also been suggested that socialized social capital gives us a much more complex and useful view of the interplay between social capital and economic development. From this we might begin to guess that Fukuyama's idea of disposable and infinitely renewable social capital is both misguided and unnecessarily brutal.

In Fukuyama's vision of the 'creative destruction' of social capital as a consequence of economic and industrial change, the networks and norms that get people into jobs grow up in symbiosis with the markets and organizations that they serve. Typically a community grows up around a colliery or mill. Within that community networks and norms evolve which serve the purpose of fitting people into jobs in the colliery or mill. When economic conditions or technology change sufficiently, perhaps after several generations, this social capital no longer serves a purpose because the traditional industry can no longer provide employment. Those members of the community who are less well equipped to compete stay behind, still locked into their decaying and now useless networks and adhering to norms which are now clearly dysfunctional. The best and the brightest of the rest pack their U-Hauls and head for Maclean, Virginia to found new communities which will generate the social capital needed to get them jobs in the information economy.

Fukuyama asserts that industrial change makes and breaks social capital. He passes rather too quickly over the casualties of this process: '[t]he negative consequences of capitalism for community life are only part of the story, however, and in many ways not the most important one' (1995: 311–12). If we also focus on the effects of industrial change on identities we will, like Fernandez Kelly, be well placed to understand how *little* the needs of economic development and the lives of individuals are kept in equilibrium.

The identities and associated social networks which once dominated the labour markets of Fordist societies lingered long after they have ceased to be of use (Portes 1998: 14). Problems of social exclusion were exacerbated where people continued to rely on them while post-industrial society with its characteristic individuation, risk, and the return of uncertainty came into being and confirmed the loss, or irrelevance, of all accumulated social capital (Beck 1992). Thus by the 1980s in Britain adult identity was derived simply from the fact of employment yet this 'fact' was becoming ever more problematic. The way in which, amongst those who set the norms and peopled the networks, expectations and experience of employment cast such a long shadow over the transition to work was recognized by Bynner (1989). He argued that adult self-identity was so bound up with getting a job that correspondingly less emphasis was placed on learning—at exactly the time when the lineaments of the knowledge economy were becoming clear.

Drawing on Bynner, Ainley (1991: 6) argues that this was one of the main reasons why so many more people remained averse to education in Britain than in other industrialized countries. This might well account for the apparently perverse finding of Banks *et al.* (1991: 47) that there was an inverse relationship between commitment to work and liking training amongst the young people they studied. This problem was exacerbated in a deteriorating labour market (Rees, Williamson, and Istance 1996). In Britain education and training were seen as a distraction from the main aim of doing what was necessary in order to earn an adult identity or, worse still, as an obstacle in the way of achieving this aim, something that kept people in their childhood role and frustrated their ambition to reach adulthood (see also R. Harrison 1993; Taylor and Spencer 1994).

Perhaps such evidence that 'obsolete' identities linger on long past their sell-by date might be no surprise to Fukuyama but what would surprise him is the idea that these identities are not being *replaced* as part of the creation of a new stock of social capital. In fact at the start of the new century it is becoming clear that the role of social capital in the transition to work—whether as identities, norms or networks—is being usurped by more commodified forms. It is no exaggeration to say that capitalism is now manufacturing its own synthetic substitute for social capital.

Fukuyama would be surprised by this suggestion because he does not suspect that the sort of relationship between social capital and economic development that he assumes to be timeless has in fact a very determinate history, and indeed belongs to a time that now appears to have passed. The power of social capital to get people into jobs was a phenomenon of Fordist societies; and although people continue to rely on networks, norms, and identities, social capital has to be supplemented more and more as society changes.

There is no need to take seriously Fukuyama's notion of the spontaneous creation of social order which is, magically, helpful to economic development because we no longer have to accept that one, dysfunctional, sort of social capital has to be replaced by another functional sort which will facilitate the transition to work in the new knowledge economy. What is clearly needed for the knowledge economy is the sort of identity which demands self-transformation but where is it to come from in circumstances of extreme individuation? Instead of putting our faith in the infinite renewal of social capital which is supposedly guaranteed by human biology, we should be thinking hard about where our aspirations to social identities are being produced if they are no longer being created as part of the process which produces social capital.

In pre-capitalist societies, identity was derived from family, village, and religion—and much more rarely from a craft or trade. In industrial capitalism work identity became paramount; and at the extreme of 'social class' it determined all other aspects of culture (Beck 1992). There was a period of transition in which the rural-urban shift meant that many fates became uncertain but in settled industrial societies identity in the sense that the term is used in this chapter came into its own. The communities of these societies acted as repositories of social capital which, in this case, consisted of the alternative identities to which one would discover one was equipped, or not, to aspire. Why cannot this type of social revolution simply be repeated?

According to Fukuyama, new social capital for the information age should be coming into being all around us. Yet all that we know about the differences between the new society and Fordist society raises doubts about whether it is really going to be possible for new identities and associate networks and norms to be built up as new jobs are created. For one thing, Fukuyama claims that post-industrial societies have little room for stable, lifelong identity. For another, we are told that identities are coming adrift from work altogether. In future you may belong to a community but that community is not going to get you a job and indeed its members probably understand very little about the work you aspire to (Beck 1992; Castells 1997). In the 'network society' other sorts of identities become important once more because this is all that social life is now able to create. If there are to be no relevant identities because of individuation on the one hand and the disappearance of lifelong careers on the other, how will people make the transition to work?

The south Wales study cited above offers some more emerging evidence which might give a clue to the answer to this question (Gorard *et al.* 1997). During the long postwar boom the transition to work could always be described in very concrete terms and identity was usually synonymous with job title (Gorard, Rees, and Fevre 1999*b*). Over time, however, the formal education system has become a much more important component of an extended transition to work. This has been associated with the obsolescence of the old social networks and family influences on the transition to work (Gorard, Rees, and Fevre 1999*b*). Since the 1980s actors' accounts of the transition to work have become still more abstract—with little mention of networks—and have begun to introduce what might be called 'commodified identities'.

If one ponders the sort of identities that will be needed to get people into the work that the network society is creating, it is entirely feasible to anticipate the disappearance of any relationship between social capital and economic development. What is going to be required to get people into higher education and into labour markets when most people do not know anyone who is in the sort of job they will end up in and indeed, they do not really know where they are going to end up? Perhaps what we need to make this new world work are fictional idealizations of possible labour-market goals rather than real identities possessed by real people that an individual knows and trusts? Contrary to Fukuyama's expectations (1995: 321) this may be exactly what is now beginning to happen.

In one possible future scenario social capital—both identities and social networks—no longer underpins the transition to work. Social capital in the form of identities and networks has been replaced by the economic capital of 'characters' (MacIntyre 1985) and markets (Keep 1997). The replacement of

networks by markets, in education as well as the allocation of labour, is familiar but the idea of characters is new to this branch of sociology. Postmen,
nurses and engine drivers serve as characters for children but young adults are
more likely to refer to managers, lawyers, and other professionals. These characters rarely count as social capital because '[s]ocial capital is a product of
embeddedness' (Portes 1995: 13; see also Granovetter 1985: 481).

Once you no longer actually know anyone who makes a living in the manner to which you aspire, adult identities have clearly become disembedded.
MacIntyre explains that characters come about with rationalization and it is
clear that some of these substitute identities are created and disseminated by
bureaucracies, like careers advisers, but the form that describes them most
accurately is 'commodified identities'. Whereas modernity entailed the progressive operationalization of identity, postmodernity has entailed its
progressive commercialization and commodification. In contrast to Arrow
(quoted by Fukuyama 1995: 151–2), we can now see that social capital itself
can be cashed out for commercial gain and that it even makes sense to talk
about the *commodification* of social capital.

The principal agent of commodification of identity, and source of information on available characters, is television This may be one rather less obvious
reason why Putnam is right to find television strongly implicated in the
decline of social capital (Putnam 1995*a, b*). Indeed, the creation of characters
and commodified identities in television shows is a perfect example of television supplanting social capital. This all means that capitalism has taken on the
job of substituting identities and networks itself rather than letting 'spontaneous sociability' work the magic that Fukuyama predicts for it. In the new
society a kind of *ersatz* social capital is created instead of the real, embedded
social capital of identities and networks.

Conclusions

The fact that sociology's stock-in-trade of networks and norms, especially
norms of reciprocity, is now receiving so much attention from other social scientists still might suggest that social capital presents a heaven-sent opportunity for the discipline (Portes 1995; Woolcock 1998). Non-sociologists now
appear to see this stock-in-trade not simply as interesting to their discipline
but as central or, at least, very important, to achieving the policy aims they
value most highly. Yet Fine (1999*c*: 416) feels the balance of the evidence is
against the optimistic view, and I am inclined to agree with him, even though
there may still be a future in the interdisciplinary study of social capital with
a restored and robust sociological contribution.

The idea, central to the social capital literature since Coleman (1988*a*), that
social capital could be a vital contribution to economic growth and prosperity
is not the most important in sociology. *The* sociological question remains:
how did the things that are here being called social capital come about? In

other words, how do communities, groups, societies come into being and change and what part do networks, norms, and so on play in all of this? Behind this question lie all the other questions about social order. To the extent that political scientists, economists, and other non-sociologists bother with the reproduction of social capital at all their treatment is usually cursory and shallow.[6] Many writers simply treat social capital at or near the level of tastes or preferences. Without a revitalized sociological contribution the literature will repeat fundamental mistakes even in understanding the relationship, if indeed there is one, between social capital and economic performance. Social capital is not guaranteed renewal or always necessary to economic development. Sociology allows us to grasp the possibility of a shift from embedded identities and the social networks necessary to achieving them towards commodified identities—characters—and market arrangements.

One of the consequences of socializing social capital is that networks, norms, and identities are rescued from relegation. There is a welcome irony in the fact that when this is done we seem to learn more about economic development than we do when working with the reductionist conceptions of economics. It seems that by refusing to succumb to the logic of economic rationality we might begin to understand more about the way in which development occurs. Readers of this volume will not be shocked by the suggestion that the extent and nature of any relationship between social capital and economic development should always be a matter for empirical enquiry, but this chapter has suggested that we are now witnessing the drastic attenuation of this relationship. When we reclaim the idea of social capital we are able to place the link between social capital and economic development or prosperity in an historical, and quite limited, context.

Failing to incorporate a proper sociology into the study of social capital is not only bad for the field but bad for sociology. In the discussion of economic rationality earlier in this chapter it was pointed out that social scientists were not immune to general cultural shifts and this explained why they had succumbed to the imperialism of economics. In the case of social capital this cultural shift is particularly dangerous because social capital risks turning sociology into a mere stripped-out instrument for the other social sciences. The problem that is described here is a more serious one for sociology than other social sciences because the nature of the concept of social capital seems to make sociology central while at the same time subordinating sociology's interests to those of other disciplines. This is a problem that other disciplines that have made the running with the concept, political science for example, do not have. This can be briefly illustrated.

Political scientists find in social capital that the ends of two other disciplines, sociology and economics, are neatly rolled into one and made to serve as the means to political science's own ends of more democracy or

---

[6] More generally, the reason that economics does not worry about the problem of social order lies in its assumption that the way the actions of optimizing individuals work out means the 'problem' is already solved.

participation. For economics itself the situation is even simpler. The end—the more efficient distribution and use of resources—of the discipline is now met in the new concept, with the means borrowed from another: sociology. For sociologists, however, the situation is far from simple. The *end* of our discipline is understanding the biggest and most numerous phenomena of social life, in other words society and all the smaller phenomena that go to make it up: communities, associations, groups, and families. Sociologists must avoid an instrumental attitude to all of this but to the extent they take on board the economists' version of the idea of social capital this becomes problematic. To the extent that they turn their attention to social capital as a means to increase prosperity or improve democracy they risk turning their unique focus into a mere tool, and a faulty one at that.

6

Social Capital, Innovation, and Competitiveness

PETER MASKELL

Introduction

T HE contemporary process of globalization has dramatically enhanced the economic importance of what a diverse group of current scholars (Bourdieu 1980; Coleman 1988*b*; Burt 1992; Putnam 1993*a*; Fukuyama 1995; Woolcock 1998) has called 'social capital'. Social capital refers to the values and beliefs that citizens share in their everyday dealings and which give meaning and provide design for all sorts of rules. The use of the word 'capital' implies that we are dealing with an asset. The word 'social' tells us that it is an asset attained through membership of a community. Social capital is accumulated within the community through processes of interaction and learning. But social capital is not a commodity for which trade is technically possible or even meaningful. Social capital is at the same time in part accumulated as an unintended and even unanticipated consequence of economic activity as people often spend more of their waking hours 'bowling' with their workplace colleagues than with their family and friends. Norms, codes, trust, solidarity and other vital elements of social capital are built and reinforced when sharing a common goal or a mutual fate even in the most hierarchical economic structures imaginable, like the globally operating multidivisional corporation, and not just when people mingle, organize and achieve with peers in their spare time.

The chapter focuses on the relationship between social capital and economic development. Social capital enables firms to improve their innovative capability and conduct business transactions without much fuss and has, therefore, substantial implications for economic performance. The interrelatedness between social capital and economic activity includes the prospect that positive feed-back loops can make initially insignificant differences in the stock of social capital a factor of major importance for the competitiveness of firms. Social capital might seriously influence a community's long-term

The author would like to acknowledge the helpful comments from Nicolai J. Foss, Henrik Sornn-Friese, and Bengt-Åke Lundvall when writing this chapter.

economic performance through such chains of circular causation with trust as its pivotal element. A distinction is made between the trust built in inter-firm networks and the mutual trust that forms part of a community's stock of social capital. It is argued that social capital is economically superior to built trust as it increases flexibility while reducing investments. These superior qualities significantly increase the economic import of social capital as globalization proceeds. Social capital enhances the division of labour by reducing the costs of coordination and it remains a source of valuable heterogeneity between communities when former localized inputs are converted into ubiquities as borders become porous.

Different approaches give significance to social capital as an instrument of economic development but the soundness of attempted cross-community collations and assessments of the stock of social capital is questioned in the final section of the paper.

Innovation and Forms of Trust

There is little doubt that deliberate efforts of knowledge creation influence and shape the economy far more today than 15 or 20 years ago. A knowledge-based economy (OECD 1996) is materializing, where the competitive edge of many firms has shifted from static price competition towards dynamic improvement, favouring those who can create knowledge faster than their competitors. Knowledge creation includes activities such as investment in R&D and the development and adoption of leading-edge technology. Equally important is, however, the 'low-tech' learning and innovation (Maskell 1998) that takes place when firms in fairly traditional industries are innovative in the way they handle and develop resource management, logistics, production organization, marketing, sales, distribution, industrial relations, and so forth. Following Carter (1994), the shift towards a knowledge-based economy might be characterized by three elements: (1) the growing importance of economic transactions focused on knowledge itself; (2) the rapid qualitative changes in goods and services; and (3) the incorporation of the creation and implementation of change itself into the mission of economic agents.

Numerous studies (see Rosenberg 1972; Lundvall 1992; De Bresson 1996; OECD 1999) have identified strong and stable relationships of inter-organizational coordination and cooperation as the solution to the somewhat puzzling question of product innovation. On the one hand, most product innovations take place in some kind of interaction between firms, but without a general transformation of markets into hierarchies as proposed by transaction cost theory. The emerging conclusion is that the process of innovation and learning is fuelled by the interaction between distinct bodies of knowledge developed in independent organizations pursuing objectives of competitiveness. Furthermore, there is reason to suspect that inter-firm learning is subject to both thresholds, before the knowledge bases of separate firms have grown sufficiently apart for interacting to imply learning, and ceilings, after which the cognitive distance becomes too great for firms to bridge, and where inter-firm learning, consequentially, will cease.

On the other hand, pure market interactions have generally proved incapable of transmitting the qualitative information needed in developing new products in interaction between firms due to the asymmetrical distribution of information between the seller and the buyer regarding the main characteristics of what is offered for sale. First of all, the potential customer wants to make sure that the knowledge offered is not already in his or her possession, in which case any asking price will be too high. One unit of any piece of knowledge is clearly enough, and the price for additional identical units of knowledge is always zero. Next, the potential buyer will want to ascertain the specific merit of the knowledge offered before purchasing it. The problem is that when fully informed of the content of the knowledge offered, she/he has in effect acquired it for free (Arrow 1970). The awareness of this foreseeable outcome might easily discourage the seller from offering the knowledge on the market in the first place.

These and other market failures for the exchange of knowledge between firms can only be overcome if and when the open market relations are superseded by stable and reciprocal exchange arrangements based on some element of trust. Following Glaeser et al. (1999) trust is defined as the commitment of resources to an activity where the outcome depends upon the cooperative behaviour of others. Without trust that the business partner will eventually pay for valuable knowledge transferred, no knowledge will be forthcoming and the innovative capability of both partners will be hampered. Trust is an excellent mechanism to overcome intricate market failures. Empirical studies of the process of building such stable and reciprocal exchange arrangements suggest that at least three distinctive stages usually have to be travelled sequentially in order for firms to learn to trust each other, or at least behave as if they trust each other (Maskell et al. 1998).

In the first stage, the transfer of knowledge involves the employment of a very old-fashioned, pre-capitalist exchange mechanism: barter. Knowledge is here exchanged directly, without the use of money, between partners who both suspect that they might benefit from obtaining some knowledge that the other possess. Such pair-wise exchange arrangements limit the firm's possible loss of competitive advantage when making knowledge available to others, though it does not completely eliminate the risk. Barter implies that each party needs to produce new knowledge in order to get access to new knowledge. Though the use of this old mechanism is not uncommon for exchanging knowledge—within and between academic research groups, for instance—it is often very costly and inefficient to use. It is costly in both money and search time because the seller will have to identify a potential buyer, who at the same time wants to exchange knowledge that might be useful; and it is inefficient as many potentially beneficial exchanges will not take place simply because buyers and sellers do not find each other.

In the second stage a more efficient arrangement has evolved as the partners in previous transactions save some or all the search costs by keeping in contact with each other, thus initiating a 'dyadic', semi-stable relation. Former misunderstandings and suspicions are gradually eliminated, and the exchange can encompass a still wider range of subtle pieces of knowledge. By repetition of knowledge exchanges, both parties thus benefit from a decrease in cost and an increase in quality of the knowledge transmitted. Each new link created, each new experience with the partner's peculiar ways, and each adaptation and modification accomplished in order to facilitate future exchange represent the sinking of costs in building the routines and conventions that reduce the friction of interaction. Gradually, not only fully explicit—codified—pieces of knowledge can be exchanged but also knowledge with some portion still tacit. As the deepening of the relationship continues, the perception is intensified and the received tacit knowledge better understood while both parties benefit from the somewhat idiosyncratic investment of learning to work together.

In the third stage, the dyadic partnerships interconnect in building network-relations through which each participant might access knowledge bases still further afield while benefiting from the trust-enhancing investments made by the initial sinking of costs in one or a few relationships: 'your friend is my friend'. Any infringement of trust by firms in such closely knitted business networks is so severely penalized that in effect malfeasance becomes a non-option. The collective awareness of this mechanism makes it possible to exchange knowledge even between competitors within a network, to an extent that no outsider can aspire to achieve.

What market relations are unable to accomplish inter-firm networks can. The explicit and tacit knowledge needed to uphold a continuous stream of innovations can thus be exchanged through networks of long-term inter-firm relations secured by relation-specific sunk costs under the assumption that any present imbalance in the exchange-related benefits will be equalized in the long run. In the quaint terminology of economic parlance, trust will thus characterize a relation between firms when each is confident that the other's present value of all foreseeable future exchanges exceeds the possible benefits of breaking the relation. The larger the sunk costs, the greater the confidence and the trust. The time and resources needed to build a relationship varies, however, with the stock of social capital that the firms in question might attain through membership of a community.

We still know very little about the actual process by which social capital is produced and accumulated, beyond suspecting that it might be a mainly unanticipated consequence of doing something else—just like, for instance, learning by doing. It appears, however, that an important transmutation sometimes take place as firms and other economic actors constantly demonstrate their ability and willingness to submit to the local rules of the game by their day-to-day operations and established business practices. By proving their continued trustworthiness they also produce or reproduce a local climate of mutual trust, where the 'default' dominant attitude towards a new and unknown potential partner might shift from distrust to trust. In such fortunate circumstances very little new investment is needed when firms decide to engage in new innovation-driven exchange relationships.

While trust built through relation-specific investments between and among firms is beneficial to the investors only, mutual trust represents a collective investment adding to the stock of social capital of the whole community. The result of building trust through network formation might have a superficial resemblance to the benefits accruing from membership of a community with a stock of social capital based on mutual trust. But the latter has major additional advantages: it is cheaper and more flexible as little or no relation-specific investment is needed. When building trust, firms have to invest in the specific relationship, establishing tight limitation on the flexibility of its future actions and, when breaking a relation, the investment cannot be recaptured. Not so with firms utilizing social capital where the minimal relation-specific sunk costs make it uncomplicated to relate to new firms if circumstances make it propitious, as long as any decisions to discontinue old partnerships are carried out in a proper manner and in accordance with the community's beliefs about good behaviour. The risk of becoming a victim of a lock-in (David 1985; Arthur 1989) is thus substantially larger for firms relying on trust built only in network arrangements than for firms able to attain and utilize social capital through membership of a community.

Even if examples of non-collaborative attitudes might be plentiful among firms in communities that are generally characterized by a large stock of social capital, their conduct is usually constrained by their knowledge of the unattractive consequences of misbehaving. Information about any kind of misbehaviour will sooner or later be available to most potential partners in the community, who in the future will tend to take their business elsewhere. Worse still, by becoming a local outcast a firm is deprived of the flow of knowledge, including its tacit parts, which can prove very difficult to substitute. The combination of incentives and penalties acts as the crucial component in a transmission mechanism preparing new generations to accept the inheritance and concede to its behavioural constraints. This is why communities such as Silicon Valley continue to accumulate social capital and prosper even though 'nobody knows anybody else's mother there. There is no deep history, little in way of complex familial ties and little structured community. It is a world of independent—even isolated—newcomers' (Cohen and Fields 1999: 2).

In other communities newcomers might be facing a *rite de passage* before they are allowed to enjoy the full benefits of the social capital accumulated (Dei Ottati 1996; Shearmur and Klein 1997). However, with the right economic incentives even newcomers constantly fell obliged to prove their continued trustworthiness in order to pursue their objectives (Saxenian 1994). By doing so they contribute to the stock of social capital, the rents of which are appropriated by present and future generations of both incumbent firms and newcomers (Axelrod 1981; Coleman 1984; Winter 1987).

In a knowledge-based economy the perhaps most significant rents originate from the way in which the easy exchange of knowledge, only partly understood, between and among a constantly changing configuration of firms within the community dramatically enhances their innovative capabilities. Reducing your development or commercialization time is often worth virtually whatever you have to pay and social capital contributes by cutting the expenses and reducing the time needed to benefit from knowledge residing elsewhere. As innovative capabilities become increasingly important so does social capital.

Globalization and Coordination

As well as its increasingly important contribution to innovation, social capital has mainly been seen as contributing to economic performance by reducing inter-firm transaction costs, that is, search and information costs, bargaining and decision costs, and policing and enforcement costs. Lower search and information costs improve the efficiency of resource allocation. Reduced costs for bargaining and decision making facilitate the coordination of diverse activities between firms and enable an even further division of labour (Richardson 1953; 1972). Diminishing costs of policing and enforcement free up resources to be used in more productive ways. Firms in communities with a large stock of social capital will, of course, always have a competitive advantage to the extent that social capital helps reduce malfeasance, induces reliable information to be volunteered, causes agreements to be honoured, enables employees to share tacit information, and places negotiators on the same wave-length. This advantage gets even bigger when the process of globalization deepens the division of labour and thus augments the need for coordination between and among firms (Loasby 1992; Foss and Loasby 1998).

The scale, scope and numbers of international economic interactions have undoubtedly increased in recent decades, reaching an unprecedented level at the beginning of the new millennium. Today only a few firms, if indeed any at all, span the entire range of activities necessary to convert a natural resource into a commodity ready for final consumption. The vast majority of firms reap the multitude of economic benefits of continuous specialization by concentrating their resources and competencies on the production of those goods or services they perceive as contributing to the firm's future competitive advantage, while at the same time leaving the rest of their former activities for others to take up. They outsource as a means of becoming agile, lean, and purpose-oriented.

The process of globalization, and therefore the division of labour, is furthered every time inter-governmental agreements—General Agreement on Tariffs and Trade, World Trade Organization, European Union, North Atlantic Free Trade Agreement, and so forth—reduce former barriers to the exchange of goods, services, knowledge and capital *and* every time innovations and investments in transport and communication systems reduce the friction of space, *and* every time the diffusion of common technical standards or the levelling of consumer preferences enlarges homogeneous market segments across countries. As the division of labour deepens with every step taken on the road towards globalization, all final products will include contributions from an increasing number of firms, each producing for smaller and smaller segments of a geographically expanding market. The division of labour is, however, limited not only by the extent of the market, but also by the rising costs of coordination between the increasingly specialized firms.

Social capital reduces the cost of coordination and, consequently, impacts directly on the boundaries of the firm, by placing them in a better position than their competitors to outsource and specialize still further, and to appropriate the excess rents flowing from the resulting deepening of the division of labour. However, social capital reduces only the cost of coordination taking place between members of a community. This might be why we see a proliferation of globally operating national corporations, but still have only a handful of truly international enterprises. American-based firms have almost exclusively American-born managers just as foreign directors in European or Japanese firms are extraordinary rare.

Some communities are not confined to a single geographical locality, but most are very place-specific. In order for interacting firms to attain the social capital of geographically embedded communities, they usually need to co-locate within the boundaries of the community. The concept of social capital might thus contribute to current theoretical and empirical work on clustering (Malmberg and Maskell 1997; Enright 1998) and help to explain why some regional and national patterns of economic specialization are so surprisingly 'sticky' (Dalum, Laursen, and Villumsen 1998). The advantages when attaining and utilizing a large stock of social capital are probably also among the reasons why low-tech firms can continue to prosper in high-cost regions and even dominate the economy of most countries in western Europe (Maskell and Törnqvist 1999).

Ubiquities and Competitiveness

As a repercussion of the ongoing globalization, most formerly localized inputs, crucial to the competitiveness of firms, have been converted into ubiquities making the input equally available at more or less the same cost to all firms almost regardless of location. A large domestic market is, for instance, of no advantage when global transport costs are becoming negligible; when the loyalty of customers toward national suppliers is dwindling; and when most trade barriers have eroded. Likewise, are domestic suppliers of the most efficient production machinery no longer an unquestioned blessing, when identical equipment is available world-wide and at essentially the same cost? The omnipresence of organizational designs of proven value makes, furthermore, a long industrial track record less valuable.

When an input becomes ubiquitous all competing firms are placed on an equal footing. What everyone has cannot constitute a competitive advantage (Dierickx and Cool 1989; Prahalad and Hamel 1990). Firms cope with this problem of former important inputs converted to ubiquities by basing their competitiveness on unique in-house competencies and capabilities gradually developed over time and supplemented with any remaining heterogeneous input. In order to contribute to the competitiveness of firms, such an input must be valuable and difficult to imitate, replicate, or substitute (Barney 1991). Social capital is such an input. It is increasingly valuable as globalization progresses. It is not abundant in all communities. It cannot be bought or acquired. And, most significantly, it is impossible to imitate, replicate, or substitute for three different but interrelated reasons.

First, asset mass efficiencies are present since communities that already possess a large stock of social capital are often in a better position to accumulate additional social capital than communities with a limited initial stock. To become a late starter on the right track and to match the first movers' rate of social capital accumulation might require more than luck and blind reliance on the possible beneficial but unanticipated consequences of doing something else.

Second, the accumulation of social capital is at least in part the unintended and unanticipated outcome of activities performed to achieve another purpose. This gives rise to all sorts of causal ambiguity, the disentangling or unravelling of which might prove impossible (Lippman and Rumelt 1982; Reed and Defillippi 1990). Unlike uncertainty, ambiguity cannot be reduced by the collection of more facts. A community's stock of social capital represents a complex web of relationships and linkages woven over time while leaving the precise nature of the means-ends relationship blurry. Initially significant institutions might even over the years mutate or interact in the origination of derivatives with profound influence on the specific qualities of the social capital of a community. Many aspects are 'in the air', but not easily contributory to any specific institution, formal or informal. For instance, the discrepancies between scholars when attempting to identify and decode the decisive elements in the Italian industrial districts are unmistakable, even when their studies are based on interviews with subsets drawn from the same pool of local managers (Harrison 1992). Precisely because of the labyrinthine qualities of social capital, the members of the local managerial class have no universal or generally accepted understanding and interpretation of the inner workings of the apparent locational advantage of their district.

Third, social capital accumulation always requires time-consuming reiteration and habituation and no short cuts are generally available. Attempts to catch up with first movers, already in possession of a large stock of social capital, are faced with time-compression dis-economies, a phenomenon illuminated in the classical dialogue between a British lord and his American visitor, the latter asking:

'How come you got so gorgeous a lawn?' 'Well, the quality of the soil is, I dare say, of the utmost importance.' 'No problem.' 'Furthermore, one does need the finest quality of seed and fertilizers.' 'Big deal.' 'Of course, daily watering and weekly mowing are jolly important.' 'No sweat, just leave it to me!' 'That's it.' 'No kidding?!' 'Oh, absolutely. There is nothing to it old boy; just keep it up for five centuries.' (Dierickx and Cool 1989: 1507)

As the process of globalization gradually has converted most of the previously important localized inputs into ubiquities, the competitiveness of firms exposed to international competition is therefore increasingly associated with the only major heterogeneous inputs that remain largely immobile: labour and social capital.

Firms in high-cost regions in Western Europe, the Antipodes, North America and Japan have often experienced a loss of competitiveness as new low-cost competitors entered the game. With open global markets, current newcomers often possess the same technologies and organizational designs, and have access to the same customers and the same suppliers of capital, goods, and intangibles, as the incumbents. Some firms in high-cost environments cope with the challenge of cheap labour available to foreign competitors by raising their capital/labour ratio through massive investments, while others take advantage of the global differences in labour costs by relocating their production. 'Automate, emigrate, or evaporate', as the saying goes. Fortunately for the high-cost regions, the majority of firms are able to compensate for their disadvantage in labour costs by utilizing the stock of social capital while reducing internal and external transaction and coordination costs. Even more importantly, they utilize social capital to enhance their innovative capability.

How Can We Know the Dancer from the Dance?

The idea of social capital as instrumental for economic development has been adopted by Third-World theorists who recognize that standard top-down approaches simply do not work. Expectations raised by international development organizations were rarely satisfied and confidence in the Third-World state as a powerful vehicle for change evaporated. Gradually, the real developmental potential was thought to reside in locally embedded institutions and community-based social connections of kinship, neighbourhood ties, and so forth (Miller 1998).

Economic historians, among others, have for quite some time identified such aspects of social capital—using related labels—as a localized capability of considerable significance for long-term economic development. The Scandinavian welfare societies of Denmark, Norway, and Sweden, for instance, advanced from being a part of the underdeveloped periphery of Europe to reach a GDP per capita among the highest in the world, while other countries with a much stronger resource endowment remained backwaters (Kuznets 1971; Olson 1982; Morris and Adelman 1988). In-depth studies of the process have had different foci, but they have one result in common: the crucial role of social capital when explaining the shift in economic level, with trust, egalitarianism, and consensus-seeking as central variables (Menzel 1980; Senghaas 1982). A common and distinct language, a shared cultural heritage, and a sense of unity and participation have all reinforced a tendency towards consensus-seeking (Hernes 1979; Nielsen and Pedersen 1988; Amin and Thomas 1996). Few who have witnessed Scandinavian consensus-seeking processes at close quarters will probably feel tempted to praise their simplicity or effectiveness (Maskell 1997). Their merit lies, however, on another level: in the way whereby the process of reaching an agreement or decision simultaneously increases the insight into, and understanding of, the other participants' positions, interests, and visions. Negotiation does in this sense imply learning, which makes the next round of negotiation slightly easier and which enables not just the elites but sometimes even the society at large to reach a common perception of present and future challenges and of the way that the society might proceed. When imported disruptions necessitate rapid restructuring and unlearning, the necessary framework can already be in place.

Despite the insights provided by such case studies of localities, regions, or nations it is commonly maintained that the economics of social capital will only advance if we find more adequate and systematic ways of measuring it. Admittedly, it is not uncomplicated to submit social capital to the test of more rigorously developed and applied models utilizing standardized international datasets. The development and extended usage of more refined concepts and techniques of national accounting in recent decades has initiated a tradition for cross-country comparisons within economics (Denison 1967; Barro 1991), but studies of the relative performance of countries with different economic, political and social systems have usually found a large residual when all present and past investments is taken into account. Recent level accounting exercises have, additionally, shown how a large variation across countries in output per worker with seemingly similar levels of physical capital and educational attainment must indicate the existence of factors crucial to economic performance residing outside the realm of mainstream economics (Hall and Jones 1999). Many labels have been put on the residual. Abramovitz (1986) coined the expression 'social capability' to describe the aptitude to make institutional changes leading to divergence in growth rates. Hall and Jones (1999) talk of 'social infrastructure'. Others have discussed the import of 'social fabric' or emphasized the role of national or regional 'culture' favourable to innovation and change. In spite of such difference in focus and terminology the studies signify a growing awareness and recognition of non-monetary factors' significance for economic growth. But what we would really like to measure is not only the effect or outcome of social capital, but the input: each community's stock of social capital.

It has, however, proved immensely difficult to move beyond the stage of crude indicators of cooperation and trust across communities, such as those used by Morris and Adelman (1988), Putnam (1995a), or Fukuyama (1999). The general feeling within mainstream economics about entities such as social capital or social capability is thus still that '. . . no one knows just what it means and how to measure it' (Abramovitz 1986).

In principle, things should have changed as a result of theoretical advances in the modern so-called 'increasing returns endogenous growth models' (Romer 1987). These theories focus on the returns on inputs that can be accumulated and treat the rent-seeking innovative efforts of firms as a cardinal mechanism of economic progress. Social capital can be accumulated in communities and utilized by rent-seeking firms in their innovative efforts. However, current versions of this new growth theory usually model the inputs as monetary investments and R&D expenditure only, disregarding the possible contribution of social capital while focusing the scholarly and political interest on the each locality's, region's, or country's ranking within the so-called high-tech industries. This current state of affair appears to be less than totally satisfying, both from an analytical point of view and when considering the options available to the vast majority of developed and developing countries and regions in the world (Maskell *et al.* 1998).

Final Remarks

It is tempting to conclude that the economic significance which the process of globalization has granted social capital is pivotal for the contemporary revival of interest shown in this old concept. In an optimistic vein it could, furthermore, be argued that social capital's significance for competitiveness provides managers and shareholders with incentives to engage in a dialogue with policy-makers on how to avoid nurturing a low-skill equilibrium where inadequate qualifications and training for employment in the knowledge-based economy guarantee inferior life chances. Without creating jobs, securing income and preventing exclusion of the less skilled, the continued accumulation of social capital is endangered together with the economic benefits that spring from it. The increasing strong interlinkage between social capital and economic growth might, therefore, be one of the driving forces behind the present broad political interest in experimenting with 'third way' national welfare policies.

In the present essay, social capital has been treated as an analytical category in its own right, independent of civic society and democracy. Yet it is often assumed that investment in social capital is necessary to achieve democracy and, only by implication, economic growth. There is a peculiar American ring to the prominence given to democracy and civic society in the currently prevailing discourse on social capital. Europeans, typically influenced by Locke or Hegel rather than by de Tocqueville, tend, perhaps, to have a more pragmatic view of social capital, keeping their reflections on democracy and civic virtues largely separate from the somewhat mundane issues of economic development and growth (Hydén 1997). In American academic and political thinking, civic society is often perceived as good in itself because it is on the cultural bedrock of civic society that democratic norms are founded and from which the society's economic vitality emanates. This, in part, also helps explain why, for instance, Putnam's writings have had an impact in the US far beyond the mainly scholarly interest shown in the rest of the world, in spite of problems with logical circularities (Portes 1998), historical flaws (Sabetti 1996) or internal contradictions (Lemann 1996). How can we, for instance, account for the fact that the asserted ebb in confidence and other social virtues of crucial economic significance coincides in time with the longest and strongest economic upturn on record in the US?

From a European small-country perspective there is also something slightly disturbing about the way in which the state is commonly perceived in the contemporary discourse. Putnam (1993*b*), for instance, believes that anything that takes place outside the state realm counts as part of civic society and contributes to the building of social capital. By taking this dichotomy too literally we run the risk of failing to appreciate the strong interrelation between the evolution of the state and the formation of social capital. A major role of the state may, actually, be to help accumulate, reproduce, and protect valuable social capital—some of which might originate from local pre-industrial traditions (Lundvall and Maskell forthcoming) , and the lack of state agency is one of the major flaws of Putnam's explanatory model (Tarrow 1996; Rothstein forthcoming). It takes a nation to fight poverty, and belief in government has been and still is a decisive element in a nation's stock of social capital when dealing with issues of conflict and social exclusion.

The editors of this volume asked all contributors to offer some final reflections on the heuristic power of the concept of social capital. The present chapter has argued that we need a concept such as social capital to capture a number of economically significant phenomena. At the same time a number of analytical shortcomings have been identified, curtailing the present explanatory potential of the concept and signalling the scope for future work.

There are many similarities between the contemporary stage of social capital's conceptual development and the situation in the mid-1950s when the later Nobel laureate Robert M. Solow identified the concept of 'technology' as responsible for the large share of economic growth unaccounted for by the standard measures then used. It took generations to get a proper grasp of what technology is really about and how it might be decomposed, measured, or influenced by managerial efforts and policy instruments. Actually we still have a bit to do before we can feel completely comfortable with the way we apply the concept of technology in economic analyses and other investigations within social science. Social capital started to gain significance less than 15 years ago. Little wonder that we haven't solved all the puzzles yet.

However, some puzzles might not be solvable at all. For instance, the limited amount of research focusing on the development of quantitative measures of social capital could, perhaps, be explained by the fact that mainstream economists are seldom experts on social capital and those who know a lot about social capital have only rarely 'toiled in the salt mines of general equilibrium theory'. It is, nevertheless, possible that the main reason lies in the nature of social capital itself. Following the line of argument in the strategy literature on causal ambiguity, introduced above, there are strong reasons to suspect that relevant dimensions of social capital may not be formally specifiable at all. The economic structure and the portfolio of challenges and opportunities differ from one community to the next and social capital, while being accumulated, is attuned to such differences. Specific features of social capital that might be valuable or even crucial in one context can, therefore, be useless in the context of another community with a different economic structure and facing other challenges and opportunities. Any endeavour rigorously to decompose social capital in the sense of reducing it to context-free basic elements might thus run up against an infinite regress. If this is indeed the case, then all attempts to obtain accuracy, completeness, and consistency when measuring and collating the stock of social capital across communities are bound to fail.

7

Are Refugees Social Capitalists?

PETER LOIZOS

Introduction

THERE are several ways of thinking about refugees: victims of trauma, needy persons, development resources, political integration problems, and many more. This essay approaches refugees from the framework of their potential for the conservation and creation of social capital. Some authors who have used this term are concerned with institution-building, democracy, effective service delivery, political and administrative accountability, and ideas about citizen participation. Others are concerned with even broader issues in societal integration, and with the differences between those for whom a political system works and those whom it might be said to fail, and who fail to thrive in it. My intention is more limited: it is to employ certain themes in social capital thinking to see if they illuminate the understanding of refugees. Can refugees can be usefully understood as coping with their unsought dislocation and destitution through the conscious conservation of social capital, and by the creation of new stocks of it?

The phrase 'social capital' unites a term from sociology and anthropology with another from economics to produce a concept which seems to integrate two approaches traditionally treated as opposed. At the heart of the concept of capital is a latent power to generate new production. 'Social' is harder to specify by abstract definition, without invoking a variant of the term itself, but it is easy enough to use—perhaps too easy. It evokes linkages, associations whether of family, friends, or other interest groups. The cognate phrase 'human capital' clearly seeks to play off the classic distinction between capital and labour, but does so in such a way as to make us appreciate the sense of skilled human beings in a workforce as being as vital to successful production as are investment funds, machines and raw materials. 'Social capital' points away from the issue of material production of goods and market-led services

I am grateful to Ayhan Aktar, Onur Yildirim, and Sophia Kouphopoulou for permission to draw upon unpublished material; to Renée Hirschon for access to papers from the conference she organized on the Compulsory Exchange of Populations between Greece and Turkey, at Queen Elizabeth House, Oxford, 17–20 September 1998; to participants in the Anthropology Seminar, Sussex University, for stimulating comments; and to Gill Shepherd for contributions to the conclusion.

towards wider issues of societal integration. The scarcity of economic capital is a main brake on development in the poorest societies, and the development of human capital through education is a critical issue for societies which seek to compete effectively with their rivals. If productivity is more easily secured, but economic competitiveness leads to unemployment, we often find a low-pay sector and problems of political and social alienation among the have-nots. Radical redistribution of capital and employment opportunities no longer appear to northern electorates as a persuasive political option because, in Galbraith's term, there is a dominant 'culture of contentment' (Galbraith 1993). Differences in social capital access offer themselves to centre-ground politicians as helping those who are a post-industrial awkward class, needing much, but hard to help in ways which the rest of the electorate will accept. There are real dangers in seeing top-down programmes to 'enhance social capital' as a quick fix for the unwanted effects of market economics. If people need jobs, a living wage, better housing, a better diet, more autonomy, more self-respect and less stress, then tinkering with their social relations is unlikely to make the vital differences (Wilkinson 1999).

But the phrase 'social capital' clearly has attractive resonances. The preoccupations of the social capital approach have been the preoccupations of classical sociologists and anthropologists. They have been 'social capital theorists' since the early days of their discipline because of the centrality of their concern with core social institutions and with the constitution of society: that is, with kinship and the family, with marriage, with local political and religious organizations, and with friendship through the concepts of exchange and trust in all its forms between equals and between unequals. The functionalists, from Durkheim and Malinowski, were preoccupied with the way in which social systems bound their members into something more than the pursuit of individual interests. Some of their key assumptions were in due course challenged, but their interest in factors promoting coherence and integration have entered into the collective thinking of the discipline. However, the strongest criticisms were introduced later by political economists, who argued that the 'social' was itself strongly determined by political power and the economy. In my view, the social capital emphasis cannot be plausible as comprehensive social theory: it can only add some harmonies to the melodic themes of political economy.

To move from general issues to the particular concern of this essay: refugees, however they themselves experience their condition, are instructive for theorists because they have often experienced near-total destitution, and are faced with continuing their economic and social lives after events which may have called into question some of their key certainties. In comparison to the problems of non-refugee citizens—labour migrants, for example, who may be unemployed and poor but not dislocated—refugees seem to face exceptional problems. But although a small number of particular individuals who experience the pains of involuntary dislocation may be permanently incapacitated, many observers have been impressed by the general resilience of refugees, as if the central disruption had been redefined as a challenge. This does not mean that most refugees become entrepreneurial and prosperous. Dramatic success stories are seductive but unlikely to be typical, and some long-term follow-up studies to be discussed later suggest that many children of poor refugees continued to be insecure and disadvantaged economically 50 years after the original parental dislocation.

In this chapter, I draw on material concerning long-term follow-up studies of groups of people who became refugees or involuntary migrants at the start of the twentieth century as a result of a common set of regional conflicts which accompanied the ending of the Ottoman Empire (Loizos 1999). The studies are not perfectly suited to the task in hand; there are unavoidable gaps in the accounts, as they were produced with other theoretical concerns in mind. In understanding how refugees transcend their dislocations and destitutions, we may gain an insight into processes of social construction which have a quasi-experimental value. Why? Because although refugees very often lose their economic and material capital, they rarely lose nearly as much of their human and social capital. Even when their stocks of both are greatly reduced, or devalued by dramatic changes in contexts where they could be applied, the refugees may with time, determination, and support, replenish them. It is, I argue, their characteristics as 'social capitalists' which assist significantly in the issue of their longer-term adjustment (James 1997; de Berry 1999; Hirschon 1989; 2000), and government policies which ignore or disrupt such processes inflict additional penalties upon them.

Imperial Collapse, Nationalist Conflict, and Social Dislocation

The material is drawn in the main from four studies, all framed by dislocations which were produced by the ending of the Ottoman Empire. Two studies are of Christian Greeks from Asia Minor, who were forced to resettle in Greece. A third is of Armenian survivors of massacres in south-east Turkey, who settled in Cyprus; and the fourth concerns Muslims expelled from Crete who settled in Turkey. The Ottoman Empire was a vast system of government which at the height of its powers dominated half the Mediterranean states, from Morocco eastwards to Anatolia, and then west through the Balkans to near Vienna. It was opposed by the Hapsburg and Russian Empires, and in the nineteenth century by the increasingly aggressive trade and imperial aspirations of Britain, France, and Germany. European powers intervened on the side of Christian peoples ruled by the Ottomans, and through such interventions the Serbs, the Greeks and the Bulgarians were helped to liberate themselves. The Armenian nationalists hoped that they too could adopt similar strategies and thus enjoy decisive European support. But south-east Turkey was not then within the same geopolitical framework as the Balkans, and the powers declined to act as the Armenian nationalists wished. They failed to detach their own state from Ottoman Anatolia and experienced massive punitive slaughter, particularly in 1915, which they insist was the first genocide of the twentieth century, a view still denied by contemporary Turkish nationalists.

Slaughter of non-combatants was a feature of all these ethno-religious conflicts. To simplify somewhat: both combatants and civilians were routinely killed, villages burned and their surviving inhabitants driven out, in order to create ethnically homogenous nation states. The rebellious Christians and the Ottoman state equalled each other in ferocity. This meant that millions of survivors fled from natal homes and moved, sometimes a number of times, to areas where they felt more secure, particularly in the period 1890–1925. For not only were there a series of Balkan Wars, but World War I saw Greece and Turkey on opposite sides. Turkey had an historic alliance with Germany, Greece with Britain and France. Russia was concerned to carve out portions of Ottoman territory, particularly on the borders of what is now south-east Turkey.

Those who had been subject to murderous attacks, or who had reason to fear that these would soon begin, sold their lands to neighbours if they could, often for very poor prices, and left with whatever they could carry. They were very often made to hand over their portable possessions under threat of violence before they reached places of safety, thus deepening their destitution. The wealthy were sometimes able to make their exits in a more deliberate way, conserving their portable wealth, but their estates were usually lost to them.

The Christian refugees from Asia Minor became in the 1923 Treaty of Lausanne the subjects of a Compulsory Exchange of Populations between Greece and Turkey. This meant that they had no right of return to Turkey, and that they were accorded citizenship in Greece. Greece had newly conquered territories to the north: Greek Macedonia, the Serres Basin, and the area including eastern Thrace. Muslims who had been leaving these regions were now compelled to do so by a deadline—eastern Thrace being an exception. The Greek state directed many of the Asia Minor Christians to settle in this zone, and the Refugee Settlement Commission—an initiative of the League of Nations, but financed by international bank loans—made support packages available to them in these areas. There was also a major land reform by the Greek state in favour of small-holders which freed up land at the expense of large estate owners.

Such measures allowed many refugees to be settled, although only after much hardship, and often in the face of competition for land from local people (Kontogiorgi 1996). But not all the Christian refugees were farmers. Some were urban dwellers who had left behind small businesses and who had been set down in either Salonika or Athens. Hirschon (1989) cited a survey of refugees in the Piraeus vicinity of Athens which included many labourers and pedlars and a high proportion of female-headed households. When Hirschon herself carried out field research among these people and their descendants more than 30 years later, they were still a population of manual workers, artisans, street traders. And their income had remained significantly lower: only 70 per cent of the national average.

The initial situation, then, for these involuntary migrants involved threats to life and health; disruption of communities of origin and established social networks; losses of both economic capital and social capital; and disruptions in the field of application for their knowledge and skills. The economic consequences lasted a long time. But what of the initial social disruption? Here the evidence is quite different, and important in its social capital implications.

Transcending Dislocation and Dispersal: Refugees in Piraeus

The political processes which had led these refugees to depart from Turkey did not usually lend themselves to an orderly exit in solidary organized groups. In general we can infer that the family, nuclear or extended, was the unit of survival, although groups of families or neighbours sometimes have journeyed together. Some families had lost members during conflicts and flight. Ladas (1932) suggested that, during the first year, refugees in Athens were dying at the rate of 6,000 a month from malnutrition and epidemic diseases. People were camping wherever they could, living on the streets. They were a heterogeneous assembly of people from many parts of Anatolia, speaking different dialects of Greek or Turkish. The things they had in common were their insecurity, destitution and memories of danger. Certain themes in their subsequent individual narratives suggest they often experienced similar rebuffs from the local Greeks, who often reportedly saw them as a problem rather than as a welcome addition to the Greek nation—the official view from Greek nationalist leaders. On the ground it looked and felt different.

Much of this is accessible in Hirschon's thoughtfully analysed ethnography. But now let us reflect on this situation of initial destitution and social disorganization in terms of the question of social capital. The condition of sudden destitution, and arriving as strangers in an unfamiliar place is unusual and extreme. Like famine, which is often an element in the process, it strips people down to their human essentials, to conditions of exposure and vulnerability. But—and here is the fundamental point—dislocation and destitution do not usually damage the deepest early learning or core values. Social identity, a belief in and understanding of kinship relations, religious commitments, technical knowledge, such things normally survive.

During a famine on the Pacific island of Tikopia, Raymond Firth (1967) noticed that acute scarcity meant people could no longer manage the luxury of making substantial ceremonial gifts of food. One solution was to drastically reduce the quantities of food given to the gods in religious rituals, a small quantity having to stand symbolically for the previous much larger one. A second solution to the food gifts problems was to curtail the range of people with whom one remained in active reciprocity. Firth suggested that kinship relations had to be collapsed to the core loyalties, with everything optional being placed on hold. But kinship was not abandoned: the Tikopians did not turn into an agglomeration of ruthless individual survivalists who 'forgot' their core kinship loyalties (cf. P. Levi 1959).

In Athens, in conditions of initial disruption, with food scarcity and disease also present when people hardly knew each other, it must have required a deliberate act for families of refugees to start talking to each other, to share and compare their experiences, to note that their new next door contacts—it is too early to write of 'neighbour'—had lost a husband and father, a son, a grandmother, and to say to themselves, 'At least we did not lose anyone from our family'. I feel able to extrapolate, to project back inferences because of my own study of Greek Cypriot refugees in Cyprus in 1975 (Loizos 1981). In Cyprus I observed refugee families who had not known each other before their dislocation, and were from different villages of origin, settling into a warm and mutually supporting set of relationships on the basis of their shared dislocation experiences. And people said very often, 'Only a refugee can understand a refugee. Those who are living in their own properties can have no idea what it feels like.'

The suggestion, then, is that in conditions of extreme vulnerability people are faced with contexts in which they can if they so decide act as if they are indifferent to those in their milieu, and some, the most demoralized, those habitually mistrustful, may do this; but they may also give recognition to the existence and needs of other people outside the sphere of their own close families. The starter mechanisms are micro exchanges: greetings, perhaps a cigarette, opinions and information, the loan of a cooking pot, help in putting up a shack or in minding a child.

The time frames in which people perceive and act upon these possibilities can be anything from the first moments of contact to months and years. Getting to know one's neighbours is a highly variable process even in the best of circumstances. In 1968 I observed a young man in Cyprus who had become engaged in a village ten miles from his home. Because his wife and her family had built a dowry house in her village, he knew he would be spending the rest of his working life among 1,500 people he did not yet know. During the several years of his engagement, he set to work to learn the names of all the adult males of the village, some 450 in number; and because they were usually related to each other by kinship and marriage he often learned these connections as well. This expansion of his social knowledge was not one way, either, because in the process the villagers in their turn learned who he was: that he was the son-in-law of Stout Yiannis, that he was from Trimiklini village, that he was a builder by trade.

The exercise which he carried out as part of normal engagement and commitment to his wife's village must be an enlarged version of what the Piraeus refugees also had to accomplish in their new residential neighbourhoods. Clearly, it would have to have started 'small' by getting to know the immediate neighbours on each side of one's shack, then some people on the other side of the road. As women were expected to stay in their residential neighbourhoods, they would not have walked to the more distant neighbourhoods. But men were expected to learn about other zones. About possible work opportunities, and about coffee shops where other men would assemble. Gradually those coffee shops came to have regional identities associated with the communities of pre-refugee origin. People from Smyrna came to know that others from Smyrna assembled at one particular coffee shop. Old social linkages—acquaintanceship, distant kinship—might have been re-established. But new relationships were formed in which a modicum of trust was extended simply because a person was linked to a known community, and the knowledge of that community was both shared—a test of each other's knowledge and social linkages—and a basis for future association. There is no need to suggest that people extended blank cheques to each other on the basis of common origins. The problem is to suggest the micro indicators which would eventually enable the randomly assorted assemblage of Asia Minor refugees in Piraeus to get some social order into their relations, and the evidence of many studies of both labour migrants and other refugees makes it clear that, in a matter of months, this commonly starts to happen.

Social Capital Conservation during Flight and Re-Settlement

A second case study, of Christians who were expelled from islands in the Sea of Marmaras, is also instructive in social capital terms, but in a quite different way. The political context was, as before, the political conflicts between Greece and the Ottoman Empire. From the Balkan War of 1912, for the next ten years, Ottoman leaders started to treat Greek Christian minorities as disloyal, and their flight was encouraged. When Greece and Turkey took opposite sides in World War I, the pressures on Greek minorities intensified, and the Marmaras islanders were removed from their strategic locations and sent to other parts of Turkey. When this war finished the survivors were allowed to return, but Greece soon launched a military campaign into Asia Minor in 1919, and when, several years later her armies were defeated, the Marmaras Christians, fearing they would be punished for the sins of the invading Greeks and for those of their numbers who had joined in the brutalities, decided to flee.

These Marmaras refugees came from a small number of villages where a dominant economic activity had been fishing from large boats owned by merchant-patrons. These communities had a three-class structure, and there were patron-client ties which obliged the rich to extend credit to the poor while benefiting from interest payments and their purchases as grocery customers. In these communities (Salamone 1987; Salamone and Stanton 1986) there was a strong tradition of the wealthy patrons acting as community leaders, so that when the time came from these villagers to leave their homes they left in large boats which had been chartered by village committees, and they attempted to stay together when they arrived in Greece; and even when dispersed, different groups remained in touch with each other.

Salamone's historical study has followed one sub-set of these islanders, several hundred men and women who, after trying several other locations, both urban and rural, settled on an uninhabited remote island, Ammouliani, off the coast of Mt Athos at intervals between 1922 and 1930. His study focuses on male livelihoods, and follows his informants up into the early 1970s. There are a number of points that are of interest in terms of the conservation of social capital and its re-creation. First, it seems as if staying together was important to these villagers and that for the first years, at least, traditional leaders were expected to take prominent roles in decision-making. When some of their initiatives proved unsatisfactory the villagers did not disperse, but turned to other leaders from the same communities of origin. Second, when they reached the island, they were encouraged by the Refugee Settlement Commission, an agency acting with the authority of the League of Nations and the Government of Greece, to allocate available land in a way which gave the farmers access to equal quantities and gave everyone a house and vegetable plot. Here was a strategy of social inclusiveness which, while externally driven, met their basic needs. One of the patrons had brought his fishing boat from Marmaras, and he took numbers of the destitute villagers with him as crew: the boats were rowed, with seven oarsmen on each side. The extra men came along in the hope of getting fish to feed their families. When the day's catch was divided, they employed the same methods as had been used in the Sea of Marmara (Salamone 1987: 132–5). So conservation of previous practices and values was important. Many of the men worked away from the island as labourers on the estates of Mt Athos.

The contribution of Ammouliani women to the conservation of social capital was marked in a number of ways. Salamone and Stanton (1986) present the relations between husbands and wives as involving notions of complementarity of roles, since they were united in the explicit shared goal of provisioning and perpetuating the household unit—*nykokirio* in demotic Greek. This was done through child-rearing, but also through the ability of wives to be thrifty and to produce savings from the incomes brought in by their husbands, no matter how tight the budgets. Men boasted of the ability of their wives in careful management of household expenditure, and the skills they possessed in making essential items of clothing, as well as the luxury display items which their daughters would need for marriage.

The authors noted that the Ammouliani villagers preserved a strong sense of continuity of identities, customs and values, in spite of their dislocation and resettlement, and that this was still in place 50 years after their initial exile. And even though not all the original six Marmaras villages had settled together in the 1920s, by the 1970s and 1980s they were in touch with relatives in several cities of Greece. The importance of maintaining ties of kinship and marriage had not atrophied in the resettlement situation. And the family as the preferred unit of economic cooperation remained paramount:

In Ammouliani, material success is judged only in the context of the economic success of the family. The family is regarded as a form of basic capital to be invested to its greatest advantage in some type of familial enterprise. This view is manifested in the recent boom in tourist enterprises that are frequently initiated and generally managed by the women of the family, and in familial decisions to emigrate and do wage labour abroad for a number of years for the purpose of accumulating sufficient capital to establish family businesses that can provide work for present and future generations. (Salamone and Stanton 1986:103)

The social capital aspects to this case include the tendency of the villagers to 'stick together' both for flight and subsequently; to regroup together; to expect initiatives from known and trusted traditional leaders; to conserve patron-client ties while they got through the most difficult period; and to keep previous gender roles and marriage related customs for many years after the original dislocation. In short, it is the package of customs, beliefs and practices from before their dislocation which continued to serve them in diasporic adjustment.

Armenian Massacre Survivors in Cyprus

To turn now to a third example: Armenians had been settling in Cyprus early in the nineteenth century, but those who came between 1895 and 1915 did so in a different spirit, escaping massacres in Turkey. They did not do as the Marmaras villagers had done and arrive in large groupings of people who had lived and worked together before. Their condition was more like that of the arbitrarily assorted refugees in Piraeus. Their most pressing concerns inevitably were, initially, housing and survival incomes, and they seem to have sought these as individuals and families. At first, to keep expenses down, they would take a house, and a whole family would crowd into a single room, and let the other rooms out to other refugee families. Many were artisans, and managed to start up their artisanal activities again: 'copper- and tinsmiths, potters, bakers, carpenters, jewellers, mechanics, soap makers and leather-workers' (Pattie 1997: 62). Others took work in the asbestos mines, a few as pedlars carrying goods for sale on their backs into the more distant villages. Women crocheted or made lace, took in laundry, cleaned houses or worked as cooks. The one occupation which few went into was agriculture, because the capital outlay was too great and because at that point many believed they would soon return to their own land.

At this point, then, the commitment to families and the re-activation of old skills in the new context are the issues to be noted. But the issues for these Armenian massacre survivors were not only economic. There were questions about their identities as Armenians which needed management. Although many of them had spoken Turkish as their first language, their collective reaction to their persecution in Turkey was to commit themselves more strongly to an emergent identity as Armenians, and this, gradually, between 1915 and 1940, involved the setting up of schools for their children where the language of instruction was Armenian. The acquisition of Armenian became a marker of diasporic ethnic identity (Pattie 1997: 69–70, 184–97). The endowment of an

Armenian Church was another important move, and Church leaders were closely involved in the administration and curriculum of the Armenian schools. Later there were cultural and political clubs, where in addition to social and recreational activities there were lectures on Armenian history and political issues.

Pattie's monograph is titled *Faith in History: Armenians Rebuilding Community*. From the standpoint of social capital theory, we can see that the refugees who started to reach Cyprus from many different towns and villages in south-east Turkey were, like the Asia Minor Greeks in Piraeus, faced with the loss of previously supportive communities and extended kinship networks. They had to survive first as individuals and families, and then, as they produced children, they had to consider how those children would be educated and eventually whom they would marry. They created schools and church and cultural clubs in which their distinctiveness was both ensured and nurtured. These were the basis for communities of partially shared values and emergent trust. I say 'partially' because Pattie stresses political divisions and class and regional distinctions as continuing to operate. Such developments are not inevitable: they depend on the reception framework. The British colonial administration had no grand scheme for turning colonial subjects into anglophone British citizens. Compare the situation of migrants to America who have been encouraged to learn English and become American, and Jewish migrants to Israel who have been encouraged to learn Hebrew and become Israelis. Nor was there an option of easy assimilation to the Greek population of Cyprus, still less to the Turkish population. The Armenians were forced to turn to each other to meet their needs: they turned outwards from their own immediate families to find marriage partners and to create bonds of trust and collectivities and institutions with other co-ethnic survivor families. This is to describe a process of social capital formation. Those scholars who normally see only the destructive power of ethnic sentiments must consider that, in such situations as those faced by the Armenian refugees, co-ethnicity was the only external social resource freely available to them at that time and in those places. It offered forms of security not otherwise available.

Cretan Muslims

The fourth main ethnographic example involves the Cretan Muslims. The Treaty of Lausanne had meant that not only would the vast majority of Greek Christians leave Turkey and become citizens of Greece, but that nearly all the remaining Muslims in Greece would leave to become citizens of Turkey. There had been a significant Muslim population in Crete, and, as the Greek nationalists on the island saw themselves close to realizing their dream of detaching Crete from Ottoman rule and having it joined to Greece, so conditions for local Muslims became more and more insecure. First, they retreated from the countryside, and regrouped in towns. But after the Lausanne Agreement they left the towns and were conveyed to Turkey. They were briefly feted on arrival, as 'Turks' 'returning' to the Turkish heartland, and they were directed by the state to sites where they should settle. There were small assistance packages provided by the state, but on a much smaller scale than took place in Greece, partly because Turkey could not secure international aid and had been thoroughly devastated by a decade of war and revolution (Yildirim, personal communication). The refugees were usually directed to areas from which Christians had departed. However, like the Asia Minor Christians seeking to settle on former Muslim land in northern Greece, the Muslim refugees found that local people, sometimes government officials, had already occupied the best land and housing, and what was left over for them was often of poor quality (de Planhol 1968; Toumarkine 1995).

One of the few available studies which examines in detail a community in which Cretan Muslims settled is Mansur's (1972) study of Bodrum. The local people were inclined to focus on agriculture and to take little interest in the sea or trade. The incoming Cretans were interested in the sea. Most of them arrived with no money or goods, did not have access to land, and were unaffected by Ottoman perceptions of certain crafts and trades as being of low status. For example, there was a local belief that Muslims should not work with lime or stone, and so house building was closed for them. The Cretans were free from this belief. This meant they had to take any opportunity for income which came their way, and, indeed, to innovate. They started to buy tobacco from local peasant farmers, curing it, packing it and sending it to wholesale merchants in Izmir. They were soon able to lend the peasants advances against future crops, which put them in a stronger position in the market as they had guaranteed suppliers. They involved themselves in similar fashion with trade in olives and figs to both Izmir and Istanbul. Their understanding of the sea and knowledge of Greek meant they could take part in the informal and untaxed trade between Turkey and Greece.

The ethnographer went as far as to insist that 'the Cretan is a harder working man than the local. He is also more able to find and do any odd jobs and change trades than the local. There are no jobs that he finds distasteful or beneath him' (Mansur 1972: 163). There is one other notable feature in how the Cretan refugees in Bodrum behaved over the long haul. It seems they married each other significantly more than they married with the local people. Of 50 marriages for which Mansur had data, not more than five were 'mixed' with the locals. We shall examine the wider implications of this for all the other refugees studied in the following section. For the moment, let us note that to marry within the category of refugees is to double up and consolidate relations between the incomer families at the expense of creating new links to the locals. At first sight, this is 'irrational' in that, if the local people had land and produced food, it might have been advantageous to seek to marry with them. There is, also, the question of whether local people were willing to make marriages with the incomers. In fact, they produced a proverb on this question: 'Give your girl to a Cretan, but do not yourself marry a Cretan girl.' The rationalization offered to Mansur was that the Cretan women were unwilling to work in the fields, and that the Cretans knew how to make money without the toil of agriculture, so a farmer's daughter who married one could expect an easier life. The attitude of the Cretan women is consistent with other studies (for example, Kouphopoulou, work in progress) in which the Cretans regarded themselves as more modern and European in gender relations than the local people. Kouphopoulou's informants continued to speak Greek and preserve a distinctive cuisine for more than 50 years after their original arrival.

We can infer that the Armenians and Cretan Muslims faced the same fundamental issues of rebuilding damaged and disrupted social networks as already discussed for the refugees in Piraeus. As in all such situations, refugees enter into social systems where the indigenous population is already entrenched, embedded, and operating in a social environment of established networks and on-going commitments. Normally the local people have their hands socially and transactionally full. They typically have most if not all the exchange relationships, obligations, and reciprocities they need. In a few cases, some refugees may 'fill a gap' for some locals: in a situation of labour or skills scarcity, the refugees may offer attractive cheap labour opportunities. But these may not be costless if, in general, buyers are looking for cheaper goods and employers are looking for cheaper labourers, then, when refugees come forward, they arouse tensions with their local competitors, who are now placed at a disadvantage. In this sense, the economics of refugee incorporation are prone to create specific hostilities, and those hostilities are likely to incline refugees seeking social support outside of the immediate family to turn to each other. An economist might stress that the refugees are also competing with each other, and this will likely be the case. An anthropologist must reply that in addition to short-term competition, there is a middle and longer term in which the refugees need each other and will legitimize each other socially. It is to this issue, an issue of 'disguised' social capital formation, which I now turn.

Marriage Partners and the Emergence of Communities

We can now move beyond issues of immediate physical survival, which would involve labour market economics, housing stocks, forms of aid, and human capital skills, to issues which have a more flexible biological basis and a cultural expression: the issues of marriage and bio-social reproduction. In conditions of severe famine, women may cease to ovulate and the incidence of infant mortality rises sharply. However, populations returning to normal food production and consumption after a famine have been observed to increase the number of children conceived, as if they are 'making up' for the lost children. Refugee migrations are often accompanied, as we have noted, not only by destitution but by chronic hunger, illness and increased mortality. When

food and future prospects slowly become less insecure, younger people in particular can allow themselves to think about something as normal as courtship
and marriage. All this is, after all, what normal social life has usually been
about. But there is a major sociological difference between courtship and marriage in conditions of cumulative economic and social 'steady state' security,
and those conditions which occur when a group of people have been through
some 'year zero' experience, have been thrown together as an agglomeration
of 'unknowns', are surrounded by settled populations who may regard them
as unwelcome and uncouth. It is sometimes possible, however, that if, among
the locals, either brides or grooms are in short supply, the incomers will be welcomed as they will be able to supply the deficit 'cheaply'.

Conditions of economic depression generate especially difficult problems
for the young-who-would-marry, and even among non-refugee populations,
when the economics of householding are disadvantageous, marriage has to be
seen as a major achievement 'against the odds'. O'Neill (1987) has described a
northern Portuguese peasant community in the late 1970s where people were
so poor, and their labour so vital to the wellbeing of their natal families, that
a couple might marry but fail to set up a conjugal household together for anything from five to ten years. The husband would leave his wife's bed and set
out for his own home 'without breakfast', O'Neill's informants insisted. And
these people were not even refugees. In London, in the late 1940s, when as a
result of war damage there was an acute housing shortage, young couples married but continued to live in the natal home of the bride or groom. This was
described as 'We're living with his mother'. In Hirschon's (1989; 2000) account
of refugee families in Piraeus, such arrangements were commonplace,
although further complicated by the hope of future state compensation.

In the peasant and urban societies of Greece, the Balkans, and Turkey marriage was not until recently a matter for two young people alone. There was
usually a significant parental interest in matching the two families whose children would be joined. Marriage was more than marriage: it was affinity, in the
fullest anthropological senses of this term (Levi-Strauss 1969). When anthropologists employ the term 'affinity' they are consciously thinking of the
enduring bonds which subsequently tie two families through marriage: the
complex precommitment negotiations, the obligatory gifts which are
exchanged, and the asymmetries implicit in the flows of wealth from one
party to the other. Sometimes women systematically marry higher-status men;
sometimes men systematically marry higher-status women. There can be
structural significance in these directional flows and often enduring changes
are made to the two corporations which are so linked by the marriage of two
young people. Such links of alliance resemble in miniature the dynastic marriages in which the monarchs of Europe were wont to indulge. When so much
is at stake, and a 'bad marriage' can be so socially destructive for the high con-
senting parties, then knowledge of the family one might marry into is at a premium. There would be concerns about the health history of the family as a
whole—for example, mental illness? TB? fertility problems?—any signs of

social unpredictability such as sexual promiscuity, gambling or addictive drinking are particularly to be avoided.

We must focus here on the difficulties faced by an agglomeration of refugees who have been thrown together largely by chance, who are deprived of the stock of information concerning the reputations of other people—so-called 'gossip'—which is available in long-settled communities. For new refugees, if it comes to seeing their children married off, the leap may be into a more impenetrable darkness than usual. To give consent to a marriage is a major step of faith, of risk, of conditional trust. So the stock of knowledge about reputations which must slowly accrue to an agglomeration as it becomes a set of people who are marrying each other is an example of developing human capital. The in-law relations which follow on become social capital for those directly related by the contracts. And as more and more marriages, over decades, take place within a neighbourhood or across the boundaries of adjacent neighbourhoods, so the families which may have started social life in this space as so many potatoes in a sack become structurally and intimately linked by consanguinity and affinity; and the general pool of information about reputations becomes more historically informed, contains more 'case histories' to be drawn on.

When we turn to the ethnography of the Marmaras fishing communities resettled in Ammouliani, we find that for many decades there was a marked tendency to endogamy—marrying within the local community (Salamone and Stanton 1986:102) and it was only eventually a lack of local partners which caused this pattern to change. Not only was there endogamy but, as was mentioned earlier, there was a commitment to a pattern of trousseau and dowry property accumulated by women and their families as a contribution to a new marriage. This was known by a Greek word *ruha*, which literally means 'clothing' but also had the expanded sense of women's property in cash or kind. Back in the Marmaras islands, these wedding contributions had included ornately embroidered display clothing. During the early years of refugee destitution, the *ruha* was reduced to 'shadow' contributions—cf food gifts to the gods in the Tikopia famine—and went from involving luxury to necessity items. The authors are strongly impressed by the continuity of the dowry pattern from pre-1930 to the 1970s. They suggest it contributes to firming up the distinctive social identity of the refugee group.

Not only was the creation of the dowry a major part of the daily schedules of teen-age girls, it also clearly helped to sustain a strong bond between the generations, and, though competitive in nature, a bond between the women in the community. In fact, dowry showings, attended by a large proportion of the women in the community, were one of the few remaining community-wide events, attracting even greater numbers than weddings themselves. (Salamone and Stanton 1986:112)

Nothing analogous to the individualism of Putnam's 'Bowling Alone' was to be seen in Ammouliani, 1980.

Similar issues have been touched upon by George Agelopoulos, writing about Asia Minor refugees who settled in a district in northern Greece where there were several other identity groups present. In the 1920s, the community of Nea Krasia, north-west of Salonica, contained five named groups of people, each with a different history, mode of livelihood and language and dialect skills. Each of these groups at first married within the group to a high degree. There was conflict between certain groups over access to land and rights of abode. A 'new village' was constructed under the supervision of the Refugee Settlement Commission. Agelopoulos provides data on many aspects of the last 70 years, and—of particular interest for this chapter—on marriage patterns within and between the groups. He lists a number of changes which affected the village and the region. His main theme is the transition from a situation of groups looking predominantly inward for security and sociality to one in which all agree that they have become 'one village'.

A key indicator of the change, and one on which his informants place great weight, is the increasing acceptability of marriages between the five groups and the sense in which the groups have lost much of their sociological salience. The frequency of 'mixed marriages' blurs the boundaries, and although the identity groups have not vanished, they no longer designate well-defined and mutually antagonistic sets. There has been a definite increase in the stock of social capital, the numbers and social characteristics of persons with whom collaborative relations may be constructed. This can be rephrased as an expansion of the pool of people who are recognised as social equals and to whom trust is conditionally extended.

Close friendships, business collaboration and love affairs between villagers from the old and new villages have been reported as existing since the very first days of the establishment of the village. But until the late 1940s these relationships were rare, subject to criticism, and not socially accepted. Such friendships and business collaborations were perceived as suspicious, and such love affairs were not allowed to develop into marriages. (Agelopoulos 1997: 139)

Putnam's account of how long it took northern Italy to develop its participatory civic trust—1,000 years—linked to the suggestion that southern Italy will need a very long time to 'catch up' has been criticized by other scholars of Italian development (see Putzell 1997). His time scales may perhaps be reconsidered in light of the Nea Krasia data. For not only did these previously stranger groups overcome their social isolation and become more closely related; they were also, when the time came, able to act generously, not, it is true, to total strangers, but to distant kin from whom they had been separated for a very long period. In 1991–2, when the state boundaries between Greece and Bulgaria relaxed as the eastern European communist system broke up, the Nea Krasia villagers learned that some distant kin in Bulgaria were experiencing hardship, and that food was scarce in their community. They collected up relief supplies of food, and transported them some hundreds of miles to the Bulgarian village. These re-activated links later became a trade network, employed for mutual benefit. The social capital that was conserved in the remembrance of kinship ties was, in due course, traded upon to produce economic capital as well. Reflecting on the case, Agelopoulos notes that the Nea Krasia Greeks were surprised, and, it seems, a little disappointed, to find how 'Bulgarian' their relatives had become. He implies that their initial food relief mission was motivated partly by Greek nationalist romanticism, partly by humanitarian motives, and partly by a need to reaffirm their own specific historical connection to the identity of the now-Bulgarian village. Perhaps this is too complex a motivational package to be subsumed under social capital theory. But it is certainly about norms, networks, and trust, and shared objectives: profit from predictable trade partnerships. And none of this involved the 'dark side' unless all instances of ethno-nationalist sentiments are classified in this way. (On the 'dark side' see Putzell 1997.)

To recap: marriage partners and family attitudes to them seem implicated in the conservation or creation of social capital. In several other studies of refugees in this region (for example, Mansur 1972; Pattie 1997) there has been data suggesting preferential endogamy. We cannot push this too far, since labour migrants, sub-castes in India, and Mediterranean peasants have all opted for preferred endogamy in circumstances different from the initial dislocation and destitution of the refugees discussed here. Endogamy is certainly a strategy by which securely privileged groups close their ranks to would-be entrants from below. But conditions of general or specific deprivation may put such social practices high up the list of priorities. The more unpredictable and threatening things are, the higher the premium on creating relationships of institutionalized trust, and endogamy may be said to do this. This means that what started as a random assemblage of unrelated families will, over three or four generations, become a highly inter-related collectivity, busily ranking members in terms of social attributes, but offering re-enforcing normative conformity and the capacity for collective action. Inevitably, some individuals will experience such a society as coercive, indeed claustrophobic.

A recent study of elderly refugee exiles in the UK makes the fundamental point about constructing social capital persuasively. It describes a group of Poles who came to the UK during or shortly after World War II and stayed on.

. . . non-blood kinship has developed among older Poles, many of whom arrived as single individuals and married from within their ethnic group, and the small numbers who married outside it. In this context, . . . extended 'family networks' are created through affiliations between exiles and realized through a series of symbolic adoptions, for example, importance is given to godparents under Catholic rite. This specific affiliation, like blood kinship, raises expectations about inter-generational support and also provides maintenance and semblance to the reconstituted family. (Scott and Bolzman 1999: 175–6)

Conclusion: Implications for the Reception of Refugees

Refugees, in the first weeks and months following forced migrations, usually need help with food, housing, medicine, and education for their children.

These things are normally provided in Britain by central government deciding on entitlements, and local government on delivery of services. Those material allocations are subject to political debate, and refugees are all-too-easy targets for populist politicians and thugs alike—they are often unpopular, vulnerable, and often cannot fight back. The refugee relief agencies such as UNHCR and Oxfam learned in the early 1980s that it was politically hazardous to refugees for them to receive targeted help if the neighbouring local people were them-selves poor, and unaided. It proved less divisive not to think about the needs of refugees in isolation, but to think of 'refugee affected populations', and to make sure that the local non-refugees were not excluded from health centres, or other valued aid inputs, that 'matching funds' could be used to make the presence of the refugees an asset, and not, in local eyes, merely a cost. Has such thinking been carried across to how refugees are received in Britain, and the rest of Europe?

In Britain, the Labour Government's new Immigration and Asylum Act gives the Home Secretary powers to direct new entrants to the UK to reside in par-ticular towns, if they need housing, food vouchers, or other necessities, while their status is being determined. This policy is driven by the wish to avoid refugees being concentrated in a few places, and social friction resulting due to pressure on housing stocks, and in the labour market.

Rather than rely upon a policy of direction and dispersal, perhaps govern-ment should take bolder steps to make the arrival of refugees more acceptable wherever they go? For if there is available public housing, there will often be local unemployment, too. Instead of allowing new arrivals to be perceived negatively as more families to be housed, 'more mouths to feed', labour mar-ket competitors, there should be transparent and well advertised schemes in which for every refugee family received and housed, there will be several new jobs created, or an upgrading of public housing units for non-refugee local families. In this way, it will be possible to argue that the new arrivals do not come 'empty-handed' but bring in significant central government benefits over and above their own short-term needs. The arguments about the future economic contributions refugees may provide when settled, will still have its place, but 'jam now' is much easier to sell to the sceptical than 'jam to-morrow'.

But in addition to these political economy arguments, there are the social capital implications. Policies which deliberately disperse members of a partic-ular group, so that they will not be a burden on local government resources, or a target for local anti-immigrant groups, could inhibit refugee social capital formation, if they prevent people making contacts with those with whom they have a great deal in common. If there are thought to be strong political reasons for policies of dispersal, it might be less problematic to encourage one ethnic category to settle in one particular town, and another in a second town, rather than engineer matters so that every family is sent more or less randomly somewhere different. In this way, those disposed (or paid) to assist refugees in a particular town will have a better chance to get well informed about a particular ethnic category, and the town's social services could develop the specialist knowledge needed to support this cultural group, rather than being forced to have a diffuse responsibility for many groups, which will almost certainly spread local knowledge and skills too thinly. Some local groups may start to feel hospitable in a grounded way to newcomers about whom there would develop a stock of local understanding. Here, church, mosque, and temple might have their parts to play, if they are not in tension with the affiliations of the newcomers.

This essay has been an exercise in the application of the social capital concept, with a focus on adaptation and social reconstruction of livelihoods. It has not been my intention to suggest that the creation or conservation of social capital—understood as social networks, shared values, and emergent trust—are in any sense a substitute for basic economic support. The concept of social capital is a useful reminder that there is more to life than market or marxist economics, which is one of the reasons why Bourdieu's practice theory has proved so popular. But it was never part of Bourdieu's programme that we should forget the priorities of economic life, and allow social relations to pretend to replace a more comprehensive social theory. Social capital is a complementary concept, and not a plausible contender for a primary theoretical role.

8

Social Capital Trumping Class and Cultural Capital? Engagement with School among Immigrant Youth

JON LAUGLO

W HY do certain groups cope much better with school than one would expect, given their humble social class position and their lack of familiarity with the culture transmitted by school? Special talents and particularities of life histories can be invoked to explain the case of individual persons. But how to explain the relative success of groups? Is social capital a productive analytic tool that is useful for that purpose? As noted in the introductory chapter of this volume, the concept of social capital as initially sketched out by Bourdieu (Bourdieu 1997; Bourdieu and Passeron 1970) tended to be presented as yet another resource that was possessed disproportionately by groups who in other respects also would be advantaged. However, in the more recent conceptualization by Coleman (1988a), which has been especially influential in social science in 'Anglo-Saxon countries', there is emphasis on the democratic distribution of these resources: the poor and the relatively unschooled might even be quite well-endowed with social capital. It is in only in this latter case that social capital can compensate for disadvantage that is related to social class or that is due to lack of cultural capital of the 'high culture' type.

With regard to education, the present study will show that social capital has explanatory value in research on immigrant youth's adaptation to school, and that in this particular case social capital works to alleviate disadvantage rather than to compound it. This finding is in the footsteps of Coleman, but it will also be asserted that the concept of social capital does not sit easily in the methodological individualist framework within which Coleman sought to lodge it.

In the research literature to be examined below, two broad perspectives on immigrant youth's adaptation to school will be discerned. First, there is the argument, which can be derived from mainstream theory on social inequality,

This report is from a research project which is based at NOVA-Norwegian Social Research and funded by the Norwegian Research Council.

that the odds are so heavily stacked against immigrant youth that they will perform poorly and easily become apathetic or hostile. As will be shown, social reproduction theory can be construed as pointing towards this expectation. Second, there is the argument that, in social contexts in which 'social capital' for educational achievement is beginning to run low, immigrant youth will benefit from superior resources in this respect and do relatively well. If these seemingly countervailing social forces both are at work, which is the stronger?

First, this essay will delineate the pessimistic former perspective and examine findings which will contradict it: immigrant youth engage more, not less, constructively with school than their peers do. Second, the paper will probe the question of whether this consistent pattern could be due to 'more social capital'. Finding that this is only part of the explanation, the essay ends on the question mark, that if certain categories of immigrant youth engage more constructively with school than the 'natives', could it simply be because they rightly perceive schooling to be particularly important for their future and because they need to work harder than others to ensure that schooling serves such purposes for them?

The focus in this study will be on attitudes to school and on efforts and behaviours which seem either helpful or harmful for educational performance: positive and negative indicators of *constructive engagement with school*. It should be emphasized that it is not 'success in school' which is to be examined in this investigation. Especially when learning tasks seem daunting to a learner, then a positive engagement can reduce the chance of failure, notwithstanding the looming difficulties. But other conditions are of course important and have been the subject of much earlier research on school achievement and attainment: for example, the effect of individual ability and a range of sociocultural and institutional circumstances which determine how hard it is to learn and the level of ambition.

The present study makes use of data from a survey that was conducted in Oslo in 1996. In this study, 'immigrant youth' refers to young persons whose parents both immigrated. Thus, it will also include some young people who were born in Norway but who none the less belong to the population of immigrant households, defined as such by the immigrant status of the adults who are in charge of these households.

Before considering reasons why immigrant children might adapt well to school—optimism about their social capital assets would be among them—reasons for expecting maladaptation, or eventual 'exclusion' in the most recent parlance, will be considered.

Reasons for Expecting Poor Adaptation to School

A mainstream view of the relation between education and social inequality is that social class advantage breeds education advantage. According to this view, poor performance and low attainment are mainly due to socially structured disadvantage. Some groups are favoured because the social circumstances of their upbringing and the resources which their families possess make it easier for them to succeed in school and to stay on longer in the system in order to reap its rewards. In principle, not all educationally important 'advantage' would need to be produced by the social class system, but the centrality of social class is pre-eminent in social reproduction theory, though the perspective can be extended to race and gender as basic forms of social inequality that are not reducible to class. Further, with respect to race and gender too, the key argument concerns the advantage gained by those who wield power over others. According to conflict theories of social reproduction, whether mainly Weberian (for example, Collins 1979) or Marxist (for example, Bowles and Gintis 1976), powerful groups shape the school system to suit their own interests and at the expense of the powerless. If this line of reasoning is extended to immigrants, one would infer that their children would do poorly in school because immigrants are hardly in a position to exert much power on behalf of their own interests. Moreover, if immigrants arrive without material wealth and without the kind of educational credentials which have much currency in the country to which they migrate, their children will also be vulnerable on account of low social class.

One influential social reproduction argument concerns the special importance of cultural capital (Bourdieu and Passeron 1970; Bourdieu 1997 [1983]): that the odds in school are stacked particularly heavily in favour of children and youth whose parents are the well-placed insiders in a society's educational and cultural institutions, the cultural elite. Not only can such parents urge their children on in school and help them with the schoolwork. Bourdieu's particular claim is that in order to succeed, especially in the selective stages of the system, you also need to be at ease with the life style which is taken for granted among those who have high status in this social field: the nuances of language, the aesthetic preferences, and other symbolic expressions which mark the insider against the outsider. Such elements are not just accoutrements of cultural privilege, according to Bourdieu; they serve as prerequisites for success. It would seem that the further one's origin is from a country's cultural elite, the fewer are one's chances of doing well in school. By this line of reasoning, immigrant children should be destined to fail in school.

Very often, immigrant parents do not speak with ease the language of the country to which they have moved, let alone master its more socially exclusive nuances. Not being familiar with the education system from their own experience, immigrants should be at a disadvantage in helping their children navigate through it. Excepting those few who belong to a jet-setting international elite, the parents' grasp of the life-style subtleties of the form of cultural capital into whose ambit they have moved would be poor. Apart from the disadvantage due to having an immigrant background as such, the chances of failing in school are greater when the parents are poor, when parents secure only menial jobs, and when parents have had little schooling. Insofar as many immigrant groups are disproportionately in these social categories, the educational prospects of youth from immigrant background should be dim.

Further, if the family belongs to a 'visible minority' typical of those who have migrated to the 'the North' from a developing country, there is racist exclusion which could cause outright opposition to the 'white man's school' and channel immigrant youth towards a future in an ethnically distinct new 'underclass'. Social reproduction theory would also imply that *among* immigrants the principles of reproduction would broadly apply as among non-immigrants: that the relative educational success of children would mirror their family's social class and relative possession of cultural capital.

Does the weight of research evidence support such pessimistic hypotheses?

Immigrant Youth Doing 'Surprisingly Well'

Findings of poor achievement are not dominant in international research literature on the educational achievement of immigrant youth. Sometimes immigrant youth from certain backgrounds lag behind others in school, but they typically do better than might be expected when account is taken of their parents' social class circumstances and level of schooling.

The theme of 'trying hard' is common to the ethnographic studies on immigrants to the United States, reported in a compendium edited by Gibson and Ogbu (1991). Many of these studies fit Ogbu's (1991) distinction between immigrant minorities and 'involuntary' minorities. Youth from the former background do better in school. Quantitative survey research in the United States has corroborated the theme of immigrants trying harder and having high educational ambitions (Rumbaut 1997a; Fuligni 1997). In the UK, Tomlinson (1991) similarly claims that immigrant minority pupils show greater persistence and motivation than non-immigrants. An earlier Norwegian youth study (Lauglo 1996) found that, compared with ethnic Norwegians, immigrant youth of non-Western background did more homework and had more positive attitudes to school.

Concerning educational performance and attainment, the consistency of positive results is less internationally complete. Before controlling for social class and/or parental education, some immigrant groups match the native majority but others lag behind (Gillborn 1997 on the UK; Portes and MacLeod 1996 on the US; Engen, Kulbrandstad, and Sand 1997 on Norway; Løfgren 1991 on Sweden). In those studies that control for socio-cultural class conditions, the findings present a more optimistic view. In the case of American research, the focus has been on the predominantly Asian and Latin American nationalities in the new wave of immigration since the early 1980s. Most of the immigrant groupings examined outperform their peers (Fuligni 1997; Rumbaut 1997a, b; Portes and MacLeod 1996). Immigrant youth also seem to perform better than non-immigrant peers from the same ethnic background (Rumbaut 1995).

European results are more mixed. British studies show that whilst Asians perform well after social class controls, youth of West Indian background do not perform as well as the majority white population (Gillborn and Gipps 1996). The few nationwide surveys which have been carried out elsewhere in Europe seem to show that performance differences from the majority grouping in secondary school achievement disappear once social class is controlled for. Vallet and Caille (1996) found such results in France, and Lauglo (1996; 1999) in Norway. In Sweden, in a study of whole cohorts of people born in Sweden during 1953–70, Similä (1994) found that those of immigrant background obtained higher rates of upper academic-secondary schooling than those of non-immigrant parentage, after controlling for parental socioeconomic status (SES). Intriguingly the sole exceptions were those of Finnish, Norwegian and Danish parentage, groups which had come from just across the border.

However, in the 1996 Oslo youth survey data, which the present study utilizes, Krange and Bakken (1998) conclude that the lower secondary performance—that is, results—of youth of non-Western origins seemingly does not quite match the performance of non-immigrant youth after controlling for parental SES. They assumed, however, that missing data meant relatively weak performance because most of these cases of missing data were students who had answered a shorter version of the questionnaire due to poor command of the Norwegian language, and in the short version they were not asked about their marks. However, if these cases accordingly are deleted from the analysis, then Helland (1997) has shown that the ethnic Pakistanis—the largest immigrant group in Oslo—do not deviate significantly from the majority after controls for SES, place of residence, and intact nuclear family. By the same approach, those of Vietnamese background would slightly outperform the 'natives' in mathematics and science. Other sources (Engen, Kulbrandstad, and Sand 1997) indicate that, for whatever reasons, there is a greater achievement gap in Oslo than in the rest of Norway between ethnic Norwegians, who perform better, and immigrant youth from non-Western backgrounds when no control is used for socio-cultural class.[1]

There is of course no reason why there would be uniformity of results across countries and nationality groups. Assuming that school is 'harder' for immigrant youth, the extra hardship could be greater in some countries than in others, depending, for example, on the nature of the educational programme, the extent to which immigrant youth from particular backgrounds suffer social exclusion, and what educational measures are taken to assist them. For example, in order to keep up with others, more homework is probably demanded

---

[1] Controlling for effects of, for example, parental education in assessing such adaptation is of some theoretical interest—though there are problems in how to interpret the results. But it is of limited policy utility because if a certain group evinced, say, a high illiteracy rate among the mothers, and if their children were to perform poorly in school mainly *because of* this trait, that would not make such an achievement gap any less important as a policy problem. Conversely, it is only if adaptive success were demonstrated *before* any social background controls that it documents actual success rather than reasons why success is wanting.

in, say, Japan than in Norway. Similarly, some immigrant groups muster greater efforts than others to 'make it' in spite of adversity. In a model of such countervailing social forces, and there is no reason to expect uniformity as to the direction of results across time and place. But it is important to examine the conditions which promote a constructive engagement with school, because these would be the conditions which help, rather than hinder, adequate coping.

Data

The data derive from a questionnaire survey of youth in the city of Oslo. The survey's multiple purposes did not include examination of social capital, but some relevant indicators could be identified. The survey was carried out in 1996 and aimed to reach all students who were in the two top grades of compulsory basic education and all students in the first grade of post-compulsory upper secondary education, which commences at age 16 plus and receives about 95 per cent of the age group. All the public schools in Oslo were included, and so were the few private schools which taught the grades concerned. Of the total target population, 94 per cent was successfully reached, a total of 11,425 young people. About two-thirds of this sample are in grades eight or nine; one-third are in the upper secondary schools. Of all respondents, 96 per cent were within the 14–17 age range. A small percentage—7.2 per cent—were given a shortened version of the questionnaire designed for those who for various reasons would have had problems completing the long version. Of these, five-eighths were either in special reception classes for newly arrived immigrants, or their command of Norwegian was deemed by their school to be too weak to cope with the longer version. The other three-eighths of these 'short version' respondents were in separate special education classes/institutions. Some of the questions to be used in the analysis below were only included in the 'long' version, indicated in the tables by starred text.

Immigrant families are strongly concentrated in Oslo. The proportion of students with partial or complete parental 'immigrant background'—one or both parents being from abroad—is much higher among Oslo youth—33 per cent—than in the country as a whole—about 6 per cent. But about one-third of these 'immigrant background' students have in fact mixed Norwegian-foreign parentage. Students whose parents are *both* immigrants, this study designates 'immigrant youth' (N=2,444), constitute 22 per cent of our Oslo sample. There is a wide range of nationalities in the sample. Going by the father's nationality,[2] 98 different countries are represented. The most common immigrant background is Pakistani (32 per cent). Then come the successor

---

[2] Or the mother's, in those cases where no information was obtained on the father's nationality. When there is information on both parents and when both parents are from abroad, 91% of the cases come from the same country.

states of former Yugoslavia—together 8 per cent, the largest contingent (2.3 per cent) being from Bosnia; Morocco (7 per cent), Turkey (6 per cent), Vietnam (6 per cent), India (4 per cent), Iran (4 per cent), and Somalia (4 per cent).

Nationalities

Only 6 per cent of immigrant youths have parents who both have immigrated from what may be termed a 'Western country'. Nearly all of these are from western Europe; and not surprisingly, four-tenths of them come from the neighbouring countries of Sweden and Denmark. In terms of ethnic identification, cultural background political traditions, and conditions of living, this group of *Westerners* would be the immigrants that most Norwegians perceive to be closest to themselves. In physical terms these are the 'invisible' immigrants. It should be easy for them to blend into the mainstream of Norwegian social life, if they so desire, once they master the language—easy for Swedes and Danes. The 6 per cent referred to above would understate how frequently Oslo youth have *some* immigrant background of this kind. Of those 81 per cent of the total sample who will be classified as 'ethnic Norwegians' in this study—at least one parent being Norwegian—4 per cent have one parent from another Nordic country, another 6 per cent from another western country. But we shall treat these mixed backgrounds as Norwegian in order to simplify the analysis and because earlier analysis on national survey data (Lauglo 1996) showed no significant differences between such 'half-Norwegians' and the 'complete natives' in terms of adjustment to school, after adjustments for social class.

Most immigrant youth—65 per cent of them—have an Asian background, 17 per cent have a background from an African country and only 3 per cent a background from a country in South America. We shall group this blend of quite diverse backgrounds in the category 'developing countries'. Eighty-five percent of the immigrant youth in the sample fall into this broad category. They share a key characteristic: they usually differ from ethnic Norwegians by their physical appearance and thus they are 'visible minorities' who risk being racially stereotyped.

Another grouping are those who have come from the former socialist countries in Europe. These countries are also economically less advanced than Norway. Their political history during the postwar era in which most present Norwegians have had their formative years is quite different from that of the Western countries. But they are much less likely to be a visible minority by appearance. We shall call this group 'Eastern Europe' because they all come from the former Communist countries whose political centre of gravity was in Eastern Europe. But fully two-thirds of this category comes in fact from the successor states of Yugoslavia, which geographically would place them as southern European.

Thus, these are the parental nationalities to be compared: Ethnic Norwegian,[3] Western countries, Eastern Europe, and developing countries. It is likely that these groupings form a continuum as to how far they are perceived as 'close' or 'remote' in ethnic and cultural terms by the ethnic Norwegian population onto whose turf the immigrants have moved.

The sub-samples of immigrants from particular nationality backgrounds are large enough so that one could compare particular country groups in this sample. However, the complexity of the intended analysis is already testing the limits of the paper format; and other reports from this sample will deal with particular nationalities, as is already the case with Helland (1997).

Valuing School

How do the immigrant youth compare with the majority population in terms of attitudes to school? Table 8.1 maps the prevalence of attitudes by nationality category and for boys and girls separately.[4] The seven items relate to appreciation of school, support for orderly learning conditions in school, and personal prioritization of school work.

The findings clearly show that it is youth from a developing country background who most often display attitudes indicating a constructive engagement in their school work, and that it is the ethnic Norwegians who least often display such traits. This applies to: valuing school as a well functioning institution (items 5 and 7), accepting and supporting orderly conditions for learning (items 3 and 4), prioritizing school work ahead of one's social life (item 6), and generally liking life at school (item 1). The sole exception is item 2: being 'nervous about going to school'.[5] Immigrant youth from a developing country background may not have an especially easy life at school—as their response to item 2 suggests—but that does not deter them from engaging constructively with school. The more positive engagement of the developing country grouping generally holds for boys and girls alike. The other immigrant youth categories are usually in an intermediate position.[6] The z-score is based on the cumulation of these items, each of which is scored on a 0–1 scale and shows the same pattern along the bottom row. In keeping with much earlier research, there is some tendency for girls to be more positive to school than boys are, but this tendency is neither strong nor consistent across all items and nationality comparisons.

[3] This term is an attempt to signal that these are not the only Norwegians. Immigrant youth are also Norwegian citizens in the overwhelming majority of cases.

[4] Thus, on item 2, 18% of the girls of ethnic Norwegian background 'agreed' more than they 'disagreed', on a four-point scale, that 'I am often nervous about going to school', as compared with 23% of the boys from the same background.

[5] The Norwegian original—*grue seg til å gå på skolen*—lacks a precise English equivalent. 'Dread going to school' would be another possibility but too strong.

[6] In these two 'intermediate' categories, especially the 'Western' group, the number of cases is so small that random fluctuations also will make trends less apparent.

Table 8.1 Attitudes to school by parental nationality and gender

		Parental nationality					(b-coefficient) on z-score score of grade point average
		Norwegian	Western countries	Eastern Europe	Developing countries	Total sample	
1. I like school (% strongly agrees on 4-point scale)	Girls	29	31	36	46	32	.28
	Boys	29	31	43	46	32	.43
2. I am often nervous about going to school (% agrees on 4-point scale)	Girls	18	26	21	23	19	-.26
	Boys	23	24	24	31	24	-.34
3[a] Teachers should be shown respect – also if one disagrees with them (% agrees more than disagree on 10-point scale)	Girls	49	58	60	70	52	.09
	Boys	47	55	62	66	50	.19
4. Teachers should be stricter to disruptive students (% agrees on 4-point scale)	Girls	48	48	52	58	50	.22
	Boys	49	48	43	52	(49)	.30
5. School is boring (% agrees on 4-point scale)	Girls	58	62	48	32	54	-.10
	Boys	61	62	39	37	57	(-.04)
6[a] Being with friends is more important to me than learning everything and doing well at school (% agrees on 4-point scale)	Girls	41	36	22	15	37	-.21
	Boys	44	29	28	22	41	-.20
7. Much time is wasted at school (% agrees on 4-point scale)	Girls	48	39	29	22	43	-.06
	Boys	56	46	30	31	51	-.09
Total numbers: range for the seven items	Girls	3,969-4,232	57-62	99-128	618-887	4,743-5,309	
	Boys	3,944-4,261	47-62	92-136	591-894	4,674-5,353	
Range of response rate for the seven items	Girls	93-97	93-95	88-96	83-92	92-96	
	Boys	92-96	76-91	79-91	75-86	89-93	
Index of valuing school: z-scores	Girls	-0.04	.05	.32	.64	.06	.13
	Boys	-0.14	.08	.20	.43	-0.06	.16

[a] Item not included in short version of questionnaire—about 7% of total sample.

The relevance of these attitudes for educational achievement is indicated in a rough and ready fashion by the coefficients from a series of bivariate regressions (the right hand column). Positive attitudes to school seem to matter for successful performance, but since the b-coefficients are of modest magnitude, they confirm that it takes more than positive attitudes to succeed there. The greatest effect is among boys and on item 1. Those who don't like school have a predicted achievement score four-tenths of a standard deviation lower than those who do. On the other hand, on item 5, disagreeing with 'School is boring' has no significant positive effect among boys. There is an effect among girls but it is weak, only one tenth of a standard unit on the achievement scale.

The main finding in Table 8.1 is that ethnicity matters more than gender in shaping attitudes to school, and that this ethnicity effect is strong. Rather than distancing themselves from, or even being hostile to, an institution in relation to which they might appear to be particularly 'disadvantaged' in the logic of cultural capital theory, it is the putatively most culturally 'remote' students who value school the most.

Table 8.2 examines behaviour deemed relevant for engagement in schooling. The nationality pattern resembles that in Table 8.1. But it is stronger; and the 'effects' of these traits on academic performance is greater. Though the putatively 'culturally closer' categories are not always in an intermediate position, the contrast between ethnic Norwegian and developing countries is clear throughout, for both boys and girls. When these items are combined into a simple additive scale and converted to z-scores (positive behaviour), one sees again that gender matters but that ethnicity matters more. At one extreme are the diligent girls of developing country background, at the other extreme are the relatively laid back 'fully Norwegian' lads. Between lies nine-tenths standard deviation on the scale, a dramatic gap.

Self-reported 'problem behaviour' (items 6 to 9) is negatively correlated with performance in school. Whenever statistically significant differences are found—five out of eight comparisons—youth from developing country background either have *the* lowest frequency or they match the lowest one. The other nationality categories show no clear pattern. The summary scale for these four items—the z-scores for problem behaviour—shows no significant nationality differences among boys. But the girls from a 'developing country' background stand out by their low score on the misbehaviour scale.

Neither the 'positive behaviour' scores nor the 'problem behaviour' scores have a distribution that is well suited for statistical analysis. By subtracting the former from the latter and thus producing a measure of 'net positive behaviour', a scale with better characteristics is obtained—kurtosis –0.46 and skew –0.28. For greater ease of interpretation, the scale is converted to z-scores. The scale correlates extremely strongly (0.98) with the first factor extracted in factor analysis of all the items involved. It has an alpha-coefficient of 0.64 . As the bottom row in Table 8.2 shows, girls have higher 'net positive behaviour' scores than boys; and immigrant youth from developing countries and ethnic Norwegians are at opposite ends: the former have the highest scores and the

Table 8.2 Homework and other behaviour which affects performance at school

		Parental nationality				Total sample	B (Regression on achievement)
		Norwegian	Western countries	Eastern Europe	Developing countries		
1. % did homework 'during free time' at least 4 times last week	Girls	47	50	62	79	51	.22
	Boys	44	44	48	57	46	.24
2a % 'often' does homework during holidays and weekends	Girls	26	33	29	31	26	.45
	Boys	18	19	22	25	19	.46
3a % does homework every day at home	Girls	64	73	67	83	67	.32
	Boys	63	64	64	72	65	.35
4. % read at least 3 books (apart from schoolbooks) last month	Girls	30	41	33	46	33	.22
	Boys	14	18	22	38	18	.21
5a % went at least twice to the public library during the last month	Girls	16	24	31	53	22	.11
	Boys	15	28	27	39	18	(.01)
6. % skipped school at least once last year	Girls	51	48	43	32	47	-0.26
	Boys	41	39	37	34	40	-0.33
7. % had at least one vehement quarrel with a teacher last year	Girls	16	22	10	7	14	-0.21
	Boys	16	18	19	13	(15)	-0.34

Item	Sex						
8a 'I am often spoken to by the teacher for disturbing the class' (% agrees on a 4-point scale)	Girls	27	21	31	20	26	-0.44
	Boys	32	39	36	31	(32)	-0.38
9. % sent to the principal's office last year for misconduct, at least once	Girls	9	6	6	7	9	-0.54
	Boys	24	30	30	26	(25)	-0.37
Total number ranges for the nine items	Girls	3,952–4,265	55–63	100–130	631–930	4,738–5,388	
	Boys	3,885–4,223	54–65	92–139	579–977	4,610–5,353	
Range of response rate for the nine items	Girls	93–98	90–97	89–97	83–97	92–98	
	Boys	90–96	87–93	79–93	74–94	88–96	
Index of positive behaviour. Z-score (based on items 1–5)	Girls	.03	.26	.27	.71	.13	.20
	Boys	-0.19	-0.04	-0.13	.33	-0.13	.21
Index of problem behaviour. Z-score (based on items 6–9)	Girls	-0.02	-0.03	-0.09	-0.31	-0.06	-0.21
	Boys	.06	.18	.14	.02	(.06)	-0.20
Index of Net positive behaviour (positive behaviour minus problem behaviour) Z-score	Girls	.03	.17	(.19)	.64	.10	.25
	Boys	-0.15	-0.09	-0.12	.21	-0.21	.27

[a] Item not included in short version of questionnaire—about 7% of total sample.

Note: Except when indicated by parentheses, the differences among the nationality groups are statistically significant at the .05 level or better, for all comparisons along the rows in this table, and for all regression coefficients—which in this case are from bivariate regression in each case, not multiple regression.

latter the lowest, whilst the other immigrant categories score in an intermediate position, in much the same way as they did on the scale of 'valuing school'.[7]

Adjusting for Social Class and Cultural Capital

How would the findings be affected by social class and cultural capital? We shall proceed by using multiple classification analysis (MCA) which has the advantage of producing results that make it easy to compare mean scores in each classification of independent variables, before and after effects of other classifications. To simplify the analysis, we delete gender, for in Tables 8.1 and 8.2 it is apparent that the differences among the nationality groups are not due to gender effects. For the moment, we shall retain as dependent variables all scales generated so far: valuing school, positive behaviour, problem behaviour, and net positive behaviour. These are already in the form of z-scores, which is convenient since MCA in any event presents the results in the form of deviations from means and in standard deviation units.

Three sets of independent variables are included in the form of classifications: parental nationality (as before); 'social class' which is based upon occupation, usually of the father; and 'cultural capital' which here is indicated by the magnitude of books in the home—there were fixed response options.[8] For each dependent variable, first is shown the mean z-scores for each classification analysed separately, with the attendant Eta-coefficient. For parental nationality, these merely restate in some detail what has been presented earlier.

It can be seen that the zero-order relationships of all these dependent variables with social class are distinctly weak, and do not fit the notion of a hierarchy of advantage and 'closeness' to the educational enterprise. For example, middle-class backgrounds do not invariably go with positive attitudinal and behavioural adaptation to school, and it is not the offspring of those who have been marginalized from gainful employment altogether who score highest on problem behaviour.

Cultural capital does not predict these scales much better; and the pattern is not always what social reproduction theory would have us expect. In fact, it is the cultural outsiders to the school, those with few books at home, who value school most. Those who value school most are *not* youth whose parents have well-stocked home libraries—and who therefore probably also have high frequency of higher education.

---

[7] To perform a sensitivity test on the patterns noted in Tables 1 and 2, we made the deliberately extreme assumption that any item-specific non-response represents such traits as, respectively for the different items: negative attitudes to school, low effort, no leisure reading of books, no use of libraries, and consistently high scores on problem behaviour. But it was found that the main contrast between the ethnic Norwegians and youth from developing-country nationality background persisted—even under these extreme assumptions.

[8] The data collected did not include information on the parents' level of schooling.

After the effects of social class and cultural capital also are taken into account, the already quite strong immigrant effects are strengthened, not weakened, as evinced by comparing the predicted means with the unadjusted ones. The boosting effect of having parents who have immigrated from a developing country is quite strong, especially on valuing school and positive behaviour.

Moving from zero-order relationships to MCA reveals increased effects of cultural capital and social class and serves to make the pattern of these effects fit better with the derivations of social reproduction theory: that is, high class and high cultural capital is shown to be advantageous for engaging with school in a positive way, as social reproduction theory would predict. But it is striking, in this sample where fully 22 per cent come from immigrant homes, that in the zero-order relationships these patterns were obscured by the much stronger effect of ethnicity. Further, it should be noted that these classical 'social reproduction' variables have only weak effects.

One notes that when it comes to valuing school the results show that the class grouping that should be socially and culturally closest to schools, the humanistic-social middle class, does not outshine other groups. Rather, the adjusted means hint that youth from this background might be slightly more jaded about school. Perhaps they take school so much for granted that it takes more for them to respect the teachers, and to like it there, and not to be bored?

The most striking finding in Table 8.3 is that parental nationality trumps both social class and cultural capital in predicting young people's constructive engagement with school; in Tables 8.1 and 8.2 it trumped gender as well. As noted, constructive engagement is not tantamount to results. But it is a measure of how far young people seek to make the most out of such resources as they possess. It is quite independent of social class.[9] It serves as an equalizer which works particularly in favour of immigrant youth from the type of background which at first glance would seem to be most remote from the majority population. Why should this be the case? One possible explanation is that these immigrant adolescents belong to families which provide them with much valuable social capital for the purpose of doing one's level best at school.

Social Capital

The themes captured by the concept of social capital have long antecedents in social science (cf. the discussion in Portes 1998). The present widespread usage of the term owes much to Coleman (1988a), who pointed to the importance of strong social regulation for the formation of human capital in the school system. He actually *defined* social capital in wider terms, as elements of social

---

[9] The Eta squares of the full social class classification were minuscule. They were for the respective dependent variables: .001 for 'Valuing school', .004 for 'Positive behaviour', .001 for 'Problem behaviour', and .003 for 'Net positive behaviour'.

Table 8.3 What matters most for a constructive engagement with school: Ethnicity? Social class? Cultural capital?

| | Four multiple classification analyses (MCAs) | | | | | | | |
| | Valuing school | | 'Positive behaviour' (homework, books, library) | | Problem behaviour | | Net positive behaviour | |
	Number range inthe four MCAs	Mean score	Predicted mean	Mean score	Predicted mean	Mean score	Predicted mean	Mean score	Predicted mean
Parental nationality									
Ethnic Norwegian	6,576–7,434	−0.08	−0.09	−0.08	−0.10	.02	.04	−0.06	−0.09
Western	87–100	.09	.08	.14	.11	.05	.07	.05	.06
Eastern Europe	147–174	.33	.38	.06	.20	.01	−0.06	.05	.19
Developing countries	893–1116	.54	.60	.53	.69	−0.16	−0.25	.43	.60
Eta-coefficient		*.21*		*.19*		*.06*		*.16*	
Beta, in MCA			*.23*		*.26*		*.10*		*.22*
Social class									
Higher managerial	748–843	.02	.08	.02	.04	.01	.00	.00	.02
Technical-economic middle class	2,540–2,877	−0.03	.01	−0.02	.01	−0.03	−0.04	.01	.03
Humanistic-social middle class	1,563–1,770	−0.06	−0.04	.09	.07	−0.01	.00	.07	.05

	N	(1)	(2)	(3)	(4)	(5)	(6)	(7)	(8)
Lower white-collar	820–948	-0.03	-0.04	-0.10	-0.09	.02	.02	-0.07	-0.05
Manual workers	1,764–2,030	.04	.00	-0.06	-0.06	.04	.04	-0.07	-0.06
Unemployed, or on welfare	268–356	.37	.05	.28	.00	-0.02	.06	.19	-0.03
Eta		*.08*		*.08*		*.03*		*.06*	
Beta, in MCA			*.03*		*.05*		*.03*		*.05*
Cultural capital (how many books are there in your home)									
More than 1,000	1,356–1,505	-0.01	.05	.16	.21	-0.06	-0.07	.13	.17
500–999	2,261–2,531	-0.01	.04	.07	.11	-0.02	-0.03	.06	.10
100–499	2,557–2,932	-0.03	-0.01	-0.11	-0.07	.01	.00	-0.07	-0.05
20–99	1,240–1,448	.09	-0.04	-0.02	-0.15	.04	.07	-0.04	-0.15
Fewer than 20	289–408	.02	-0.26	-0.23	-0.50	.15	.23	-0.27	-0.51
Eta		*.04*		*.11*		*.04*		*.09*	
Beta, in MCA			*.07*		*.16*		*.07*		*.15*
Number for multiple classification			8,646		8,280		8,824		7,703
Multiple R in MCA			.22		.26		.10		.22

Notes: All etas and betas are significant at .05 level. The betas differ from the 'β' or beta that is used in ordinary least squares (OLS) regression, in that in MCA they refer to the relative effect of the whole classification, but they are not directly comparable with the Eta coefficients.

structure 'that facilitate certain actions of actors, whether persons or corporate actors, within that structure' (Coleman 1988a: 98). This definition is so wide that it not only includes benefits derived from strong social solidarity, but in principle it could accommodate the view that freedom from group restraints also can serve actors' purposes, an idea which equally has a long history in sociology. Thus, Park (1928), in launching the concept of the 'marginal man', was interested in the opportunities for innovative behaviour which inhered in detachment from group solidarity. More recently, Granovetter (1973) argued that, for many purposes, people derive benefits from having distinctly weak but widely scattered social ties rather than strong ties within 'closed' networks. However, in exemplifying and actually using the concept of social capital Coleman focuses exclusively on the benefit of having strong ties and closed networks: the bonds that better enable people to give strong support to each other and act together for common purposes. That is also the way that other theorists have interpreted Coleman's definition, for example Fukuyama (1995) in his monograph on the importance of trust for economic development, or Putnam's (1995a) work on participation in civic activities. In practice Coleman's conceptualization comes close to what Bourdieu (1997[1983]: 51) earlier offered as a definition of social capital: advantages derived from membership in networks through which a person benefits from collectively-owned resources.

One reason why there is at present special interest in the kind of social capital that is connected with strong ties is the suspicion that modern society, with the US at the head of the column, increasingly shows a deficit of social regulation, allegedly as indicated by, for example, high crime rates, declining memberships in civic voluntary organizations, less public-mindedness, more general narcissism, and more children growing up in broken homes. It has long been a suspicion among conservatives and socialists alike that modernization and its economic engine, market capitalism, could end with individualism running rampant. Worries about excessive individuation have become a major theme in recent diagnosis of the ills of contemporary society. Well-known contributors are Robert Bellah, Amitai Etzioni, Christopher Lasch, Robert Putnam, and Thomas Ziehe.

But liberals have been optimists. The position that most clearly derives from the liberal tradition in social philosophy is methodological individualism. 'Rational choice' has been the model of action associated with that position. It has all along served as the engine of action in economics. In recent years it has become increasingly important as a model of the person in political science and sociology too. Over the years, Coleman increasingly positioned himself in this liberal tradition and came to view instrumental rationality as the engine both of individual action and of institutional evolution. However, his turning to social capital could be construed as a return to the more Durkheimian concerns which he had early in his career, for Coleman used the concept to show that high-school drop-out could be due to insufficient social regulation by parents and community. He here comes full circle back to concerns he developed in *Adolescent Society* (1961): that in order to engage constructively and purposefully with school, adolescents need sufficient social regulation by the responsible adults, lest they be led astray from what in the long term is in their interest by their ties to the peer group and by the kind of activities which were socially rewarded in the 'adolescent society' of the United States in the late 1950s.

But social capital, like social regulation more generally, raises the question of the purpose it serves. That would depend on the kinds of beliefs and normative patterns which prevail in a group and on the effective enforcement of the norms. Coleman's view has been that the norms which responsible adults subscribe to would help adolescents engage with school, but he suspected that this would not be the case with adolescent peer groups, in the context of his particular time and society. Indeed, peer group solidarity can under certain conditions lead to outright opposition to school, a theme pursued by conflict theorists who perceive school to serve as an instrument of oppression and control (for example, Willis 1977). Thus, whether strong ties to a particular social group will help or hinder a person in furthering a particular goal is of course something not something to be assumed; it needs to be examined, for what serves as 'capital' is, to follow Coleman (1988*a*), 'defined by its function'.

In Coleman's version of social capital, which has been so influential in recent years and which in practice concerns the benefits of *strong* social bonds, there remains an ambiguity. Coleman sought to develop the concept within a methodological individualist framework. In keeping such a stance, Coleman referred to social capital as a resource which the actor *makes use* of—as if it were an asset that is deliberately deployed. But he also refers to norms and their effective enforcement as resources which can serve the actor's purposes; and he toned down the importance which internalization of norms would have for shaping social action. But it would seem that social regulation can serve as a resource only when it is *internalized* by most people whose relations serve as a resource at any one time, for any given individual. However, that concession might prise the concept of social capital loose from the methodological individualist framework for which Coleman sought to refashion this previously existing concept.

Do Immigrants Muster More Social Capital for Education?

The corollary to worries about excessive individuation in modern society is the view that immigrants from more traditional places carry with them the kind of social capital which Coleman thought was in increasingly short supply: cohesive families, backed up by a community, capable of effective social regulation of adolescents so that they buckle down to what it takes to do well in school and persevere there. In keeping with Coleman, Steinberg's (1997) research in the US concludes that immigrant families have got what others have lost.

Social capital has explicitly been invoked as an explanation for the strong effort and school performance among immigrant youth by Zhou and Bankston (1994) and by Portes and MacLeod (1996). But themes of 'strong immigrant families' and of their 'strong support for education' have long been prevalent. In the case of studies of immigrant families from east Asia, these themes are typically also interpreted as derived from the Confucian cultural tradition (Yap 1986 in England; Caplan, Whitmore, and Choy 1989 in the US).

Research on diverse groups has stressed the great importance that immigrant parents attach to educating their children. Suarez-Orozco (1991) exemplifies this in his ethnographic study of immigrants to the US from Central American countries. Not infrequently, the act of migration was itself motivated by the desire to secure better educational opportunity for the children. It may also be that the very condition of being an immigrant creates an urge to educate the children. Both by self-selection and by the need to build a new life, immigrant families are future-oriented, and are thus induced to see education as an investment for their children as individuals and also for the whole family. Education can become a means by which the entire family seeks to advance from humble circumstances and become part of the new society. In the process, old barriers may erode. Gibson and Bhachu (1991) noted about Sikh families in England and in California that schooling for girls can fairly quickly become important when parents begin to perceive a future for their daughters as gainfully employed.

Thus, there is good reason to believe that immigrant families value education for their children. It is also likely that family, and community, solidarity is strengthened by the shared distinction which immigrants experience from the surrounding society and by the perceived need to stick together in that situation. Immigrants from developing countries may also come from countries in which families are strongly cohesive to begin with.

However, whether immigrant families stand much apart from other families as to cohesion depends not only on the immigrants but also on how cohesive the families and communities are in the society to which they have migrated. Conditions might differ between Norway, California, or Florida, where some of the major US studies have been conducted, in this regard. Another question is whether immigrant families, notwithstanding their degree of *internal* cohesion, in fact will be particularly effective in socially regulating the life of their offspring at school and in other meeting grounds *outside the family*.

Table 8.4 is an attempt both to compare the nationalities in our Oslo sample with respect to social relations, or ties, which might serve as social resources for education and, at the same time, to assess whether these relations in fact make a difference for how youth engages with school. These are the types of social relations examined: cohesive family ties, effective monitoring by parents of their offspring, parental backup for school work and involvement with the school, participation in a religious community, and intensity of peer relations. On all these types of relations, the differences among the nationality categories are statistically significant.

On every indicator of cohesive family relations, there is a contrast between ethnic Norwegians and immigrant youth of developing countries parentage: the latter are part of more cohesive families. Also, those of Eastern European background evince signs of stronger family ties. But the Westerners seem quite similar to the ethnic Norwegians. Family cohesion does help youth to engage constructively with school. In terms of bivariate regression coefficients, all indicators of such relations are positively associated with both measures of constructive engagement with school.[10]

Immigrant youth are more often part of a religious community, and the more remote the immigrant background seemingly is from Norway, the stronger the religious involvement seems to be. Also, this type of involvement is conducive to a positive engagement with school.

Contrary to mass media reports on juvenile delinquency, of ethnic immigrant youth running in gangs, those from a developing country background are *more rarely* part of a gang than are other young people. In general, they seem to be less intensely involved with peers and friends. But there is no clear difference between the 'intermediate' immigrant groups and the majority population with respect to this set of indicators. It turns out on this count too that the most 'culturally remote' immigrant youth may be at an advantage. For in keeping with Coleman's perspective on the US, the intensity of peer-group relations seems to have adverse effects on engagement with school in Norway too. There is of course an inevitable trade-off between time spent with friends and time spent on schoolwork or on reading books. More surprisingly, two of the items also have weakly adverse effects on valuing school.

The 'social capital' advantage of immigrant youth from a developing countries background is not consistent across the board. Their parents are less able to monitor them *outside* the family. And effective monitoring by parents is important for young people's engagement with schooling. Adolescents whose parents usually know what their offspring is up to score fully 0.63 of a standard deviation higher on 'net positive behaviour'. Finally, immigrant parents less often involve themselves personally in their children's school and school work, a probable disadvantage for their children, though Helland's (1997) analysis of this Oslo survey has already shown that parents attending meetings at school does not seem to boost the marks of students of Pakistani or Vietnamese background.

The balance sheet of social capital contains mostly advantages for the immigrants, but there are also minuses. Immigrant parents, being themselves less integrated into the larger society, are also less able personally to back up adolescents' schoolwork; and they have greater problems keeping track of

---

[10] The coefficients are b's, not standardized 'betas', since the concern is with magnitude of effect, not with contribution to prediction. The dependent variables are already standardized. These are bivariate regressions. Thus, youth 'living with both parents' score .34 of a standard deviation higher on the Net positive behaviour scale than those who do not live with both parents.

Table 8.4 Social ties by parental nationality and the 'effects' which social ties have on positive engagement with school

	Parental nationality					Effects on positive engagement with school (b coefficient)[b, c]	
	Norwegian	Western countries	Eastern Europe	Developing countries	Total sample	Appreciation of school	Net positive behaviour
Cohesive family relations (%)							
Lives with both parents	63	55	74	76	66	.14	.34
Visited relatives at least twice last week	26	21	41	49	30	.20	.18
Helped at home, more than 3 times, last week	29	40	45	59	34	.33	.38
Looked after siblings at least twice last week	11	16	19	34	15	.24	.30
Spent leisure time on some joint family activity on at least two occasions last week	22	23	34	33	24	.40	.44
Agrees: In our family, we don't let each other down[a]	68	67	77	72	69	.44	.41
Agrees: In our family we help each other[a]	65	65	76	75	67	.46	.45
Disagrees: In our family, we often quarrel[a]	76	74	80	86	78	.46	.48
Monitored by parents (%)							
Agrees: My parents usually know where I am and what I am doing, during my spare time[a]	78	78	75	71	77	.52	.63

Agrees: My parents know most of my friends[a]	72	71	70	65	71	.35	.44
Agrees: My parents know quite well who I am with, in my spare time[a]	78	77	65	62	75	.36	.50
Parents back school up (%)							
Agrees: My parents always go to parents' meetings[a]	57	50	40	40	55	.15	.21
Agrees: My parents often help me with my schoolwork	59	57	49	51	58	.19	.30
Disagrees: My parents rarely talk to me about my schoolwork	37	31	43	41	38	.35	.35
Religious participation (%)							
Goes to church/mosque at least once a month	7	14	29	39	12	.41	.40
Intensity of peer relations (%)							
Has definitely at least one friend 'you trust completely'	61	63	57	52	59	(.03)	-0.14
Been with friends, at a home, at least 3 times last week	60	62	56	41	57	-0.26	-0.40
Is part of a 'gang', when with friends	48	43	38	31	45	-0.20	-0.40

a Item not included in short version of questionnaire—about 7% of total sample.
b b coefficients from bi-variate regression.
c Parentheses indicate that coefficient is not significant at .05 level.

what their children are up to, out there in the larger world.[11] Beyond the walls of Fortress Family, immigrant youngsters seem to be more on their own.

The Importance of Social Capital

We are now in a position to assess the net effect of the relative magnitudes which immigrant youths seem to possess of these forms of social capital in order to see if social capital in fact can explain the type of patterns revealed in Tables 8.1 and 8.2. Table 8.5 presents the findings.

Ordinary least squares (OLS) regression is used to examine the effect of these traits. For ease of presentation, simple additive scales are used to sum up the social capital items which have just been examined. Since the predictors are a mix of dummy variables and continuous variables, both b and beta coefficients are now presented. Models 1 to 3 in the table, which are re-runs of relations examined in Table 8.3, merely repeat the finding that ethnicity is much more important than social class and cultural capital. Adding the social capital indicators in model 4 greatly boosts R^2—though it still remains at a modest level—and shows that both classifications still matter for engagement with school. Since the significant regression coefficients of ethnicity are weaker in model 4 than in model 2, we can conclude that the net effects of social capital influences are helpful to immigrant youth from a developing country background. This is most clearly true for *behaviour*. Thus, in engagement with school too, action speaks louder than words.

When in model 5 the 'social reproduction predictors' of social class and cultural capital are added as well, there is not much change. The only effect is then to drive slightly up again the magnitude of ethnicity effects, for the same reasons as already shown in Table 8.3. That the social capital effects are unaffected by these social reproduction predictors merely goes to suggest that the net balance of these social resources is indeed fairly 'democratically' distributed—as Coleman thought they would be.

We are left with the conclusion that social capital indeed helps to explain the differences among nationality groupings as to engagement with school. But since nationality differences remain, it cannot be the whole story.

The Necessity of Strong 'Agency'

The analysis in Table 8.5 failed to explain fully why youth from a developing country background engage more positively with school than do ethnic Norwegians. Why should they value school more and behave towards school in a more positive manner after social capital, cultural, capital, and social class all have been taken into account?

[11] Adding gender to Table 8.4 showed that girls help a bit more at home, and parents keep a bit more track of girls; but the ethnicity differences were much the same for boys as for girls.

Table 8.5 Does social capital explain differences among nationality groups on positive engagement with school? Ordinary least squares regression analyses of 'School appreciation' and 'Net positive behaviour' scales

Predictor	Dep. variable: z-score on 'Valuing school' scale					Dep. variable: z-score on 'Net positive behaviour' scale				
	Model 1 (B / β)	Model 2 (B / β)	Model 3 (B / β)	Model 4 (B / β)	Model 5 (B / β)	Model 1 (B / β)	Model 2 (B / β)	Model 3 (B / β)	Model 4 (B / β)	Model 5 (B / β)
Parental nationality (three dummy variables with Ethnic Norwegian as reference category)										
Western		(.15) / (.02)	(.16) / (.02)	(.16) / (.02)	(.17) / (.02)		(.11) / (.02)	(.14) / (.01)	(.11) / (.01)	(.13) / (.01)
Eastern Europe		.41 / .06	.43 / .06	.39 / .05	.39 / .05		(.11) / (.01)	(.22) / (.08)	(.02) / (.00)	(.09) / (.01)
Developing country		.63 / .20	.67 / .22	.51 / .16	.53 / .16		.50 / .16	.63 / .20	.26 / .08	.36 / .11
Cohesive family (scale)		.15 / .15			.15 / .15		.18 / .18			.17 / .17
Monitoring by parents (scale)		.19 / .19			.19 / .18		.22 / .22			.22 / .21
Parents' involvement with school (scale)		.11 / .11			.11 / .10		.12 / .12			.11 / .11
Religious participation (dummy variable)			.13 / .04		.13 / .04			.16 / .05		.15 / .05
Intensity of peer relations	-.09 / -.04		(-.08) / (-.08)		-.09 / -.09			-.22 / -.22		-.22 / -.23
Social class: middle class (dummy)				(.02) / (.01)	(.01) / (.00)				.12 / .06	.10 / .05
Cultural capital: more than 500 books at home (dummy)	(.01) / (.00)			.07 / .04	(.02) / (.01)	.16 / .08			.22 / .02	.15 / .08
R	.04	.21	.21	.38	.38	.08	.16	.21	.45	.46
R²	.00	.04	.05	.14	.14	.01	.03	.04	.21	.21
Constant	.06	-.09	-.13	-.08	-.10	-.08	-.06	-.25	-.06	-.21

Note: Parentheses indicate that coefficients are not significant at .05 level.

If school is more difficult for them, then perhaps they work harder simply because they need to do so in order to keep up? Is not working harder the rational response to flashing warning lights? Is it not justified to lie back a bit and rest on your laurels when you get good marks? But if these were the mainspring of effort at school, then marks would be negatively correlated with effort, not moderately positively as we see in Table 8.2, items 1–3. Further, it is hard to see how putatively 'greater difficulties' also could explain strongly appreciative attitudes to the very arena in which these difficulties would be experienced. It is also hard to see how this explanation could account for the difference between visible and invisible immigrants which runs through most of the findings. Why, for example, should the 'developing country' category engage even more positively with school than do the 'Eastern Europe' grouping, most of whom are fairly recent family arrivals from former Yugoslavia?

What youth from developing country backgrounds have in common is that they are part of a visible minority and that they are likely to encounter social reminders of this sometimes when they least expect it, ranging from acts of hostility to simply being treated as part of a social category that is 'not really Norwegian' solely on the basis of appearance. Unlike other immigrants, they cannot blend into the majority population simply by acquiring the full register of linguistic nuances and enough local life-style elements that symbolize belonging: skis, walks in nature, boating, school bands, football matches, brown cheese. Norwegian nationalism remains quite strong and rests on a populist concept of national identity. It differs from those few countries—the USA, France, the former Soviet Union—in which national identity historically had strong infusions of universalistic ideas. Neither does the historical construction of Norwegian national identity stress new groups arriving, settling, adding their particular contribution to the nation—as even the British concept of national identity would in a long historical perspective. In short, Norwegian national identity is not something that is easily joined. If you 'look different' you never know how welcoming a stranger will be, but even when the natives are friendly the chances are you will be perceived as an outsider even if you may have been born in the country.

In such circumstances, it is realistic for immigrant youth from a developing country background to perceive that the labour market they eventually will enter is one in which the odds are stacked against them, especially during rounds of impersonal job applications. More than others, immigrants are thrown back on personal networks in order to find their way in the job market, in order to be personally introduced and sponsored. Immigrant youth and their families are likely to be deficient in the 'weak ties' version of social capital (Granovetter 1973) which leads to job possibilities outside such niches. And yet it is likely that they more than others depend on such ties in order to get a hearing with employers unknown to them.

School matters in order to get a job. But for those who in Norway are part of a visible minority, schooling acquires added importance because it appears to them as the one available ladder to the labour market. And in order to compete with others in that market, such immigrant youth may need to climb a bit higher than their competitors.[12] Such a view of the surrounding society may help explain the special urgency that schooling seems to acquire for such youth.

In the Weberian view, echoed in Coleman (1988a), the key element in modernity is the advance of instrumental rationality. This could be construed to imply that a strong 'agency' is a distinctly modern mindset. But trying to cope with necessity is a basic human trait that has nothing uniquely modern about it. Purposive engagement with the world is activated in most human beings whenever there comes a clear and present need. And our findings support the view that there is no necessary conflict between this seemingly individualistic trait and strong family ties: immigrant youth, for example, stand out from others by their stronger family ties *and* by their 'stronger agency' in relation to schooling.

A weakness of social reproduction theory is that it fails to explain such social fluidity and social advancement as does occur in a society. In particular, it offers little help in explaining educational success among individuals who lack the very class-related background resources which are deemed to be of decisive importance. Other conditions of social structure—especially social capital—and culture also structure social action. In addition to the individual exceptions, it is also possible to trace particularly strong social ascent over generations by certain cultural groups. Social history is replete with examples concerning certain religious minorities as well as certain immigrant groups who in the space of two to three generations have risen from humble beginnings to a preponderance in middle-class professions: for example, Japanese Americans, Chinese Americans, immigrant Jews who started in the sweatshops of New York's garment district or in London's Spitalsfield. Social reproduction is a reality, but so also are the forces that defy it. Coleman suggested the more 'democratically distributed' force of social capital.

It should be noted that not all kinds of strong social ties are an advantage for engaging constructively with school—just as not all kinds of strong social ties are helpful if the goal is to keep away from crime. Whether strong ties serve as a beneficial support or not depends on the group concerned, and presumably on the norms that prevail in these groups—norms for which there regrettably are no direct measures in the present research material. As noted, there are numerous contributors to theory on how immigrant families cope who have suggested that the mentality of showing 'strong agency' becomes part of the norms that emerge among many immigrant families. These would be norms which are born out of necessity. But normative regulation, important though it is, did not fit all findings in this study. It is likely that, at the individual level, a stronger agency is activated simply by necessity—striving hard to learn to swim, lest you sink.

---

[12] Lødding (1997) found, in a study of the transfer to apprenticeship in the city of Oslo, that the chances of immigrant youth obtaining an apprenticeship place matched the chances which non-immigrants had only in the achievement category which had very high marks in school. In the other achievement categories, the odds were indeed stacked against immigrant youth.

9

Social Capital, Schools, and Exclusions

PAMELA MUNN

[The] principle that we live by entering into relations with one another, provides the basic structure within which all human experience and activity falls,
whether individual or social. For this reason the first priority in education . . .
is learning to live in personal relation to other people. Let us call it learning to
live in community.

I call this the first priority because failure in this is a fundamental failure that
cannot be compensated for by success in other fields; because our ability to
enter into fully personal relations with others is the measure of our humanity.
For inhumanity is precisely the perversion of human relations.

McMurray 1958, quoted in M. Fielding (1996: 162)

Introduction

THIS chapter explores the usefulness of the concept of social capital in
relation to understanding school practices, particularly those aimed at
tackling social exclusion. It is in four main parts. First, it briefly describes the
enduring concern to explain why schooling seems to do little to change patterns of disadvantage, as the background to the emergence of the concept of
social capital. Although schooling does provide the main meritocratic route by
which individuals can escape from poverty, in itself no mean achievement,
the emphasis on educational attainment which necessarily accompanies
notions of meritocracy tends to individualize explanations for success and failure in examinations and to distract attention from structural explanations of
disadvantage. This part notes the congruence of concerns of Marxist theorists
of education with those of mainstream British politicians who explicitly call
for a closer correspondence between schools and economic and social structures, albeit from a different theoretical basis. Politicians see schools as one of
the main drivers of change of social and economic structures, rather than

I am grateful to the editors and to Lindsay Paterson, Gwynedd Lloyd, and Ian Martin, colleagues at
the University of Edinburgh, for comments on an earlier draft of this paper.

social and economic structures determining the role and functions of schooling. 'Social capital and schooling' explores the usefulness of social capital in explaining the underachievement of disadvantaged children, in promoting social control, and in examining school practices in personal and social development. This part concludes that the concept is a helpful analytical tool. 'Schools and social exclusion' takes this view further and gives examples of the ways in which social capital can be helpful in analysing policies and practice to promote social inclusion, particularly in the area of exclusion from school. The argument of this part is that social capital is value neutral and that, in using it analytically, one needs to be clear about the norms and values which create and sustain particular networks. The chapter concludes by warning of the risks of developing ever more sophisticated models of school improvement designed to help underprivileged children and raise their levels of attainment, so diverting attention from the need to develop a coherent anti-poverty strategy which would bring more immediate and longer term benefits to children in need.

As the epigraph from McMurray makes clear, sociability is part and parcel of what it means to be human. This raises the question of the nature of sociability, of the kinds of relations in which one should live with others. Drawing on the tradition of Scottish Enlightenment thinkers of 'moral sense' and 'moral duty' (see Paterson in this volume), McMurray was pointing to the need for education to develop a sense of mutual obligation among children and between children and teachers, a kind of social capital. Enlightenment thinkers also pointed to the instrumental role of social capital to help the realization of shared goals, such as efficiency in the conduct of business and the maximization of profits. The modern example, commonly quoted, is that of New York diamond traders who rely on shared norms and trust (see Chapter 1). Thus the concept is not new but, as applied to schools as part of the explanation for underachievement, it draws attention to the importance of family networks and to school culture. It helps to synthesize school-level explanations for achievement and to link these to social structures.

The focus of the chapter as a whole, then, is on the instrumental function of social capital in helping to explain the differential access to educational qualifications among children, thereby helping to sustain social—and economic—stratification. Educational qualifications are a positional good in terms of entry to further and higher education and of access to employment. Social capital can also help explain 'mobility through occupational ladders and entrepreneurial success' (Portes 1998: 12), but this is not the concern of this chapter, save that we may note in passing the familiarity of the term 'old boy network', often a reference to men who have been at the same—independent—school to explain the persistence of male, upper-class occupation of key positions in British society. Neither is the chapter concerned with social capital as a feature of networks among schools and its utility in terms of understanding the sociology of policy, though is has potentially much to contribute to this field.

Schooling and Society

The connections between schooling and society have long been a matter of debate. Three main kinds of connections are briefly sketched here to provide a backdrop against which the idea of social capital has emerged and flourished. The suggestion is that the emergence and take-up of social capital as an analytic tool is part of a continuing attempt by some educational sociologists to link the micro processes of school life with macro economic and social structures. This is a huge and difficult task but nevertheless a key—some would say *the* key—one for educational sociology. It was elegantly expressed by C. Wright Mills (1959) who defined the core features of the sociological imagination as the ability and desire to connect the personal and private with the broader social structures which help to shape people's everyday lives. Mills was writing about sociology in general but his definition of the sociological imagination applies no less to schools than to other *milieux*.

Unsurprisingly, those sociologists who have been most prominent in theorizing connections between schooling and society have tended to come from a Marxist or quasi-Marxist standpoint. Thus Althusser (1971), for example, argues that schooling serves to reproduce the social relations of production. It does so not only by determining what counts as really useful knowledge through the formal curriculum, but also by instilling values such as respect for authority and obedience and by giving pupils a sense of their own worth. He suggests:

Children at school also learn the 'rules' of good behaviour i.e. the attitude that should be observed by every agent in the division of labour according to the job he is destined for: rules of morality, civic and professional conscience, which actually means rule of respect for the socio-technical division of labour and ultimately the rules of the order established by class domination. (Althusser 1971: 245, quoted in A. Hargreaves 1980: 175)

Hargreaves (1980) summarizes the main criticisms of Althusser's model of schooling; in positing a direct reproduction of capitalist social and economic relations it is overly deterministic. Teachers and pupils are seen as passive, helpless and unable to resist the roles in which they have been cast. In brief, there is little attempt to explain how direct reproduction of class relations takes place and no empirical evidence of daily life in schools and classrooms to underpin his theory. Where empirical evidence has been provided, as in the case of Bowles and Gintis (1976), it tends to mask the subtlety and dilemmas of relations among and between pupils and teachers. There is no account, for instance, of anti-school sub-cultures which may equip pupils with strategies to resist dominant ideologies outside school.

An approach which sees the prime job of schools as directly influencing economic and social relations can also be detected in mainstream British politics. The need for an educated, flexible workforce so that Britain can compete successfully with other advanced economies in the world runs through the rhetoric of both Labour and Conservative parties from at least the 'Great Debate' instigated by James Callaghan in the late 1970s, through Margaret Thatcher's attempts to revolutionize the school curriculum in the 1980s, to Tony Blair's focus on 'education, education, education' as the main priority for the Labour government elected in 1997. This rationale has underpinned a number of major education policies, such as the accountability of schools for educational standards, the introduction of a national curriculum, the introduction of the literacy and numeracy hour, and the expansion of pre-school education. As we shall see below, social capital has emerged as an idea at a time when policy makers are particularly interested in making schools more effective and when educational sociologists are continuing to seek ways of explaining the connections between schools and society. This state of affairs may focus undue attention on the school as the cure-all for economic and social problems and divert attention away from the 'bigger picture' of the underlying causes of these problems.

A rather different way of conceptualizing connections between schooling and society but still in the Marxist tradition is that of the relative autonomy of schools from social structures. In this formulation, the connection is 'indirect, mediated and complex' (A. Hargreaves 1980: 180) rather than direct and determined. Reproduction of economic and social relations still takes place, but according to the proponents of this view, this happens relatively indirectly. Bernstein (1977: 186, quoted in A. Hargreaves (1980: 178) describes it thus: 'only a small fraction of the output of education bears a *direct* relation to the mode of production in terms of the appropriateness of skill and disposition'.

As Chapter 1 makes clear, Bourdieu and Passeron (1977), in developing the concept of cultural capital and habitus sought to explain how schools, despite their relative autonomy from social structures, reproduced economic and social relations. As with the straight reproduction model, however, empirical evidence for this explanation is weak. Similarly, the treatment of the cultural capital of elites as unproblematically dominant without any attention to resistant other cultures means that we are still far from understanding how cultural capital works in theory as well as practice.

A third way of thinking about connections between schooling and society is to see the two, for all practical purposes, as disconnected. This is an approach adopted by those working in the phenomenological or interactionist traditions, whose focus is on the meanings and interactions in particular classrooms in particular schools at particular times. Such researchers and theorists, like Schutz (1967) and Goffman (1975) do not disclaim connections but rather doubt the ability of empirical work in their theoretical tradition to throw light on their nature and extent. A recent example of this stance is the debate in education journals between D. Hargreaves (1996; 1997), calling for more evidence based practice in teaching, and Hammersley (1997), who contends that the very nature of teaching makes it unlikely that research will be able to offer solutions to problems of practice. How much less, then, might such research be able to shed light on connections between school and social structures. One might note in passing that major funders of educational research in Britain have been more interested in the practical relevance and immediate utility of findings than in 'grand theorizing' about the links between schools and society. The argument is that teachers, parents, and policy makers are primarily interested in 'what works' in so far as teaching and learning are concerned. The focus of funding has thus been on understanding individual and institutional agency rather than on social and economic structures or even on the interaction between structure and agency. Major emphases have been on school effectiveness and school improvement, mapping studies of the implementation of various curriculum and other developments, and on process-product studies of teaching and learning.

This brief foray into the historical antecedents of social capital in relation to schooling has highlighted a number of issues. These are: (1) the gap between providing theoretical insights into connections and demonstrating at a theoretical level how these connections operate in practice; (2) the weak empirical base on which these theories rest; (3) the difficulties of operationalizing concepts and hence (4) of exploring their utility in understanding school and classroom policy and practice. Social capital as a concept is a product of the continuing search to understand the connection between schools on the one hand and social, economic, and political structures on the other. It can be seen as an elaboration of the concept of cultural capital, and by giving greater analytical purchase on that concept provides a useful analytical tool in understanding school practices, at a time when there is a heavy political emphasis on the need to improve the levels of pupils' educational attainments and on the role of schools in promoting a sense of social interdependence.

Social Capital and Schooling

Social capital has been developed as a concept by Bourdieu and Coleman to help explain the reproduction of social inequality. Bourdieu explains the reproduction of elites through social capital, while Coleman uses social capital to explain the higher than expected attainment by poor children in Catholic schools. The concept can thus be used to help to understand the underachievement of poor children in school and hence the continuing under-representation of people from poor backgrounds in higher education and 'white collar' jobs. Since success in school examinations is a positional good, opening doors to further and higher education and to the labour market, the development of the concept can be seen as part of the continuing work to develop the sociological imagination referred to above, to synthesize private troubles and relate them to social structures. Underachievement would thus be explained not only in terms of these children's lack of material resources—financial capital—such as would provide good quality housing, a decent diet, warm winter clothing and so on; nor yet only in terms of a lack of cultural capital, the predispositions and schemes of thought which influence achievement in school—see Chapter 1; but also in terms of children's lack of access to familial, peer and other networks which reinforced aspiration to learn, and which could help overcome learning difficulties and gain qualifications. Social capital is conceived as a property of individuals and families in networks that they use to promote learning, and as a property of schools themselves. Thus Coleman, for example, draws attention to the higher expectations of teachers in Catholic schools in relation to pupils' behaviour and academic performance, suggesting that this helped children from poor families attain higher test score than comparable children in state schools—see Chapter 1. In drawing attention to the social networks which schools could generate to help children's achievements, Coleman helps to analyse aspects of what school effectiveness researchers have identified as school ethos (for example, Rutter *et al.* 1979; Mortimore *et al.* 1988; Sammons, Thomas, and Mortimore 1997) and what other researchers have called school culture, as a variable explaining differences in attainment among schools with similar pupil populations. Thus Catholic schools create a climate in which pupils are expected to achieve. They do so by promoting a sense of a pupil's individual worth and value through faith and, through faith, uniting home—regardless of background—and school and the school community in a shared moral purpose. Non-denominational schools do not have the basis of a shared religion on which to construct social capital and so their task is more difficult. Such schools, in poor communities, have to work hard to raise expectations among pupils and parents of what can be achieved and can make no assumptions about shared values in the way that Catholic schools can. Coleman's formulation helps make explicit that a positive school ethos compensates for disadvantaged pupils' lack of social capital outside school, at least as far as social capital relating to attainment is concerned. Social capital then, may be summed up as follows: '[Social capital] stands for the ability of actors to secure benefits by virtue of membership in social networks or other social structures' (Portes 1998: 6).

By using the concept to help explain underachievement and the school's role in the reproduction of social inequality, Bourdieu and Coleman direct attention to the *instrumental* role which social capital can play. The benefits or resources obtained relate to learning that will result in certification and a positional good. For example, a child unable to do mathematics homework can turn to parents for help who in turn may approach friends if they themselves cannot help with the mathematics. Similarly, a school might seek to develop peer tutoring or after-school homework clubs to promote learning through the stimulation of networks of children or of adults and children. We might indeed assume that such actions on the school's part would be especially beneficial to children—actors—who did not have access to such social capital. The benefits accrue both to the individual, in terms of facilitating achievement, and to the familial network which can be seen as consolidating its broader social and economic advantage. Benefit also accrues to the school in this formulation. The more it can help children achieve, the higher up performance tables it will move, achieving local and perhaps even national approbation. It might also secure additional funding as more parents choose to send their children there as its reputation for facilitating achievement grows. Bourdieu and Coleman's starting point also draw attention to the *positive effects* of social capital. As Portes (1998) and Gamarnikov and Green (1999) point out, however, social capital can be used for undesirable ends, ranging in the school context from exclusion of outsiders, a common form of bullying (Mellor 1999; Smith *et al.* 1999), to networks which reinforce resistance to schools, exemplified by truanting or violence towards pupils who comply with school norms and standards (Munn 1999*a*).

Portes (1998: 9–12) further points out that it is possible to distinguish from a range of empirical studies 'three basic functions of social capital, applicable in a variety of contexts: a) as a source of social control; b) as a source of family support and c) as a source of benefits through extra-familial networks'. As far as schools are concerned those studies relate to compliance—or to non-compliance—with school rules and educational attainment. However, schools are concerned with more than discipline and attainment as measured in public examinations. Are there ways in which social capital might be a useful analytic tools in other areas of school life?

Schools have always been concerned with the personal and social development of pupils as well as with their cognitive-intellectual development. Provision for personal and social development has been made through the formal curriculum, with slots on the timetable, through the informal curriculum of school clubs, sports, drama productions, and so forth, and through the hidden curriculum, the routines, rituals, and practices which govern school life and send messages about who and what are valued. Social capital is a useful tool here. At a basic level one might explore whether such provision exposes children to ideas about the functions of networks and whether personal and social development in schools helps to facilitate the creation of new networks rather than reinforcing the networks of those pupils who are already network rich. Likewise, the part played by social capital in children's emotional development promoting a sense of belonging, well being, and self-esteem seem fruitful areas for exploration. Such questions seem important when considering the role of schools in combating social exclusion. It is to this topic which we now turn.

Schools and Social Exclusion

Social exclusion is a slippery concept but it is typically seen as a multi-dimensional. The Social Exclusion Unit set up by the Labour administration as part of the Cabinet Office defined it thus:

social exclusion is a shorthand label for what can happen when individuals or areas suffer from a combination of linked problems, such as unemployment, poor skills, low incomes, poor housing, high crime environments, bad health and family breakdown. (Social Exclusion Unit 1999)

The combination of linked problems underlines the approach to tackling social exclusion which emphasizes a multi-agency approach, public services working together to minimize the risk of social exclusion happening and reacting to existing social exclusion through joined-up working among these services and with the private sector. The Scottish documentation setting out the government's approach to tackling social exclusion emphasizes the need for coordination: 'it is essential that the action taken by the various agencies across Scotland should "fit together" to form a truly comprehensive and coherent programme to promote social inclusion . . . Most importantly, action should be based on a clear understanding of "what works" and what more can be done' (Scottish Office n.d.: 5).

It is worth noting that the Scottish strategy has been developed by a Social Inclusion Network, formed in 1998, consisting of representatives of government and other national public and private sector organizations, alongside individuals with direct experience of tackling social exclusion (Scottish Office n.d.: 4) and chaired by a government minister, Lord Sewel. The network is supported by a small team of civil servants. This arrangement might be seen as an attempt to model inter-agency working and it is in its early stages. Interestingly enough, however, it has so far adopted a project-based approach like its counterpart south of the border, although some projects in education— for example, Educational Action Zones in England and New Community Schools in Scotland—stress multi-agency working. Thus, at one level, the idea of social capital may throw new light on the operation of networks across and within professional agencies and be an explanatory variable of the success or otherwise of multi-agency approaches. Bids for funding for new community schools and Educational Action Zones require evidence of inter-agency collaboration. As bids are renewed or extended for new phases of these initiatives a consequence may be (1) the reinforcement of existing networks, especially if bids are successful, and (2) the development of new networks as a response to specifications for projects. The social capital of professionals will thereby increase as new professional links are forged and trust is reinforced by success in securing funding for projects. The social exclusion emphasis on inter-agency working provides the impetus for 'investment strategies orientated to the institutionalization of group relations usable as a reliable source of other benefits' (Portes 1998: 3). Garmanikov and Green (1999: 60) point out the potential irony of 'the institutional redesigning of authority for the network-rich to have a role in managing the network-poor and thus may provide yet another manifestation in the long tradition of the professionalizing of *noblesse oblige* in which teachers are likely to find themselves ambiguously placed'.

Can the concept of social capital help us analyse school-focused attempts to tackle social exclusion? Schools certainly feature prominently in government policy in their own right and as an important element in multi-agency or 'joined-up' approaches to tackling disadvantage. Thus early intervention schemes to support children—and families—with difficulties in reading, writing, and number, alternatives to exclusion from school projects, schemes to promote good attendance at school as well as educational action zones and new community schools mentioned above—the latter in Scotland modelled on the full-service school in the USA—are designed to raise attainment and promote a sense of belonging at school. These schemes often feature curriculum flexibility to make 'additional opportunities for work-related learning and community work or . . . literacy and numeracy' (DfEE 1997: 8). In Scotland national guidance on curriculum design for secondary schools and on exclusion from school also recognize the need for curriculum flexibility (SCCC 1999; Scottish Office 1998).

Space does not permit a detailed exploration of all these initiatives but a brief consideration of alternatives to exclusion from school may serve to illustrate the usefulness of social capital as a concept in analysing policy and practice to combat social exclusion more generally.

Exclusion from School

Exclusion from school is the most serious sanction a school can use in response to disruptive behaviour. Schooling is denied the excluded pupils for a specified time and re-admittance may be made conditional on the pupil and/or parent(s) undertaking to change their behaviour. In the most serious cases, exclusion can be permanent and alternative education arrangements have to be made. It can be seen at once that exclusion from school is salient to social exclusion. Attainment is influenced by attendance at school and so an excluded pupil, especially if excluded repeatedly or for long periods, is at risk, and so is progression to further and higher education or to employment. Moreover, feelings of low self-esteem, stupidity, and rejection can be engendered. A number of psychological studies in the USA has shown the association between these feelings, aggressive behaviour, and youth crime (see Goleman 1996: 234–7 for a useful overview; Cullingford and Morrison 1995). Research also reports the stress which exclusion can cause in families, adding to other stresses being experienced such as poverty, bad housing, bereavement, and illness (Cohen *et al.* 1994; Commission for Racial Equality 1996; Lawrence and Hayden 1997).

It is difficult to obtain accurate figures on the extent of exclusion from school in Britain because there is wide variation in the kinds of statistics which local authorities collect. Furthermore local authorities have to rely on information supplied by schools, and schools do not officially record all exclusions (Stirling 1992; Imich 1994; C. Parsons 1996; 1999; Munn *et al.* 1997; Lawrence and Hayden 1997).

As far as England is concerned, it is estimated that about 13,500 permanent exclusions had taken place in 1996–7. Parsons estimates that 10,890 pupils were permanently excluded from secondary schools, 1,856 from primary schools and 707 from special schools. The absolute numbers were worrying in themselves, but of greater concern is that numbers have grown. There was a 45 per cent increase between 1993–4 and 1995–6 in primary schools and an 18 per cent increase over the same period in secondary schools (C. Parsons 1996; Lawrence and Hayden 1997). Fixed-term exclusions are about eight times more numerous than permanent exclusions (C. Parsons 1999).

No equivalent statistics yet exist for Scotland. Research based on a sample of secondary and primary schools revealed that over an eight month period almost 5,000 pupils had been excluded. Most of these pupils had been excluded once and for three days or fewer, although 30 per cent of pupils had been excluded for longer periods (Munn *et al.* 1997). An analysis of the characteristics of excluded pupils both in England and Scotland showed that boys are around four times as likely to be excluded as girls and exclusions peak towards the end of compulsory schooling (year 10 in England and Secondary 3 and 4 in Scotland). In England, African-Caribbean pupils are excluded proportionately between three and six times more often than their white peers.[1] It is hardly surprising that alternatives to exclusion from school should feature in government policy to tackle social exclusion more generally.

One kind of alternative to exclusion that seeks to build social capital is the KWESI project in Birmingham. This project is run by black men and provides mentoring support for African-Caribbean boys. The project has seen exclusion rates falling by 23 per cent with two-thirds of the reduction comprising ethnic minority pupils (Social Exclusion Unit 1998; Osler and Hill 1999). Although not conceptualized explicitly in terms of building social capital, the project can be seen as attempting to provide a source of benefits—emotional and perhaps employment related—to African-Caribbean boys through extra familial networks, which in turn begins to impact on the social control function of networks. Similarly 'buddy systems', whereby older pupils befriend younger pupils transferring from nursery to primary and primary to secondary schools or other pupils new to the school, can be seen as a strategy to extend the network of the new pupil(s) and to secure the benefit of more rapid induction into the school's norms, values, and disciplinary codes than would otherwise be the case. Such strategies can help to prevent bullying and promote compliance with school rules (Munn 1999*b*).

More generally, the extent to which alternatives to exclusion from school seek to promote open or closed networks among pupils within mainstream schools could be a variable explaining their success. A common alternative to exclusion is the provision of a unit or base within the school to meet the needs of disaffected pupils. Units vary as to their purpose, size, the way in which pupils are allocated, and the ways in which staff are recruited. A hypothesis would be that those units which sought to extend pupil's networks outwith the unit and set out to demonstrate the advantages of such networks would be more successful in reducing the use of the unit—other things being equal—

[1] Sample size and the lack of a significant percentage of African-Caribbean children in Scotland made it inappropriate to calculate this comparison.

than units which did not attempt to build networks at all or confined them to regular pupil users of the unit. Such a closed network might produce a sense of social solidarity within the group but also risk the development and maintenance of a culture resistant to attainment. Such a hypothesis awaits testing empirically, although many studies of units and bases have found pupils referred to them as socially marginalized, and the lack of reintegration into mainstream of pupils in off-site special units is well documented (for example Gray and Noakes 1993; Ofsted 1995; Kinder and Wilkin 1998). Furthermore, the promotion of open networks links to the issue of sociability mentioned in the introduction to this chapter. A justification of separate provision for disaffected pupils is the collective welfare of the majority of pupils in mainstream schools. They need to feel safe and secure and to avoid distractions from learning which troubled young people can engender. This seems common sense. Nevertheless, separate provision may insulate the generality of pupils from a sense of social responsibility for the excluded and send a message that difference is best handled through rejection. The notion of social capital encourages empirical exploration also of this kind of hypothesis.

A further strategy to combat exclusion from school is the more active involvement of parents in school affairs. Munn, Lloyd, and Cullen (2000) report this as the strategy most frequently cited by headteachers as a way of preventing exclusion; and Osler and Hill (1999: 49) describe one school's attempt to canvass parents' views about behaviour with a follow-up survey one year later asking parents how they felt the school had developed. 'By asking parents about what they understood as acceptable, normal and good behaviour in schools, the school had also won the approval of many pupils who indicated that the parents' questionnaire had opened up a debate about the issue as well as those of parents.' Could this be construed as one school's attempt to develop social capital through community networks as it seeks to improve school discipline and render the use of exclusion obsolete, building social capital among parents as well as between parents and the school? If so, what happens to those parents and children who refuse to conform to the consensus on acceptable, normal, and good behaviour in school? Vincent and Tomlinson (1997: 373) argue that the dominance of the rhetoric of partnership in home-school relations 'acts to conceal a continuing professional concern to control the manner and degree of parental involvement'. They go on to argue that the underlying agenda is a 'harder-edged attempt to direct family life and the behaviour of both children and their parents'. They cite Jack Straw's plans to introduce a national system of parenting classes and could also have mentioned the provisions surrounding the 1997 Education Act which characterizes parents of pupils permanently excluded twice as 'unfit persons' who are *ipso facto* denied the right to choose a school for their children. Thus, more active parental and community involvement in schooling as envisaged under social inclusion policies can be involvement that ensures conformity and control rather than negotiation, debate, and the promotion of learning for active citizenship which Ranson (1993) envisages. Indeed Riddell

(1997) suggests that one reason for the concept of social capital gaining currency in the USA is a response to the growing concern with social alienation, disaffection, and violence. If so, then there is a risk that networks will adopt authoritarian and hierarchical values, apparent in some zero-tolerance campaigns.

Alternatively social capital might be used to challenge political orthodoxies, as Ranson (1993) contends. For example, the social capital of parents and teachers in Scotland was used successfully to resist government policy on national testing by organizing a very successful public campaign, and by the large-scale withdrawal of children from school when national testing was due. This is rather in striking contrast to the examples of conformity and control given above. A key point, therefore, in using the idea of social capital in analysing school approaches to promote social inclusion is that social capital can be used to engender and solidify rather different values. In itself the concept is value neutral and any analysis would need to make explicit the shared norms and values which permeated the network under study.

It has been suggested in this section that social capital can be a helpful analytic tool in understanding schools' approaches to tackling exclusion. It is by no means the only tool, however, and it would be mistaken to see it in isolation. In a study of the different rates of exclusion used by schools with similar pupil populations in terms of social class the following four aspects proved analytically productive in explaining differences between 'matched pairs' of schools in their use of exclusion: (1) ideology: teachers' beliefs about the nature of schooling and the kind of pupil they were willing to teach; (2) teacher perceptions of the cause of learning and behaviour difficulties, distinguishing 'real' difficulties from those which pupils had brought upon themselves. The former were 'worthy' and the latter 'unworthy' pupils; (3) the curriculum on offer in terms of flexibility and differentiation to meet pupils' needs; and (4) decision-making structures in the school (Munn, Lloyd, and Cullen 2000). Furthermore, schools have to operate in a context of competing priorities and public accountability through the publication of performance indicators of which by far the most important politically are pupils' performance in national tests and public examinations. An analysis of alternatives to exclusion which relied only on social capital explanations, failed to take the policy context into account and also failed to consider teacher traditions of professional autonomy would be telling a rather partial story. For instance, Clark *et al.* (1999), in a study of inclusive schools, identify four different kinds of explanations drawn from theory for the complex picture of inclusion which emerged from in-depth case studies of a small number of schools originally identified for study as examples of 'best practice'. The schools turned out to be less inclusive than the researchers had been led to believe. Inclusion was largely conceptualized as the integration of pupils with special educational needs into the day-to-day academic and social life of the school. The schools' attempts to be inclusive were beset by difficulties and ambiguities and the theoretical explanations available for this state of affairs were found to be inadequate. The research team argued that traditional explanations such as those relating to organizational change and the nature of professionalism need to be supplemented 'by a perspective which sees responses to diversity as being beset by dilemmas arising from contradictory imperatives within mass education systems' (Clark *et al.* 1999: 157). The schools were faced with what they construed as contradictory demands. These included the demand to raise levels of achievement, juggle resources, respect specialist expertise, and integrate all pupils in mainstream classes. This reinforces the importance of using a number of theoretical lenses in attempting to understand the complex world of schools and the multi-faceted nature of teaching.

Conclusion

This chapter has suggested that the concept of social capital has grown out of attempts to understand why schooling tends to reproduce economic and social structures. The implication is that if schools are aware of the advantage which social capital confers on middle- and upper-class children then schools can compensate for this by developing their own support mechanisms to help poor children achieve. The remainder of the chapter has sought to demonstrate that social capital is indeed a useful analytic tool in understanding and comparing school practices but that it is value neutral as a concept. It can be used for ethically competing purposes. It has also suggested that social capital is only one set of lenses through which to view schools if one wants to understand inclusive or effective attainment practices.

The potential danger in the current fashion for the concept is that it focuses attention too firmly on the school as a vehicle for combating social disadvantage. The more we understand about how schools reproduce social and economic structures, the more tempted policy makers may be to focus on schools as the cure-all for society's ills, including raising levels of attainment, inculcating moral values, and educating children for active citizenship. It is remarkable, for example, how prominently schools feature in the Labour government's policies to promote social inclusion. Halsey, writing in 1972 about the introduction of Educational Priority Area, said that we should avoid treating 'education as the waste paper basket of social policy—a repository for dealing with social problems where solutions are uncertain or where there is a disinclination to wrestle with them seriously' (1972: 8). Similarly Hopmann and Konzali (1997), reflecting on schooling in Sweden, conscious of its similarities to many other Western countries, exclaim that common social problems which are difficult to resolve have come to be blamed on schools with little thought about what is appropriate or realistic to expect of schools or the purposes for which schools are actually resourced. Social inclusion policies which genuinely see schools as part of a larger jigsaw are to be welcomed especially if that jigsaw also has pieces labelled macroeconomic policy. The danger is that as economic growth in individual nation states becomes more difficult to secure and control in the context of the globalization of economic activity, politicians will focus on those aspects of national life which it seems easier to control and on which to construct reputations for achievements. Schooling is one such aspect. Moreover, the attractions of social—and cultural—capital lie not only in their applications to school improvement and social inclusion but in '[the] premium [placed] by employers on employees with the appropriate social and interpersonal skills alongside their technical know-how' (Brown and Lauder 1997: 190). Thus developing social capital has important educational and economic advantages for individuals, schools and companies.

It is salutary to remind ourselves that 'Britain stands out internationally in having experienced the largest percentage increase in income inequality between 1967 and 1992' (Dennely *et al.* 1997: 280, quoted in Mortimore and Whitty 1999: 81) and that 'the proportion of children living in poor households is now 32 per cent compared to the European Union average of 20 per cent' (Eurostat 1997, quoted in Mortimore and Whitty 1999: 81). In Glasgow, for example, over 40 per cent of children are entitled to free school meals, the indicator of disadvantage used in performance tables of schools (Clark and Munn 1997). While schools may help in creating a skilled and flexible workforce, they can do nothing about the demand side of the economy which is critical for the creation of employment opportunities. Clearly it is easier for modern governments to intervene in schooling than in the global economy. It is equally easy for academics, teachers and others to develop and implement ever more complex models of school improvement designed to help poor children attain at higher levels. These have been valuable and have removed complacency that there is nothing that schools can do to help individuals overcome disadvantageous circumstances in which they find themselves. It would be ironic indeed, however, if theorists of social and cultural capital who are committed to the success of disadvantaged pupils in the school system succeeded in diverting attention from the need to develop anti-poverty strategies by providing new analytic tools only to drive school improvement.

10

Social Capital and Health: Contextualizing Health Promotion within Local Community Networks

CATHERINE CAMPBELL

> On the one hand, millions of dollars are committed to alleviating ill-health through individual intervention. Meanwhile we ignore what our everyday experience tells us, *i.e.* the way we organize our society, the extent to which we encourage interaction among the citizenry and the degree to which we trust and associate with each other in caring communities is probably the most important determinant of our health.
>
> J. Lomas (1998: 1181)

THIS chapter examines the potential contribution of the concept of social capital to our understandings of the social determinants of health, and to current debates in the design and evaluation of health promotional intervention and policy. Historically, information-based health education has been the preferred method of health promotion in many countries and contexts. However, much research points to the limitations of health education, which is believed to change at best the behaviour of one in four, generally the more affluent and better educated (Gillies 1998). This is because health-related behaviours, such as smoking, diet, condom use, and exercise, are determined not only by conscious rational choice by individuals on the basis of good information, as traditional health educational approaches assumed, but also by the extent to which broader contextual factors support the performance of such behaviours. Against this background, the challenge for health promoters is twofold. First, they need to develop policies and interventions that promote social and community contexts that enable and support health-enhancing behaviours. Second, there is a need for the development of measurable indicators of what constitutes a health-enabling community, to assist in the planning and evaluation of such policies and interventions.

Thanks to Anna Ziersch, Brian Williams, and Virginia Morrow for critical comments on an earlier version of this chapter.

However, our understandings of what constitutes a 'health-enabling community' are still in their infancy. Recently much enthusiasm has been generated around the hypothesis that levels of health might be better in communities characterized by high levels of social capital. Such discussions have tended to draw on Putnam's (1993) definition of social capital, where social capital is defined as the social or community cohesion resulting from the existence of local horizontal community networks in the voluntary, state and personal spheres, and the density of networking between these spheres; high levels of civic engagement/participation in these local networks; a positive local identity and a sense of solidarity and equality with other community members; and norms of trust and reciprocal help, support and cooperation (see Chapter 1 of this volume for an account of Putnam's work). Unless otherwise specified, it is Putnam's notion of social capital that forms the context for this chapter.

High levels of social capital have been found to be associated with a range of positive political and economic outcomes in contexts as diverse as Italy (Putnam 1993) and Tanzania (Narayan and Pritchett 1997). Most of the social capital research in the Putnam tradition falls within the disciplinary boundaries of economics and political science. More recently a range of authors (such as Baum 1999; Gillies 1998; Kawachi *et al.* 1997; Lomas 1998; Wilkinson 1996) have suggested that social capital might also be associated with positive health outcomes, and argued that Putnam's ideas might usefully be imported into the field of health promotion. If support could be found for this hypothesis, the implication would be that health promoters should put less energy into health education and the provision of information about health risks, and more energy into developing programmes and policies that enhance levels of social capital in low-health communities.

The concept of social capital has generated much enthusiasm in health promotion circles, but also many criticisms, with even its most enthusiastic supporters pointing to its shortcomings. Baum (1999) warns that in its present state of development the concept is vague, slippery, and poorly specified, and in danger of 'meaning all things to all people' on both right and left of the political spectrum. As such it urgently needs clarification. Gillies (1998) emphasizes that social capital is a descriptive construct rather than an explanatory theory, and that much work remains to be done in accounting for the mechanisms underlying the alleged health-community link. Other less sympathetic critics argue that those who seek to import social capital into the field of health promotion research are simply reinventing the wheel, and that most of the so-called insights the concept would allegedly bring to health promotion are already well established in both research and practice in this field (Labonte 1999).

The most strongly articulated criticism is that the concept of social capital has been so enthusiastically grasped by health professionals, ranging from local and national government representatives to overseas development agencies, because it points towards a convenient justification for a retreat from

expensive welfare spending. Cynical critics point out that despite the abundance of strong research linking material deprivation and health inequalities,
such as Gordon *et al.* (1999), social capital proponents prefer to place their
emphasis on the, as yet only hypothesized, link between health and social capital. Critics suggest that social capital is popular because its implications for
policy—for example, that ordinary people should be encouraged to participate
in the local civic community in the interests of improving community levels
of health—are cheaper than the goal of reducing income inequalities. They
also argue that such thinking potentially incorporates an element of victim-
blaming, implying that that poor people are unhealthy because they do not
devote enough energy to participation in community activities (Muntaner
and Lynch 1999).

In response to such criticisms, it has been argued that rather than seeing a
focus on social capital as a means of displacing attention from the strong evidence for the impact of poverty on health, a focus on social capital could contribute to much-needed research into the mediating mechanisms whereby
material deprivation impacts on health. Empirical research into the health-
social capital link is still in its infancy. However, a preliminary analysis of existing health survey data in England (Cooper *et al.* 1999) suggests that while
material living conditions and socio-economic position remain stronger
predictors of adverse health than various indicators of social capital, people
living in materially deprived circumstances are more likely to live in communities that are low in social capital. Furthermore, the same study suggests that
the statistical relationship between material deprivation and poor health is
weakened by controlling for variation in neighbourhood social capital.
Against the background of similarly suggestive evidence for possible links
between income, social capital and health inequalities in Australia, Baum
(1999) points to the work of Bourdieu (1986), with his emphasis on the role
played by different forms of capital in the reproduction of unequal power relations, as a useful starting point for urgently needed research into the role that
social capital might play in mediating between material deprivation and poor
health.

Along similar lines, Gillies, Tolley, and Wostenholme (1996) emphasize that
the primary cause of health inequalities is poverty and that the economic
regeneration of deprived communities is essential for reducing such inequalities. However, they qualify this claim with their argument that since that one
of the effects of poverty is to undermine community networks and relationships, economic regeneration must be accompanied by social regeneration—
that is, projects to enhance social capital—if they are to have optimal success
in improving health.

In the light of the controversies that the concept has generated, the remainder of this chapter examines the role the concept of social capital might play
in developing actionable understandings of what constitutes a 'health-
enabling community', a community context that enables or supports health-
enhancing behaviour. The first two sections locate the concept within the

context of current debates in the practical fields of health promotion and public health, and seek to illustrate how social capital fills an important gap in existing academic understandings of the health-society interface by analyzing the preliminary research seeking to link health and social capital. The third section examines recent research into the appropriateness of Putnam's conceptualization of social capital as a tool for characterizing local community life in real-world social settings in England. The fourth section raises the potential negative effects of 'anti-social capital' on health. The chapter concludes by highlighting the urgent need for further research if social capital is to serve as a useful conceptual tool for health promotion.

Social Capital and Current Debates in the Practice of Health Promotion and Public Health

This section outlines the potential role the concept of social capital could play in addressing a number of currently unresolved issues in the applied fields of health education and public health. Each of these areas is considered in turn. Within the area of health education, the limited successes of didactic information-based methods, including posters, school lessons and television programmes, has led to a 'paradigm drift' away from the provision of health-related information by experts to a passive target audience towards a community development perspective (Beeker, Guenther Gray, and Raj 1998: 831). Such approaches involve the participation and representation of local people in health promotional interventions. They have gone hand in hand with the proliferation of non-governmental organizations which aim to empower members of groups particularly vulnerable to health problems, working at the local level in projects which aim for 'community ownership' as their highest goal.[1]

Despite the fact that the concepts of community-level 'participation' and 'representation' have become virtual articles of faith in health-promotion circles, little is known about the psycho-social and community-level processes whereby participation and representation have their alleged benefits. This gap severely restricts the extent to which the benefits of successful programmes can be documented and disseminated, and to which lessons can be learned from less successful programmes (Milburn 1995).

Drawing on the social psychological concepts of social identity and perceived self-efficacy/empowerment, participatory health promotion programmes succeed to the extent that they facilitate two inter-locking processes. First, they succeed to the extent to which they facilitate opportunities for people to make collective decisions to change their behaviour in negotiation with

---

[1] This move towards participatory community-based approaches to health promotion has been formally articulated in a range of internationally subscribed declarations of intent, spearheaded by the World Health Organisation, including the Alma-Ata Declaration of 1978, the Ottawa Charter of 1986, and the Jakarta Declaration of 1997.

liked and trusted peers. Health-related behaviour is shaped by collectively negotiated social identities rather than by factual information about health risks as traditional health education programmes assumed (Stockdale 1995). Second, they succeed to the extent that they increase the sense of perceived self-efficacy and confidence—or 'empowerment'—experienced by target group members. This occurs as the result of people's participation in programme planning and implementation—given that people are most likely to take control of their health if they feel they are in control of other aspects of their lives (Bandura 1996).

It is hypothesized that both of these processes are facilitated within community contexts characterized by a rich tapestry of trusted and valued social networks. Such networks would provide opportunities for the collective re-negotiation of peer identities which are believed to influence health-related behavioural norms. Furthermore, high levels of participation in effective horizontal networks are likely to maximize general levels of perceived self-efficacy amongst community members. The concept of social capital emphasizes the positive value of high levels of civic participation in dense horizontal local networks. As such it provides a potentially useful starting point for conceptualizing those features of community that serve to enable and support the identity and empowerment processes that are most likely to facilitate health-enhancing behaviour change.

As critiques of traditional educational approaches gain wider acceptance within health education circles, there is a shift in discourse. People are speaking less of 'health education' and 'behaviour change' and more of 'structural interventions' and 'enabling approaches'. Tawil, Vester, and O'Reilly (1995) define enabling approaches as those that, rather than trying to *persuade* people to change their behaviour, seek instead to create circumstances that *enable* behaviour change to occur. Such approaches focus on the community, or social, or political factors that facilitate or impede behavioural choice, and they aim to remove structural barriers to health-protective action as well as constructing barriers to risk taking. Tawil, Vester, and O'Reilly illustrate their argument by discussing the context of HIV transmission through heterosexual sex in developing countries. They argue that enabling approaches should focus on the economic development of at-risk groupings as well as on development policy. In their view, the crucial issue at stake in HIV-transmission in their countries of interest is the economic powerlessness of many women to protect themselves against HIV-infection in the face of male reluctance to use condoms. They discuss a number of economic and policy strategies aimed at improving women's access to resources and reducing their financial dependence on male partners.

While few would disagree with the substance of this argument, their analysis illustrates a common tendency to polarize health promotion possibilities in terms of micro-social individual behaviour-change mechanisms on the one hand, such as persuading individuals to use condoms, and macro-social structural and economic interventions on the other hand, such as the economic empowerment of women. Concepts such as social capital enhancement, which focus on formal and informal networks at the local community level of analysis, represent an important intermediary stage between the micro-social individual and the macro-social levels favoured in such polarizations.

Turning away from a focus on health education to consider the broader field of public health, the Healthy Cities Movement (HCM) has aimed to enhance and build health-promoting networks and practices in a number of cities throughout the world (Kelley and Davies 1993). The HCM is based on the insight that the promotion of health must include the adaptation and trans-formation of those social structures that foster ill-health, and that community participation is the most powerful method of attaining this goal. The Healthy Cities Movement (HCM) attempts to maximize involvement of a wide range of community representatives in health promotion, backed up by the devel-opment of appropriate health policies at both the local and national levels. Accordingly, the movement seeks to foster the development of health-pro-moting social relations within cities, including strong local government, broad community ownership, effective committees, strong community par-ticipation, inter-sectoral collaboration, and political and managerial account-ability (see Tsouros 1990 for a more extensive list).

Advocates of the HCM highlight the lack of appropriate research techniques and concepts to document and evaluate the processes underlying the approach (Hancock 1993). The HCM's emphasis on the promotion of citizen participation in strong local community networks resonates strongly with insights from a social capital framework. If hard research evidence could be gathered to demonstrate a link between health and social capital, the concept could form the basis of measurable indicators of some of the processes which the HCM seeks to stimulate. It could also play a key role in the design and evaluation of future public health programmes.

Social Capital and Current Debates in the Academic Study of the Health-Society Interface

This section locates social capital within the broader context of existing aca-demic research into the health-social relations interface, in the interests of assessing the potential of the concept of social capital to contribute to such understandings. Copious research, in fields such as public health, epidemiol-ogy, medical sociology, and the social psychology of health, has highlighted the links between health and social relations at a range of levels of analysis, including the macro-social—for example, socio-economic status, area of resid-ence, ethnicity, gender; the organizational—for example, status within organ-izations; the small group—for example, social support; and the psycho-social—for example, empowerment, perceived self-efficacy. However, very little is known about the community level networks and relationships that mediate between these levels. Social capital forms a fruitful starting point for filling the current gap in our understandings of community-level determinants of health.

Attention to the concept of social capital in the area of health is relatively recent, and as yet little hard empirical evidence exists linking social capital to health. Here we need to distinguish between research into social capital and the related research field of social support and social networks, where much research has been done (Berkman 1995). This research has measured social support as a property of individuals. In comparison, social capital is a property of communities. Kawachi *et al.* (1997) emphasize the distinction between the individual-level construct of social support and the community-level construct of social capital. They provide an example of a widow, living on her own, and with few friends, who would qualify as socially isolated using a measure of individual social support. However, she would still benefit from residing in a neighbourhood with high levels of social capital 'in which neighbours organized and mingled at block parties, transported elderly residents to voting booths on election days, made sure the sidewalks were cleaned when it snowed, and so on' (Kawachi *et al.* 1997: 1496).

One reason for the dearth of empirical research linking social capital to health is that, at the early stage of its conceptual development, the task of developing instruments to measure social capital in the context of health is still in its infancy. Much work remains to be done in this regard (see Morgan 1999; Onyx and Bullen 1997; and Kreuter 1997 for discussion of measurement issues in the context of health promotion in England, Australia and the United States respectively).

Within discussions of social capital and health, the most frequently cited empirical research is Wilkinson's (1996) analysis of the link between health and comparative income distribution between countries, and Kawachi and colleagues' work on comparative income distribution between regions within the US (Kawachi and Kennedy 1999) and Russia (Kennedy, Kawachi, and Brainerd 1998). The concept of social capital serves as a major explanatory construct in Wilkinson's (1996) book, *Unhealthy Societies: The Afflictions of Inequality*. Wilkinson examines the relationship between health—as measured by mortality statistics—and social inequalities, arguing that in the developed world it is not the richest countries that have the best health but those with the smallest income differences. Drawing on a rich and diverse array of research from a variety of disciplines, Wilkinson suggests that the concept of social capital might serve as a potential explanation for his findings that relative income levels have a greater impact on health than absolute income levels. He suggests that egalitarian societies are more socially cohesive, with the public arena serving as a source of supportive and health-promoting social networks rather than a source of stress, conflict, and ill-health. On the other hand, social inequality increases social instability, crime rates and violence, and undermines the likelihood of densely overlapping horizontal social networks, imposing a burden which reduces the health and well-being of the whole society.

Wilkinson suggests that his claims about the health-enhancing benefits of social capital presuppose a particular level of economic affluence, and that these principles are likely to hold only in countries that have achieved the level of wealth necessary to make the 'epidemiological transition', where the main causes of death have changed from infectious diseases to degenerative diseases, and where there is a shift from direct material pathways to disease, to a more complex pattern which includes psychosocial pathways. The extent to which social capital might constitute a positive social resource in developing countries or in conditions of extreme poverty is currently a source of much research and debate (for example, Campbell and Mzaidume 1999; Gillies, Tolley, and Wostenholme 1996; Moser 1998).

Kawachi *et al.* (1997) seek to provide hard statistical support for Wilkinson's preliminary arguments about the role of social capital through their study of the correlation between mortality, social capital, and income inequality in 39 US States. Their statistical analysis isolates social capital—measured in terms of levels of trust of fellow citizens and the extent of membership in voluntary groupings—as a causative variable in this relationship, arguing that income inequality exerts its negative effect on health through the social capital variable. Although further studies are clearly needed to test the validity of this causal model, which has been strongly criticised in some circles (for example, Coburn 2000), it does provide suggestive support for a link between health and social capital.

Lomas (1998) hails current interest in Putnam's notion of social capital as a welcome antidote to the individualistic focus of much research and practice in the field of public health. He compares the potential of six progressively less individualized and more community-focused interventions to prevent death from heart disease. These range from, at the most individualized end of the continuum, measures geared towards: the rescue of sick individuals; routine medical care; improved access to care; traditional public health approaches; increased social and family support services; and—the most community-focused end of the continuum—measures to improve social cohesion. Lomas uses the terms 'social capital' and 'social cohesion' interchangeably in his study. He finds that measures to increase social support and measures to increase social cohesion fare well against more traditional individualized medical care approaches.

A plethora of other small-scale specialized studies provide evidence for links between a variety of measures of social cohesiveness and a range of health-related outcomes, such as resistance to the common cold (Cohen *et al.* 1997) and satisfaction with health care services (Ahern, Hendryx, and Siddarthan 1996). However, despite the excellent quality of many such studies of health and community cohesion, they work with a piecemeal variety of conceptualizations and measures of what constitutes positive community resources. As a result of this, there is a lack of conceptual coherence when one attempts to integrate their findings, and any cumulative impact these studies might have is severely diluted. In particular, Kawachi, Kennedy, and Wilkinson (1999) emphasize that although they themselves often use the concepts of 'social capital' and 'social cohesion' interchangeably in their own research, these terms do not mean the same thing, and urgent work needs to be done in distinguishing between them.[2]

The claim that social capital has any role to play in our understandings of the community-level determinants of health is a controversial one. Labonte (1999) argues that community level determinants of health have already been well researched and investigated, and that social capital adds nothing new to a long tradition of interest in this area. Related concepts include, amongst others, community empowerment (Shiell and Hawe 1996), sense of community (McMillan and Chavis 1986), community competence (Eng and Parker 1994), community capacity (Goodman *et al.* 1998), and collective efficacy (Sampson, Raudenbush, and Earls 1997). Each of these concepts has been linked to health both within health promotional research and practice. In particular, since the classic work of Freire (1970), a large health promotion literature has postulated 'empowerment' as the mechanism through which successful community-based health promotion has its effects (Israel *et al.* 1994; Schultz 1995). Health-enhancing empowerment is generally agreed to derive from participation in and representation on those community and political structures which shape people's lives. This focus on empowerment is consistent with a large social psychological literature on the health-promoting effects of self-efficacy (for example, Bandura 1996). However, little consensus exists regarding exactly what is meant by the empowerment of local people, or which community networks and relationships are most likely to promote this empowerment, despite the fact that this is the key goal of most community-based health promotion programmes. Rissel (1994) argues that the field of health promotion undoubtedly has much to gain from better understandings of the process of empowerment. However, he suggests that at its present state of conceptual development, the use of the concept of empowerment is hampered by 'the lack of a clear theoretical underpinning, distortion of the concept by different users and measurement ambiguities' (Rissell 1994: 39).

There is an urgent need for energies to be pooled in the establishment of consensual definitions of what constitutes health-enhancing community resources. Otherwise work in this field will continue to be undermined by the fragmentary array of conceptual tools used from one study to the next. It is argued here that the concept of social capital, which resonates with the insights of the fragmentary range of concepts cited above, is particularly suitable for such a task. At a pragmatic level, the concept is particularly suitable because of the unprecedented amount of ground it appears to have captured in contemporary political discourse. At this particular moment in history there is an unusual degree of sympathy for concepts such as 'community' and

---

[2] 'It is important to note that social capital and social cohesion are not the same thing. In a well known example, gangs may provide social capital to their members without contributing to the level of social cohesion in a community' (Kawachi, Kennedy, and Wilkinson 1999a: 730). The issue of anti-social capital is taken up in the fourth section of this chapter.

'participation', and a heavy emphasis on the importance of 'the local'. Partly as a result of this, social capital has captured more research and political interest than has been the case with any of the piecemeal community-level concepts referred to above. Furthermore, the concept holds particular promise for health researchers and practitioners because of its inter-disciplinary nature, in a context of growing emphasis on the complex array of determinants of health. These include features of the local environment as diverse as housing, transport, air quality, the reputation of an area, and the quality of policing (MacIntyre and Ellaway 1999).

Many such factors lie outside the conventional scope of a biomedical conceptualization of health or of the traditional scope of public health departments. In the current general climate of 'joined up thinking' increasing attempts are being made to dissolve boundaries both between traditionally separate academic disciplines, such as political science, economics, and medical sociology, as well as across traditionally separate sectors of local and national government, such as housing, transport, and health. Within such a context, a multi-disciplinary concept such as social capital could serve as a useful bridging tool both for academics and practitioners in the field of health promotion.

To What Extent is Putnam's Conceptualization of Social Capital Applicable to Small Local Communities in England?

Ongoing attempts to develop the notion of social capital for use by health promoters in England currently take two forms. The first is re-analysis of existing health surveys, most of which were developed before the concept of social capital became current, but included questions which are now being pulled together as composite proxy measures of social capital. For example, Cooper *et al.* (1999) create social capital scales by pulling together existing survey questions such as 'involvement in community activities', 'availability of facilities for young children', 'personal experience of theft, mugging, break-in or other crime', and various social support measures. A variety of further large-scale studies of this nature are currently in progress.

As an antidote to this 'top-down' large-scale quantitative research, a number of studies are using micro-social 'bottom-up' qualitative research methods to explore social capital at the level of small local communities. In a recent study, this author and colleagues conducted micro-qualitative exploratory research into social capital in two wards—administrative districts—in the town of Luton, England. We did this in the interests of examining the suitability of Putnam's conceptualization of social capital as a tool for characterizing local community life in England (Campbell, Wood, and Kelly 1999). We justify our choice of a micro-qualitative approach by reference to our view that too much thinking and writing about social capital and its potential as a resource for improving health—or governance, or economic performance for that matter—has been done in a top-down way by researchers, politicians, and policymakers. Such actors often make unproblematized assumptions about the existence of such resources at the small local community level.

In the field of health and social services, historical experience of 'care in the community' policies suggests that these policies made intellectual and political sense. Despite this, many of them were less than successful because they rested on a series of over-optimistic and untested assumptions. In particular they, overestimated the extent to which supportive community networks existed in local communities and the extent to which these networks were capable of providing adequate care and support for previously institutionalized people (Barnes 1997). We argue that if, by the same token, health promoters are going to work at enhancing social capital or community cohesion in order to advance their goals, they need to have clear understandings of what resources exist in local communities as the basis for their policies and interventions.

Our Luton study involved in-depth interviews and focus groups with 85 residents, and sought to explore their experiences of social capital in their local communities. On the basis of our data analysis, we conclude that those resources that do exist in local communities might be fewer, and take a different form, than is commonly assumed by social capital advocates. Our study highlights a number of ways in which Putnam's notion of social capital needs to be developed in order to serve as a useful conceptual tool for health promoters in local communities in England.

First, we query the appropriateness of Putnam's highly essentialist notion of a cohesive civic community characterized by generalized levels of trust and identity. We argue that this is a romanticized and inaccurate starting point for characterizing contemporary community life in the early twenty-first century. Informants gave an account of local community life as characterized by high levels of mobility, instability, and plurality. Under such conditions the likelihood of widespread community cohesiveness was low. Those community-level relationships of local identity and trust that did exist in our communities of interest were present in a far more restricted form than Putnam's definition of social capital would suggest. They were generally limited to small exclusive face-to-face groups of people—friends, relative, and/or neighbours—who were personally known to one another, and they excluded community residents who fell outside one's personal acquaintance. This is in strong contrast to Putnam's concept of generalized levels of trust, which includes trust of community members one is not personally acquainted with.

Second, we query the extent to which Putnam's emphasis on organizational membership is a useful way of characterizing local English community life. Putnam's (1993a; 1995a) research findings draw on research conducted in very different conditions of local communities in Italy and America. In these contexts, civic engagement, characterized in terms of high levels of citizen involvement in voluntary associations such as choral societies, literary societies and bowling leagues, is a key component of social capital. Voluntary organizations of this kind played little or no role in the lives of the Luton informants. People's major community networks took the form of the small-scale exclusive informal networks of friends and neighbours referred to above, which Putnam does not include at all in his account of social capital. Most informants in our Luton study said that the multiple demands of day-to-day contemporary life—in particular the demands of making a living in a context where employment was often hard to come by and badly paid, as well as the multi-faceted demands of caring for a family—meant that they had little time, energy or interest in involvement in voluntary organizations or in community affairs (see Higgins 1999 for similar findings in grass-roots communities in Canada). Furthermore, people emphasized that they had little faith in the power of ordinary people to exert any influence over any aspect of local or national government, and thus took no interest in these. Interviews suggested that informants were guided by a strongly individualistic outlook, which was counter to the more collectivist and community-oriented culture which forms a building block of Putnam's concept of social capital.

Third, in our comparison of stocks of social capital in the two Luton wards, one of which was characterized by higher levels of health than the other, we hypothesize that certain dimensions of Putnam's social capital might be more health-enhancing than others. In particular, we argue that levels of trust, civic engagement, and 'perceived citizen power' might be more important for health than a strong local identity or numerous council-provided community facilities. We also suggest that certain network types—diverse and geographically dispersed networks—might be more health-enhancing than others—narrow, local, and inward-looking networks. This is within the context of our more general point that sources of social capital often cross the boundaries of geographically defined communities.

Finally, we emphasize that social capital is not a homogenous resource that is equally created, sustained, and accessed by all members of a particular community. People are embedded in local networks in different degrees and in different ways. Our pilot study data highlight age and gender-related differences in people's perceptions and experiences of community life. In the conclusion to our exploratory study, we hypothesize that income and ethnic differences might also be associated with differences in the forms of social capital available to different identity groups within particular communities (see also Morrow 1999 for a discussion of social capital in relation to children). Within-community difference is an aspect of social capital which Putnam's work does not take account of, and one that would have definite implications for those seeking to develop health promotional policies and practices aiming to enhance levels of social capital in local communities.

In short, our study illustrates the way in which Putnam's notion of social capital serves as a useful heuristic device for exploring the existence of grass-roots networks and resources in local communities in England. However, much conceptual and empirical refinement remains to be done to tailor the concept into a conceptual tool for planning and evaluating services and policies aimed at promoting health-enabling communities.

Anti-social Capital?

Another area where conceptual refinement is needed relates to the task of distinguishing between positive and health-enhancing social capital on the one hand, and negative 'anti-social capital' on the other hand (see also Portes and Landolt 1996; Levi 1996). Baum (1999) warns that cohesive communities might be characterized by distrust, fear, racism, and exclusion of outsiders, and as such may not be healthy for those who are not part of them, or for insiders who disagree with the majority.

In a survey study of the links between social capital and sexual health in the southern African mining community of Carletonville, Williams, Campbell, and MacPhail (1999) argue that the impact of varying associational memberships on sexual health is a complex one. While levels of HIV infection were lower amongst members of church groups and sports groups, they were higher amongst members of *stokvels*, savings clubs associated with high levels of alcohol consumption and multiple sexual partners, both of which place people at increased risk of HIV-infection.

In another micro-qualitative study of social capital and sexual health promotion, again in the Carletonville region, Campbell and Mzaidume (1999) examine the contradictions of assuming that strong local networks are necessarily beneficial for health. This work is conducted as part of their process evaluation of a community-led condom promotion programme amongst female commercial sex workers in a deprived shack settlement. On the one hand, members of their study community expressed a strong sense of local identity. They described their daily community relations as better organized and with higher levels of social control and policing of criminals than other similar communities in the area. However, this organization was orchestrated by groups of heavily armed gangsters who wielded absolute control over community residents through the threat and use of violence. In order to facilitate the development of a sexual health promotion programme, health development workers had to gain the support and approval of these gangsters, who serve as community gate-keepers. The authors discuss the contradictions involved in having to collaborate with a violent and hierarchical group of armed male gangsters in a sexual health promotion programme aiming to empower female sex workers to insist on condom use in the face of reluctant male clients. These findings highlight the way in which social capital might be closely interlinked with unequal and exploitative power relations, in this case relations between men and women (see also Beall 1998). The directive by health promotion and development agencies that health workers should seek out latent and existing indigenous sources of social capital as the basis for their work might make theoretical and intuitive sense. However, those charged with implementing these directives frequently become trapped in ambiguities regarding the potentially positive and negative effects of social capital, as well as the potential links between social capital and unequal power relations, which need to be researched and theorized.

Conclusion

In this chapter it has been argued that the concept of social capital fills important gaps in our understandings of the interface between health and social relations. In the applied arena of policy and intervention, concepts such as 'community', 'participation' and 'empowerment' often have the unquestioned status of articles of faith. However, much work remains to be done in developing understandings of the mechanisms whereby community-level interventions and policies wield their effects on health, and in developing ways of measuring the extent to which such interventions or policies succeed or fail. Such understandings are needed for the key tasks of explaining the patchy results of current community-based health promotion programmes, and for documenting and disseminating the lessons that need to be learned from successful programmes. At the level of academic research, much work has explicated various aspects of the health-social relations interface at the behavioural, physiological, psycho-social, and macro-social levels of analysis. However, much room exists for conceptual development and empirical research into community-level determinants of health, and it is here that the concept of social capital could make an important contribution.

Although social capital is a potentially important concept, research into health and social capital is still in its infancy and much work remains to be done. First, there is an urgent need for further hard empirical evidence for a health-social capital link in order to move current health-social capital debates beyond the level of conjecture and hypothesis. Much work remains to be done developing measurement tools to facilitate the quest for such hard empirical evidence. There is a need for a two-pronged approach to the development of such tools and such evidence. On the one hand, there is the need for rapid 'top-down' quantitative investigation of existing data sources. Existing health-related survey data often contain items relating to issues such as trust of neighbours, perceived quality of the local area, or involvement in community activities which serve as excellent interim measures (see Cooper et al. 1999; Kawachi et al. 1997). On the other hand, there is an urgent need for micro-qualitative 'bottom up' studies of the forms social capital takes in particular local communities. Both the Luton and Carletonville micro-qualitative studies referred to above highlight the urgent need for development and refinement of the concept if its relevance is to extend beyond the discourses of academics and politicians. Studies of this nature warn of the need to guard against simplistic and unproblematized assumptions. For example, high levels of civic participation in strong local community networks are not necessarily beneficial for the health of a community. Furthermore, it does not necessarily make sense to assume the possibility of cohesive community relationships in the multiply fragmented and mobile communities that characterize life in the early twenty-first century.

We have already pointed to Gillies' (1998) description of social capital as a descriptive construct rather than an explanatory theory. Levi (1996) has highlighted the poor explanatory power of the construct of social capital in Putnam's 'home discipline' of political science. She argues that Putnam has, as yet, failed to explicate the mechanisms whereby high levels of involvement in voluntary associations and networks, and the allegedly associated relationships of trust, reciprocal help and support, lead to more effective local government. Ironically, while this problem is such an acute one in Putnam's 'home discipline' of political science, which seeks to link social capital to good government, this might not be the case when we import the idea of social capital into the area of health promotion. Reference has already been made to a large research literature in the various health disciplines, including medical sociology, the social psychology of health, epidemiology, and public health, which has highlighted a range of potential mechanisms at the individual, inter-individual, organizational, community, and macro-social levels of analysis which provide a starting point for hypotheses regarding possible mediating mechanisms between health, community-level social capital, and broader macro-social relations.

Much qualitative and quantitative work remains to be done exploring possible interactions between social capital and broader macro-social factors in perpetuating health inequalities as well as other forms of social exclusion associated with differences in socio-economic position, ethnicity, and gender. Our understanding of the role played by social capital in perpetuating unequal power relations is still in its infancy.

11

Local Social Capital: Making it Work on the Ground

ALEX MACGILLIVRAY AND PERRY WALKER

Introduction

WE are the country mice in this collection of town mice, wondering if our wellington boots look out of place amidst the soft black shoes and the academic gowns. For our interest is in measuring the social capital created by some very practical regeneration projects. We do this despite believing that no exact measure is possible, since how we do so affects the results. We do this because we know that such measures act as flags, drawing attention to aspects of regeneration previously invisible. We want these flags to be available to policymakers, but also to the residents affected by these projects. How we have tried to do this, and the dilemmas we faced, is the subject of this chapter.

On the Shoulders of Giants

Is social capital a new concept in community development? Novelty is relative. In a book published by the press of a university that attaches the word 'New' to a college 500 years old, a phrase coined only a few generations ago certainly seems novel. The first mention of the term 'social capital' seems to be in L. J. Hanifan's *The Community Center*, published in Boston as recently as 1920.

Time is to the history of ideas as wind and rain are to stone. The soft parts of stone are steadily eroded, leaving the harder parts to stand out. So time wears away thinkers and ideas until only the outstanding remain. Isaac Newton said that he stood on the shoulders of giants, but his figure is all the more imposing to us because we no longer discern most of his intellectual ancestors. Much apparent novelty in ideas is due to a similar forgetfulness.

The giants we do remember in the context of social capital—Burke, Weber, and, de Tocqueville foremost—emphasised the link between private and public life. Burke stated that, 'To be attached to the subdivision, to love the little platoon we belong to in society, is the first principle, the germ, as it were, of public affections. It is the first link in the series by which we proceed toward a love to our country and to mankind' (Burke 1987: 100). Time hasn't yet weathered our century in the same way. None the less, there seem to be, again, three candidates for gigantism. These are Bourdieu, Coleman, and Putnam, commonly agreed to represent the 'three relatively distinct tributaries of social capital theorizing [that] are evident in recent literature' (Foley and Edwards 1999: 141).

Our work is on social capital at the local level, among the 'little platoons'. Here, the inspiration is from two other people, each supplying rather different strands of applied theory. The first is that doyenne of urban planning, Jane Jacobs. She was an immensely practical woman who led successful campaigns against freeways in both New York and Toronto. This pragmatism shows in her early identification (1961: 83) of social networks as a form of capital: 'Lowly, unpurposeful and random as they may appear, sidewalk contacts are the small change from which a city's wealth of public life may grow.' Jacobs equated this small change with trust.

The sum of such casual, public contact at a local level—most of it fortuitous, most of it associated with errands, all of it metred by the person concerned and not thrust upon him by anyone—is a feeling for the public identity of people, a web of public respect and trust, and a resource in time of personal or neighbourhood need. The absence of this trust is a disaster to the city street. Its cultivation cannot be institutionalised. And above all, *it implies no private commitments*. (Jacobs 1961: 67)

We are with Jane Jacobs almost to the end. With her comment that such trust cannot be institutionalised, however, we disagree. We are in distinguished company, for Jacobs herself provides our evidence. Her book is full of instances of how civic design can either encourage or deter such contacts.

Here is a British example:

And once the mothers got out for that couple of hours a week you'd find that they were better to the children. They'd got more time for the children, having had the break. But now they have got no outlet [because developers pulled the hall down]. They are tensed up, the mothers, and they haven't got time for the children. Going round the estate you can see the difference in the kids. (Gibson 1979: 47–8)

Paul Ekins, one of the most distinguished of new economists, finds his way not to Jacobs, Bourdieu, Coleman, or Putnam, nor to sidewalks, academia, Catholic schools or Italian towns, but to J. F. Tomer and his Ph.D. thesis of 1973 on organisational capital in private enterprise, since published as Tomer (1987). Building on Tomer, Ekins incorporates social capital alongside environmental, human and physically produced capital into a four-capital model of wealth creation. In this four-capital model, only the definition of manufactured capital is left substantially unchanged from the three-capital model of conventional economics. Ecological capital is a broader and more realistic concept than 'land' to cover the wealth of the biosphere which sustains the economy. Human capital emphasises the role of health, knowledge, skill and motivation in wealth creation. Finally, the new category of social and organisational capital 'is to be taken to be quite distinct from human capital, being embodied in the structures, rules, norms and cultures of organizations and society at large, which enable people to be jointly productive' (Ekins 1992: 150).

In short, we discern two additional strands to the intellectual provenance of social capital: Jacobs and Ekins. From Ekins we take the connection between social capital and sustainability that for us is the ultimate reason for using the concept. From Jacobs we take this chapter's street-level, grass-roots viewpoint.

From Intellectual Roots to Grass Roots

If social capital is a form of wealth that can be enjoyed by all at the local level, then it might have public policy implications. Although Jacobs warned that social capital could *not* be cultivated by institutions, Ekins sees the role of public policy precisely to nurture it, as well as the other three forms of capital. So can the concept be used in UK communities? In other words, can social capital be measured on the ground? More interestingly, if it can be measured, then, in management jargon, it can be managed.

Researchers are divided on this question. Statisticians are beginning to question the robustness of the most famous attempt at measurement, by Robert Putnam and colleagues in Italy (Foley and Edwards 1999). In the UK, and drawing on a large number of local studies in East London, Greg Smith has concluded that 'the notion of social capital is a useful one in evaluating the resources to be found in a place like Newham'. However, he continues, it is 'totally impossible and probably misguided to reduce the concept of social capital in its many varies forms to a single measurable index. It is also beyond the scope of any existing research project in East London to make statistically valid, comparative or longitudinal conclusions' (Smith 1998: 67).

Elsewhere, researchers have been more ambitious—or more misguided, according to Smith's camp. Deepa Narayan and her team undertook a Participatory Poverty Assessment involving more than 6,000 people in 87 villages across Tanzania. With characteristic World Bank understatement, Narayan observed that the logistics of mounting such an exercise 'are by no means simple'. Even so, she managed to produce a Social Capital Index and concluded that 'many social and psychological dimensions often considered to be too "soft" to be measurable *can* be measured to increase understanding of social, political, and institutional factors linked to poverty' (Narayan 1997: 65; emphasis added).

So can it or can't it be measured? Suspecting that the answer lies somewhere between these two extremes, the authors and our colleagues at the New Economics Foundation embarked in 1998 on the boldest effort in the UK actually to measure social capital in different places over time. This intensely practical undertaking is admittedly a bit of a departure from the academic discourse. If the notion of social capital is to be accessible beyond the realms of policymakers and academics, it must become a tool that communities can use to improve their quality of life.

We have been working with Groundwork, Britain's largest environmental regeneration organization, to measure the effect on people who become involved in, or benefit from, projects sponsored by Barclays Bank PLC under a programme called Barclays SiteSavers. Barclays SiteSavers was launched in 1996 to transform derelict and redundant land on deprived estates in urban and rural areas throughout Britain. It was a response to a 1995 MORI poll, which found that 71 per cent of respondents believed that derelict land reduces the quality of life. Asked how this land could be improved, two out of the three most popular areas were the creation of recreation or play spaces. The survey also showed overwhelming support for the involvement of local people in the regeneration process.

Since its inception in 1996, Barclays SiteSavers has supported some 200 projects, transforming 348 hectares of derelict and under-used land into new community leisure and recreation facilities. The process has involved 11,000 young people and 7,500 adult community members, as well as over 800 Barclays staff. It has created:

- 45 new gardens attached to youth and community centres;
- 53 new adventure and toddlers play areas;
- 26 projects focusing on access improvements;
- 35 new wildlife parks; and
- 41 new community parks.

In 1999, the Barclays SiteSavers programme was redesigned in line with the current regeneration agenda, neatly summarized by Richard Rogers and his task force as the *urban renaissance* (Urban Task Force 1999). It began to focus specifically on three objectives. The first is sustainable development, tackled through partnership working that can link environmental, social, and economic regeneration. The second is participation and skills, to be developed through community capacity building. The third objective is inclusion, which means encouraging people on the margins to participate, as well as equipping them to do so.

Over the previous three years, each Barclays SiteSavers project had collated quantitative and anecdotal evidence of its impact on communities and the environment. However, the methods used were not sufficient to establish the full social, economic, and environmental benefits, and this was felt to restrict the learning potential. To overcome this, Barclays and Groundwork commissioned us to work with Groundwork Trusts and local communities to develop sustainable impact measurements, to be trialled on 16 of the 66 projects which received funding from Barclays SiteSavers in 1999.

There were two particular reasons why we identified social capital as what we wanted to measure. First, it provided a way of linking the effect of Barclays SiteSavers projects on people with the effects on the environment already measured. This link is through the 'four capital model' described above. Second, there is increasing evidence linking increasing social capital with a variety of benefits. These include: finding a job; social integration; better health; falls in crime; better performance at school; better government; and higher economic growth. So we can be pretty sure that Barclays SiteSavers projects that lead to improvements in social capital now will generate more benefits in future years.

Ways to Measure Social Capital

The stated ambition of many social scientists and economists is to measure social capital objectively. Our experience suggests, however, that there are no robust practical ways of assessing social capital behind peoples' backs. Heisenberg's Uncertainty Principle, that the observer can affect the observed, seems to hold good on deprived estates. So the act of measuring social capital can, and probably will, affect the stock of capital that is being assessed. With most evaluations of community projects, done *to* the community, not *by* the community, the chances are that the stock will be diminished. This may be due to questionnaire fatigue, suspicion of outsiders or lack of timely feedback. These are all especially likely in deprived neighbourhoods, where the existing stock of social capital may already be low. Exacerbating these problems is the fact that outside researchers may simply not record much of what is going on, and mis-understand what they do record. A member of staff at Groundwork summarized the situation by saying, 'The history of evaluation is the history of fear'.

The alternative is, on the face of it, rather unorthodox. This is a measurement process that unabashedly sets out to increase the stock of social capital in the community. There is growing evidence that the act of measuring, done right, can itself contribute to community development along with every other aspect of a community project. People enjoy choosing indicators, gathering data and arguing over the results in the pub (MacGillivray, Weston, and Unsworth 1998). A simple example is that the measurement increased the number of local people who came to the launch of one of the Groundwork projects. Most of the people who came were people who had been surveyed. The survey had acted as awareness raiser as well as information gatherer.

More surprisingly, perhaps, the information generated by local people can be more robust than those generated by experts. As one Lancastrian participant in a 1995 focus group said: 'It comes back to local knowledge. People have said that the beaches are more polluted than what they've been for years. I could have told you that. Because I've seen from upstairs for 30 years and looked out the window every day and seen the colour of the sand change colour. Whereas it used to be like everyone imagines sand, it's now a browny colour' (Macnaghten *et al.* 1995: 64).

One of the most reliable data sets used by the UK government as a head-line indicator of sustainable development has been gathered by hundreds of amateur bird watchers over 30 years. A crime survey undertaken by local schoolchildren in Merthyr Tydfil in 1996 was recognized to be more reliable than the local police records because people were prepared to tell them the truth (Platt and Treneman 1997: 8). One of the Groundwork Trusts found that young people started by saying that everything was fine, but that after a while their real feelings started to emerge. A professional market researcher allowing ten minutes per interview wouldn't have got past that initial response.

The burden of our argument, more familiar to natural scientists than to social scientists, is that independent researchers cannot say, objectively, that any community has a particular level of social capital. The answer would depend on which approach to measurement is adopted.

Any Colour So Long as it's Black

Tensions arise in a participative multi-locality longitudinal study between free-dom and comparability. In this project, these tensions first arose when the consultants came together in February 1999 with representatives of the 16 localities, about half of whom had brought with them local people involved in their projects. We wanted this group to feel free to choose their indicators, but we also wanted each indicator to have a clear relationship to social capital and we wanted the set of indicators to span the spectrum. This last was a par-ticular challenge: we wanted a total of only a dozen or so indicators, since more would have meant a questionnaire too lengthy for volunteers to admin-ister on the streets.

We tackled this with a framework that laid out the component parts of social and human capital. Table 11.1 is a simplified version, which attempts to assign key concepts from the social capital literature into a coherent matrix. This framework is pretty pragmatic. It is, for example, designed to reflect the bilingual nature of the project, where we talk about 'social capital' to policy-makers and 'trust' to people on estates. This desire for appropriate language may be a source of bias. It may cause us to emphasise trust over networks within social capital. Our wish to describe human capital also in the language of trust may have led us into a looser definition than academics would allow. Our defence is that the acquisition of elements of a tighter definition of human capital—skills and attitudes—depends very much on the extra attrib-utes in our definition—self-confidence and self-respect. Many training pro-grammes fail for lack of recognition of this fact.

Also pragmatic is the split in social capital. A simple way of describing the three columns is that the first is about 'me', the second is about 'us' and the third is about relations with 'them'. It is clear that friends and family are 'us' and the council is 'them'. Local self-help groups are mostly 'us'. National vol-untary organizations with local branches are harder to allot. The distinction isn't hard and fast.

Table 11.1 A matrix of human and social capital components

Type of capital	Human	Social (informal)	Social (formal)
Type of trust	Trust in ourselves	Trust in each other	Trust in organizations
Components	Self-esteem, self-respect, self-confidence	Level of trust	Number of organizations
	Attitudes	Norms	Services provided
	Skills and knowledge	Reciprocity	Effectiveness
	Behaviour	Networks and connections	Community involvement
			Networks and partnerships

Each of the components of the framework can be further broken down, until we reach something that can be measured. For example, social capital is about trust in each other, which in turn is about social networks, and these networks are evident in meeting places; so a relevant indicator is the use made of community centres.

There is a surprising range of indicators of social capital in circulation. What is even more surprising is that they can be found in relatively 'mainstream' publications such as British Social Attitudes Surveys and the English Survey of Housing. However, they have still got a way to go in penetrating the public and policy-making psyche. The research team has collected well over 100 indicators that had been proposed, and in most cases used, elsewhere.

Table 11.2 illustrates some of these indicators, and, where data is available on a national level, gives pointers to the current state of social capital in the UK. With the framework as background, we brainstormed and voted our way to the following core set of 13 survey indicators—expressed as statements with which people were invited to agree or disagree—and two others:

- I feel I can help bring about change locally.
- I am proud of this area.
- This is a good place to live.
- I have learned/used new skills in the past six months. (If so) I have used them.
- My neighbours in my street or block look out for each other.
- There is somewhere I can go to work with others on ideas for action.
- I have met new people on the project.
- I have enjoyed conversations with new people from a different age or background within the last six months.
- Usage of the facility provided by the project: who and when? (Non-survey indicator.)

- I know who to contact to help me bring about change in: voluntary groups; council; other agencies.
- How many new people have been involved in the project? (Non-survey indicator.)
- Have you benefited from being involved in the project?
- Have you spent more than 15 minutes on the project? If so, has it led to action?
- Do you think the [name of facility] will survive?
- I feel safe out and about in my community/using the facility.

We didn't force the group to find indicators for the various elements of the framework. It is pleasing that they fit so well. A couple, though, are ambiguous. 'I am proud of this area' is an attitude, so part of human capital. Yet it also expresses a relationship and a sense of connection. Similarly, 'I feel I can help

Table 11.2 Existing British survey indicators of social capital

Indicator	Source	Details
Generally speaking, would you say that most people can be trusted or that you can't be too careful in dealing with people?	British Social Attitudes 1999 (BSA)	Overall, 44% of the British public take the view that most people' can be trusted (38% of Americans take the same view).
Percentage of adult population undertaking formal voluntary activity in the past 12 months	National Survey of Volunteering 1997	The idea (supported by the UK Department of Environment, Transport and the Regions) is that voluntary activity can promote social cohesion. In the UK this figure was 51% in 1991, but dipped to 48% in 1997.
Percentage of people using some community centres	Demos	Anecdotal evidence suggests that in communities only 15% use their community centre.
Percentage of householders who think their area has a 'lot' of community spirit	Department of Environment Transport and the Regions	In 1997/98, 46% of all households thought that their area had a lot of community spirit. This has not changed from surveys in 1992 and 1994/95.

bring about change locally' is a statement of self-confidence, but the inclusion of the word 'locally' makes it less my attribute and more about my relationship with my area.

We have found many small difficulties with language. In one place, people did indeed 'look out for' their neighbours—to make sure they weren't being burgled. Words like 'background'—'I have enjoyed conversations with new people from a different age or background'—and 'agencies'—'I know who to contact to help me in other agencies'—usually needed explaining. Our use of local people or local Groundwork staff was an advantage in this.

Each of the 16 localities was asked to use this core set, and to organize surveys to ask the questions and gather data on the responses. We wanted the core set to be widely tested and we wanted to be able to make comparisons, both between places and over time. The localities were also encouraged to work with local people to choose additional indicators that suited their particular project. This was an attempt to strike a balance between participation and rigour.

The project team urged the individual locations not to hire professional market researchers to gather the data, and also discouraged Groundwork staff from doing it all themselves. Instead, they were encouraged to involve local people, and guidance was provided for Groundwork staff to use with their local volunteers. For example, interviewers should carry out their interviews in areas with which they are unfamiliar, lest they interview people they knew, biasing the results. This guidance was followed as far as possible in practice.

The Barclays SiteSavers projects ran throughout 1999, with some running on into early 2000. Two surveys were planned: the first when each project was getting under way in early summer, and the second three months after the physical work was completed, though no later than June 2000. Here we report on the results of the first baseline survey, which attempted to measure levels of social capital in communities before the projects had made their contributions.

There were a total of 1,246 interviews, of which 16 per cent—199 interviews—were with people who would be directly participating in the projects, say in planting trees, and 84 per cent—1,047 interviews—with the wider community, whose involvement was limited to, say, using a park that was being restored.

Bright Eyed and Bushy Tailed: Comparing Participants with Others

There are some interesting differences between project participants and the wider community. Taking the average responses from the 16 localities, project participants are much more likely to be proud of the area—55 per cent—than the wider community—46 per cent. There are also marked differences in some of the reasons why people feel proud, or not, illustrated in Table 11.3 below.

Table 11.3 Percentage of respondents giving reasons to be proud or not proud of their area

	Project participants	Wider community
Reasons to be proud		
Lots going on	29	13
Places to walk and play	45	24
People willing to get involved	35	18
People make an effort to make it look nice	29	21
Reasons not to be proud		
Vandalism	72	51
Nothing to do	53	37
Boarded up shops	54	35

On the other hand, there were several positive factors about which project participants and the wider community were in close agreement. Around 40 per cent of each group agreed that there were 'great people' involved, while roughly 30 per cent of both groups thought that there was 'good community spirit'.

The research does not fully explain why such differences exist. Does an existing strongly held attitude towards, for example, vandalism, make some people want to participate in regeneration projects? Or does the experience of participating in a project bring about a new perspective? The answer is probably that both factors are at work. Over half the participants—56 per cent— were aged under 25, compared with a third—32 per cent—of the wider community, which perhaps explains why participants feel more acutely than their neighbours the lack of 'anything to do'.

These age differences probably explain most of the differences in economic status. Just under a quarter of the wider community were employed and just under a quarter were unemployed. The proportions for participants were 15 per cent in each case. Conversely, 'student/unspecified' was 19 per cent for participants, only 6 per cent for the wider community. There were no other major differences between participants and the wider community. As Table 11.4 shows, there were more white participants than their proportion of the wider community justified. Apart from Afro-Caribbeans, the opposite was true for other ethnic groupings. These differences do not seem enough to explain the differences in attitude listed above. As far as we could tell, the proportion of whites in the wider community was the real state of affairs and did not reflect interviewer bias. Gender also provides no explanation. Women were 56 per cent of the wider community and 57 per cent of participants.

Table 11.4 Ethnic groupings (%)

Grouping	Wider community	Project participants
White	90.9	96.6
Indian	1.4	0.0
Bangladeshi	0.7	0.0
Pakistani	3.1	0.7
Black African	0.9	0.7
Afro Caribbean	1.2	2.1
Chinese	0.1	0.0
Asian	0.5	0.0
Other	1.2	0.0

Where the Grass is Greener: Comparing Localities

It was also possible to compare the 16 localities. One of the key questions was about pride in the area, with three clearly discernible types of community:

- less than half the respondents feeling proud;
- between half and two-thirds of respondents feeling proud;
- over two-thirds of respondents feeling proud.

Pride is highly variable across these 16 communities, ranging from the Dearne Valley where less than one in five people felt proud—17 per cent—to Camden in London where three-quarters of respondents were proud—77 per cent. It was beyond the scope of the research to identify reasons for these differences, such as levels of income, social exclusion and/or dereliction of the environment. On average, though, more than half of local people—57 per cent—were already proud of the area before the projects got under way.

Patterns are hard to make out. Table 11.5 demonstrates every possible combination of high and low for two indicators that one the face of it sound quite similar. At the moment, we can only understand these combinations anecdotally. Bridgend, for example, is a small estate in the Llynfi Valley that the local council thoughtfully built on top of a bog. Almost every house shows damp on the outside walls. Bizarrely, the estate won awards for a design that gave no one a garden. The Groundwork project is starting to rectify this. Attitudes are starting to change as residents see that change is possible. The Groundwork member of staff showing us round pointed to a new greenhouse and said, 'They wouldn't have dared to put that up six months ago'.

Despite the damp and lack of gardens, this is a close-knit Welsh community. When Groundwork asked 'If there was a new house elsewhere in the valley, would you move', most people answered 'No'. This has been reinforced by a lack of people either arriving or leaving. Hence they look out for each other.

Table 11.5 Linking human and social capital

	Locality I am proud of this area (%)	My neighbours and I look out for each other (%)
Bridgend	35	82
Macclesfield	33	34
Camden	77	75
West London	72	33

Figure 11.1 shows a scatter diagram of the twelve communities for which data are comparable on levels of pride and neighbourliness. For each group A, B and C, the intention of the community regeneration projects currently under way is to advance the community as a whole towards the top right of the chart.

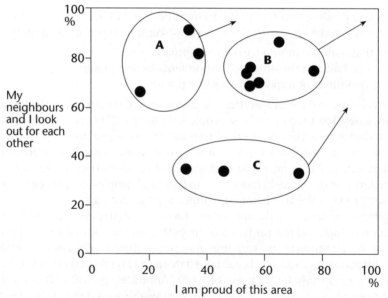

FIGURE 11.1 Percentage of local people in twelve communities agreeing with questions on pride and neighbourliness

Comparisons Over Time

While the project as planned and described is far from intending to yield definitive statistical results, it seems likely that careful analysis of the responses to the follow-up surveys will show that each community has made different progress towards its goal. Inevitably, a single project lasting less than a year cannot be expected to yield very dramatic changes in the stock of human and social capital, but there will be intense interest in any changes that are discernible.

Here are two examples of developments of the sort that we hope the indicators will track over time. The first is an arts project: 'Batley Bands Coop had inspired young people to help develop similar opportunities for other people in the town. Forming a band had been a struggle: having reclaimed their self-esteem, they were fired up to fight back on behalf of the town. Batley had become a place where they had the opportunity, as someone put it, "to live with their dreams" ' (Matarosso 1997: 40).

Two tangible results from this project were that the proportion of people on the estate feeling safe from crime rose from 56 per cent to 67 per cent, and that there was a dramatic fall in council spending on vandalism.

The second example is a Barclays SiteSavers project. Residents of terraces backing on to an open courtyard in Openshaw, Manchester, were suffering from a weekly assault on their homes through attempted burglaries, joy riding, dumping, and youth nuisance. The neighbours also didn't know each other, adding to the climate of fear and isolation. After witnessing a Barclays SiteSavers project elsewhere in Openshaw, three residents decided to take action and persuaded other residents of the 'croft' to form an action group. Twelve months on, the group had changed the courtyard into a secure community garden, cutting off the access to burglars and joy riders. Residents now hold keys and have drawn up agreements over behaviour within the communal space. Hanging baskets and other personal additions are in evidence, but, most importantly, there has not been a single successful burglary in the six months since the courtyard scheme was put in place. Previously, every house on the croft had suffered at least one attempted burglary during the year.

The gain in social capital generated through the courtyard project has also yielded other significant outcomes. Because of the networks created, residents have set up a home watch scheme and phone each other if they hear and see suspicious behaviour. When going on holiday, residents also trust neighbours with keys and possessions. The number of people in the action group is still growing.

A Few Conclusions About Social Capital

We take Arrow's point, quoted in Chapter 1, about the lack of deliberate sacrifice. An alternative metaphor to 'social capital' that gets closer to the heart of the matter is that of 'social energy'. This was developed by Albert Hirschman (1984: 42–57) to account for the dynamism of grass roots development projects in Latin America supported by the Inter-American Foundation. Hirschman's description of the components of social energy makes for a fascinating contrast with those of social capital. The first element is friendship. This is a 'friendlier' word than 'norm' and 'network': more the language of trust than that of social capital. More analytically, the term 'friendship' has its weaknesses, such as under-emphasising the value of 'weak ties'. But it has the great strength of pointing up the personal impact of social capital. I feel differently about a person when he or she becomes a friend. Re-read the brief description of Openshaw above. Is not the growth of friendship one of the main drivers of the changes?

This brings us to another, agreeably paradoxical, conclusion. A vicious circle is a wonderful thing. For if it can be turned around, as was the case in Openshaw, it becomes virtuous. Isolation led to crime and more isolation. Connection led to a lack of crime and more friendship.

In Fig. 11.2, quadrant I represents the self-reinforcing behaviour of a vicious circle: quadrant IV does the same for a virtuous circle. The essence of friendship is that it shifts us from I towards IV, because it teaches us to have regard for the well-being of other people (Uphoff 1996: 379). The same is true, in a less individual way, for Hirschman's second component of social energy: ideals. For us, ideals are the big gap in much writing on social capital, and the reason why such writing is often pessimistic about the possibility of transcending historic forces. We believe that the form that ideals most powerfully take is that of shared vision. Vision is well described as 'a statement of values projected as a future reality' (Institute of Cultural Affairs International 1998: 194).

ORIENTATION TO ACTION

Cooperative

		III. Self-regarding cooperation	IV. Other-regarding cooperation	
ORIENTATION TO OUTCOMES	*Selfish*			*Generous*
		I. Selfish individualism	II. Individual generosity (charity)	

Individualistic

FIGURE 11.2 Virtuous and vicious circles in community development
Source: Uphoff (1996: 341).

How does vision shared between people work? Marjorie Parker charted a visioning exercise in Hydro Aluminium, part of Norsk Hydro, Norway's largest industrial group. She argues that 'the desire to act was a result of being tuned into values. Work life takes on new meaning when we are aware of our values—what we care about most' (Parker 1990: 45). At one point in 1987 the highest values that emerged were good health, a meaningful work place, and a balance between work and family life. The employees also envisioned good health as being manifested in 1992. By the spring of 1989 the accident rate had been reduced by more than half. The company's Safety Inspector stated that 'A lot more people here are just taking responsibility for their own health' (Parker 1990: 78).

Hirshman's third and last component of social energy is ideas. These, like ideals, help us to escape from the trammels of the past. Norman Uphoff (1996: 360–1) gives the example of an intervention to stimulate farmer organization for water management in Sri Lanka:

Something as simple as the designation farmer-representative, instead of the widely used term farmer-leader, affected the behaviour of thousands of people. Farmers acting as 'representatives' rather than as 'leaders' saw themselves, and were seen, in quite a different light. The latter, widely used designation had made fellow farmers into followers, not what a programme promoting self-reliance needed. Officials could not make deals with farmer-representatives to be enforced from the top down. A process of negotiation and consensus building resulted from the introduction of a new word, conveying a powerful new idea.

We hope and believe that the participative measurement of social capital will also prove a powerful new idea. That leads us on to our final section.

A Few Conclusions About the Project

1. The project will stand or fall on whether the indicators do indeed track what communities and outside observers think is going on.
2. In saying this, we have to remember that the aim of the project is to make visible something previously invisible: the effect of regeneration projects on people. The indicators and the framework of social and human capital on which they are based therefore provide part of the language that people use to reflect on what is going on.
3. Social capital appears to provide the relevant concepts from which to derive the indicators.
4. We don't at this stage know how sensitive the indicators are.
5. The indicators will pick up the cumulative effect of all the influences on an area. It may well not be possible to discern the effect of any given project.
6. We don't know if the argument in favour of communities measuring themselves will prevail, or whether the desire for supposed objectivity will win out.

So there's a lot to play for. Let us know if you want to play too.[1]

---

[1] The authors welcome comment from any readers interested in discovering the results of this work in progress. The New Economic Foundation can be contacted at Cinnamon House, 6–8 Cole Street, London, England SE1 4YH; Telephone +44 20 74077447; http://neweconomics.org.uk. Full documentation on the project is available to all interested parties on request from The Barclays SiteSavers Manager, Groundwork National Office, 85–87 Cornwall Street, Birmingham, England B3 3BY.

12

Social Capital and Associational Life

WILLIAM A. MALONEY, GRAHAM SMITH, AND GERRY STOKER

Introduction

FUNDAMENTAL to debates about social capital is the belief that the quality of democratic politics in modern societies is dependent upon the performance of organizations such as interest groups, intermediary associations, civic associations, social movements and voluntary associations (van Deth 1998: 1). A thriving civil society is perceived as acting as a check on state activities: a strong civic community creates strong government, and strong democracy which '. . . rests on the idea of a self governing community of citizens [which] . . . challenges the politics of elites' (Barber 1984: 117). While voluntary associations are not the only vehicle for the political mobilization of citizens, they are generally seen as fostering the development of democratic values and attitudes. As Putnam argues:

Civil associations contribute to the effectiveness and stability of democratic government, it is argued, because of their 'internal' effects on individual members and because of their 'external' effects on the wider polity. Internally, associations instil in their members habits of co-operation, solidarity, and public-spiritedness . . . Participation in civic organizations inculcates skills of co-operation as well as a sense of shared responsibility for collective endeavours . . . Externally, what twentieth-century political scientists have called 'interest articulation' and 'interest aggregation' are enhanced by a dense network of secondary associations. (Putnam 1993a: 89–90)

The vibrancy of associational life, according to commentators such as Putnam (1993a; 1995a, b), Fukuyama (1995), and Jones (1998), is positively correlated with the stocks of social capital a society possesses. The higher the stock the greater the vibrancy, and vice versa.

Social capital is a complex resource which offers an explanation of how the 'dilemmas of collective action' can be overcome (Putnam 1995a: 67). In

The research reported in this paper was supported under the UK Economic and Social Research Council Cities Programme, award number L 130251052.

the absence of norms and expectations of reciprocity, 'co-operation is confined to the narrow predictions of the collective action theory' (Boix and Posner 1998: 13). Social capital, unlike physical or human capital, is not the 'property' of individuals or institutions: it inheres in the relations between actors and is drawn upon to facilitate collaborative actions. Trust-building networks of civic engagement such as neighbourhood and community associations, sports clubs, cultural associations, and other voluntary organizations are frequently highlighted as potential sources of social capital generation. These networks provide channels along which information flows and support the development and application of norms and sanctions. Such networks of civic engagement are not the only source of social capital (Newton 1997), but they are seen by many interested scholars as having direct policy relevance in areas such as health, crime, welfare, economic growth, the performance of political institutions, and the development of effective and democratic governance (see Coleman 1988a; 1990a; Fukuyama 1995; Halpern 1998; Putnam 1993a; 1995a, b; 1998b). However, many other academics are sceptical of the 'panacea for all ills' school of thought (Berman 1997; Foley and Edwards 1997; 1998; Maloney, Smith, and Stoker forthcoming; and Portes 1998). For example, Portes (1998: 2) somewhat dismissively claims that: 'Despite its current popularity, the term does not embody any idea new to sociologists. That the involvement and participation in groups can have positive consequences for the individual and the community is a staple notion' that dates back to the work of Durkheim and Marx. We, however, are not concerned with the novelty of the concept, but are keen to explore the substantive elements and to assess its heuristic value in examining the structure of network relations.

This chapter examines the relationship between associational life and social capital. First, we offer a clearer, more analytically useful definition of social capital than that typically offered in political science research. Second, we analyse the relationship between social capital and civic associations, identifying four main areas of debate. Third, we outline the utility of a more contextualized approach, identifying the important role political institutions and political structures have on the creation, maintenance, and distribution—and, at times, destruction—of social capital.

Clarifying the Concept

Portes (1998: 2) argues that the concept of social capital has gained such popularity that ' . . . the original meaning of the term and its heuristic value are being put to severe tests by these increasingly diverse applications'. Similarly, Foley and Edwards (1997: 551, 553) are also critical—most notably of the Putnam-school approach—arguing that there is both a lack of clarity about the concept and ' . . . a failure to appreciate the complexities of the theoretical tradition . . . Putnam's conception like that current in contemporary popularized versions both narrows the field of what might constitute or generate social capital and bestows on it a valorization that Coleman's concept cannot sustain by itself'. They identify three main faults in current usage. First, in general social capital is undertheorized and oversimplified. Second, contemporary writings have under-emphasized the conflictual nature of civil society. Third, '. . . these (mis)understandings conjoin in the suppression of the economic dimension of contemporary social conflict'.

Juxtaposing the Putnam and Coleman perspectives on social capital research, we see that Putnam wishes to accentuate forms of social capital based on democratic values and attitudes, whereas Coleman seeks to explain a wider field of actions: the civic or uncivic nature of social capital is not really a central issue. We are drawn to Coleman's conception because it enables us to understand the success of, for example, the extreme right in France in terms of its ability to generate high levels of social capital amongst its supporters.[1] It also directs attention to the distributive dimension of social capital and facilitates analysis of the way social capital is distributed: recognizing the possibility that 'some may be organized "in" and others "out" by the same set of developments' (P. Hall 1999: 434; see below, Foley and Edwards 1998). Putnam side-steps such issues.

Coleman (1988a: 98) argues that:

Social capital is defined by its function. It is not a single entity but a variety of different entities, with two elements in common: they all consist of some aspect of social structure, and they facilitate certain actions of actors whether persons or corporate actors within the structure. Like other forms of capital, social capital is productive, making possible the achievement of ends that in its absence would not be possible. Like physical capital and human capital, social capital is not completely fungible but may be specific to certain activities. A given form of social capital that is valuable in facilitating certain actions may be useless or even harmful for others . . . Unlike other forms of capital, social capital inheres in the structure of relations between actors and among actors.

Coleman (1988a: 102–4) then moves on to a deeper analysis of the components of social relations that constitute useful social capital resources. He identifies three components: obligations, expectations and trustworthiness of structures; information channels; and norms and effective sanctions. Taking pains to warn that social capital both facilitates *and* constrains actions, he highlights two types of structure that generally facilitate social capital. The first of these is closure of social networks which creates the conditions for (1) the emergence of effective sanctions that can monitor and guide behaviour and (2) trustworthiness of social structures that allows the proliferation of obligations and expectations (Coleman 1988a: 105–7). The second social structure he identifies as social organizations, such as voluntary organizations: '. . . organizations, once brought into existence for one set of purposes, can also aid

[1] Berman (1997: 571) argued that, 'Militia movements, business improvement districts, and home schooling societies all arise out of dissatisfaction with how public institutions are doing their jobs; all of them should be seen as signs of sickness rather than signs of health'. In our work on the politics of race in Birmingham, UK, we found that poor institutional design and governmental intransigence was the catalyst for the creation of mass community-level social capital (Maloney, Smith, and Stoker forthcoming).

others, thus constituting social capital available for use' (Coleman 1988*a*: 108). Following Coleman removes many of the normative problems associated with Putnam's conception and provides for a clearer description and analysis of the structure of relationships.

Social Capital and Civic Associations: Four Major Debates

Four main areas of debate surrounding the relationship between social capital and civic associations can be identified: (1) the correlation between social and political involvement; (2) the correlation between associational vitality—and, hence, levels of social capital—and 'good government'; (3) whether social capital is always a beneficial resource; and (4) the nature of the evidence for the decline in social capital thesis.

The Correlation between Social and Political Involvement

The Tocquevillian perspective sees political and civil associations as thriving through reciprocity:

In all countries where political associations are forbidden, civil associations are rare . . . It is hardly likely that this is due to accident, and it is wiser to conclude that there must be some natural, perhaps inevitable connection between the two types of association . . . civil associations pave the way for political ones, but on the other hand, the art of political association singularly develops and improves this technique for civil purposes . . . . It is through political associations that Americans of every station, outlook, and age day by day acquire a general taste for association and get familiar with the way to the use the same. Through them large numbers see, speak, listen, and stimulate each other to carry out all sorts of undertakings in common. Then they carry these conceptions with them into the affairs of civil life and put them to a thousand uses. (de Tocqueville 1969 [1835]: 520–1; 523–4)

It is from such an inspirational sources that Putnam advances his claim that a vibrant civil society facilitates and encourages a vibrant political society: associational vibrancy in the political sphere is the by-product of associational vibrancy in the social realm. However, it is unclear how social involvement positively enhances the willingness to become politically involved: what is the causal link between bird watching or choral society performing and political activism? How does membership of one organizational type facilitate the negotiation of the 'free-rider' obstacle in another? (M. Levi 1996). Galston and Levine (1997: 4) also claim that data in the US suggests that civic involvement may be shifting 'from official politics to the voluntary sector'. Bennett (1998: 747) highlights data from the Needham Life Style Studies, which showed that between 1975 and 1997 respondents reported substantial decreases in organized group memberships, but increases in volunteering. The Gallup data quoted by Bennett showed that, between 1987 and 1995, 54.4 per cent of the

US population claimed to be volunteering. He concluded that 'these data do not paint a picture of selfish Americans walled off from each other inside their electronic bunkers. Rather, they suggest that something has happened that makes structured groups less attractive to citizens leading increasingly complex, individualistic lifestyles'(1998: 747). Galston and Levine (1997: 4) also argued that, 'the classic Tocquevillian thesis would have to be modified: local civic life, far from acting as a school for wider political involvement, may increasingly serve as a refuge from (and alternative to) it'. Social participation could be presented as absorbing the time and energy of citizens and leading to a process of demobilization within the traditionally conceived political sphere.

Social Capital and Good Government

It has been argued that the correlation between associational vitality and good government is over-simplistic (see Maloney, Smith, and Stoker forthcoming; Tarrow 1996; and Berman 1997). There are a number of problems here. First, Putnam confuses policy performance with democratic practice. As Tarrow (1996: 395) comments in a review of *Making Democracy Work*, 'performance is as likely to be positive in non-democratic states as in democratic states'. Second, associational activity may actually be a response to poor governmental performance. As Berman (1997: 569–70) argues: 'A flourishing civil society under these circumstances [i.e. 'poor government'] signals governmental and institutional failure and bodes ill for political stability and democracy'. More generally it would seem reasonable to suggest that the activities of political institutions or other agencies might help or hinder the creation of social capital.

In general Putnam appears to neglect the role public authorities play in the creation and destruction of social capital. In his work on Italian regions, Putman perceives 'the character of the state as external to the model, suffering the results of the region's associational incapacity, but with no responsibility for producing it' (Tarrow 1996: 395). But, as we argue in more detail below, public authorities are deeply implicated in the shape and activities of voluntary associations, whether it is in terms of the institutions they create or the resources they provide to encourage participation (see below, 'The Importance of a Contextualized Approach to Social Capital Research').

Finally, there is a problem with Putnam's understanding of the challenge of governing in modern complex societies. There is a wide-ranging debate about a shift from government to governance (Stoker 1998). The emerging pattern of governance has to do with partnerships and networks. The key is the interrelationship between a range of voluntary, private, and public bodies. Elected governments remain significant actors but they have to collaborate with other organizations to achieve their goals. In short, institutions in civil society do not simply underwrite the capacity for good government, they are incorporated into the processes of governing.

Social Capital and Social Benefit: Trust and Distribution?

Many scholars see trust in political institutions and political office holders as a key indicator of the health of democracies: the higher the levels the more healthy the democracy. For example, Nye argues that 'cynicism about the political process and the elected government . . . may reduce participation and the quality of our democracy' (1997: 5, quoted in Kazee and Roberts 1998: 2). However, measuring levels of social capital in terms of levels of trust in political institutions is problematic.

As Kazee and Roberts (1998: 3) point out, while over the last 30 years or so many scholars have provided extensive and detailed 'evidence of a precipitous decline in political trust and developed plausible hypotheses about the consequences of that decline, for both individuals and for the system in general. What is lacking . . . is compelling evidence of the link between trust and political behaviour'. Kazee and Roberts' (1998: 9–10, 24) data shows that:

Membership in cultural, fraternal, recreational, religious or political groups seems to be unrelated to political trust . . . In sum, then, the analysis shows that political trust is not related to a host of behaviors and attitudes relevant to involvement in the political system. Those who professed to distrust the government are very much like those who claim to trust it: most citizens claim to vote, to discuss politics, to care about elections, and to pay a reasonable amount of attention to campaigns. Most do not get involved in campaigns, listen to talk radio, or join a large number of groups. To be sure, a number of factors account for the rather substantial amount of variation in measures of political participation and engagement but political trust is not one of them . . . If declining trust is associated with eroding social capital, we saw no evidence of it.

On the basis of this evidence one could argue that low levels of political trust might actually be a positive and healthy aspect of modern democracies. Scepticism about government may not be inimical to democracy and it may, in fact, be a consequence of increasing educational attainment that encourages greater governmental scrutiny. As Kazee and Roberts (1998: 28) point out, low levels of trust actually conform to Madisonian principles: citizens must keep a watchful eye on the governors, because leaders can't be trusted 'to do what is right' unless they are carefully scrutinized and held to account for their actions. Similarly, Fukuyama (1995: 51) persuasively argues that US citizens have a relatively strong anti-statist tradition, with many opinion polls showing that they have 'lower levels of confidence in and respect for government than do citizens of other industrialized nations. But anti-statism is not the same as hostility to community'. Thus he maintains that while Americans may dislike and distrust 'Big Government', they are 'extraordinarily co-operative and sociable in their companies, voluntary associations, churches, newspapers, universities'. The issue is not one of whether or not citizens are anti-statist, but whether they are prepared to place their own individual interests below those of intermediate social groups.

The existence of social capital does not necessarily entail just or democratic outcomes. Access to stocks of social capital may well help to reinforce economic, social, and political cleavages. Foley and Edwards (1997: 550–1) argue that 'superior resources of social capital might be more characteristic of highly polarized or fragmented societies than of smoother functioning ones'. We should be aware that all networks, including civic networks, are mechanisms for both inclusion *and* exclusion. As Whittington (1998: 25) says, 'social capital is valuable in part due to its scarcity and exclusivity. Those within a given association have access to it, but non-members are excluded from its benefits . . . The exclusion problem suggests the possibility that social capital can be an antidemocratic force in the polity and a potentially disruptive one'. Membership of one network does not necessarily breed trust and feelings of reciprocity towards others outside; these may be reserved for insiders. Those outside may be viewed with even greater disdain because of the dynamics of group formation and maintenance. Prejudice and distrust of others may be heightened through continual reinforcement within a group setting: a process that may be self-reinforcing.

An extreme but instructive example here could be certain areas of Northern Ireland where there is certainly a high level of intra-community trust and associational activity within the Protestant and Roman Catholic sub-cultures, perhaps generating a great deal of social capital. However, such intra-community trust is generally located within the two communities and has generated high levels of inter-community distrust and intolerance. The Northern Ireland example also provides us with a clear example of two types of social capital: bonding and bridging (Putnam 1998*b*). Bonding relates to the generation of social capital within relatively tightly drawn groups, be it the family, a community or some other form of association. Bridging refers to the social capital built up when these more closed groups interact beyond the limits of their own world and interface with other groups. Thus bonding social capital is built up within the distinctive religious subcultures in Northern Ireland, whereas bridging social capital is that which is generated with the interaction between people from these two sub-cultures.

It is important then to stress the differential ability of groups and communities to access social capital. As Foley and Edwards (1998: 2) argue, access to social capital resources 'is neither brokered equitably nor distributed evenly'. From his research into social capital in Britain, P. Hall (1999: 458) concludes that we should 'be attentive not only to aggregate levels of social capital but also to its distribution, that some may be organized "in" and others "out" by the same set of developments'. The 'distributive dimension' of social capital needs to be recognized, a fact that much of the cross-national research on national levels of, for instance, social trust and other democratic attitudes and values tends to ignore or overlook (Foley and Edwards 1998: 7). Differentials in ability to create and access social capital are likely to reinforce existing social, political, and economic inequality.

The Decline of Social Capital

Putnam's (1995*a*, *b*) 'disappearance of civic America' thesis has been strenuously challenged by several commentators. Skocpol (1996), Schudson (1996), and Ladd (1996) have questioned his interpretation of the General Social Survey (GSS) data. Skocpol (1996) maintains that Putnam's description of the 'disappearance of civic America' is too strong, arguing that US citizens are more likely than their counterparts in other advanced democracies to join churches or other voluntary associations. Skocpol (1996: 21) further argues that: 'The GSS asks respondents about "types" of organization to which they belong, not concrete group memberships; as groups have proliferated within certain categories, the extent of individuals' involvements may well be undercounted'. What is more, newer types of involvements such as parents congregating on Saturdays at children's sports events, or several families going together to the bowling alley, may not be captured by the GSS questions. Whitehead (1996: 21) maintains that Putnam's study of Italian regions focuses solely on the activities of 'official' associations known to the regional authorities themselves: 'It can be argued that such lists, to a great extent, reflect "official" activity, and that a large amount of associational activity is, by its nature, relatively autonomous and unofficial'. Along similar lines, M. Levi (1996: 52) criticizes Putnam's conservative analysis which highlights the decline of parent-teacher associations and the rise of working mothers without acknowledging alternative forms of organization and support that now exist. Schudson (1996: 17) cites data by Verba, Schlozman, and Brady (1995) showing an increase in local civic engagement. In 1987, 34 per cent of their national sample reported active membership in a community problem-solving organization and 34 per cent reported working with others on a local problem. The respective figures for 1967 were 31 per cent and 30 per cent. Ladd (1996) boldly states that there is 'Not even one set of systematic data to support the "Bowling Alone" thesis'.

Our data on civic associations in Birmingham, UK, suggests that there has been a significant increase in civic involvement over the last 30 years and not a precipitous decline. Our 1998 data here are compared with data from Newton's earlier study (Newton 1976; on the data sources, see Maloney, Smith, and Stoker forthcoming). While we are aware that our findings in this city may not be reflective of the general trends throughout the UK, there is no *a priori* reason to assume that Birmingham is a special case. The data in Table 1 show an increase of at least a third in the number of voluntary associations in Birmingham over the last three decades. If we were to disregard sports clubs,[2] where the figure for 1998 is a *substantial underestimate*, then there is at least a

---

[2] No specialist sports lists are available and no recent systematic analysis of sports associations has been undertaken in Birmingham by the relevant local administrative bodies. It is clear from discussions with local administrators and development officers that there are thousands of sports groups and associations in the city. For example, Birmingham Sports Council estimates that there are around 2,000 football teams playing regularly in the city. This is itself a conservative estimate of activity since there has been a huge rise in more informal five-a-side as compared with the 1970s.

doubling in the number of groups. In 1970 there were 2,120 non-sport voluntary associations; in 1998 this figure was up to 4,397. While we are mindful
that the sheer number of associations tells us nothing about levels of individual membership and involvement (van Deth and Krueter 1998), information
about individual involvement cannot necessarily be directly equated with
levels of social capital. Further, focusing purely on the activities of individual
members fails to account for the development of social capital between groups
and other institutions (see Table 12.1).

Table 12.1 Comparison of number of voluntary associations in Birmingham in 1970
and 1998

Type of association	Number in 1970	Number in 1998
Sports	2,144	1,192
Social welfare	666	1,319
Cultural	388	507
Trade Associations	176	71
Professional	165	112
Social	142	398
Churches	138	848
Forces	122	114
Youth	76	268
Technical and Scientific	76	41
Educational	66	475
Trade Unions	55	52
Health	50	309
Not Classified	—	75
TOTAL	4,264	5,781

Source: Maloney, Smith, and Stoker (forthcoming).

Our data shows some relatively predictable shifts in the numbers of associations across different fields over the last 30 years or so, largely a consequence
of the changing political environment (see Stoker 1997; Taylor 1997). For
example, as local government powers and functions have been progressively
eroded in traditional service delivery areas such as housing, existing or new
voluntary and community organizations have taken over some of these
responsibilities and developed new areas of work. This in turn has opened up
new opportunities for arms-length providers. In other areas, there has been a
shift to a more enabling role rather than direct provision of social services. The
doubling of the number of groups in the social welfare category reflects the
impact of such trends. This category includes not only social-care providers
but also associations within the areas of community economic and social

development, housing, employment, and training as well as civic advocacy groups. The growth in education groups reflects a rise of parent-teacher associations, and of nurseries, play schemes and after-school clubs. A similar trend can be observed in the youth sector. Health is another area where we see dramatic rises in numbers that include 'friends' of hospitals and other support groups. Finally, local government has also moved into new policy fields such as economic development, environmental protection and crime prevention and has done so in cooperation with a range of 'third force' organizations (see Stoker and Young 1993). The impact of these trends is reflected in the growth in the social welfare, social and health categories.

We would also argue that the quality of contemporary democracy requires a broader conception of political 'involvement' and 'participation'. We would also emphasize modes of citizens' participation which go beyond the traditional concepts of both 'conventional', institutionalized modes of participation and 'unconventional', non-institutionalized protest activities. For example, 'consumer democracy' based upon a reciprocal relationship between public service providers and their clients has shifted attention from the realm of 'big' politics to issues of everyday life. Active involvement in areas such as schools, work places, or health systems might actually be seen as important contributions to democracy.

However, Putnam (1995a) is pessimistic about the changing organizational structure of many interest groups and voluntary associations. This includes the decline of 'classic secondary associations'—that is, sports clubs, trade unions, professional associations—and the growth of what he terms 'vertically ordered', 'tertiary associations'—including staff groups, mail order groups and protest businesses. Such associations tend towards hierarchy because membership simply entails the payment of dues. The ties that exist are to 'common symbols, common leaders, and perhaps common ideals, but not to one another' (Putnam 1995a: 71). These organizations are seen as taking advanced democracies closer to mass societies (Hayes 1986). They are 'a symptom of a sick society in which individual citizens choose to abandon true democratic participation where persons meet and debate face-to-face. Instead, they select ersatz political participation in which the electorate responds only to a national elite that communicates through direct mail' (Topolsky 1974, cited in Godwin, 1988: 4–5). Ultimately these processes lead to depletions in social capital resources because the direct social link between people is taken to be crucial to engendering tolerance, accommodation and mutual understanding.

However, Schudson (1996: 18) has argued that checkbook participation may

be a highly efficient use of civic energy. The citizen who joins may get the same civic pay-off for less personal hassle. This is especially true if we conceive of politics as a set of public policies. The citizen may be able to influence government more satisfactorily with the annual membership in the Sierra Club or the National Rifle Association than by attending the local club lunches.

Similarly, Godwin (1988: 50) maintains that if checkbook participation stimulates and motivates the public to pay attention to important issues and the actions of their representatives, then it could be perceived as strengthening democracy. In addition to this, Whiteley (1999: 30–1) has hypothesized that social capital can or may be generated 'by membership of "imaginary [or abstract] communities", that is communities which individuals identify with, but which they never actually interact with on a face-to face basis'. Imaginary communities are large and geographically dispersed and individuals within them can socially interact only with a very small fraction of the group. In spite of this 'social barrier', Maloney (1999: 116) argues that 'individuals within these groups can develop very strong levels of group identification: "joining like-minded people" in pursuit of a cause may develop a sense of "community" or belonging. Membership of these groups may not be as detrimental to the generation of social capital as the Putnam/Tocqueville model suggests . . .'.

Clearly the contribution—be it negative, positive or neutral—of tertiary associations to social capital remains an open question requiring detailed empirical investigation.

The Importance of a Contextualized Approach to Social Capital Research

Insufficient attention has been paid to the variety of locations where social capital can be generated, inhibited, and appropriated, and the role played by other actors, such as public institutions, in this process. It is clear that the complex forms of interaction between public bodies and institutions of civil society have not received the attention they deserve. Thus, it is necessary to take a wider and more contextual perspective on social capital, and not only to focus on numbers and activities of voluntary associations but also to take into account the relationship between different voluntary associations and political institutions. Some accounts in the social capital debate imply that influence flows only in one direction—civil society to state—rather than reciprocally. As Tarrow (1996: 395) points out, Putnam generally perceives the nature of the state as an exogenous factor. This neglects the role played by political structures and institutions in shaping the *context of associational activity* and hence the creation of social capital.

A top-down perspective recognizes that the governance of an area is affected by social capital, but is itself an influence on social capital. Indeed, we argue that political institutions have a significant role, at least in helping to sustain civic vibrancy and probably also in stimulating its growth. Public authorities are deeply implicated in the shape and activities of voluntary associations. For example, Maraffi (1998: 16) argues that the vibrancy of associational life he found in north-eastern and central Italy 'is not so much the result of spontaneous, horizontal, "bottom-up", social activity; rather it is the result of purposive, vertical "top-down", efforts by political parties to mobilize the population . . . the presence of voluntary associations in a given area is a complex phenomenon as to its genesis and development'.

However, it is important to note that our argument is not that the political system determines civil society, as a counterpoint to Putnam's bottom-up model. Rather, the key point is the interpenetration of state and civil society.

Skocpol (1997: 16) argues that 'recent research by historians underscores the enduring importance of the U.S. federal government in promoting a vibrant civil society'. Walker's (1991: 49) data shows that one of the most important reasons for the rapid expansion of the citizen groups sector in the US was the growth of patronage. His 1980 survey found that 89 per cent of citizen groups had received financial assistance from an outside source in order to start its operations. In the UK, P. Hall (1999: 443) notes that:

not only have British Governments made substantial efforts to ensure that voluntary activity flourishes, they have also adopted an approach to social policy that makes extensive use of volunteers, alongside professionals, for the delivery of social services. This commitment has been accompanied by large public expenditures, via grants and fees for services, to the kinds of associations that mobilize voluntary action on the local level. All the indications are that these government policies have made a major contribution to sustaining the kind of associations that augment the level of social capital in Britain.

At the local level, Lowndes *et al.* (1998: 16) have argued that encouraging participation is an everyday element of English local government practice. Their 1997 study found that local government in the UK was engaged in a wide range of public participation initiatives. These ranged from more traditional public meetings and the cooption of community representatives on to committees, to more innovative community planning exercises. Although the effects of such initiatives will differ, such activities on the part of political institutions cannot be ignored and may well have important effects on the creation or enhancement of social capital.

Our work on civic associations in Birmingham demonstrates that Putnam's approach overlooks the level of inter-penetration of public authorities and voluntary and community associations. The noticeable shifts in the numbers and activities of associations across different fields of operation mirror many of the changes in the local political environment over the last three decades. Our survey of voluntary associations in Birmingham illustrates the high levels of contact between the public and the voluntary sectors; the importance of information flows between the City Council and associations; and the high level of financial and other informal support given to voluntary and community associations. 'Research on social capital should not only focus on the effect of community-level social capital on government performance, but also the effect of government-associational relationships on social capital. A top-down perspective needs to supplement the more usual bottom-up approach championed by Putnam' (Maloney, Smith, and Stoker forthcoming).

In addition, our work on the politics of race in Birmingham further demonstrates the significant impact of institutional design on associational life and the level of inter-community and inter-organizational social capital. Briefly, in the 1970s, no formal structures existed to engage ethnic minority organizations (Newton 1976: 208), thus forcing these communities to mobilize at the grassroots. Poor institutional design acted as a stimulus for the generation of social capital at the local level. By the mid-1980s ethnic minority communities and their associations were highly active and the local authority was forced into creating institutions that provided a formal avenue for engagement (Solomos and Back 1995: 193–7). As the informal attitude toward ethnic minority associations became more responsive and cooperative, opportunities for developing and accessing social capital between ethnic minority associations and the local authority increased. A decade later, the institutional mechanisms for engaging ethnic minority associations are under review and are likely to change. Whatever form the emerging structures take, the new governance of race equality in Birmingham will restructure opportunities for engagement and thus for access to and generation of social capital (Maloney, Smith, and Stoker forthcoming). It seems clear to us that a contextualized approach that is more sensitive to the formal and informal aspects of relations between actors, and that recognizes the reciprocity that exists between civil society and state, is crucial to gaining a fuller understanding of issues such as generation, maintenance, and destruction of social capital.

Conclusions

While we have identified several problems with the neo-Tocquevillian/Putnam perspective on social capital, we still believe the concept has great utility. It invites us to explore the infrastructure of civil society and suggests that within it we may find an explanation of why in some polities political activity, and, more broadly, social and economic activity, displays greater vitality and appears to be more effective. Nevertheless, we conclude with two critical comments. First, we are persuaded by Portes's (1998: 21) views that the current enthusiasm for studying the concept of social capital is:

partially warranted because the concept calls attention to real and important phenomena. However, it is also partially exaggerated for two reasons. First, the set of processes encompassed by the concept are not new and have been studied under other labels in the past. To call them social capital is, to a large extent, just a means of presenting them in a more appealing conceptual garb. Second, there is little ground to believe that social capital will provide a ready remedy for major social problems, as promised by its bolder proponents. Recent proclamations to that effect merely restate the original problems and have not been accompanied so far by any persuasive account of how to bring about the desired stocks of public civicness.

Second, the work of Verba and Nie (1972), Parry, Moyser, and Day (1992) and Verba, Scholzman, and Brady (1997) based on extant data found that the more economically prosperous participate to a much greater extent than poor or disadvantaged groups, with the result that policies may be skewed in favour of 'the particular participant groups and away from the more general "public interest" ' (Verba and Nie 1972: 342). Verba, Scholzman, and Brady (1997) argue that debates about declines in civic vitality and civic participation have missed—arguably—the key issue: the focus should not simply be on the amount of civic activity but its distribution, that is, who within the citizenry takes part and who does not. Differential participation rates appear to us to be one of the most significant aspects of social—and political—exclusion and of central concern to the social capital debate. For scholars such as Putnam who are concerned about the health of democracy and the decline in 'civicness', their critiques and remedies might be better aimed at identifying the causes, consequences, and possible cures for facilitating the meaningful engagement of the politically, socially, and economically disadvantaged.

13

Human Capital, Social Capital, and Collective Intelligence

PHILLIP BROWN AND HUGH LAUDER

A SIGNIFICANT feature of the late twentieth century is the heightened importance attached to human capital. Globalization, technological innovation, and the increased demand for 'knowledge' workers are typically cited to explain why the wealth of nations now depends on the quality of their human resources. Reich (1991), for example, argues that in a global labour market income from employment will reflect the 'true' market value of labour; this, he suggests, explains the dramatic shift in the incomes of different categories of workers. Those who are able to sell their skills, knowledge, and insights in the global market place have witnessed a significant rise in income, while those who in the past relied on high-waged, low-skilled jobs have seen their wages stagnate or decline as this work is transferred to low wage regions of the world economy. Equally, corporate restructuring and the rapidity of technological innovation have increased the need for life-long learning. Workers are expected to invest in their 'employability' regardless of whether they are in employment or looking for work. As the British government report *Our Competitive Future* has noted:

Successful modern economies are built on the abilities of their people. People are at the heart of the knowledge driven economy. Their knowledge and skills are critical to the success of British business. People are the ultimate source of new ideas. In a fast moving world economy, skill must be continually upgraded or our competitiveness will decline. (Department of Trade and Industry 1998: 28)

Many of the key insights into the knowledge-driven economy are derived from human capital theory. The basic tenets of this theory were established by Schulz (1961*b*) and Becker (1964). They include the proposition that skills inhere in individuals; that they are measurable, such as in terms of the years of formal education; and that the motivation to enhance one's human capital is based on a rational calculation of individual rates of return. Human capital theory is also informed by a 'technocratic' approach which assumes that the more technologically advanced a society becomes, the greater the demand for technical, managerial and professional workers and the fewer jobs there will be for those with little formal education and training (Kerr *et al.* 1973). In other words, the creation of a high skills economy is a matter of an evolutionary process of technological progression.

Problems associated with human capital theory are well-known (Klees 1986; Fevre, this volume). These include behavioural assumptions of utility maximization (Fine 1999*c*), difficulties with calculating rates of return to investments in education, and a failure to recognize that skills are socially defined and constructed. Underlying these criticisms is the fundamental issue of power relations and their influence on reward structures and motivation. For example, Reich's analysis of globalization causing the polarization of income ignores the fact that not all Western societies have polarized in the way he assumes. Brown and Lauder (1997) argue that New Right policy reforms offer a better explanation for polarization in the English-dominated societies of Britain, America and New Zealand than does the global development of a near-perfect market. In many ways the success of the New Right in the 1980s can be seen as the triumph of capital over labour.

Equally, the question of motivation is understood primarily as a question of getting the 'incentives' right, between rewards—increased pay, promotion, status—and punishments—pay cuts, unemployment, stigma. But the motivations for academic success or to train, for example, are only partially explained in these terms. There is a long tradition of sociological theory which has interpreted achievement as a social duty given a normative commitment to society (T. Parsons 1959). Research on working-class youth has shown how cultural understandings of 'being' and 'becoming' can lead young people to restrict their commitment to education and training, irrespective of 'rational' considerations of self-interest. Such self-assessments are not made in social isolation (P. Brown 1987; Rees *et al.* 1997; Lauder and Hughes 1999). The weight of evidence suggests that issues of motivation and commitment are tied to social and cultural questions of economic involvement and to 'emotional intelligence' (Goleman 1996). To put it crudely, if people do not share a sense of involvement or commitment in what they do, they may be able to fulfil a mechanical task such as attaching widgets on an assembly line under close supervision, but they will not use their creative powers or work effectively in a team.

James Coleman is also critical of mainstream economic analysis because it ignores the fact that individual actions are embedded in a social context and that 'norms, interpersonal trust, social networks, and social organization are important in the functioning not only of the society but also of the economy' (1997: 80). Coleman uses the term 'social capital' to distinguish it from physical or human capital, although like all forms of capital he suggests that social capital is productive, it is able to make possible the achievement of goals that would not be possible in its absence. 'If physical capital is wholly tangible, being embodied in observable material form, and human capital is less tangible, being embodied in the skills and knowledge acquired by an individual, social capital is less tangible yet, for it exists in the relations among persons' (Coleman 1997: 83). Although Coleman does not view human and social capital as competing concepts, they can lead to significant differences in policy terms. Whereas the emphasis on human capital leads to issues of investment in education, training, and life-long learning, the emphasis on social capital extends the policy framework to include urban regeneration and community networks.

The scale of social inequalities and economic polarization in Britain and American has also raised the idea of social capital up the political agenda as concerns have grown about the urban 'underclass' and social disorder. The concept is being used by centre-left governments in these countries in an attempt to re-unite the principles of social justice and economic efficiency. However, there are fundamental problems in the rhetorical use made of the concept by politicians on both sides of the Atlantic. At a time when there seems little hope of expanding public provision, social capital seems to provide a panacea for underwriting new forms of social solidarity at little extra cost to the exchequer.

Moreover, while politicians have readily taken up the rhetorical use of 'social capital' they have ignored one of the fundamental conceptual problems associated with it: the inherent danger that the development of social capital will lead to social closure rather than inclusion. This is because the strong ties that bind communities with agreed norms, high trust and dense social networks may serve to exclude those that are not part of them. As Etzioni (1996: 9) has noted, they have 'identities that separate and a sense of sociological boundary that distinguishes members from non-members'. That said, it is also the case that the social capital developed in one context can be transferred to another. Fukuyama (1995) has pointed out that in the Asian 'tiger' economies family and religious affiliations can be transferred into work organisations. As Naphapiet and Ghoshal (1997) put it, social capital networks are 'appropriable'. The challenge at the macro policy level is to devise policies which acknowledge the limitations of closure while supporting those elements which are appropriable. Consequently, the translation of concepts of social capital into policy formulations will not be straightforward in the way that politicians and their advisers would have us believe.

The purpose of this chapter, therefore, is to argue that the ideas associated with social capital are vital to the development of progressive social change but not within the parameters defined by centre-left politicians. The concept needs to be located within a broader framework which we define as the struggle for collective intelligence.

The Politics of Social Capital

The fundamental concern with the way the term 'social capital' has been converted into political currency is that it is being used to rationalize cheap remedies for problems which require new ways of thinking and considerable redistribution of income. For example, in his Fabian pamphlet, *The Third Way:*

New Politics for the New Century, Tony Blair has this to say: 'We can only real-ize ourselves as individuals in a thriving civil society, comprising strong fami-lies and civic institutions buttressed by intelligent government . . . This Third Way . . . will build its prosperity on human and *social capital'* (Blair 1998: 3, 20; emphasis added).

   But this social capital is to be built on doubtful foundations: there has been some redistribution of income but it is limited. Government spending on some of the key budgets relating to social capital such as education and ele-ments of social welfare is less under the Blair administration than under the previous Conservative government. While measures so far have taken 800,000 children out of poverty, another 4,200,000 remain in poverty (Piachaud 1999). At the same time a battery of social initiatives to regenerate inner cities and run-down estates has been introduced. However, we shall argue that these ini-tiatives are unlikely to trigger the development of social capital. Ian Gough has argued persuasively that 'cooperative labour, including unpaid care work is a defining feature of all social groups . . . Participation in universally socially significant activities, including work, is a crucial contributor to autonomy and human welfare' (Gough 1996: 82–3).

   Underlying Gough's claim are motivational issues relating to dignity and respect and, perhaps more fundamentally, identity. While Bourdieu (1997) has drawn attention to the crucial role played by social capital in identity forma-tion, it is an insight that has not been elaborated upon in discussions of social capital, yet in our view it is helpful in understanding why the centre-left mod-ernizers' approach to social capital is flawed.

   Government policy in Britain and America is targeted primarily at only one form of participation in society: paid work. This means that the fundamental source of an individual's self-respect and identity is to be derived from his or her role as a wage earner. Consequently, the identity of those who are excluded from the labour market or for whom life there is highly uncertain is under threat (Burchell *et al.* 1999). These are not the conditions under which social capital is likely to be built. However, we have argued elsewhere that full employment under present global economic conditions is a chimera and that we now have the wealth to expand our definitions of what counts as a valid contribution to society and to pay for it (Brown and Lauder 1997; 2000).[1] Yet while the British and American governments make small inroads into income polarization, the kinds of redistributive policies needed to support the build-ing of social capital networks remain absent. With these criticisms in mind we turn to the development of a conceptual framework of collective intelligence necessary for the reconstruction of social solidarity.

----

   [1] There are those who will argue that full employment has to all intents and purposes been attained in the US and that it is close to being attained in Britain. But full employment now means something quite different from what it did in the 1950s and 1960s. In contrast to that period, it now means that many are only employed on poverty wages, which require governments to subsidize low-paying employers with tax credits. Work for many is also highly irregular and there are high levels of insecurity. Finally, some 15% of British households in which adults are eligible to work do not do so, and a large minority work part-time.

The Social Construction of Intelligence

The first step in the move towards a definition of collective intelligence is to reclaim 'intelligence' from the grip of IQism (Bowles and Gintis 1976). Here it is assumed that intelligence is measurable, largely decided by nature rather than the social environment, and largely immutable or fixed, which means that it can be predicted at an early age; and that high intelligence is in limited supply as suggested by the metaphor of the bell curve (Herrnstein and Murray 1994). Despite the dominance of this view, the social distribution of intelligence has remained an active battleground for debates about equality of opportunity and social justice. On the centre-left of the political spectrum there have been those who have developed counter-arguments about the nature of IQ and intelligence. This tradition of research has been important for refuting what has been at best a narrowly mechanistic and naive approach to questions of intelligence. It has drawn attention to the all important influence of social inequalities, in determining educational and occupational achievement, even when measures of IQ are taken into account (Lauder and Hughes 1990; Fisher et al. 1996; Sternberg 1996) and in exploring the legitimizing myths used to justify inequalities based on intelligence (Bowles and Gintis 1976; Gould 1981).

What is implicit in much of this work is the fact that intelligence is a social achievement. As Dewey suggests, 'the conception of mind as a purely isolated possession of the self is at the very antipodes of the truth. The self achieves mind in the degree in which knowledge of things is incarnate in the life about him; the self is not a separate mind building up knowledge anew on its own account.' (Dewey 1916: 344). As individuals, we possess only the potential for intelligence. It is developments in the social world that stimulate the mind's potential for new forms of feeling, reasoning, and understanding which, as we shall show, have to be learned.

At the heart of our argument is the proposition that what counts as intelligence is historically variable. The way work and family life are organised, the way we interact with one another, and the tools we use to create wealth and communicate have changed dramatically. Intelligence is not, therefore, a fixed capacity, as is so frequently asserted; rather the capacities and potentials of what we consider intelligence and intelligent action change in relation to new demands and practices of any given age. It follows that new forms of intelligence will be invoked as the institutions and practices of society change. Perhaps the most telling point about the way our ability to develop more powerful mental capacities has evolved socially comes from the work of Hacking (1975; 1990), who has shown how styles of reasoning have emerged at specific times in history. For example, he is concerned with notions of probability, which he argues came into being around 1660. However, the notion of a representative sample within probabilistic thought was 'unthinkable during most of the nineteenth century' (1990: 6). The 'thinkable' could occur only when an entire style of scientific reasoning had evolved. Crucially, he argues that this emergence was connected to the development of the Western concept of community.

Historically, the IQist view of intelligence reflected the way the world of paid work, education, and everyday lifestyles were arranged throughout much of the twentieth century. In the postwar period economic activity was organised on the basis of giant corporate hierarchies and Fordist assembly lines. This involved a clear division of labour usually with an elite at the apex making policy decisions, and a large number of white-collar workers overseeing a reluctant army of blue-collar workers whose tasks could be performed best when 'their minds were least consulted'. This division of activity was mirrored in the education system where it was only the managerial and professional elite that received an extended period of formal education beyond the age of 18. Hence, the normal curve depicting the distribution of IQ mapped quite well on to this distribution of corporate decision-making power.

Earlier in the twentieth century, Terman asserted that there was indeed a good match between the spread of job opportunities and the pool of talent. He argued that IQ tests not only had the power to predict future intellectual potential but also served as a measure of an individual's suitability to succeed in different sorts of jobs:

preliminary investigations indicate that an IQ below 70 rarely permits anything better than unskilled labor: that the range from 70 to 80 is pre-eminently that of semi-skilled labor, from that of 80 to 100 that of the skilled or ordinary clerical labor, from 100 to 110 or 115 that of the semi-professional pursuits; and that above all these are the grades of intelligence which *permit* one to enter the professions or the larger fields of business . . . This information will be of great value in planning the education of a particular child and also in planning the differentiated curriculum here recommended. (Terman 1923: 27–8)

But equally important was the view that intelligence was in the main cognitive and that different levels of cognitive ability mapped on to differing types of educational curricula which were neatly subdivided into 'subjects' and offered according to the perceived future destination of the student. Hence the academic curriculum of the sciences and humanities was deemed suitable for those of relatively high IQ, while technical and craft knowledge was assumed to require less intelligence. At the same time, the acquisition of tacit knowledge, especially by people of colour, women, or the working class, stood beyond the conventional definition of intelligence dominated by the precepts of scientific reason. As Western societies have moved into a more technologically advanced and knowledge-intensive world, the limitations of this understanding of intelligence have become more obvious with the decline in bureaucratic work structures, more flexible labour markets, and negotiated roles in the home, at school, and paid work (Beck 1992; Giddens 1991).

In the postwar 'factory' model of Fordism and bureaucracy, roles were carefully delimited both at home and at work. Knowledge of oneself and of others in the exercise of work roles was discouraged as unprofessional or irrelevant, beyond an evaluation of the individual's job title, authority, or certified expertise (Merton 1964). Pre-existing roles prescribed the way individuals should act and it was only from the late 1960s that these were subjected to serious challenge. Now, knowledge of oneself and of others is necessary to function adequately. Under such conditions the interpersonal skills which come from such knowledge are at a premium. In the corporate world, hierarchies of roles have been replaced by team work in which the 'person' is as important as the technical skills he or she may possess, indeed the two have become inseparable (Brown and Scase 1994).

Howard Gardner's (1993) *Frames of Mind* is indicative of a sea change in our understanding of what constitutes intelligence in a post-industrial world. He argues against the unitary idea of intelligence as represented by the IQist tradition and instead outlines a theory of multiple intelligence, numbering among them linguistic, musical, logical and mathematical, spatial, bodily-kinesthetic and personal intelligence. Our concern here is not with the way Gardner has delimited different forms of intelligence but to note how the changing social world has made a theory of multiple intelligence relevant, if not inevitable. Of particular interest is his theory of personal intelligence. For Gardner, personal intelligence involves access to one's own feelings and an ability to notice and make distinctions between the moods, temperaments, motivations, and feelings of others. Crucially, this involves greater personal 'reflexivity' (Giddens 1991) since it is by monitoring our behaviour and that of others that we can develop the interpersonal relationships necessary for functioning in the modern world. As Giddens describes his notion of reflexivity: 'decisions have to be taken on the basis of a more or less continuous reflection on the conditions of one's action' (1991: 86).

In this sense reflexivity refers to the use of information about the conditions of an activity as a means of regularly reordering and redefining the activity, including the constant re-adjustment of our understanding of relationships. The emergence of the concept of personal intelligence in Gardner's work and reflexivity in Giddens's provide clear examples of how our understanding of what constitutes intelligence is historically invoked.

For some time feminists have been pointing out that personal intelligence has been the prerogative of women precisely because as 'homemakers' they have been the keepers of subjectivity and the emotions (Pateman 1989). But with the increasing flexibility of gender roles within the home and at work, some feminists have also pointed out the stunted nature of the male psyche because of the absence of personal intelligence. The emergence of personal intelligence as a necessary quality for *all* individuals can, therefore, be seen partly as a consequence of the breakdown in the division of labour between women and men. The net results of these changes in the division of labour and our modes of interaction has been that our ideal of the intelligent person has changed, especially for men. A well-rounded personality is one in which emotional or personal intelligence is as important an attribute as logical and mathematical intelligence.

Since the Enlightenment, emotions including fear, anger, sadness, love, and happiness have been bracketed off as expressive, and therefore seen as irrational in an age of scientific rationality. The labelling of the emotions as 'feminine' has been used by male elites as a convenient way of demonstrating the inferiority of women in a scientific world. This mind-numbing interpretation of intelligence is far removed from Aristotle's philosophical enquiry into character, virtue, and the good life. Here the issue is not cast in terms of how to eliminate emotions from everyday interactions and activities, but rather one of how to manage our emotions with intelligence. And this, as Goleman (1996) suggests, will include self-control, zeal, persistence, and the ability to motivate oneself.

It follows from this account that intelligence in post-industrial societies will include the ability to solve problems, to think critically and systematically about the social and material worlds, to apply new skills and techniques, and to empathize and communicate with others. Above all, in a society characterised by risk and insecurity, it means being able to imagine and assess alternative futures. In turn, this means being able to go beyond established paradigms of thought. As Lacey has suggested, intelligence has to do with making judgements about when it is appropriate to create new courses of action or avenues of thought, which 'involves the development of a morality that is capable of guiding action' (1988: 94).

Towards a Definition of Collective Intelligence

Axiomatic to the idea of collective intelligence is a belief that human intelligence has been limited by social hierarchy and cultural learning, which has led to feelings of inferiority, stupidity and incapability among the majority at the same time as a minority has staked its superiority on membership of nature's aristocracy of talent. The historical limitations on the capacity for intelligence are not congenital but a cultural and institutional problem within society's power to correct, as each period in history can be characterised by both its mode of economic organization and its model of human nature. As Marx argued:

In this society of free competition the individual appears free from the bonds of nature, etc., which in former epochs of history made him a part of a definite, limited human conglomeration. To the prophets of the eighteenth century, on whose shoulders Smith and Ricardo are still standing, this eighteenth century individual, constituting the joint product of the dissolution of the feudal form of society and of the new forces of production which had developed since the sixteenth century, appear as an ideal whose existence belongs to the past; not as a result of history, but as its starting point. Since the individual appeared to be in conformity with nature and [corresponded] to their conception of human nature, [he was regarded] not as a product of history, but of nature. (Marx 1961: 136–7)

Our argument, therefore, is that post-industrial possibilities exist for the creation of productive, just and cohesive societies, which offers the prospect of a significant improvement in the quality of life for all. But the exploitation of these possibilities depends on redefining our cultural assumptions about intelligence, human nature, and the relationship between the individual and society. The dim view of intelligence of the majority inherent in the IQist tradition, and the technicist view of skill inherent in human capital theory, are now impediments to the creation of such a society. They continue to be used as a way of legitimizing inequalities but only at the cost of wasting human talent. Just as inequality has depressed the capacity of individuals to exercise intelligence according to measures of IQ, so it will militate against the exercise of multiple intelligences.

The concept of collective intelligence, however, not only draws attention to the idea that 'intelligence' is socially constructed but that what is central to the quality of life is the way people combine their 'intelligence', whether at home, school, work, in the community, or in the individual's relationship to the broader society in which she or he lives. Collective intelligence can be defined as empowerment through the *development and pooling of intelligence* to attain common goals or resolve common problems (Brown and Lauder 2001). It is inspired by a spirit of cooperation rather a Darwinian survival of the fittest. In a society that eulogises the virtues of competition, self-interest, and acquisitiveness, rather than cooperation, common interest, and the quality of life, it is difficult to maximize human potential or to coordinate opportunities for intelligence action in an efficient matter. The struggle for collective intelligence therefore involves more than a democratization of intelligence; it involves making a virtue of our mutual dependence and sociability which we will need to make a dominant feature of post-industrial society based on information, knowledge, and life-long learning.[2]

To develop our understanding of the social foundations of collective intelligence, at any given historical moment, a distinction can be made between the *capacity for intelligence* and what we call *relations of trust*. The capacity for intelligence describes the raw materials on which the development of intelligence depends. It includes the state of knowledge, scientific discovery, technology, and learning techniques, on which societies can draw. In many respects the capacity for intelligence has become global in scope as new ideas, fashions, technologies, and sources of productivity traverse the globe in real time through the media, the Internet, and multinational companies. At a societal level the capacity for intelligence also includes the scale of investment in knowledge, learning, and research infrastructure in the form of schools, colleges, universities, community workshops, libraries, museums, training centres, research institutes, and information superhighways.

As human capital ideas have come to dominate government policies there has been a considerable emphasis on increasing post-compulsory access to tertiary education, adult training, and wiring-up schools to the Internet. This

---

[2] Our definition also highlights the fact that the acquisition of intelligence and the ability to use it depends on the learning potential of individuals—and institutions—in all spheres of life and is not restricted to the formal learning which goes on in our schools, offices or factories.

kind of capacity building is important, but inadequate, as such policies fail to take account of how the raw materials of post-industrial economies are woven into the social fabric. The nature and distribution of intelligence will be shaped by the social groups to which an individual belongs and the cultural, economic, and political institutions of society more generally. In low-trust societies, for instance, education, knowledge, and learning are treated as part of a zero-sum game, where extending opportunities to less privileged groups and the pooling of intelligence are seen as a threat to the positional advantage of social elites (Hirsch 1977). Therefore, the development and pooling of intelligence are severely restricted for less advantaged social groups and for society as a whole, unless high-trust relations can be fostered.

The inter-relationship between capacities and relations is vital because it is within the nexus between these two forces that the 'space' or possibilities for individuals to develop their capabilities for intelligent action will be created. The relationship between capacities and forces also addresses the extent to which people are institutionally encouraged to pool their capacity for intelligent action. Capacities and relations are interwoven in the way that concrete is reinforced with steel rods to create the infrastructure on which the development of collective intelligence depends.

Relations of Trust

In the remainder of this chapter we will focus on the social relations of trust since it is closely allied to debates about social capital discussed in this book. We have suggested that relations of trust refer to whether the development and pooling of intelligence are encouraged in the relationships between individuals, groups, and classes that are embedded in classrooms, offices, households, neighbourhoods, welfare policies, and taxation systems. As Fox (1974: 15) has noted, we need to focus on the way social relationships are embedded 'in the institutions, patterns, and processes themselves which are operated by people who are capable of choosing differently'.

Relations of trust have had a profound impact on the organization of economic life in the early decades of the twenty-first century. This is because they shape the nature of cooperation between economic actors, whether as employers, employees, trade union representatives, government policymakers, or consumers. Historically, the nature of this cooperation has changed since in pre-industrial societies cooperation involved acting for purposes of economic production or distribution on established routines described by Durkheim as 'mechanical' solidarity. Cooperation in the labour process involved little scope for human freedom, as Marx observed: 'the individual has as little torn himself free from the umbilical cord of his tribe or community as a bee has from his hive' (1976: 452).

Marx also noted that there were few examples in ancient times of cooperation on a large scale; and where this did occur it was founded on slavery. With the rise of industrial capitalism new forms of economic cooperation developed, based on the 'free' wage-labourer who sells her or his labour-power to employers and the development of production on a large scale, which presupposes new forms of cooperation. The factory system involved a fundamental change because workers had to be disciplined to coordinate their working day (Thompson 1967), which greatly increased productivity, a process graphically outlined in Adam Smith's discussion of the division of labour. Marx (1976: 451) recognised that the socially productive power of labour develops as a 'free gift' to capital whenever the workers are placed under certain conditions.

He therefore saw this form of social cooperation in economic affairs as a valuable source of capital—although he did not use the term 'social capital'. He also believed it to be exploitative since the owner and controllers of production appropriated the fruits of this collective activity, but as workers came to understand the injustice of capitalist production they would seek to overthrow the system. But the development of Fordism in the twentieth century not only enhanced corporate efficiency and profitability; it also gave workers the chance to mobilize collectively in order to claim an increasing share of the fruits of productive cooperation. The legitimacy of industrial capitalism depended on its ability to deliver prosperity to large sections of the population and the development of formal opportunities for all rather than a few.

However, by the 1970s the low-trust relations inherent in Fordism inhibited the patterns of commitment and communication which made it difficult to compete with Japan and the Asian 'tiger' economies. Low-trust relations in Fordist organizations led to worker resistance, minimum levels of commitment, high rates of absenteeism, and wildcat strikes (Sabel 1982). These responses have traditionally been interpreted by management as a manifestation of the feckless and irresponsible nature of most workers. Indeed, managers have typically recognised these responses as a justification for the introduction of intensive surveillance and the threat of sanctions in the control of the workforce. A more plausible interpretation is that they are a rational response to working conditions where little is expected of workers and little is given in return (Fox 1974). One of the key features of the low-trust relations of Fordism was the lack of opportunity for workers to learn and, as important, for managers to learn from them (Zuboff 1988). It was precisely because the Asian 'tigers' developed productive systems of learning and continuous innovation that they gained a superiority in the manufacturing sector.

However, we are at the dawn of a third phase of post-industrial, if not postcapitalist, development, requiring new forms of cooperation and foundations of trust. Within business organizations it is the way these are combined to produce constant innovative solutions to problems that holds the key to economic competitiveness. It is no longer enough to bring people together to generate the 'socially productive power of labour'; cooperation which leads to profitability depends on the development of collective intelligence.

There is a growing body of literature which suggests that in circumstances where employees are given room for individual discretion and see some point in what they are doing, they will show a strong tendency towards cooperation because it leads to individual and collective growth. Goleman has noted that the single most important element in what he calls group intelligence is not the average IQ in the academic sense but social harmony: 'it is this ability to harmonise that, all other things being equal, will make one group especially talented, productive, and successful, and another—with members whose talent and skills are equal in other regards—do poorly' (1996: 160).

In one the most interesting papers on social capital and business innovation, Naphapiet and Ghoshal (1997) build on these insights to argue that the development of social capital within organizations is necessary for the creation of intellectual capital and hence innovation. At the heart of their argument is the view that innovation is the product of collective problem-solving leading to the development of new ideas. These are facilitated by three dimensions of social capital: the structural, which refers to network ties and the way they are configured and appropriable; the cognitive, of shared codes, meaning and narratives; and the relational, of trust, norms, obligations and the personal identity which emerges from being part of a network. Brought together these dimensions facilitate the development of intellectual capital and innovation based on collective knowledge. They suggest that some of this knowledge is 'objectified' such as that found in scientific communities, while social tacit knowledge 'represents the knowledge that is fundamentally embedded in the forms of social and institutional practice and that reside in the tacit experiences and enactment of the collective' (Naphapiet and Ghoshal 1997: 7).[3]

The key point here is that, without these tacit forms of knowledge which are shared through the cooperation of the network or organization, new intellectual capital is hard to generate. Hence the collective intelligence of the organization is based on a structure of cooperation and trust. In what is perhaps a sign of a fundamental intellectual shift in our understanding of the significance of cooperation to contemporary capitalism, Naphapiet and Ghoshal (1997) go on to argue that the formation of social capital in and between organisations is more efficient than market competition in generating innovation.

Developing high-trust relations in paid work is of course only part of the story. The social networks built in corporations may not be directly appropriable to the democratic life of the community; but, given that it is the education system that has assumed responsibility for the socialization of the 'model' workers of the future, they are likely to be closely connected. As Tawney reminds us, it is impossible to achieve social or economic change without changing the 'scale of moral values which rules the minds of individuals'

---

[3] Here they rely on Spender's (1996) matrix which delineates four types of organisational knowledge: individual explicit knowledge, individual tacit knowledge, objectified knowledge and social tacit knowledge. The first two of these inhere in individuals while the latter two are inherent in organizations.

(1982: 10). It is, perhaps, not surprising that the growth of mistrust in politicians over the past 20 years in Western societies has occurred at the same time as there has been increased mistrust in the labour market, with the introduction of 'flexible' labour market polices leading to corporate and public sector 'downsizing', non-standard forms of employment, increasing job insecurity, and job intensification (Burchell *et al.* 1999).

Building high-trust relations is at the heart of the struggle for collective intelligence across society, in that it is a way of moving towards a form of associated living which involves making experience more communicable. This conforms to Dewey's (1916: 101) notion of democracy which is more than a system of government because it defines the way people live together and pool their intelligence. Collective intelligence is exercised through the development of the art of conversation which gives an authentic voice to all constituencies in society. This in turn depends upon the breakdown of social divisions which inhibit the free communication and interaction between people and groups and applies equally to social barriers constructed around class, race, gender, or religion, whether in the workplace, home, or community. Such barriers serve to undermine the potential for collective intelligence. But it is not only the powerless who lose out in these circumstances. The evils thereby affecting corporate executives may be less material and less obvious, but they are equally real in their consequences. As Dewey notes, 'their culture tends to be sterile, to be turned back to feed on itself; their art becomes a showy display and artificial; their wealth luxurious; their knowledge over-specialized; their manners fastidious rather than humane' (1916: 98).

In such a society all social groups lack the relations of trust upon which conversation is possible (Habermas 1987*b*). It denies a society of novel and challenging ideas which frequently stem from diversity in social experiences. Collective intelligence involves a 'widening of the circle of shared concerns and the liberation of a greater diversity of personal capacity' (Dewey 1916: 87).

The development of high-trust relations therefore offers the best chance of making a positive feature of cultural pluralism and of meeting post-modern calls for a politics of difference. What is recognised in the struggle for collective intelligence is that different voices which reflect the rich diversity of cultural identity and social experience are the lifeblood which fuels the collective effort to resolve common problems in an attempt to improve the quality of life for all. Equally, this involves recognizing that there are different ways to live a life. But in polarized and divided societies people come to feel isolated and fearsome of groups with which they share little in common, and with whom they rarely come into contact. Hence, social inclusion is vital to communication across social networks at all levels of society.

Proximate Equality and the Building of Social Capital

Recent research supports the view that the more inclusive a society is, the less likely it is that a range of medical and social pathologies, including a failure to learn, will manifest themselves. Wilkinson has demonstrated in his international study of *Unhealthy Societies* that 'egalitarian countries are more socially cohesive. They have a stronger community life and suffer fewer of the corrosive effects of inequality . . . The public arena becomes a source of supportive social networks rather than of stress and potential conflict' (1996: i). Social polarization in the 1980s led to a growth in the number of poor people dying prematurely, committing suicide, getting divorced, and with children underachieving at school. Wilkinson is able to show that these social pathologies were less a direct consequence of material deprivation than a symptom of a collapse in trust.[4] As he acutely observes 'whenever we leave our homes, we face the world with two perfect symbols of the nature of social relations on the street. Cash equips us to take part in transactions mediated by the market, while keys protect our private gains from each other's envy and greed' (Wilkinson 1996: 226).

Learning, however, can take place only where ideas and practices are diffused throughout the society rather than hoarded and 'privatized' as in a cash and keys society. Here the work of Coleman and another eminent American sociologist, William Julius Wilson (1987), is relevant. Coleman thought that social capital inheres in the relationships between individuals in a community which is characterised by high-trust relations and shared responsibilities. An example would be a network of the parents of kindergarten and primary-school children, who share the duties of ferrying kids to and from school, and who share the responsibility of looking after each others' children when the need arises. This leads to the creation of social capital because these activities also involve communicating to children an agreed set of expectations about appropriate standards of behaviour, the value of education, and the benefits of sharing resources including cars and time. This form of informal learning may not be overt or even oral, but is achieved by prompting such as 'have you got homework today?', or by parental interest in what the children did at school that day. It is the messages of the community in sum that is significant in the creation of social capital. The relative wealth of communities in this respect is reflected in the performance of their children in school, as Coleman and Hoffer (1987) have attempted to demonstrate empirically.

The impact of inequality on the development of informal learning is not difficult to understand, although it often operates in subtle and complex ways. Communities or networks which are rich in social capital, for instance, take

---

[4] When his work first appeared it was subjected to considerable criticism, but subsequent work by him and others has provided further evidence for his findings such that they are now taken as well established. See Kawachi, Kennedy, and Wilkinson (1999*b*).

time, energy, and resources to build. They also depend on a high degree of stability in the family and neighbour context. This is highlighted in Coleman and Hoffer's research, where they found that the most significant impact on educational failure was the number of times a child moves school. The point is that every time a child moves school the parents or caregivers of that child have to re-establish the networks necessary to social capital. Failure to do so is to render the child as an atomised and 'anomic' individual. Significantly, the instability associated with high turnover of students in schools is most frequently found in poor school districts (General Accounting Office 1994). This is not the only malign effect of poverty in the creation of social capital.

The impact of the ghettoization of American inner-cities on the decline in social capital is graphically portrayed in the work of Wilson (1987). He shows how a perceptive ghetto youngster in a neighbourhood where some people have been able to keep good jobs, even in a context of increasing joblessness and idleness, can continue to see a meaningful connection between education and employment. The problem is that these neighbourhoods show signs of becoming even more polarized when those who are able to find decent jobs leave the neighbourhood. As a consequence, ghetto children find there are no role models of adults in work or higher education, the only lessons they learn are those of the informal economy. These insights demonstrate the necessity of a proximate equality to building a society in which incomes and opportunities are more equally distributed.

A narrowing of inequalities will not be achieved without a different approach to social policy. The labour market can no longer be left to resolve distributional questions. This is not only because we do not believe the problem of unemployment can be solved in the way it has been suggested by the modernizers on both sides of the Atlantic, but because of the huge disparities in earning power and wealth that now characterize the Anglo-Saxon dominated societies.

The distribution of rewards can no longer be left to a division of labour in which a large minority have to survive on poverty wages and others are excluded from finding meaningful employment altogether. Equally, whereas the world of paid work once provided the cornerstone of family security, it no longer can. Ways need to be found to increase real incomes to eradicate poverty and improve job security for all. This is especially so in relation to child poverty, since we know that if children are born into poverty they are penalized in terms of educational outcomes and life chances (Brown and Lauder 2000). Together, a more equitable distribution of rising incomes, along with greater job security, would provide the impetus for a more open society in which people could seize opportunities and feel a commitment to it.

In this respect, a key task is to question current policy, which draws a sharp distinction between productive and unproductive work. Productive work is assumed to be waged work and the measure of an individual's contribution to society is typically based on how much they earn. Unproductive work includes all activities which do not generate an income. In post-industrial societies, where collective intelligence is based on the intelligence of all, the educative role of parents has become far more important because the early years of a child's life set the platform for subsequent learning. This role clearly produces a major return to the society and it should be recognised as doing so. Therefore, the definition of productive work and what constitutes social responsibility needs to be extended to include not only those who are directly involved in the production of goods and services, but also those who contribute to economic competitiveness and the quality of life of communities, through the pre-school and home-based education of children (Halsey and Young 1997).

However, even this extension does not go far enough to address the needs of such a society, for it fails to take into account the unemployed. Periods of unemployment up to twelve months should not be seen as down time or wasted time but necessary in a high-skills economy in order that individuals have the time to upgrade their skills. Viewed in this way unemployment is not a matter of fecklessness or a reflection on past poor performance. The corollary to this is that unemployed people need a relatively high level of compensation so that they can focus on taking the opportunities to retrain rather than be distracted by the question of where the next family meal will come from.

There seems little doubt that this must also involve the development of a 'third sector' of employment opportunities distinct from established patterns of waged employment in the private and public sectors of the economy, 'freeing up the labor and talent of men and women no longer needed in the market and government sectors to create social capital in neighbourhoods and communities' (Rifkin 1996: 294).

These arguments lead us to the inescapable conclusion that a society based on collective intelligence, geared to more efficient high-skills production, must be a society with a very significant element of redistribution of income and wealth.

Conclusion

In British and American the contradiction between the *capacity for intelligence* and *relations of trust* lies at the heart of the struggle for collective intelligence. Millions of people are failing to benefit from post-industrial possibilities as a result of a cultural, economic, and political system which remains locked into the principles of market individualism. We have argued that the concept of social capital represents an important advance in that it brings into question the excesses of Western individualism and the need to rebuild divided, excluded, and deprived neighbourhoods. Debates about social capital also recognize the importance of a vibrant civil society, but in order for this to be achieved we have argued that it needs to be located within a broader vision of society which, to reiterate Tawney, holds out the prospect of changing the core assumptions which rule the minds of individuals (Tawney 1982: 10).

The overarching concept of collective intelligence is required because building social capital networks at the macro policy level is unlikely to work because of the problem of group or community closure which may inhibit the development of an inclusive society. Moreover, a fundamental cause of closure has to do with the extreme inequalities in the Anglo-Saxon dominated societies and the pathological impact they have on learning. We have argued that seeking to resolve the distributional question of 'who gets what?' through driving all those deemed able into the labour market is likely to fail, particularly in deprived neighbourhoods where 'social capital' is seen to be the remedy. This is because in the absence of paid work in the traditional labour market these groups lack the motivational drivers of positive identity formation and financial resources to build social capital networks. In our view the distribution of rewards, status, and identities built on contribution and participation in society need to be extended.

The need to view social capital within the context of the struggle for collective intelligence is also informed by the argument that building social solidarity in post-industrial societies is inevitably a reflexive project. In post-industrial societies collective intelligence needs to become the social glue that holds societies together. We have argued that globalization, technological innovation, and changes in psychological contract of work mean that the labour market can not serve as source of 'spontaneous' solidarity (Durkheim 1933; Smith 1976).

This will require a redefinition of social contribution extending beyond the labour market to include those who contribute to the growth potential of others. It must also be based on a new modesty that involves recognizing that individual achievement, which is usually understood as a gift of nature, is in vital respects a social gift which conveys social responsibilities for others. Reflexive solidarity, therefore, depends on individuals recognizing that their position in society is not due to their efforts alone, and that their ability to extract undue wealth from the society necessarily damages the welfare and especially the learning of others. Recognition of this kind necessarily follows from the arguments we have advanced here.

For all these reasons reflexive solidarity in such a society will depend upon the ability of individuals to reflect critically on how much they owe to the talents and contribution of strangers, and to the potential of collective intelligence to improve the quality of life for all (Brown and Lauder 2001).

14

Social Capital and Human Capital Revisited

JOHN FIELD, TOM SCHULLER, AND STEPHEN BARON

Introduction

I N this concluding chapter we address directly the relationship between human capital and social capital. In part this reflects the origins of the volume, which lie in our participation in the 'Learning Society' Research Programme, sponsored by the UK Economic and Social Research Council in the late 1990s. The second, more contentious, reason is this: the later decades of the twentieth century saw a massive swing towards the view of human capital as the royal road to economic success and social cohesion. This was based on rather simplistic linear models, which imply that investing in education yields returns in the same way as investing in stocks or bonds, with measurable, tangible results. This view is being challenged by recognition that more complex processes are at work, with multiple interactions between different social forces, and with the possibility that not all learning is individually or socially beneficial in a straightforward, aggregate fashion. In particular, we cannot simply tot up the numbers of people achieving educational qualifications and assume that we are progressing—or not—towards a 'Learning Society'.

Our argument is that social capital offers one way of apprehending and analysing the embeddedness of education in social networks. It not only offers this; it also challenges dominant human capital approaches, whether driven by policy or by theory, which concentrate on narrowly defined, short-term results or tidy analytical devices.

Our starting point is a paper by James Coleman (1988a) on the contribution, as he saw it, of social capital to the creation of human capital. Tackling as it does the issue of learning across the lifespan and across different social groups, this chapter begins with a critical examination of Coleman's views on social capital and human capital. We specifically seek to broaden out the debate from its current focus on institutionalized forms of instruction such as

We wish to thank Frank Coffield for comments on an earlier version of this chapter.

schooling. This has become an increasingly important challenge in recent years, as is witnessed in the rise of lifelong learning up the policy agenda (Coffield 2000). In scholarly circles, meanwhile, there has been a burgeoning interest in the social and economic basis of much adult learning (Lave and Wenger 1991; Boud and Garrick 1999), and particularly in the role of networks in facilitating the exchange of skills, information and ideas (Eraut 2000; Maskell *et al.* 1998).

In this analysis, we draw on evidence based on earlier empirical studies of adult learning and social capital. These have sought to examine relations between the two in the case of adults with special learning needs (Baron, Riddell, and Wilson 1999; Riddell, Baron, and Wilson 1999*a, b*; 2000), and in respect of a number of sectors of economic activity in Scotland and Northern Ireland (Field 1999; Field and Spence 2000; Schuller and Bamford 2000; Schuller and Field 1999). We conclude that only by viewing learning as embedded in networks of social capital can we begin to grasp the complex patterns of participation and outcome that are found in the field of adult learning. Rather less is known about the converse, namely, how learning creates social capital, but we suggest that more ready access to new knowledge and skills can help to build, and transform, social capital.

Social Capital as a Differentiated Resource

The relevance of social capital for the study of school attainment is well-established. While Coleman proposed the concept of social capital as the key generic tool in his wider project of integrating rational choice theory with an understanding of social structure, his empirical studies were largely concerned with pupil performance at school. Indeed, Coleman frequently provided definitions couched precisely in the language of schooling. In an early essay, subsequently reprinted, Coleman proposed the following:

What I mean by social capital in the raising of children is the norms, the social networks, and the relationships between adults and children that are of value for the child's growing up. Social capital exists within the family, but also outside the family, in the community . . . in the interest, even the intrusiveness, of one adult in the activities of someone else's child. (Coleman 1990*c*: 334)

In his late attempt at a theoretical synthesis, Coleman virtually restated the position: 'Social capital is the set of resources that inhere in family relations and in community social organization and that are useful for the cognitive or social development of a child or young person' (Coleman 1994: 300). Education represented, for Coleman, not simply a neat example of a general proposition, but rather the strongest expression of the resources generated by the relationships, values, and trust that constitute social capital.

Coleman's work in this field has been particularly influential, not least because it appears to offer a useful communal and value-dependent counterweight to the individualism and narrow instrumentalism of human capital theory. Coleman himself, however, drew no such direct opposition. Rather, his account explicitly seeks to establish a direct and causal connection between the two forms of capital, as is clear in the title of his paper, which refers to 'social capital in the creation of human capital'. Social capital, Coleman suggested, deserves attention precisely because it helps us understand the nature of human capital (Coleman 1988a; among replication studies see Teachman, Paasch, and Carver 1997; on relations between sociology and economics, see Granovetter 1985: 507). Indeed, Coleman treated social capital, which parallels the development of financial, physical, and human capital in economics, as a central factor in the formation of human capital. The chief difference from the point of view of economic theory is that whereas financial, physical, and human capital are normally private goods, according to Coleman, social capital is mainly a public good; it followed that somewhat different policy approaches might be appropriate in order to bring about increases in social capital (Coleman 1988a: 116). Moreover, social capital is not completely fungible; for many purposes it may be impossible to transpose the benefits of social capital across different contexts (Coleman 1994: 302). For Coleman, social capital is highly distinctive, and the idea that it is a form of *capital* is not simply a helpful metaphor; rather, it defines the substance of the concept.

Coleman's treatment of social capital has been subjected to widespread discussion and critique, as in Chapter 1. We wish to focus here on three areas where, we think, his use of the concept is inadequate, and requires development. The first concerns the variable value of social capital; while Coleman rightly emphasized the contribution of social capital to equity and justice, he wrongly downplayed the ways in which social capital may also serve to underpin social hierarchies and create new sources of inequality—Bourdieu's work, by the same token, is vulnerable to the reverse criticism: namely, that he downplays how social capital can indeed contribute to greater social equity (Bourdieu 1997). Second, Coleman placed too much emphasis upon primary connections such as kinship, and too little upon secondary connections such as social networks and civic engagement—here, Putnam may be vulnerable to the reverse criticism. The downside of social capital as embodied in such networks was not addressed by Coleman, especially how it may act to constrain and limit individuals. Third, and very much in connection with the weight that his theory places upon family relationships, Coleman appeared to be blind to highly specific forms of inequality such as gender and disability. Below we consider the implications of the concept for women and for a group—adults with learning disabilities—that tends to be marginalized within the labour market, and is largely neglected in human capital theory.

Concerns for equity stands at the core of Coleman's work on education. An able advocate and practitioner of public policy research, he frequently emphasized the ways in which social capital can help counter racial and social inequality. Perhaps as a result, the schooling literature has rarely acknowledged the effects of inequalities in the distribution of social capital (but see

Edwards and Foley 1997: 677). As Stanton-Salazar and Dornbusch have suggested in their studies of Mexican-origin students in US high schools, this may point to a flaw in Coleman's formulation. Their studies found that the level of association between social capital and students' grades and aspirations was generally positive, but relatively weak. They attribute this to the nature of the social capital available to Mexican-origin students, which may be good at transmitting some types of information highly effectively, but is relatively poor when it comes to providing information on college admission or school qualifications. They conclude that Coleman's work overplayed 'the "role-modelling" and "cheer-leading" influences of significant others'. They advocate instead a 'network-analytic approach' that draws attention to the 'inequitable transmission of tangible institutional resources and opportunities', as well as toward the difficulties for some groups in 'forming relationships with institutional agents' who are able to negotiate access to those resources and opportunities (Stanton-Salazar and Dornbusch 1995: 116–19; see also Lauglo's chapter in this volume). Below we explore how forms of social capital may act similarly to exclude people with learning difficulties from many of the benefits of contemporary Scottish society.

A second flaw in Coleman's work is that it privileges one site of social capital. Empirically, Coleman usually treated family structures, defined in terms of parental presence and numbers of siblings in the household, as a proxy index of levels of social capital. But his view of the family was not just as a convenient statistical indicator, but also as a key set of relationships. Coleman regarded what he calls 'primordial' relationships, with their 'origins in the relationships established by childbirth', as the most robust source of social capital, as distinct from 'constructed' forms of social organization that come together for a single purpose or narrow range of purposes (Coleman 1991: 1–3). With the erosion of primordial social relations, Coleman believed that with them would vanish the 'social capital on which societal functioning has depended' (Coleman 1991: 9). Coleman largely discounted 'constructed social organization' as a source of social capital.

This led Coleman to value close networks, and to praise 'intergenerational closure' in particular, by which he meant the extent to which all parties to the relationship, children, parents, community leaders, teachers, were communicating regularly and effectively with one another (Coleman 1988a: 103–4). But intergenerational closure may also be a powerful force for conservatism, and can be perceived by actors as inhibiting rather than facilitating their development. In certain circumstances, intergenerational closure can, as we suggest below, support 'downward levelling pressures' (Portes and Landolt 1991: 19). Equally, social capital can serve as a defensive or coping device, inhibiting innovation and preventing goal-oriented forms of reciprocity, as Kolankiewicz notes in his comments on the 'amoral familism and clientelism' that underpin network reciprocity in post-communist societies (Kolankiewicz 1996: 438).

These reservations might apply with equal force to Putnam and Bourdieu. Emphasizing as he does the importance of civic engagement in creating trust, networks and norms, Putnam's conception of social capital is broader than Coleman's, and he could well be accused of understating the place of family in his analysis of social capital in southern Italy (Putnam 1993*a*). While he has briefly noted that social capital can be used for undesirable purposes as well as desirable ones (Putnam 1993*b*: 18), his overwhelming message is that social capital serves the common good, ignoring the possibility of social capital being used by one group or individual at the expense of others (Portes and Landolt 1991: 19). In his more recent work, Putnam has considered evidence that social capital has a 'dark side', but concluded that in general social joiners and civic activists tend to be more tolerant and inclusive, and make a greater contribution to equity and choice for others, than their more stay-at-home neighbours (Putnam 2000: Ch. 22). But this then requires, as Putnam tentatively acknowledges, a more differentiated understanding of social capital.

In a more individualized and fluid society, increasing weight may be placed upon what Mark Granovetter (1974) has called 'weak ties'. Like Coleman, Granovetter was interested in promoting a convergence between sociology and economics; as an economist, he acknowledged the force of Weber's view that economic action is one special, if important, category of social action (Granovetter 1985: 507). His work upon the value of weak ties originated in a study of youth labour markets, which showed the value of social networks in helping young Americans build a career. His approach was subsequently developed through an analysis of trust in modern industrial society which in many ways foreshadowed the later, lengthier book by Francis Fukuyama (Granovetter 1985; Fukuyama 1995).

Responding to the debate among economists over the levels of trust and avoidance of malfeasance required to maintain economic activities in the context of imperfectly competitive markets in modern industrial society, Granovetter argued that it was not necessary to resort to blanket explanations such as functionalism or generalized morality. Rather, trust was generated, and malfeasance discouraged, through the operations of 'concrete personal relations and structures (or "networks") of such relations', which enabled actors to indulge their 'widespread preference for transacting with individuals of known reputation' (Granovetter 1985: 490). However, Granovetter emphasized that close relationships could not of themselves provide guarantees of trustworthiness. First, the very existence of personal trust provided opportunities for new forms of malfeasance such as embezzlement; and fraud itself became easier the higher the level of trust among the thieves. Second, personal trust could never be general, but was bounded in its working, creating further potential for conflict between those outside any particular, given relation of trust. Granovetter noted the emergence of the ideal-typical Weberian bureaucracy as a means of solving this problem; ironically, though, large hierarchical organizations with well-defined internal labour markets and elaborate promotion ladders were characteristically vulnerable to 'co-operative evasion' and 'malfeasance generated by teams' (Granovetter 1985: 501).

In a highly fluid and open social system, Granovetter argued, high levels of personal trust can be economically dysfunctional. As a counterweight to the influence of close ties, Granovetter stressed the contribution of 'weak ties' in allowing actors to place a degree of trust upon one another, without necessarily having the same tight bonds as might be found among kin or neighbourhood relationships. In similar vein, Ray Pahl and Liz Spencer have argued that strong ties can also constrain social behaviour and relationships. While the 'inward-looking, strong ties of family' may help children form a 'healthy personality', they can also prevent adults from learning how 'to cope with a risk society and gain full opportunities from a flexible labour market' (Pahl and Spencer 1997: 102). Where Granovetter merely states the value of weak ties in general, Pahl and Spencer stress the role of 'bridging ties' that stretch between different communities of interest, and may be vital in accessing resources that are unavailable on the basis of strong ties alone. Below we explore these issues further in terms of bonding social capital's limiting of the ability of people with learning difficulties to negotiate a 'risk society' (Beck 1992).

Putnam and the World Bank have become increasingly concerned to address the balance between bonding and bridging, as a matter of policy as well as theoretical debate (for example Narayan 1999; Putnam 2000). The advocates of situated learning similarly emphasize that a 'community of practice' is not necessarily based upon co-presence or even 'socially visible boundaries', but may be defined as much by the existence of shared activity systems with common frameworks of understanding (Lave and Wenger 1991: 98; Eraut 2000).

Third, Coleman's interest in equity issues was combined with a curious blindness to gender, ethnicity, and disability. Much the same might be said, of course, about Putnam and Bourdieu, who have little to say on these dimensions. Yet by defining primordial relations as primary in the creation of social capital—relations, that is, that are ultimately 'established by childbirth'—Coleman's concept is unusual in the weight that it places on activities and structures that are highly gender specific.

Moreover, his view of family's importance in social capital is couched in highly traditional terms. Deficiencies in social capital, be they internal or external to the family, are harmful to the cognitive development of young people, and thus to the creation of human capital. Internal deficits do not solely refer to lower levels of parental involvement in schooling—for example, lack of interest in homework—but also such factors as single parenting. External deficits might include a low level of interaction between parents. Generally speaking, these parents are, in practice, mothers. It is mostly mothers who chat by the school gates, who care for a child without a live-in partner, or read with the child. In expressing concern over rising levels of maternal employment, Coleman (1988a) acknowledged this indirectly.

Subsequent attempts to test Coleman's own analysis, using child-mother data from the National Longitudinal Survey, found that early maternal employment appeared to have only 'minimally negative effects' on verbal facility and no effects on behavioural problems among three to six-year-olds (Parcel and Menaghan 1994: 997–9). Maynard and McGrath (1997: 136), in an extensive review of the relationship between family structure and child welfare, found that the main impact of divorce and single parenthood was the loss of income and material support, more than the absence of one parent. Empirically, then, Coleman's own propositions seem dubious. But this should not cloud the wider issue, which is the extent to which his view of social capital simply ignored issues of gender relations, and, we would suggest, of power in general. Thus it is possible, for instance, that women's stocks of social capital will grow, and certainly will change, as they move into waged employment, exposing them to a wider range of work-based networks. We explore below the extent to which Northern Ireland's strong reserves of social capital have helped inhibit the participation of women in large parts of the public sphere.

The links which Coleman sought to forge between social capital, human capital, and equity are based on a conception of cognitive development in which individuals are arrayed along a single dimension of ability and, thereby, are located in the economy according to their quantum of human capital. People with learning disabilities are defined by the attribution of impaired cognitive development and low levels of human capital and, typically, they occupy marginal positions in economic and social life (Riddell, Baron, and Wilson 2000). Addressing such marginalization not only addresses issues of equity but also allows us to understand current definitions of human and social capital and their inter-relation more clearly. Emile Durkheim (1982), in analysing the distinction between the 'normal' and the 'pathological', pointed out that deviance is not only necessary for any social system in order to define the boundaries of acceptable/unacceptable but that, in doing so, it offers a peculiar insight into the nature of the 'normality' which is being enforced. With increasing claims being made about the knowledge-driven economy, upskilling, and life-long learning, an analysis of those deemed to be unemployable, poorly skilled, and permanently impaired in their capacity for learning promises a critical perspective on the normality of a 'Learning Society'. We explore this further below.

So much for our critique of Coleman, and his application of the concept to education. We turn now to see how the concept might be used to extend the range of analysis of learning across the lifespan and across different social groups.

Social Capital and Adult Learning

In this and the next section we draw on evidence from two studies from the ESRC's 'Learning Society: knowledge and skills for employment' research programme. It is worth noting first that the programme's emphasis was mainly on institutionalized education and training, and its remit was closely tied to employment issues, as its subtitle implies (ESRC 1994). In this it reflected the dominant ideology, especially of the Conservative administration in power at the time of its conception, with human capital construed largely in a narrow and economistic sense. Our studies were not originally designed around the concept of social capital. Instead, our interest in the concept developed precisely as a means of extending the range of our analyses and the scope of the programme as a whole.[1] One of the most significant conclusions of the programme was the need to include informal learning in any account of a Learning Society. As the programme Director observed: 'there is more to creating a learning society than continually beating the drum of human capital. The more subtle claims of social capital need to be explored, and robust indicators of informal learning should be developed' (Coffield 2000: 8).

Human and social capital are not in direct opposition to each other, but in a relationship of tension, theoretically and pragmatically. In Table 14.1 we give a schematic representation of this, before turning to our empirical evidence.

Table 14.1 The relationship between human capital and social capital

	Human Capital	Social Capital
Focus	Individual	Relationships
Measures	Duration	Membership/participation
	Qualifications	Trust levels
Outcomes	Direct: income, productivity	Social cohesion
	Indirect: health, civic activity	Economic achievement
		More social capital
Model	Linear	Interactive/circular
Policy	Skilling, accessibility, and	Citizenship, capacity-building,
	rates of return	and empowerment

Focus

The key distinction between human capital and social capital is that the former focuses on individual agents, and the latter on relationships between them and the networks they form. In the case of our theme, the inclusion of social capital makes the point that individuals' training timetables are not discrete entities which exist separately from the rest of the organization. Employees may benefit from training leave and increase their own qualifications, but the impact of this on the organization's performance will

---

[1] It is significant that the Department for Education and Employment has now provided direct governmental funding for a research centre on the wider benefits of learning based explicitly on the notion of social capital.

depend on how their learning is incorporated into the activity of the work-place by their own colleagues and immediate workgroup.

Measures

Human capital is measured primarily by duration of education—almost always initial education—or by levels of qualification achieved. Social capital is far more diffuse, and is measured broadly by levels of active participation in civic life or in other networks. One example of how this might be of relevance is the way in which network membership provides access to important information and ideas, often in a relatively unstructured way. Another is the question of how far organizations actively encourage their staff to play a part in the life of the surrounding community, in the course of which they may well acquire important skills. Participation of this kind clearly raises issues about control of time in and out of work.

Outcomes

The output of human capital is generally measured in terms of enhanced income or productivity. Whilst social capital has been linked to economic performance, it also has wider outcomes, including social cohesion and the generation of further social capital. Looked at from a social capital perspective, the impact of training may be as much in the strengthening of networks and information flows as in the acquisition of individual competencies.

Models

Human capital approaches suggest a direct linear model: investment is made, in time or money, and economic returns follow in direct, if variable, proportion to the amount invested. Social capital has a much less linear approach, and its returns are more diffuse and less easily definable. In this respect, the distinction resembles that between 'training', with its defined and predictable outcomes, and 'education', with its much broader focus and variable outcomes.

Policy

Human capital thinking has strong associations with policy, and the implications are usually regarded as relatively straightforward. Investment in human capital resources is justified by an appropriate rate of return, usually measured in terms of impact upon individual earnings and organizational profitability. Although analytically human capital can be extended to encompass social benefits, in policy circles it is generally used to justify investment in those forms of skills training that have measurable consequences for earnings and profitability. It is also frequently held to imply that the costs of training should be met by those individuals and employers who benefit. Social capital is less clearly and directly associated with a tangible and measurable return; indeed, the returns on social capital may not be measurable at all. Even when measured, many of the benefits accrue to groups and institutions rather than to individuals, and are in the nature of a public good, so that responsibility for investment may lie as much with governmental actors as individuals and employers. In a stronger version, a focus on social capital may even foster the recasting of governance itself towards a concern with building networks and fostering trust and cooperation between different players in both government institutions and in civil society (Rhodes 1996; Mouqué 1999: 63–72).

For empirical illumination, our chapter draws first on a study of social capital and life-long learning in Scotland and Northern Ireland.[2] This study was rooted in the desire to explore what appeared to be a persistently skewed pattern in both societies in the relationship between schools attainment and adult learning. Stated baldly, there seemed to be strong evidence of a divergence between comparatively high rates of attainment in initial education on the one hand, and relatively low levels of participation and achievement in adult learning on the other (Field and Schuller 1995). The study involved further, more detailed analysis of statistical data combined with qualitative data gathered through fieldwork (the methodology is described further in Schuller and Field 1999). Our findings were that, for Northern Ireland, there was indeed a pattern of divergence: young people generally attained more academic qualifications than their counterparts in Britain, and were far more likely to enter higher education. Adults, on the other hand, were less likely to participate in general education, vocational training, or independent study. In Scotland, the picture was more nuanced. Our evidence suggested that, in respect of initial education, the Scottish and English systems are set on a course of convergence; and there was less difference than at first appeared in levels of adult participation (see Schuller and Field 1999).

Social capital provided one important way of trying to understand these patterns. One way of visualizing the possible relationships is the network shown in Fig. 14.1, which lists the key actors in adult learning. At its simplest, Coleman's hypothesis would suggest that the core institution in this network is that which commands greatest primordial loyalty, namely, the family. If we were to accept this hypothesis, we would therefore conclude that the ideal of a learning society is best served by the existence of strong ties between family and the other relevant actors. Our preferred approach, though, was to allow for the importance of other ties—loose ties, in Granovetter's terms—and to remove family from its privileged place within social capital. Even our simplified figure would then allow for other possible relationships between the different actors in the domain.

    [2] This study was undertaken by Caroline Bamford, Lynda Spence, John Field, and Tom Schuller, and was funded by the Economic and Social Research Council's Learning Society Programme (grant L123251043.) and Scottish Enterprise.

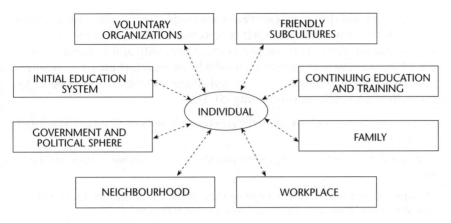

F<small>IGURE</small> 14.1 Sources of social capital

In contrast with schooling, adult learning tends to be a broad and fluid field. Some commentators distinguish between:

(1) formal education for adults, defined as intentional instruction undertaken in the education and training system;
(2) non-formal learning, which consists of planned learning undertaken outside the education and training system; and
(3) informal learning, which is largely unplanned or is incidental to another activity (Cross 1981).

Our analysis focused primarily on the first and the last of these, while allowing for the significant role of non-formal learning for those groups who are most marginalized within the formal system.

With this model in mind, what did our study demonstrate? First, the levels of social capital in both societies appear relatively high, at least in comparison with the rest of the UK (Field and Schuller 2000). In Northern Ireland, the key components of networks appear to be family, church, and neighbourhood, and to a lesser extent non-religious voluntary organizations; such values as welfare collectivism appear to enjoy higher support than in Britain (Field 1999). In Scotland, the picture is more shaded. In particular there is far greater variation between regions than in the smaller society of Northern Ireland, and church affiliations and loyalties play a weaker part in social life (see also Paterson in this volume). When it comes to the relationship between social capital and life-long learning, a selective summary account of the findings is given below, with some illustrative quotation from the interviews and an indication of whether these apply to Northern Ireland alone (NI), Scotland alone (S) or both (NIS).

First, it seems to be generally true that higher levels of social capital are indeed associated with relatively high levels of initial attainment (NIS). Thus far, the study was entirely consistent with Coleman's hypothesis. However, intergenerational closure was also associated with a highly traditionalist view of the education system and what it is expected to deliver, including the belief that education stops when one leaves the system (NI); and a strong sense of the education system as something to which responsibility for achievement is 'contracted out' to others, rather than something undertaken at least partly by the individual, family, or community (S). Thus:

Middle class families contract out to the private sector; working class families contract out to the state.

I am appalled at parents' evenings when parents say that education is up to the teachers.

My father always used to take a negative view of the Parent-Teacher Association: 'it should stop meddling and let the teachers get on with the job'.

A further telling piece of evidence emerges from the 'Status Zero' study of young people who are neither in training, work, nor the unemployment register; as one might expect in view of Coleman's hypothesis, this group is indeed comparatively small in Northern Ireland (Armstrong 1997).

Cultural influences were strongly seen in family and peer influences over learning. The decisive influence exercised by the family, and above all mothers, was visible on the educational and career choices and behaviour of young people and adults, sustaining a commitment to achievement but also encouraging avoidance of risk situations rather than a search for ways of living in risk society (NI). Men were particularly likely to share a peer culture that places a low value on organized learning, unless it results in a direct material reward (S).

The problem is men not participating. More women participate, and are keener on education. Oppressed groups see education as a way out of oppression. If you go to community education it is 90 per cent female. They can't get young men to participate at all.

Unless it's a very technical skill, men have to be actively recruited onto courses. They are much more sensitive than women about being exposed, and more going back to school.

In a context where the further and higher education system is dominated numerically and culturally by the training of young adults, women in particular faced both structural and cultural barriers to participation in adult learning; however, women are more likely to realize a joy in their learning, and are more likely to do in non-formal education (NIS).

Finally, social capital was strongly associated with a preference for informal learning (both, but especially NI).

Self-build is a very good way to build up self confidence. You have experience of dealing with a small group, and this gives you the confidence to take part in larger groups. Since finishing my house I have become involved in the School Board and the local Community Council.

This is partly a matter of opportunity; strong networks and high trust tend to facilitate the rapid transfer of information and skills, both among men and women, and often in a highly coordinated ways, reducing the demand for more formal education and training (Field and Spence 2000). It is partly because a highly academic, traditional view of initial education shades over into a perception of the institutions of transition—further education colleges, universities—as lacking either the desire or the capacity to serve more vocational and applied goals.

We still have the mediaeval gown-and-parchment approach, the sorcerer's apprentice.

This study demonstrated that social capital offers abundant opportunities for informal and incidental learning, but that it has a clear downside. It is inherently narrowing, in that it gives access only to the limited range of resources that happen to be available in any given locale or community of interest. Characteristically, familistic forms of social capital can be particularly limiting and inward-looking, making it substantially more difficult to build bridging ties (Pahl and Spencer 1997). This has particular significance for the most marginalized groups in Northern Ireland, who for security reasons among others tend to be located in relatively distinctive spatial zones, and are also bound to self-identities that emphasize reliance upon insider cultures and contacts. Scotland is not a divided community in the same way. While there is a tendency to regard one's path as set once initial education is completed, there is a stronger commitment to meritocratic patterns promoted by education. By comparison with Northern Ireland, its social and economics structures are also more diverse and in some ways more open—for example, in the range of patterns of inward migration—allowing for considerably greater and more varied forms of incidental learning, with a greater propensity for fostering innovation and change.

Social Capital and Learning Disability

The clear downside of social capital identified through Field and Schuller's focus groups in Scotland and Ireland can be illuminated further through the ethnography of another ESRC Learning Society research project, 'The meaning of the Learning Society for adults with learning difficulties'.[3] This study explored the tension in the ESRC programme's working definition of a Learning Society between the utilitarian discourse of knowledge-skills-employment-competitiveness and the humanist discourse of self development-social inclusion -equity (Baron, Riddell, and Wilson 1998). In particular it explored ethnographically the life situation of 30 adults with learning difficulties in three age groups: a transition group of people in their late teens and early twenties; a post-transition group of people from their mid-twenties to late-thirties; a delicately named, older group of people over 40 with the

---

[3] This study was undertaken variously by Stephen Baron, Sheila Riddell, Kirsten Stalker, Heather Wilkinson, and Alastair Wilson, and was funded by the Economic and Social Research Council's Learning Society Programme, grant L1123251042.

oldest person studied being 67 years of age. Six test criteria were derived from the programme's working definition and were used both to understand the life worlds of the 30 people and to assess in which respects a 'Learning Society' could be said to exist in Scotland.

In summary, our findings suggested that:

1. Access to excellent services was limited by the geographical location of services and by the dominance of segregating services.
2. Developmental progression of the individual was notable by its absence. Services did not provide the framework by which the transition to adulthood could be made fully and a process of life-long development undertaken.
3. Contribution to the social and economic whole was limited by the scarcity of suitable work, by inappropriate support services and by benefits regimes which pivoted on the dichotomy between those who 'could' work and those who 'could not'. Lack of work severely restricted personal development and opportunities for wider social engagement.
4. Social integration was limited by the dominance of special social networks and the paucity of work opportunities.
5. Participative citizenship was limited by the relatively closed nature of the social networks and by segregated provision.
6. Equity for people with learning difficulties in terms of the programme may best be defined as the combination of the previous five test criteria which, in their delineation of exclusion from mainstream social, economic and personal life-chances, suggest inequity.

For an extended summary see Riddell, Baron, and Wilson (2000).

Social capital was not a concept used in designing the research. As the field-work progressed, though, we turned to it for two principal reasons: it helped us make sense of the variegated, but consistent, pattern of marginalization, segregation and exclusion experienced by the 30 informants; and it offered a way of thinking about social relations, especially with respect to production, which did not start from the human capital assumption that people with learning difficulties were a deficit system. Figure 14.2 offers a specification of the predominant relationship of our 30 informants to different sources of social capital.

Mapping thus the principal links which our case-study individuals with learning difficulties had to different sources of social capital immediately suggests a refinement of Granovetter's argument about the strength of loose ties (Granovetter 1974; 1985). Such ties were certainly present in the lives of our case-study individuals but did not function as a flexible resource enabling individuals to negotiate their way through a risk society (Baron, Riddell, and Wilson 1999). The key deficiencies in the relationships of people with learning difficulties to these sources of social capital were, we suggest, the strength of bonding forms of social capital, the non-reciprocal nature of the ties, and the absence of bridging social capital. People with learning difficulty, in so

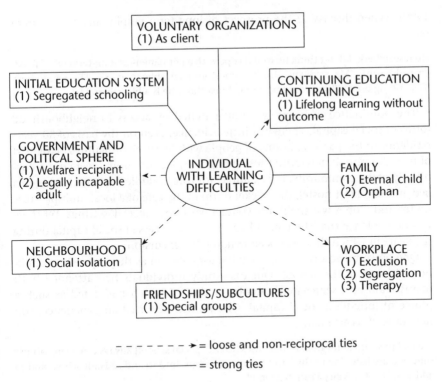

FIGURE 14.2 Principal relationship of individuals with learning difficulties to sources of social capital

far as they were connected with sources of social capital, tended to be placed in the position of dependent recipients rather than as reciprocal partners. Loose and non-reciprocal ties appear to be very different in form and effect from the loose and reciprocal ties that Granovetter uses as examples of 'loose ties'.

The dominant form of social capital to which our case-study individuals had access was that of the family of origin. The typical life trajectory of our sample was to live at home until middle age, when parental illness and death forced a move into residential care or to the home of a sibling. One person, however, was enabled to continue living in the home of her late parents through the support of his or her network of ageing friends, while another was held to be *incapax*—legally incapable—by the terms of the parental will. Such strong ties into the family of origin tended continually to redefine, implicitly and explicitly, our case-study people as eternal children, dependent on parental—particularly maternal—services, thus linking into a centuries-old construction of learning difficulties as, in contemporary terms, arrested development and low human capital (Baron, Riddell, and Wilson

1999). When discussing the prospect of long-term employment one parent said:

[To researcher]: 'I don't think he would cope with a permanent or long-term job'. [To 23-year-old son]: 'Ma says she thinks you would be able to cope'. [To researcher]: 'Depending on what he would be doing. I just think he is a bit vulnerable'.

The dominance of home was not matched by access to neighbourhood forms of social capital. There was little evidence, even on the basis of 30 years residence in the parental home, of people with learning difficulties being part of neighbourhood networks; those living 'in the community' were not recognizably *of* the community. For example, for three middle-aged men living in a bed-and-breakfast hostel, the weekend trip to the café of a local multiple store for tea and scones was their only contact with non-'special' settings. Yet there was no evidence that these men had formed or accessed social capital during the years in which they had been making this excursion.

One powerful source of social capital for children as they move into adulthood is that of the school. Our case-study individuals had attended both mainstream and segregated schools, neither of which had acted as such a source of long-term social capital. One mother reported an experience, still raw some 20 years later:

We had to sit there for hours—the buses [to the special school] always came late. All the time you are listening to this 'And so and so has got into so and so High School and so and so has got in Vairy Posh Academy'.

Those attending mainstream schools reported isolation, hostility and, often, the breakdown of the placement. Those attending special schools had sometimes formed proto-networks but, due to geographic dispersion and difficulties with travel, these appeared difficult to maintain. One woman in late middle age, recently de-carcerated from a lifetime in hospital, formed a strong friendship with someone else at the further education college, where they were placed for part of the week. Due to lack of staff to help with transport, this friendship could not develop. Ongoing education and training, through further education colleges, community education and, predominantly, adult resource centres (ARCs), was the staple daily activity of most of our sample. This provision was characterized by segregated settings and the social networks of our sample revolved almost exclusively around 'special' clubs for the clients of the ARCs. The training was characterized by a lack of outcome in terms of employment, both limiting the forms of social capital to which people had access and not enabling that which was created to enter into the circuit of production and self-expansion (Riddell, Baron, and Wilson 1999*a*). One of the older people in our study was about to 'retire', without ever having worked, from the circuit of work training in an ARC on which one of our younger informants was about to embark.

The timetable of George, a middle-aged man in a major Scottish city, is typical. George's life is governed by routine (Foucault 1977):

Table 14.2 George's weekly timetable

	Morning	Afternoon
Monday	Craft activity in Centre	Quiz in Centre
Tuesday	FE College: going for a walk	FE College: watching TV
Wednesday	Swimming: segregated session in community facility	Relaxation class in Centre
Thursday	Placement in special horticultural project: £1.50 earned	Placement in special horticultural project: £1.50 earned
Friday	Karaoke in Centre	Group meeting with key worker in Centre

The Tocquevillian legacy in political science sets great store by voluntary associations as the cradle of social capital (see Maloney's chapter in this volume). The 30 people in our study had multiple connections with voluntary organizations but these were organizations *for* rather than *of* people with learning difficulties (Stalker *et al.* 1999) with non-reciprocal and limiting ties. People with learning difficulties were the largely passive clients of the voluntary organizations—and local and central government—which, despite genuine attempts to empower the clients, could act as quasi-total institutions exercising control over all aspects of the person's life. For example, one of the very few people in our sample to have held a full-time job had to give it up and become classified as disabled because the undifferentiated funding regime between the local authority and the voluntary organization which provided the accommodation demanded it. The activity of self-advocacy, learning-disabled-led voluntary organizations such as People First had not made an impact on the particular individuals we studied.

Many of the case-study individuals were convinced, as are many social capital theorists, that access to work was the key to self-development, personal fulfilment, and social integration. Full-time work appeared, however, to be becoming increasingly difficult for people with learning difficulties to maintain as their labour-market niches have been squeezed out: another of the people who had held full-time work was, when the public utility in which he worked was being prepared for privatization, given the choice between becoming classified as disabled, thus generating a 50 per cent wage subsidy for the employer, or disciplinary action for low productivity. The nearest most people got to production was the severely limited contact allowed under the 'therapeutic earnings rule', which depends on being classified as being permanently unable to work. One person stood out from this picture, a person who had been introduced into a full-time job through the support of a job coach from a supported employment scheme. We consider the significance of such schemes below.

We suggested above that using social capital as an analytic device would enable us both to understand the patterns of marginalization, segregation, and exclusion of people with learning difficulties better than would a human capital perspective, and that social capital offered the prospect of thinking about people with learning difficulties as other than a deficit system. By way of concluding this brief account of the study, we now reflect on these issues.

A human capital explanation of the life situation of the people with learning difficulties centres on their incompetence: people are so classified because they are slow to learn and may never acquire skills which others take for granted. In the context of the developing knowledge-driven economy, such people are a poor investment, although in a polarizing workforce a minority might be ideal workers for certain types of 'MacDonaldized' jobs (Baron, Riddell, and Wilson 1998). In policy terms this generates the divide between 'work for those who can, welfare for those who can't'. This places people with learning difficulties in a welfare discourse, apart from, and 'a burden' on, the mainstream discourse of material and symbolic production.

From a social capital perspective the exclusion of people with learning difficulties may be understood in terms of both the forms of social capital to which they have access and the nature of their relationships with these forms of social capital. Figure 14.2 shows people with learning difficulties having access mainly to 'special' forms of social capital with little access to the forms of social capital which enable the transition to full adult status: employment, independent living, intimate personal relations, self-selected reference group. The relationship which people with learning difficulties have with these limited forms of social capital is both strong and asymmetric: they are tied tightly to specific forms, and the networks relationships are largely non-reciprocal, neither of which enable the negotiation of 'risk' which many hold to be the key of current social life (Baron, Riddell, and Wilson 1999). At its starkest people with learning difficulties are the passive consumers of 'rights' defined and delivered by professional others rather than active citizens forming rights in the inter-change of duties (see Baron and Dumbleton 2001).

In many ways such a social capital analysis of the life situation of people with learning difficulties is as bleak as that generated by a human capital perspective. Lives are being limited by segregation and crushing routines as surely 'in the community' as in the asylum. Where a human capital perspective can offer, as ways forward, only the prospect—at the margins—of better diagnosis and training and the welfare discourse, our social capital analysis suggests a much richer agenda. If learning depends on access to social capital, as several studies in the Learning Society Research Programme suggest (Coffield 2000), then addressing the limitation of the learning of people with learning difficulties becomes less a matter of endless training programmes than the creation, or accessing, of contexts in which more spontaneous learning can occur. Similarly, replacing the strong ties and the loose but non-reciprocal ties which currently characterize the relationship of people with learning difficulties to social capital with loose but reciprocal ties promises greater learning and the consequent benefits of social integration.

In this context, supported employment schemes with natural supports offer a generalizable model (Riddell, Baron, and Wilson 1999b). A person with learning difficulties is employed in an open market context and the immediate workgroup is supported in terms of time and staffing in introducing the newcomer both to the work routines and to the social system of the workplace. Such schemes are still in their infancy but they address the problems of both access to, and relationship with, mainstream forms of social capital and, in our view crucially, they represent the opportunity for the reciprocal development of social capital of the immediate workgroup.

Conclusions and Implications

Social capital is related to human capital, but not in a linear or monocausal manner. In our opening comments, we suggested that only by viewing learning as embedded in networks of social capital can we begin to grasp the complex patterns of participation and outcome that are found in the field of adult learning. As illuminated in the two empirical studies reported here, the relationship is both a complex and a multidirectional one which has a number of possible outcomes depending upon such matters as the context and the attributes and behaviour of actors themselves. While we agree with Coleman on the importance of social capital to the creation of human capital, then, we have tried to show that he seriously understated the complexity of this relationship. Above all, social capital can be used to exclude, or to limit participation, as well as to promote it. Even loose ties, particularly it seems if they are intrinsically not reciprocal, can be used to exclude as well as to include. It remains to be seen whether the example of disability has wider applicability, or whether perhaps the exclusionary effects of non-reciprocal loose ties take a less permanent and inexorable form than with ties marked by high degrees of closure. Effectively, though, Coleman adopted a version of functionalism which took social capital as largely benign in its consequences, neglecting the fact that social capital, as a set of resources arising from relationships and values, may become the focus of conflict and tension between different actors.

Social capital's constraining function appears to be particularly significant in the case of precisely those relationships described by Coleman as 'primordial'. Close, bounded ties and strong levels of trust appear to promote a propensity to share information, ideas, and skills, albeit within the boundaries of a defined set of networks and relations, such as those arising from kinship and neighbourhood. Given the significance now attributed to informal learning as a prized source of human capital, this insight is an important one. But there seems to be a tension, at least potentially, between the informal learning that is facilitated by close ties on the one hand and the limits that they place upon access to a wide variety of global knowledge sources and formally certified possession of codified skills on the other. Does it therefore follow that looser ties are intrinsically more likely to favour the institutionalized transmission and acquisition of skills and knowledge? Do looser ties also provide an environment that allows individuals and groups to engage in the 'negotiation of risk', possibly accompanied by an experimental disposition towards self-identity, that appear to be so vital to individual well-being in a risk society? While this is a strong possibility, we conclude that unless loose ties are accompanied by high expectations of reciprocity, the least advantaged will be subject to even greater marginalization than they already are. Attention to the differentiated nature of social capital, and its overlapping but distinctive relationship to other resources, is therefore a necessary refinement to Coleman's approach.

As well as conceptual refinement, this analysis also has implications for policy. Recent policy debate in Britain and North America has tended to blur the distinctions between social capital and older policy concepts such as community, and to treat each as almost uniformly a Good Thing. Our analysis suggests that there are serious risks in this approach, and that public policy may, entirely unintentionally, create and consolidate social divisions rather than healing them. Examples might include those regeneration strategies that focus on building social capital within disadvantaged neighbourhoods, and thereby intensifying their separation from the outside world, rather than building bridging ties that allow access to externally-controlled resources. Similarly, Blaxter and Hughes (2001) detect what they describe as a 'disciplining discourse' around the concept, particularly in respect of the 'invisibility of women's active citizenship'. The current emphasis on governance through partnership and networking (Rhodes 1996) may unintentionally lead to bureaucratization through the proliferation of quangos and committees, where what is needed are looser and more informal connections. Finally, there is the problem of measurement. Human capital was popularized among policymakers because it offered a simple set of measurable indicators by which finance ministries could judge the relative success or failure of particular policy-measures. Will interest in social capital be sustained if similarly robust indicators are not measured? And just as the measurability of human capital has a marked downside, what will be the disadvantages if social capital is similarly reduced to a small number of numerical indicators?

Our account, like Coleman's, has focused on the contribution of social capital to human capital. Rather less is known about the converse, namely how learning creates social capital, and this is clearly likely to prove a fruitful area for future studies. Existing studies have confirmed repeatedly that levels of initial education are closely associated with the propensity to participate in associational life, and indeed take leadership positions (McMahon 1998; Hall 1999). Our own investigations have led us to hypothesize that more ready access to new knowledge and skills can help to build, and transform, social capital. It is not simply that knowledge and skills can be exchanged through high-trust networks, thus helping to renew and restate their significance to their members. New information and competencies can also help build the capacity of a given network, enabling it both to function more effectively and to adapt to changing circumstances.

The outcomes of the current upsurge of interest in social capital are hard to predict. One possible future, versions of which are envisaged both by Coleman and by Fine and Green, is that social capital will become another variable alongside physical, financial and human capitals in the equations of econometricians. For Coleman, this would complete the project of linking the social action frame of reference to neo-classical economics, creating a new synthetic discipline; for Fine and Green this would complete the reduction of human phenomena to the assumptions of utility maximization, at the cost of a true political economy. Another possible future for social capital, versions of which are avowed by the majority of the authors in this volume, is that it will enable new sets of questions to be posed about the nature of economic production, its links to different forms of human sociality, and the consequences of these for different social groups. We are clear which future is preferable.

REFERENCES

Abbott, A. (1988). 'Transcending General Linear Reality'. *Sociological Theory*, 6: 169–86.

Abramovitz, M. (1986). 'Catching Up, Forging Ahead, and Falling Behind'. *Journal of Economic History*, 46/2: 358–406.

Addison, P. (1975). *The Road to 1945*. London: Quartet.

Adonis, A., and Pollard, S. (1997). *A Class Act: The Myth of Britain's Classless Society*. London: Hamish Hamilton.

Agelopoulos, G. (1997). 'From Bulgarievo to Nea Krasia, from "Two Settlements" to "One Village": Community Formation, Collective Identities and the Role of the Individual', in P. Mackridge and E. Yanakakis (eds), *The Development of a Greek Macedonian Cultural Identity*. New York: Berg,133–51.

Ahern, M., Hendryx, M., and Siddarthan, K. (1996). 'The Importance of Sense of Community on People's Perceptions of their Health Care Experience'. *Medical Care*, 34: 911–23.

Ainley, P. (1991). *Young People Leaving Home*. London: Cassell.

Akerlof, G. (1970). 'The Market for "Lemons": Quality Uncertainty and the Market Mechanism'. *Quarterly Journal of Economics*, 54: 345–64.

—— (1990). 'George A. Akerlof', in R. Swedberg (ed.), *Economics and Sociology, Redefining Their Boundaries: Conversations with Economists and Sociologists*. Princeton: Princeton University Press, 61–77.

Allan, D. (1993). *Virtue, Learning and the Scottish Enlightenment*. Edinburgh: Edinburgh University Press.

Almond, G. and Verba, S. (1963). *The Civic Culture*. Princeton: Princeton University Press.

Althusser, L. (1971). *Lenin and Philosophy: and Other Essays*. London: New Left Books.

Amin, A. and Thomas, M. D. (1996). 'The Negotiated Economy: State and Civic Institutions in Denmark'. *Economy and Society*, 25/2: 255–81.

Anderson, B. (1991). *Imagined Communities: Reflections on the Origin and Spread of Nationalism*. London: Verso.

Antikainen, A., Houtsonen, J., Kauppila, J., and Houtelin, N. (1996). *Living in a Learning Society: Life-histories, Identities and Education*. London: Falmer.

Appleby, A. (1978). *Famine in Tudor and Stuart England*. Liverpool: Liverpool University Press.

Armstrong, D. (1997). *Status 0: A Socio-economic Study of Young People on the Margin*. Belfast: Training and Employment Agency.

Arrow, K. (1970). *Essays in the Theory of Risk Bearing*. Amsterdam: North-Holland.

—— (1974). *The Limits of Organisation*. New York: Norton.

—— (2000). 'Observations on Social Capital', in P. Dasgupta and I. Serageldin (eds), *Social Capital: A Multifaceted Perspective*. Washington, DC: World Bank, 3–5.

Arthur, W. B. (1989). 'Competing Technologies, Increasing Returns, and Lock-ins by Historical Events'. *Economic Journal*, 99: 116–31.

Ashton, D. and Green, F. (1996). *Education, Training and the Global Economy*. Cheltenham: Edward Elgar.

Aspinwall, B. (1984). *Portable Utopia: Glasgow and the United States, 1820–1920.* Aberdeen: Aberdeen University Press.

Axelrod, R. (1981). 'The Emergence of Co-operation among Egoists'. *American Political Science Review,* 75/2: 306–18.

Baier, A. (1994). *Moral Prejudices.* Cambridge, MA: Harvard University Press.

Bandura, A. (1996). *Self-efficacy in Changing Societies.* Cambridge: Cambridge University Press.

Banks, M., Bates, I., Breakwell, V., Bynner, J., Emler, N., Jamieson, I., and Roberts, K. (1991). *Careers and Identities.* Milton Keynes: Open University Press.

Barber, B. (1984). *Strong Democracy.* Berkeley: University of California Press.

Barnes, M. (1997). *Care, Communities and Citizens.* London: Longman.

Barney, J. (1991). 'Firm Resources and Sustained Competitive Advantage'. *Journal of Management,* 17: 99–120.

Baron, J. and Hannan, M. (1994). 'The Impact of Economics on Contemporary Sociology'. *Journal of Economic Literature,* 32: 1111–46.

Baron, S. and Dumbleton, P. (2001). *The Politics of Learning Disability.* Basingstoke: Macmillan.

—— Riddell, S., and Wilson, A. (1998). 'The Best Burgers? The Person with Learning Difficulties as Worker', in T. Shakespeare (ed.), *The Disability Reader.* London: Cassell, 94–109.

—— —— —— (1999). 'The Secret of Eternal Youth: Identity, Risk and Learning Difficulties'. *British Journal of the Sociology of Education,* 20/4: 483–99.

—— Stalker, K., Wilkinson, H., and Riddell, S. (1998). 'The Learning Society: The Highest Stage of Human Capitalism?', in F. Coffield (ed.), *Learning at Work.* Bristol: Policy Press, 49–57.

Barro, R. (1991). 'Economic Growth in a Cross-Section of Countries'. *Quarterly Journal of Economics,* 106/2: 407–43.

Baum, F. (1999). 'The Role of Social Capital in Health Promotion: Australian Perspectives'. *Health Promotion Journal of Australia,* 9/3: 171–78.

Bauman, Z. (1998). *Work, Consumerism and the New Poor.* Buckingham: Open University Press.

Beall, J. (1998). 'Social Capital in Waste—A Solid Investment?'. *Journal of International Development,* 9/7: 951–61.

Beck, U. (1992). *Risk Society: Towards a New Modernity.* London: Sage.

Becker, G. (1964). *Human Capital: A Theoretical and Empirical Analysis with Special Reference to Education.* Princeton: Princeton University Press.

—— (1990). 'Gary S. Becker', in Swedberg, R. (ed.), *Economics and Sociology, Redefining Their Boundaries: Conversations with Economists and Sociologists.* Princeton: Princeton University Press, 27–46.

—— (1996). *Accounting for Tastes.* Cambridge, MA: Harvard University Press.

Beeker, C., Guenther Gray, C., and Raj, A. (1998). 'Community Empowerment Paradigm and the Primary Prevention of HIV/AIDS'. *Social Science and Medicine,* 46/7: 831–42.

Bell, F. and Millward, R. (1998). 'Public Health Expenditures and Mortality in England and Wales 1870–1914'. *Continuity and Change* 13/2: 221–40.

Bender, T. (1978). *Community and Social Change.* New Brunswick: Rutgers University Press.

Bennett, W. L. (1998). 'The Uncivic Culture: Communication, Identity, and the Rise of Lifestyle Politics'. *PS: Political Science and Politics,* 31/4: 741–61.

Berkman, L. (1995). 'The Role of Social Relations in Health Promotion'. *Psychosomatic Medicine,* 57: 245–54.

Berlin, I. (1969). *Four Essays on Liberty*. Oxford: Oxford University Press.

Berman, S., (1997). 'Civil Society and Political Institutionalization'. *American Behavioral Scientist*, 40/5: 562–74. (Special Edition: 'Social Capital, Civil Society and Contemporary Democracy'.)

Bernstein, R. J. (1985). 'Introduction', in R. J. Bernstein (ed.), *Habermas and Modernity*. Cambridge: Polity Press, 1–32.

Berry, C. J. (1997). *Social Theory of the Scottish Enlightenment*. Edinburgh: Edinburgh University Press.

Blair, T. (1998). *The Third Way: New Politics for the New Century*. London: Fabian Society.

Blau, J. L. (1963). 'Introduction', in F. Wayland [1835], *The Elements of Moral Science*, ed. J. L. Blau. Cambridge, MA: Harvard University Press, ix–xlix.

Blaxter, L. and Hughes, C. (2001, forthcoming). 'Social Capital: a Critique', in J. Thompson (ed.), *The Politics and Practice of Widening Participation in Higher Education*. Leicester: National Institute of Adult Continuing Education.

Bloch, A. B. and Levy, C. (1999). *Refugees, Citizenship and Social Policy in Europe*. Basingstoke: Macmillan.

Block, F. (1990). *Post-Industrial Possibilities*. Berkeley: University of California Press.

Boix, C. and Posner, D. (1996). *Making Social Capital Work: A Review of Robert Putnam's 'Making Democracy Work: Civic Traditions in Modern Italy'* (Working Paper No. 94). Cambridge, MA: Center for International Affairs, Harvard University.

—— —— (1998). 'Social Capital: Explaining its Origins and Effects on Government Performance'. *British Journal of Political Science*, 29/3: 686–93.

Bott, E. (1957). *Family and Social Network*. London: Tavistock.

Boud, D. and Garrick, J. (1999). *Understanding Learning at Work*. London: Routledge.

Bourdieu, P. (1977). *Outline of a Theory of Practice*. Cambridge: Cambridge University Press.

—— (1980). 'Le capital social: notes provisoires'. *Actes de la Recherche en Sciences Sociales*, 31: 2–3.

—— (1984). *Distinction: A Social Critique of the Judgement of Taste*. London: Routledge and Kegan Paul.

—— (1986). 'The Forms of Capital', in J. Richardson (ed.), *Handbook of Theory and Research for the Sociology of Education*. New York: Greenwood, 241–8.

—— (1988). *Homo Academicus*. Cambridge: Polity Press.

—— (1991a). *The Craft of Sociology: Epistemological Preliminaries*. New York: de Gruyter.

—— (1991b). *Language and Symbolic Power*. Cambridge: Polity Press.

—— (1997) [1983]. 'The Forms of Capital', in A. H Halsey, H. Lauder, P. Brown, and A. Stuart Wells (eds), *Education: Culture, Economy, Society*. Oxford: Oxford University Press, 46-58.

—— and Coleman, J. (1991). *Social Theory for a Changing Society*. Oxford: Westview Press.

—— and Passeron, J.-C. (1970). *La reproduction*. Paris: Les Éditions de Minuit.

—— —— (1977) [1970]. *Reproduction in Education, Culture and Society*. London: Sage.

Bowles, S. (1998). 'Endogenous Preferences: The Cultural Consequences of Markets and Other Economic Institutions'. *Journal of Economic Literature*, 36/1: 75–111.

—— and Gintis, H. (1976). *Schooling in Capitalist America*. London: Routledge and Kegan Paul.

Boxman, E.A., de Graaf, P. M., and Flap, H. D. (1991). 'The Impact of Social and Human Capital on the Income Attainment of Dutch Managers'. *Social Networks*, 13: 51–73.

Boyarin, J. (1991). *Polish Jews in Paris: The Ethnography of Memory*. Bloomington: Indiana University Press.

Braudel, F. (1973). *The Mediterranean World in the Age of Philip II*. London: Harper Collins.

Breen, T. H. (1993). 'The Meanings of Things: Interpreting the Consumer Economy in the Eighteenth Century', in J. Brewer and R. Porter (eds), *Consumption and the World of Goods*. London: Routledge, 249–60.

Brehm, J. and Rahm, W. (1997). 'Individual-Level Evidence for the Causes and Consequences of Social Capital'. *American Journal of Political Science*, 41/3: 999–1023.

Brewer, J. (1989*a*). 'Conjectural History, Sociology and Social Change in Eighteenth-Century Scotland: Adam Ferguson and the Division of Labour', in D. McCrone, S. Kendrick, and P. Straw (eds), *The Making of Scotland*. Edinburgh: Edinburgh University Press, 13–30.

—— (1989*b*). *The Sinews of Power: War, Money and the English State, 1688–1783*. London: Routledge.

Briggs, A. (1968). *Victorian Cities*. Harmondsworth: Penguin.

Brown, A. and Galligan, Y. (1993). 'Changing the Political Agenda for Women in Scotland and Ireland'. *West European Politics*, 2: 165–89.

—— McCrone, D., and Paterson, L. (1998). *Politics and Society in Scotland* (2nd edn). London: Macmillan.

—— —— —— and Surridge, P. (1999). *The Scottish Electorate: The 1997 General Election and Beyond*. London: Macmillan.

Brown, A. J. (1997). 'Becoming Skilled during a Time of Transition: Observations from Europe'. Paper to Sixth National Career Development Association Conference, Daytona Beach, Fla.

Brown, C. G. (1987). *The Social History of Religion in Scotland, 1780–1914*. London: Methuen.

Brown, P. (1987). *Schooling Ordinary Kids*. London: Tavistock Press.

—— and Lauder, H. (1997). 'Education, Globalization and Economic Development', in A. H. Halsey, H. Lauder, P. Brown and A. Stuart Wells (eds), *Education: Culture, Economy, Society*. Oxford: Oxford University Press, 172–92.

—— —— (2001 in press). *Capitalism and Social Progress*. Basingstoke: Macmillan.

—— —— (2000). 'Child Poverty, Education and Collective Intelligence', in S. Ball (ed.), *Key Papers in the Sociology of Education*. London: Routledge.

—— and Scase, R. (1994). *Higher Education and Corporate Realities*. London: UCL Press.

Brown, S. J. and Fry, M. (1993). *Scotland in the Age of the Disruption*. Edinburgh: Edinburgh University Press.

Burchell, J., Day, D, Hudson, M., Ladipo, D., Mankelow, R., Nolan, J., Reed, H., Wichert, I., and Wilkinson, F. (1999). *Job Insecurity and Work Intensification*. York: Joseph Rowntree Foundation.

Burke, E. (1987). *Reflections on the Revolution in France*. Indianapolis: Hackett.

Burt, R. (1992). *Structural Holes: The Social Structure of Competition*. Cambridge, MA: Harvard University Press.

—— (1997). 'The Contingent Value of Social Capital'. *Administrative Science Quarterly*, 42: 339–65.

—— (1998). 'The Gender of Social Capital'. *Rationality and Society*, 10/1: 5–46.

Bynner, J. (1989). *Transition to Work: Results from a Longitudinal Study of Young People in Four British Labour Markets* (ESRC 16–19 Initiative Occasional Papers No. 4). London: City University.

Calhoun, C. (ed.) (1997). *Habermas and the Public Sphere*. Cambridge, MA: MIT Press.

Campbell, C. and Mzaidume, Y. (1999). 'Social Capital and Grassroots Participation in Community Health Projects.' Paper presented to First International Conference on Critical and Qualitative Approaches to Health Psychology. St Johns, Canada, July.

—— with Wood, R., and Kelly, M. (1999). *Social Capital and Health*. London: Health Education Authority.

Caplan, N, Whitmore, J. K., and Choy, M. H. (1989). *The Boat People and Achievement in America: A Study of Family, Hard Work and Cultural Values*. Ann Arbor: University of Michigan Press.

Carter, A. P. (1994). *Measuring the Performance of a Knowledge-based Economy* (Working Paper No. 337). Waltham, MA: Department of Economics, Brandeis University.

Castells, M. (1996). *The Information Age, Volume 1: The Rise of the Network Society*. Oxford: Basil Blackwell.

—— (1997). *The Information Age, Volume 2: The Power of Identity*. Oxford: Basil Blackwell.

Chandler, A. D. (1992). 'Organizational Capabilities and the Economic History of the Industrial Enterprise'. *Journal of Economic Perspectives*, 3/6: 79–100.

Chastaing, M. (1954). 'Reid, la philosophie du sens commun et la problème de la connaissance d'autrui'. *Revue philosophique*, 144: 352–99.

Checkland, O. (1980). *Philanthropy in Victorian Scotland: Social Welfare and the Voluntary Principle*. Edinburgh: John Donald.

Cherry, S. (1980). 'The Hospitals and Population Growth: The Voluntary General Hospitals, Mortality and Local Populations in the English Provinces in the Eighteenth and Nineteenth Centuries'. *Population Studies*, 34: 59–75, 251–6.

Chitnis, A. C. (1986). *The Scottish Enlightenment and Early Victorian English Society*. London: Croom Helm.

Church of Scotland (1989). 'The government of Scotland', reprinted in L. Paterson (ed.) (1998). *A Diverse Assembly: The Debate on a Scottish Parliament*. Edinburgh: Edinburgh University Press, 183–8.

Clark, C., Dyson, A., Millward, A., and Robson, S. (1999). 'Theories of Inclusion, Theories of Schools: Deconstructing and Reconstructing the "Inclusive" School'. *British Educational Research Journal*, 25/2: 157–77.

Clark, M. M. and Munn, P. (eds) (1997). *Education in Scotland: Policy and Practice from Pre-school to Secondary*. London: Routledge.

Clarke, P. F. and Trebilcock R. C. (eds) (1997). *Understanding Decline: Perceptions and Realities of British Economic Performance*. Cambridge: Cambridge University Press.

Coase, R. H. (1937). 'The Nature of the Firm'. *Economica*, 4: 386–405.

Coats, A. (ed.) (1996). 'Special Issue: The Post-1945 Internationalization of Economics'. *History of Political Economy*, 28/Supplement.

Coburn, D. (2000). 'Income Inequality, Social Cohesion and the Health Status of Populations: The Role of Neo-Liberalism'. *Social Science and Medicine*, 51: 135–46.

Coffield, F. (2000). 'The Structure Below the Surface: Reassessing the Significance of Informal Learning', in F. Coffield (ed.), *The Necessity of Informal Learning*, Bristol: Policy Press, 1–11.

Cohen, A. (1969). *Custom and Politics in Urban Africa: A Study of Hausa Migrants in Yoruba Towns*. London: Routledge and Kegan Paul.

—— (1996). 'Personal Nationalism: A Scottish View of Some Rites, Rights, and Wrongs'. *American Ethnologist*, 23: 802–15.

Cohen, J. L. and Arato, A. (1992). *Civil Society and Political Theory*. Cambridge, MA: MIT Press.

Cohen, R. and Hughes, M. with Ashworth, L. and Blair, M. (1994). *School's Out: The Family Perspective on School Exclusion*. London: Barnardo's and Family Service Unit.

Cohen, S., Doyle, W., Skoner, D., Rabin, P., and Gwaltney, J. (1997). 'Social Ties and Susceptibility to the Common Cold'. *Journal of the American Medical Association*, 277: 1940–4.

—— and Fields, G. (1999). *Social Capital and Capital Gains, Or Virtual Bowling in Silicon Valley: An Examination of Social Capital in Silicon Valley*. Berkeley: Berkeley Round Table on the International Economy (BRIE),University of California.

Coleman, J. S. (1961). *Adolescent Society*. New York: Free Press.

—— (1984). 'Introducing Social Trust into Economic Analysis'. *American Economic Review*, 74/2: 84–8.

—— (1988a). 'Social Capital in the Creation of Human Capital'. *American Journal of Sociology*, 94/Supplement: S95–S120.

—— (1988b). 'The Creation and Destruction of Social Capital: Implications for the Law'. *Notre Dame Journal of Law, Ethics and Public Policy*, 3: 375–404.

—— (1990a). *Foundations of Social Theory*. Cambridge, MA: Harvard University Press.

—— (1990b). 'James S. Coleman', in R. Swedberg (ed.), *Economics and Sociology, Redefining Their Boundaries: Conversations with Economists and Sociologists*. Princeton: Princeton University Press, 47–60.

—— (1990c). *Equality and Achievement in Education*. Boulder, CO: Westview Press.

—— (1991) 'Prologue: Constructed Social Organisation', in P. Bourdieu and J. S. Coleman (eds), *Social Theory for a Changing Society*, Oxford: Westview Press, 1–14.

—— (1994). *Foundations of Social Theory*. Cambridge, MA: Belknap Press.

—— (1997). 'Social Capital in the Creation of Human Capital', in A. H. Halsey, H. Lauder, P. Brown, and A. Stuart Wells (eds), *Education, Culture, Economy and Society*. Oxford: Oxford University Press, 80–95.

—— and Hoffer, T. (1987). *Public and Private Schools: The Impact of Communities*. New York: Basic Books.

Collier, P. (1998). *Social Capital and Poverty* (Social Capital Initiative Working Paper No. 4). Washington, DC: World Bank.

Collins, J. C. and Porras, J. I. (1994). *Built to Last: Successful Habits of Visionary Companies*. London: Century.

Collins, R. (1979). *The Credential Society: An Historical Sociology of Education and Stratification*. New York: Academic Press.

Commission for Racial Equality (1996). *Exclusion From School: The Public Cost*. London: Commission for Racial Equality.

Cooper, H., Arber, S., Fee, L., and Ginn, J. (1999). *The Influence of Social Support and Social Capital on Health: A Review and Analysis of British Data*. London: Health Education Authority.

Coplestone, F. C. (1955). *Aquinas*. Harmondsworth: Penguin.

Cox, E. (1995). *A Truly Civil Society*. Sydney: ABC Books.

Crafts, N.F.R. (1995). 'The Golden Age of Economic Growth in Western Europe, 1950–1973'. *Economic History Review*, 48: 429–47.

Cressy, D. (1993). 'Literacy in Context: Meaning and Measurement in Early Modern England', in J. Brewer and R. Porter (eds), *Consumption and the World of Goods*. London: Routledge, 305–19.

Cross, K.P. (1981). *Adults as Learners*. San Francisco: Jossey-Bass.

Crowther, J., Martin, I., and Shaw, M. (1999). *Popular Education and Social Movements in Scotland Today*. Leicester: National Institute of Adult and Continuing Education.

Cullingford, C. and Morrison, J. (1995). 'Bullying as a Formative Influence: The Relationship Between the Experience of School and Criminality'. *British Educational Research Journal*, 21/5: 547–60.

Dalum, B., Laursen, K., and Villumsen, G. (1998). 'Structural Change in OECD Export Specialisation and Stickiness'. *International Journal of Applied Economics* 13/3: 423–43.

Darling, J. (1989). 'The Moral Teaching of Frances Hutcheson'. *British Journal of Eighteenth-Century Studies*, 12: 165–74.

Dasgupta, P. (2000). 'Economic Progress and the Idea of Social Capital', in P. Dasgupta and I. Serageldin (eds), *Social Capital: A Multifaceted Perspective*. Washington, DC: World Bank, 325–424.

—— and Serageldin, I. (eds) (2000) *Social Capital: A Multifaceted Perspective*. Washington, DC: World Bank

David, P. A. (1985). 'Clio and the Economics of QWERTY'. *American Economic Review*, 75: 332–7.

Davie, G. (1986). *The Crisis of the Democratic Intellect: The Problem of Generalism and Specialism in Twentieth-Century Scotland*. Edinburgh: Edinburgh University Press.

—— (1991). 'The Social Significance of the Scottish Philosophy of Common Sense', in G. Davie, *The Scottish Enlightenment and other Essays*. Edinburgh: Polygon, 51–85.

de Berry, J. (1999). 'Life After Loss: An Anthropological Study of Post-War Recovery, Teso, East Uganda, with Special Reference to Young People'. Ph.D. thesis, London School of Economics.

de Bresson, C. (1996). *Economic Interdependence and Innovative Activity*. Cheltenham: Edward Elgar.

de Planhol, X. (1968). *Les Fondements Géographiques de l'Histoire de l'Islam*. Paris: Flammarion.

de Tocqueville, A. (1969) [1835]. *Democracy in America*, ed. J. P. Mayer. New York: Harper Perennial.

Dei Ottati, G. (1996). 'Trust, Interlinking Transactions and Credit in the Industrial Districts'. *Cambridge Journal of Economics*, 18: 529–46.

Denison, E. F. (1967). *Why Growth Rates Differ*. Washington, DC: Brookings Institution.

Department for Education and Employment (DfEE) (1997). *Education Action Zones: An Introduction*. London: DfEE.

Department of Trade and Industry (1998). *Our Competitive Future: Building the Knowledge Driven Economy*. London: Department of Trade and Industry.

Dewar, D. (1988). 'Williamson lecture'. Stirling University, 21 October, reprinted in L. Paterson (ed.) (1998). *A Diverse Assembly: The Debate on a Scottish Parliament*. Edinburgh: Edinburgh University Press, 169–73.

Dewey J. (1916). *Democracy and Education*. New York: Free Press.

Dierickx, I. and Cool, K. (1989). 'Asset Stock Accumulation and Sustainability of Competitive Advantage'. *Management Science*, 12/35: 1504–13.

Donaldson, W. (1986). *Popular Literature in Victorian Scotland*. Aberdeen: Aberdeen University Press.

Dube, Y., Howes, J., and McQueen, D. (1957). *Housing and Social Capital*. Toronto: Royal Commission on Canada's Economic Prospects.

Durkheim, E. (1933). *Division of Labour in Society*, trans. G. Simpson. New York: Macmillan.

—— (1976) [1915]. *The Elementary Forms of the Religious Life*, trans. J. W. Swain. London: George Allen and Unwin.

—— (1982). *The Rules of Sociological Method and Selected Texts on Sociology and its Method*, ed. S. Lukes. London: Macmillan.

Dyos, H. J. and Reeder, D. A. (1973). 'Slums and Suburbs', in H. J. Dyos and M. Wolf (eds), *The Victorian City: Images and Realities*, i. London: Routledge and Kegan Paul, 359–86.

Economic and Social Research Council (ESRC) (1994). *The Learning Society: Knowledge and Skills for Employment Research Programme*. Swindon: ESRC.

Edwards, B. and Foley, M. (1997). 'Social Capital and the Political Economy of our Discontent'. *American Behavioural Scientist*, 40/5: 669–78.

—— —— (1998). 'Civil Society and Social Capital Beyond Putnam'. *American Behavioural Scientist* 42/1: 124–39.

Edwards, O. D. (1989). *A Claim of Right for Scotland*. Edinburgh: Polygon.

Ekeh, P. (1974). *Social Exchange Theory: The Two Traditions*. Cambridge, MA: Harvard University Press.

Ekins, P. (1992). 'A Four-Capital Model of Wealth Creation', in P. Ekins and M. Max-Neef (eds), *Real Life Economics: Understanding Wealth Creation*. London: Routledge, 147–55.

Elster, J. (1989). 'Social Norms and Economic Theory'. *Journal of Economic Perspectives*, 3/4: 99–117.

Eng, E. and Parker, E. (1994). 'Measuring Community Competence in the Mississippi Delta: The Interface between Programme Evaluation and Empowerment'. *Health Education Quarterly*, 21: 199–210.

Engen, T, O., Kulbrandstad, L. A., and Sand, S. (1997). *Til keiseren hva keiserens er? Om minoritetselevenes læringsstrategier og skoleprestasjoner. Sluttrapport fra prosjektet Minoritetselevenes skoleprestasjoner*. Hamar: Oplandske Bokforlag.

Enright, M. J. (1998). 'Regional Clusters and Firm Strategy', in A. D. Chandler, P. Hagström, and O. Sölvell (eds), *The Dynamic Firm*. Oxford: Oxford University Press, 315–42.

Eraut, M. (2000). 'Non-Formal Learning, Implicit Learning and Tacit Knowledge in Professional Work', in F. Coffield (ed.), *The Necessity of Informal Learning*. Bristol: Policy Press, 12–31.

Etzioni, A. (1996). 'The Responsive Community: A Communitarian Perspective'. *American Sociological Review*, 61: 1–11.

Evans, P. (1995). *Embedded Autonomy: States and Industrial Transformation*. Princeton: Princeton University Press.

Ferguson, A. (1966) [1767]. *An Essay on Civil Society*, ed. D. Forbes. Edinburgh: Edinburgh University Press.

Fernandez Kelly, M. P. (1995). 'Social and Cultural Capital in the Urban Ghetto: Implications for the Economic Sociology of Migration', in A. Portes (ed.), *The Economic Sociology of Immigration*. New York: Russell Sage Foundation, 213–47.

Fevre, R. (1989). 'Informal Practices, Flexible Firms and Private Labour Markets'. *Sociology*, 23/1: 91–109.

—— (1990). 'Sub/contracting and Industrial Development', in S. Kendrick, P. Straw and D. McCrone (eds), *Interpreting the Past, Understanding the Present*. Basingstoke: Macmillan, 196–216.

—— (1992). *The Sociology of Labour Markets*. Hemel Hempstead: Harvester Wheatsheaf.

—— (1998). 'Spirits of the Hive: Different Visions of Economic Rationality and Morality in Late Modernity'. Paper to Work Employment and Society Conference, Cambridge, 14–16 September.

Fevre, R., Gorard, S., and Rees G. (2000). 'Necessary and Unnecessary Learning: The Acquisition of Knowledge and "Skills" In and Outside Employment in South Wales in the Twentieth Century', in F. Coffield (ed.), *The Necessity of Informal Learning*. Bristol: Policy Press, 64–80.

—— Rees, G., and Gorard, S. (1999). 'Some Sociological Alternatives to Human Capital Theory and their Implications for Research on Post-compulsory Education and Training'. *Journal of Education and Work*, 12/2: 117–40.

Field, J. (1999). 'Schooling, Networks and the Labour Market: Explaining Participation in Lifelong Learning in Northern Ireland'. *British Journal of Educational Research*, 24/4: 501–15.

—— and Schuller, T. (1995). 'Is There Less Adult Learning in Scotland and Northern Ireland? A Quantitative Analysis'. *Scottish Journal of Adult and Continuing Education*, 2/2: 71–80.

—— —— (2000, forthcoming). 'Networks, Norms and Trust: Explaining Patterns of Lifelong Learning in Scotland and Northern Ireland', in F. Coffield (ed.), *Differing Visions of the Learning Society: Research Findings*, ii. Bristol: Policy Press.

—— and Spence, L. (2000). 'Social Capital and Informal Learning', in F. Coffield (ed.), *The Necessity of Informal Learning*. Bristol: Policy Press, 32–42.

Fielding, M. (1996). 'Beyond Collaboration: On the Importance of Community', in D. Bridges and C. Husbands (eds), *Consorting and Collaborating in the Market Place*. London: Falmer, 149–67.

Fine, B. (1997). 'The New Revolution in Economics'. *Capital and Class*, 61: 143–8.

—— (1999a). 'From Becker to Bourdieu: Economics Confronts the Social Sciences'. *International Papers in Political Economy*, 5/3: 1–49.

—— (1999b). 'The World Bank and Social Capital: A Critical Skinning', mimeo. London: School of Oriental and African Studies.

—— (1999c). 'A Question of Economics: Is It Colonizing the Social Sciences?'. *Economy and Society*, 28/3: 403–25.

—— (2000). 'Endogenous Growth Theory: A Critical Assessment'. *Cambridge Journal of Economics*, 24/2: 245–65.

—— (2001). *Social Capital versus Social Theory: Political Economy and Social Science at the Turn of the Millennium*. London: Routledge.

Firth, R. W. (1967). *The Work of the Gods in Tikopia* (2nd edn). London: Athlone Press.

Fisher, C., Hout, M., Jankowski, M., Lucas, S., Swidler, A., and Voss, K. (1996). *Inequality by Design: Cracking the Bell Curve Myth*. Princeton: Princeton University Press.

Floud, R. and McCloskey, D. (eds) (1994). *The Economic History of Britain Since 1700* (2nd edn). Cambridge: Cambridge University Press.

—— Wachter, K., and Gregory, A. (1990). *Height, Health and History: Nutritional Status in the United Kingdom, 1750–1980*. Cambridge: Cambridge University Press.

Foley M. W. and Edwards, B. (1997). 'Editors' Introduction: Escape from Politics? Social Theory and the Social Capital Debate'. *American Behavioral Scientist*, 40/5: 550–61. (Special Edition: 'Social Capital, Civil Society and Contemporary Democracy'.)

—— —— (1998). 'Beyond Tocqueville: Civil Society and Social Capital in Comparative Perspective: Editors' Introduction'. *American Behavioral Scientist*, 42/1: 5–20. (Special Edition: 'Beyond Tocqueville: Civil Society and Social Capital in Comparative Perspective'.)

—— —— (1999). 'Is It Time to Disinvest in Social Capital?'. *Journal of Public Policy*, 19: 141–73.

Forbes, D. (1966). 'Introduction', in A. Ferguson (1966) [1767], *An Essay on Civil Society*, ed. D. Forbes. Edinburgh: Edinburgh University Press, xiii–xli.

Foss, N. J. and Loasby, B. J. (eds) (1998). *Economic Organization, Capabilities and Co-ordination*. London and New York: Routledge.

Foucault, M. (1997). *Discipline and Punish: The Birth of the Prison*. London: Allen Lane.

Fox, A. (1974). *Beyond Contract: Work Power and Trust Relations*. London: Faber and Faber.

Freire, P. (1970/1993). *The Pedagogy of the Oppressed*. London: Penguin.

Fry, M. (1987). *Patronage and Principle: A Political History of Modern Scotland*. Aberdeen: Aberdeen University Press.

Fukuyama, F. (1992). *The End of History and the Last Man*. New York: Free Press.

—— (1995). *Trust: The Social Virtues and the Creation of Prosperity*. New York: The Free Press.

—— (1999). *The Great Disruption: Human Nature and the Reconstitution of Social Order*. New York: The Free Press.

Fuligni, A. J. (1997). 'The Academic Achievement of Adolescents from Immigrant Families: The Roles of Family Background, Attitudes and Behavior'. *Child Development*, 68/2: 351–63.

Galbraith J. K. (1993). *The Culture of Contentment*. Harmondsworth: Penguin.

Galston, W. A. and Levine, P. (1997). 'America's Civic Condition: A Glance at the Evidence'. *The Brookings Review*, 15/4: 23–6.

Gamarnikov, E. and Green, A. (1999). 'Developing Social Capital: Dilemmas, Possibilities and Limitations in Education', in A. Hayton (ed.), *Tackling Disaffection and Social Exclusion*. London: Kogan Page, 46–64.

Gambetta, D. (1988). *Trust: Making and Breaking Co-operative Relations*. Oxford: Basil Blackwell.

Gamm, G. and Putnam, R. D. (1999). 'The Growth of Voluntary Associations in America, 1840–1940'. *Journal of Interdisciplinary History*, 29: 511–57.

Gardner, H. (1993). *Frames of Mind: The Theory of Multiple Intelligences* (2nd edn). London: Fontana.

Gellner, E. (1995). 'The Importance of Being Modular', in J. A. Hall (ed.), *Civil Society*. Cambridge: Polity Press, 32–55.

General Accounting Office (USA) (1994). *Elementary School Children: Many Change School Frequently, Harming Their Education: Report to the Hon. Marcy Kaptur*. Washington, DC: House of Representatives.

Gibson, A. (1979). *People Power*. Harmondsworth: Penguin.

Gibson, M. A. and Bhachu, P. K. (1991). 'The Dynamics of Educational Decision Making: A Comparative Study of Sikhs in Britain and the United States', in M. A. Gibson and J. U. Ogbu (eds), *Minority Status and Schooling: A Comparative Study of Immigrant and Involuntary Minorities*. New York: Garland, 63–96.

—— and Ogbu, J. U. (eds) (1991), *Minority Status and Schooling: A Comparative Study of Immigrant and Involuntary Minorities*. New York: Garland.

Giddens, A. (1991). *Modernity and Self Identity: Self and Society in the Late Modern Age*. Cambridge: Polity Press.

Gillborn, D. (1997). 'Ethnicity and Educational Performance in the United Kingdom: Racism, Ethnicity, and Variability in Achievement'. *Anthropology and Education Quarterly*, 28/3: 351–74.

Gillborn, D. and Gipps, C. (1996). *Recent Research on the Achievements of Ethnic Minority Pupils*. London: Her Majesty's Stationery Office (Ofsted Reviews of Research Series).

Gillies, P. (1998). 'The Effectiveness of Alliances and Partnerships for Health Promotion.' *Health Promotion International*, 13: 1–21.

—— Tolley, K., and Wolstenholme, J. (1996). 'Is AIDS a Disease of Poverty?' *AIDS Care*, 8/3: 351–63.

Gilligan, C. (1982). *In a Different Voice*. Cambridge, MA: Harvard University Press.

Gilsenan, M. (1973). *Saint and Sufi in Modern Egypt: An Essay in the Sociology of Religion*. Oxford: Clarendon Press.

Glaeser, E. L., Laibson, C. L., Scheinkman, J. A., and Soutter, C. L. (1999). *What Is Social Capital? The Determinants of Trust and Trustworthiness* (Working Paper No. 7216). Cambridge, MA: NBER.

Godwin, R. K. (1988). *One Billion Dollars of Influence*. Chatham House, NJ: Chatham House.

Goffman, E. (1975). *Frame Analysis*. Harmondsworth: Penguin.

Goldthorpe, J. (1996). 'The Uses of History in Sociology: Reflections on Some Recent Tendencies', in M. Bulmer and G. Rees (eds), *Citizenship Today: The Contemporary Relevance of T. H. Marshall*. London: UCL Press, 101–24.

—— Llewllyn, C., and Payne, C. (1980). *Social Mobility and Class Structure in Modern Britain*. Oxford: Clarendon Press.

—— Lockwood, D., Bechofer, F., and Platt, J. (1968–9). *The Affluent Worker*, 3 vols. Cambridge: Cambridge University Press.

Goleman, D. (1996). *Emotional Intelligence*. London: Bloomsbury.

Goodman, R., Speers, M., McLeroy, K., Fawcett, S., Kegler, M., Parker, E., Smith, S., Sterling, T., and Wallerstein, N. (1998). 'Identifying and Defining the Dimensions of Community Capacity to Provide a Basis for Measurement'. *Health Education and Behaviour*, 25/3: 258–78.

Gorard, S., Rees G., and Fevre, R. (1999a). 'Patterns of Participation in Lifelong Learning: Do Families Make a Difference?' *British Educational Research Journal*, 25/4: 517–32.

—— —— —— (1999b). 'Two Dimensions of Time: The Changing Social Context of Lifelong Learning'. *Studies in the Education of Adults*, 31/1: 35–48.

—— —— —— and Furlong, J. (1997). *Learning Trajectories: Some Voices of Those in Transit* (Working Paper No. 11). Cardiff: School of Education, University of Cardiff.

—— —— —— Renold, E., and Furlong, J. (1998). 'A Gendered Appraisal of the Transition to a Learning Society', in R. Benn (ed.), *Research, Teaching and Learning: Making Connections in the Education of Adults*. Leeds: SCUTREA, 62–7.

Gordon, D., Shaw, M., Dorling, D., and Davey Smith, G. (1999). *Inequalities in Health: The Evidence Presented to the Independent Enquiry into Inequalities in Health*. Bristol: Policy Press.

Gough, I., (1996). 'Justifying Basic Income?' *Imprints*, 1: 82–3.

Gould, S. (1981). *The Mismeasure of Man*. London: Pelican.

Granovetter M. (1973). 'The Strength of Weak Ties'. *American Journal of Sociology*, 78/4: 1350–80.

—— (1974). *Getting a Job: A Study of Contracts and Careers*. Cambridge, MA: Harvard University Press.

—— (1985) 'Economic action and social structure: the problem of embeddedness'. *American Journal of Sociology*, 91, 3 (November): 481–510.

—— (1994). 'Business Groups', in N. J. Smelser and R. Swedberg (eds), *The Handbook of Economic Sociology*. Princeton: Princeton University Press, 453–75.

Grave, S. A. (1960). *The Scottish Philosophy of Common Sense*. Oxford: Oxford University Press.

Gray, P. and Noakes, J. (1993). 'Reintegration of Children with Challenging Behaviours into the Mainstream School Community' in A. Miller and D. Lane (eds), *Silent Conspiracies: Scandals and Success in the Care and Education of Vulnerable Young People*. Stoke: Trentham Books, 47–74.

Green, D. (1994). *Re-inventing Civil Society*. London: Institute of Economic Affairs.

—— (1995). *Community Without Politics*. London: Institute of Economic Affairs.

Green, F., Ashton, D., and Sung J. (1999). 'The Role of the State in Skill Formation: Evidence from the Republic of Korea, Singapore, and Taiwan'. *Oxford Review of Economic Policy*, 15/1: 82–96.

Grootaert, C. (1997). *Social Capital: The Missing Link?* (Social Capital Initiative Working Paper No. 3). Washington, DC: World Bank.

Habermas, J. (1984) [1981]. *The Theory of Communicative Action I. Reason and the Rationalisation of Society*. London: Heinemann.

—— (1987*a*) [1968]. *Knowledge and Human Interests*. Cambridge: Polity Press.

—— (1987*b*). *The Philosophical Discourse of Modernity*, trans. F. Lawrence. Cambridge, MA: MIT Press.

—— (1989). *The Structural Transformation of the Public Sphere: An Inquiry into a Category of Bourgeois Society*. Cambridge, MA: MIT Press.

Hacking, I. (1975). *The Emergence of Probability*. Cambridge: Cambridge University Press.

—— (1990). *The Taming of Chance*. Cambridge: Cambridge University Press.

Hagen, E. E. (1964). *On the Theory of Social Change*. Homewood, IL: Dorsey Press.

Hall, J. A. (1995). 'In Search of Civil Society', in J. A. Hall (ed.), *Civil Society*. Cambridge: Polity Press, 1–31.

—— and Lindholm, C. (1999). *Is American Breaking Apart?* Princeton: Princeton University Press.

Hall, P. (1999). 'Social Capital in Britain'. *British Journal of Political Science*, 29/3: 417–61.

Hall, R. E. and Jones, C. I. (1999). 'Why Do Some Countries Produce So Much More Output Per Worker Than Others?' *Quarterly Journal of Economics*, 114/1: 83–116.

Hall, S. and Held, D. (1989). 'Citizens and Citizenship', in S. Hall and M. Jacques (eds), *New Times*. London: Lawrence and Wishart, 173–88.

Halpern, D. (1998). *Social Capital, Exclusion and the Quality of Life: Towards a Causal Model and Policy Implications*. London: Nexus.

—— (1999). *Social Capital, Exclusion and the Quality of Life*. London: Institute for Public Policy Research.

Halsey, A. H. (1972). *Educational Priority: EPA Problems and Policies*, i. London: HMSO.

—— and Young, M. (1997). 'The Family and Social Justice', in A.H. Halsey, H. Lauder, P. Brown, and A. Stuart Wells (eds), *Education: Culture, Economy and Society*. Oxford: Oxford University Press, 784–98.

—— Lauder, H., Brown, P., and Stuart Wells, A. (eds) (1997). *Education: Culture, Economy and Society*. Oxford: Oxford University Press.

Hammersely, M. (1997). 'Educational Research and Teaching: A Response to David Hargreaves' TTA Lecture'. *British Educational Research Journal*, 23/2: 141–62.

Hancock, T. (1993). 'The Healthy City from Concept to Application', in J. Kelley and M. Davies (eds), *Healthy Cities: Research and Practice*. London: Routledge, 14–24.

Hanifan L. J. (1920). *The Community Center*. Boston: Silver, Burdett and Co.

Hannan, C. (1999). *Beyond Networks: 'Social Cohesion' and Unemployment Exit Rates* (Discussion Paper No. 99/28). Colchester: Institute for Labour Research, University of Essex.

Hargreaves, A. (1980). 'Synthesis and the Study of Strategies: A Project for the Sociological Imagination', in P. Woods (ed), *Pupil Strategies: Explorations in the Sociology of the Secondary School*. London: Croom Helm, 162–97.

Hargreaves, D. (1996). *Teaching as a Research-based Profession*. London: Teacher Training Agency.

—— (1997). 'In Defence of Research for Evidence-based Teaching: A Rejoinder to Martyn Hammersely'. *British Educational Research Journal* 23/4: 405–20.

Harrison, B. (1992). 'Industrial Districts: Old Wine in New Bottles?' *Regional Studies*, 26: 469–83.

Harrison, R. (1993). 'Disaffection and Access', in J. Calder (ed.), *Disaffection and Diversity: Overcoming Barriers to Adult Learning*. London: Falmer, 2–18.

Harriss, J. and De Renzio, P. (1997). 'An Introductory Bibliographic Essay'. *Journal of Development Studies*, 9/7: 919–37 (Special Issue, ed. J. Harriss: 'Policy Arena: "Missing Link" or "Analytically Missing": The Concept of Social Capital'.)

Harvie, C. (1977). *Scotland and Nationalism: Scottish Society and Politics, 1707–1977*. London: Allen and Unwin.

—— (1981). *No Gods and Precious Few Heroes*. London: Edward Arnold.

—— (1990). 'Gladstonianism, the Provinces, and Popular Political Culture, 1860–1906', in R. Bellamy (ed.), *Victorian Liberalism*. London: Routledge, 152–74.

Hawken, P., Lovins, A., and Lovins, L. (1999). *Natural Capitalism: The Next Industrial Revolution*. London: Earthscan.

Hayes, M. T. (1986). 'The New Group Universe', in A. J. Cigler and B. A. Loomis (eds), *Interest Group Politics* (2nd edn). Washington, DC: Congressional Quarterly Press, 133–45.

Hearn, J. S. (1998). 'The Social Contract: Re-Framing Scottish Nationalism'. *Scottish Affairs*, 23/Spring: 14–26.

—— (forthcoming). 'Introduction', in J. S. Hearn (ed.), *Taking Liberties: Contesting Visions of the Civil Society Project* (Special Issue of *Critique of Anthropology*).

Helland, H. (1997) *Etnisitet og skoletilpasning. En undersøkelse av norske, pakistanske og konfusianske Osloungdommers skoleprestasjoner*. Magistergradsavhandling. Institutt for sosiologi og samfunnsgeografi, Universitetet i Oslo.

Hennock, E. P. (1973). *Fit and Proper Persons: Ideal and Reality in Nineteenth-Century Urban Government*. London: Edward Arnold.

—— (1987). *British Social Reform and German Precedents: The Case of Social Insurance 1880–1914*. Oxford: Clarendon Press.

Hernes, G. (1979). *Forhandlingsøkonomi og blandingsadministrasjon*, Oslo: Universitetsforlaget.

Herrnstein, R. and Murray, C. (1994). *The Bell Curve: Intelligence and Class Structure in American Life*. New York: Free Press.

Higgins, J. (1999). 'Closer to Home: The Case for Experiential Participation in Health Reforms'. *Canadian Journal of Public Health*, 90/1: 30–4.

Hill, M. (1993). *The Policy Process: A Reader*. New York: Harvester Wheatsheaf.

Hirsch, F. (1977). *The Social Limits to Growth*. London: Routledge and Kegan Paul.

Hirschman, Albert O. (1984). *Getting Ahead Collectively: Grassroots Experiences in Latin America*. New York: Pergamon Press.

Hirschon, R. (1989). *Heirs of the Greek Catastrophe: The Social Life of Asia Minor Refugees in Piraeus*. Oxford: Clarendon.

—— (2000). 'The Creation of Community: Well-Being without Wealth in an Urban Greek Refugee Locality', in M. Cernea (ed.), *Risks And Reconstruction: Experiences of Resettlers and Refugees*. Washington, DC: World Bank, 393–411.

Hirst, P. (1994). *Associative Democracy*. Cambridge: Polity Press.

Hodgson, G. M. (1988). *Economics and Institutions*. Cambridge: Polity Press.

—— and Rothman, H. (1999). 'The Editors and Authors of Economics Journals: A Case of Institutional Oligopoly?' *Economic Journal*, 109/453: 1165–86.

Hodkinson, P., Sparkes A., and Hodkinson, H. (1996). *Triumph and Tears: Young People, Markets and the Transition from School to Work*. London: David Fulton.

Hoffer, T., Greeley, A., and Coleman, J. S. (1985). 'Achievement and Growth in Public and Catholic Schools'. *Sociology of Education*, 58/2: 74–97.

Hogwood, B. W. and Gunn, L. A. (1984). *Policy Analysis for the Real World*. Oxford: Oxford University Press.

Hollis, M. (1988). *The Cunning of Reason*. Cambridge: Cambridge University Press.

Hopmann, S. and Konzali, R. (1997). 'Close our Schools! Against Trends in Policy-Making, Educational Theory and Curriculum Studies'. *Journal of Curriculum Studies*, 29/3: 259–66.

Hughes, D. and Lauder, H. (1991). 'Human Capital Theory and the Wastage Of Talent'. *New Zealand Journal of Educational Studies*, 26: 5–20.

Hume, D. (1978) [1739]. *A Treatise of Human Nature*, ed. L. A. Selby-Brigge and P. H. Nidditch. Oxford: Oxford University Press.

Hutton, W. (1996) *The State We're In* (revised edn). London: Vintage.

Hydén, G. (1997). 'Civil Society, Social Capital and Development: Dissection of a Complex Discourse'. *Studies in Comparative International Development*, 32/1: 3–30.

Imich, A. (1994). 'Exclusions from School: Current Trends and Issues'. *Educational Research*, 36/1: 3–11.

Institute of Cultural Affairs International (1998). *Beyond Prince and Merchant: Citizen Participation and the Rise of Civil Society*. New York: Pact Publications.

Israel, B., Checkoway, B., Schulz, A., and Zimmerman, M. (1994). 'Health Education and Community Empowerment: Conceptualising and Measuring Perceptions of Individual, Organisational and Community Control'. *Health Education Quarterly*, 21/2: 149–70.

Jacobs, J. (1961). *The Death and Life of Great American Cities: The Failure of Town Planning*. New York: Random House.

James, W. (1997). 'The Names of Fear: Memory, History and the Ethnography of Feeling among Uduk Refugees'. *Journal of the Royal Anthropological Institute*, 13/1: 115–31.

Johnson, T. (1972). *Professions and Power*. London: Macmillan.

Jones, R. R. (1998). 'Conceptualizing Social Capital, Civil Society, and Democratic Consolidation'. Paper presented at the Western Political Science Association Annual Meeting, Los Angeles, California, 19–21 March.

Jordan, G. and Maloney, W. A. (1997). *The Rise of the Protest Business: Mobilizing Campaign Groups*. Manchester: Manchester University Press.

Kaestle, C. F. (1983). *Pillars of the Republic: Common Schools and American Society, 1780–1860*. New York: Hill and Wang.

Kandel, D. B. (1999). 'Coleman's Contributions to Understanding Youth and Adolescence', in J. Clark (ed.), *James S. Coleman*. London: Falmer, 33–45.

Katz, E. and A. Ziderman (1990). 'Investment in General Training: The Role of Information and Labour Mobility'. *Economic Journal*, 100: 1147–58.

Katzenstein, P. J. (1985). *Small States in World Markets: Industrial Policy in Europe*. New York: Cornell University Press.

Kawachi, I. and Kennedy, B. (1999). 'Income Inequality and Health: Pathways and Mechanisms'. *Health Services Research*, 34/1: 215–27.

Kawachi, I., Kennedy, B., and Wilkinson, R. (1999*a*). 'Crime: Social Disorganisation and Relative Deprivation'. *Social Science and Medicine*, 48: 719–31.

—— —— —— (eds) (1999*b*). *The Society and Population Health Reader: Income Inequality and Health*. New York: The New Press.

—— —— Kimberly L., and Prothrow-Smith, D. (1997). 'Social Capital, Income Inequality and Mortality'. *American Journal of Public Health*, 87/9: 1491–8.

Kay, J. A. (1993). *Foundations of Corporate Success: How Business Strategies Add Value*. Oxford: Oxford University Press.

Kazee, T. A. and Roberts, S. L. (1998). 'Eroding Political Trust in America: An Assessment of Its Nature and Implications'. Paper to American Political Science Association Annual Conference, Boston, 3–6 September.

Keane, J. (1998). *Civil Society: Old Images, New Visions*. Cambridge: Polity Press.

Keep, E. (1997). ' "There's No Such Thing as Society. . . ": Some Problems with an Individual Approach to Creating a Learning Society'. *Journal of Educational Policy*, 12/6: 457–71.

Kelley, J. and Davies, M. (1993). 'Healthy Cities: Research and Practice', in J. Kelley and M. Davies (eds), *Healthy Cities: Research and Practice*. London: Routledge, 1–13.

Kennedy, B., Kawachi, I., and Brainerd, E. (1998). 'The Role of Social Capital in the Russian Mortality Crisis'. *World Development*, 26/11: 2029–43.

Kerr, C., Dunlop., J., Harbison., F., and Meyer, C., (1973). *Industrialism and Industrial Man*. Harmondsworth: Penguin.

Kidd, C. (1993). *Subverting Scotland's Past*. Cambridge: Cambridge University Press.

Kinder, K. and Wilkin, A. (1998). *With All Respect: Reviewing Disaffection Strategies*. Slough: National Foundation for Educational Research.

Kinsley, J. (1968). *Commentary*, Vol. III of J. Kinsley (ed.), *The Poems and Songs of Robert Burns*. Oxford: Clarendon Press.

Klees, S. (1986). 'Planning and Policy Analysis in Education: What Can Economics Tell Us?' *Comparative Education Review*, 30: 574–607.

Knack, S. (1999), *Social Capital, Growth and Poverty: A Survey of Cross-Country Evidence* (Social Capital Initiative Working Paper No. 4). Washington, DC: World Bank.

—— and P. Keefer (1997). 'Does Social Capital Have an Economic Payoff? A Cross-Country Investigation'. *Quarterly Journal of Economics*, 62/4: 1251–88.

Knoke, D. and Kuklinski, J. (1991). 'Network Analysis: Basic Concepts', in G. Thompson, J. France, R. Levacic, and J. Mitchell (eds), *Markets, Hierarchies and Networks: The Coordination of Social Life*. London: Sage, 173–82.

Kolankiewicz, G. (1996). 'Social Capital and Social Change'. *British Journal of Sociology*, 47/3: 427–41.

Kontogiorgi, E. (1996). 'The Rural Settlement of Greek Refugees in Macedonia, 1923–30', D.Phil thesis, University of Oxford.

Krange, O. and Bakken, A. (1998). 'Innvandrerungdoms skoleprestasjoner: Tradisjonelle klasseskiller eller nye skillelinjer?' *Tidsskrift for samfunnsforskning*, 39/3: 381–410.

Kreuter, M. (1997). *National Level Assessment of Community Health Promotion Using Indicators of Social Capital*, WHO/EURO Working Group Report. Atlanta: CDC.

Krishna, A. (2000). 'Creating and Harnessing Social Capital', in P. Dasgupta and I. Serageldin (eds), *Social Capital. A Multifaceted Perspective*. Washington, DC: World Bank, 71–93.

Kuznets, S. (1971). *Economic Growth of Nations: Total Output and Population Structure*. Cambridge, MA: MIT Press.

Labonte, R (1999). 'Social Capital and Community Development: Practitioner Emptor'. *Australia and New Zealand Journal of Public Health*, 23/4: 430–3.

Lacey, C. (1988). 'The Idea of a Socialist Education', in H. Lauder and P. Brown (eds), *Education in Search of a Future*. Basingstoke: Falmer Press, 91–8.

Ladas, S. P. (1932). *The Balkan Exchange of Minorities: Bulgaria, Greece and Turkey*. New York: Macmillan.

Ladd, E. C. (1996). 'The Data Just Don't Show Erosion of America's Social Capital'. *The Public Prospect*, 7/4: 7–16.

Langford, C. (1989). *A Polite and Commercial People: England 1727–83*. Oxford: Oxford University Press.

Lasch, C. (1991). *The Culture of Narcissism*. New York: Norton.

Lash, S. and Urry, J. (1993). *Economies of Signs and Space*. London: Sage.

Lauder, H. and Hughes, D. (1990). 'Social Origins, Destinations and Educational Inequality', in J. Codd, R. Harker, and R. Nash (eds), *Political Issues in New Zealand Education*. Palmerston North: The Dunmore Press.

—— ——, Watson, S., Waslander, S., Thrupp, M., Strathdee, R., Simiyu, I., Dupuis, A., McGlinn, J., and Hamlin, J. (1999). *Trading in Futures: Why Markets in Education Don't Work*. Buckingham: Open University Press.

Lauglo, J. (1996). *Motbakke, men mer driv? Innvandrerungdom i norsk skole*. UNGforskrapport 6/96. Oslo: NOVA.

—— (1999). 'Working Harder to Make the Grade. Immigrant Youth in Norwegian Schools'. *Journal of Youth Studies*, 2/1: 77–100.

Lave, J. and Wenger, E. (1991). *Situated Learning: Legitimate Peripheral Participation*. Cambridge: Cambridge University Press.

Lawrence, B. and Hayden, C. (1997). 'Primary School Exclusions'. *Educational Research and Evaluation*, 3/1: 54–77.

Laybourn, K. (1990). *Britain on the Breadline: A Social and Political History of Britain Between the Wars*. Gloucester: Alan Sutton.

Lazear, E. P. (1998). *Personnel Economics for Managers*. New York: John Wiley.

Lee, F. and Harley, S. (1998). 'Peer Review, the Research Assessment Exercise and the Demise of Non-Mainstream Economics'. *Capital and Class*, 66: 23–51.

Lemann, N. (1996). 'Kicking in Groups'. *The Atlantic Monthly*, April: 1–9.

Lenman, B. (1981). *Integration, Enlightenment and Industrialisation: Scotland 1746–1832*. London: Edward Arnold.

Levi, M. (1996). 'Social and Unsocial Capital: A Review Essay of Putnam's "Making Democracy Work" '. *Politics and Society*, 24/1: 45–55.

Levi, P. (1959). *Survival in Auschwitz: The Nazi Assault on Humanity*. New York: Orion Press.

Levi-Strauss, C. (1969). *The Elementary Structures of Kinship*. Boston: Beacon Press.

Levitt, I. (1988). *Government and Social Conditions in Scotland, 1845–1919*. Edinburgh: Scottish History Society.

Lippman, S. A. and Rumelt, R. P. (1982). 'Uncertain Imitability: An Analysis of Interfirm Differences in Efficiency under Competition'. *Bell Journal of Economics*, 12: 418–38.

Loasby, B. J. (1992). 'Market Co-ordination', in: B. J. Caldwell and S. Boehm (eds), *Austrian Economics: Tension and New Directions*. Boston: Kluwer, 137–56.

Lødding, B. (1997). *For ellers får jeg ikke jobb etterpå . . ." Søkning, opptak og progresjon i videregående opplæring blant tospråklig ungdom. Evaluering av Reform 94: Underveisrapport høsten 1996*, Oslo: Norsk Institutt for Studier av Forskning og Utdanning.

Løfgren, H. (1991). *Elever med annat hemspråk än svenska*. Pedagogisk Orientering och Debatt, Malmö: Lärarhögskolan i Malmö—Lunds Universitet.

Loizos, P. (1981). *The Heart Grown Bitter: A Chronicle of Cypriot War Refugees*. Cambridge: Cambridge University Press.

—— (1999). 'Ottoman Half-Lives: Long-Term Perspectives on Particular Forced Migrations'. *Journal of Refugee Studies*, 12/3: 237–63.

Lomas, J. (1998). 'Social Capital and Health: Implications for Public Health and Epidemiology'. *Social Science and Medicine*, 47/9: 1181–8.

Lowndes, V., Stoker, G., Pratchett, L., Leach, S., and Wingfield, M. (1998). *Enhancing Public Participation in Local Government*. London: Department of the Environment, Transport and Regions.

Luhmann, N. (1988). 'Familiarity, Confidence, Trust: Problems and Alternatives', in D. Gambetta (ed.), *Trust: Making and Breaking Co-operative Relations*. Oxford: Basil Blackwell, 94–107.

Lundvall, B.-Å. (ed.) (1992). *National Systems of Innovation: Towards a Theory of Innovation and Interactive Learning*. London: Pinter.

—— and Maskell, P. (forthcoming). 'Nation States and Economic Development: From National Systems of Production to National Systems of Knowledge Creation and Learning', in G. L. Clark, M. P. Feldmann, and M. S. Gertler (eds), *Handbook of Economic Geography*. Oxford: Oxford University Press.

MacGillivray, A., Weston, C., and Unsworth, C. (1998). *Communities Count: A Step by Step Guide to Community Sustainability Indicators*. London: New Economics Foundation.

MacIntyre, A. (1985). *After Virtue*. London: Duckworth.

Macintyre, S. and Ellaway, A. (1999). 'Local Opportunity Structures, Social Capital and Social Inequalities in Health: What Can Central and Local Government Do?'. Paper presented at the 11th Australian Health Promotion Conference, Perth, May.

Mackay, F. (1996). *Women and Representation: Discourses of Equality and Difference*. Edinburgh: University of Edinburgh.

Mackintosh, J. P. (1968). *The Devolution of Power*. Harmondsworth: Penguin.

Macnaghten, P., Grove-White, R., Jacobs, M., and Wynne, B. (1995). *Public Perceptions and Sustainability in Lancashire: Indicators, Institutions and Participation*. Lancaster: Centre for the Study of Environmental Change, Lancaster University for Lancashire County Council.

MacRae, D. (1969). 'Adam Ferguson', in T. Raison (ed.), *The Founding Fathers of Social Science*. Harmondsworth: Penguin, 17–26.

Madden, E. H. (1968). *Civil Disobedience and Moral Law in Nineteenth Century American Philosophy*. Seattle: University of Washington Press.

—— (1998). 'Common Sense School', in E. Craig (ed.), *Encyclopaedia of Philosophy*. London: Routledge, 446–8.

Malmberg, A. and Maskell, P. (1997). 'Towards an Explanation of Industry Agglomeration and Regional Specialization'. *European Planning Studies*, 5/1: 25–41.

Maloney, W. A. (1999). 'Contracting Out the Participation Function: Social Capital and Checkbook Participation', in J. van Deth, M. Maraffi, K. Newton, and P. Whiteley (eds), *Social Capital and European Democracy*. London: Routledge, 108–19.

—— and Jordan, G. (1997). 'The Rise of Protest Businesses in Britain', in J. W. van Deth (ed.), *Private Groups and Public Life: Social Participation, Voluntary Associations, and Political Involvement in Representative Democracies*. London: Routledge, 107–24.

—— Smith, G., and Stoker, G. (1998). 'Social Capital and Urban Governance: Adding a More Contextualized "Top-Down" Perspective'. Paper presented to Political Studies Association Workshop, University of Bath Jean Monnet Centre of Excellence, 6 November.

———— ———— ———— (forthcoming). 'Social Capital and Urban Governance: Adding a More Contextualized "Top-Down" Perspective'. *Political Studies*.

Manns, J. W. (1994). *Reid and his French Disciples*. Leiden: Brill.

Mansur, F. (1972). *Bodrum: A Town in the Aegean*. Leiden: Brill.

Maraffi, M. (1998). 'Voluntary Associations, Political Culture and Social Capital in Italy: A Complex Relationship'. *European Consortium for Political Research News*, 9/Summer: 15–17.

Marquand, D. (1988). *The Unprincipled Society*. London: Jonathan Cape.

Marr, A. (1995). *Ruling Britannia: The Failure and Future of British Democracy*. London: Michael Joseph.

Marsden, P. V. (1990). 'Network Data and Measurement'. *Annual Review of Sociology*, 16: 435–63.

Marshall, G., Newby, H., Rose, D., and Vogler, C. (1989). *Social Class in Modern Britain*. London: Routledge.

Marshall, T. H. (1950). *Citizenship and Social Class, and Other Essays*. Cambridge: Cambridge University Press.

Marwick, A. (1964). 'Middle Opinion in the Thirties: Planning, Progress, and Political "Agreement" '. *English Historical Review*, 79: 285–98.

Marx, K. (1961). 'The Material Forces and the Relations of Production', in T. Parsons, E. Shils, K. D. Naegele, and J. R. Pitts (eds), *Theories of Society: Foundations of Modern Sociological Theory*, i. New York: Free Press, 136–8.

———— (1976) *Capital: Volume One*. Harmondsworth: Penguin.

Maskell, P. (1997). 'Learning in the Village Economy of Denmark: The Role of Institutions and Policy in Sustaining Competitiveness', in H. J. Braczyk, P. Cooke, and M. Heidenreich (eds), *Regional Innovation Systems: The Role of Governance in a Globalized World*. London: UCL-Press, 190–213.

———— (1998). 'Successful Low-Tech Industries in High-Cost Environments: The Case of the Danish Furniture Industry'. *European Urban and Regional Studies*, 5/2: 99–118.

———— and Törnqvist, G. (1999). *Building a Cross-Border Learning Region: The Emergence of the Northern European Øresund Region*. Copenhagen: Copenhagen Business School Press.

———— Eskelinen, H., Hannibalsson, I., Malmberg, A., and Vatne, E. (1998). *Competitiveness, Localised Learning and Regional Development: Specialisation and Prosperity in Small Open Economies*. London: Routledge.

Matarosso, F. (1997). *Use or Ornament?: The Social Impact of Participation in the Arts*. London: Comedia.

Maxwell, S. (1982). 'The Secular Pulpit: Presbyterian Democracy in the Twentieth Century', in H. M. Drucker and N. Drucker (eds), *Scottish Government Yearbook 1982*. Edinburgh: Unit for the Study of Government in Scotland, University of Edinburgh, 181–98.

Maynard, R. A. and Mcgrath, D. J. (1997). 'Family Structure, Fertility and Child Welfare', in J. Behrman and N. Stacey (eds), *The Social Benefits of Education*. Detroit: University of Michigan Press, 125–74.

McCrone, D. (1992). *Understanding Scotland: The Sociology of a Stateless Nation*. London: Routledge.

McMahon, W. (1998). 'Conceptual Framework for the Analysis of the Social Benefits of Lifelong Learning'. *Education Economics*, 6/3: 309–46.

McMillan, D. and Chavis, D. (1986). 'Sense of Community: A Definition and Theory'. *Journal of Community Psychology*, 14: 6–23.

McMillan, J. (1997). 'Losing Sight of Tinkerbell'. *The Herald*, 16 August: 32, reprinted in L. Paterson (ed.) (1998). *A Diverse Assembly: The Debate on a Scottish Parliament*. Edinburgh: Edinburgh University Press, 296–8.

Mead, G. H. (1967). *Mind, Self and Society*, Chicago: Chicago University Press.

Mellor, A. (1999). 'Victims of Bullying', in H. Kemshall and J. Prichard (eds), *Good Practice in Working with Victims of Violence*. London: Jessica Kingsley, 75–88.

Menzel, U. (1980). *Der entwicklungsweg Dänemarks (1880–1940) Ein Beitrag zum konzept autozentrierter entwicklung. Projekt Untersuchung zur grundlegung einer praxisorientierten theorie autozentrierter entwicklung*. Forschungsbericht No. 8. Bremen: Bremen Universität.

Merton, R. K. (1964). *Social Theory and Social Structure*. New York: Free Press.

Meyerson, E. M. (1994). 'Human Capital, Social Capital and Compensation: The Relative Contribution of Social Contacts to Managers' Incomes'. *Acta Sociologica*, 37: 383–99.

Milburn, K. (1995). 'A Critical Review of Peer Education with Young People with Special Reference to Sexual Health'. *Health Education Research: Theory and Practice*,10/4: 407–20.

Miller, C. (ed.) (1998). *Developing and Newly Industrializing Countries*. Cheltenham: Edward Elgar.

Mills, C. W. (1959). *The Sociological Imagination*. Harmondsworth: Penguin.

Mondak, J. (1998). 'Editor's Introduction', in *Political Psychology*, 19/3: 434–40 (Special Issue: 'Psychological Approaches to Social Capital').

Morgan, A. (1999). 'Developing an Index of Social Capital: Experience from the Health Education Authority, England'. Paper presented to the 11th Australian Health Promotion Conference, Perth, May.

Morris, C. T. and Adelman, I. (1988). *Comparative Patterns of Economic Development 1850–1914*. Baltimore: John Hopkins University Press.

Morris, R. J. (1990). 'Scotland 1830–1914: The Making of a Nation Within a Nation', in W. H. Fraser and R. J. Morris (eds), *People and Society in Scotland, Vol. II: 1830–1914*. Edinburgh: John Donald, 1–7.

—— (1992). 'Victorian Values in Scotland and England', in T. C. Smout (ed.), *Victorian Values*. Oxford: Oxford University Press, 31–47.

Morrow, V. (1999). 'Conceptualising Social Capital in Relation to Health and Well-Being for Children and Young People: A Critical Review'. *Sociological Review*, 47/4: 744–65.

Mortimore, P. and Whitty, G. (1999). 'School Improvement: A Remedy for Social Exclusion?', in A. Hayton (ed.), *Tackling Disaffection and Social Exclusion*. London: Kogan Page, 80–94.

—— Sammons, P., Stoll, L., Lewis, D., and Ecob, R. (1988). *School Matters: The Junior Years*. London: Paul Chapman.

Morton, G. (1996). 'Scottish Rights and "Centralisation" in the Mid-Nineteenth Century'. *Nations and Nationalism*, 2: 257–79.

—— (1998a). 'Civil Society, Municipal Government and the State: Enshrinement, Empowerment and Legitimacy. Scotland, 1800–1929'. *Urban History*, 25: 348–67.

—— (1998b). 'What If? The Significance of Scotland's Missing Nationalism in the Nineteenth Century', in D. Broun, R. J. Finlay, and M. Lynch (eds), *Image and Identity: The Making and Re-Making of Scotland Through the Ages*. Edinburgh: John Donald, 157–76.

—— (1999). *Unionist Nationalism*. East Linton: Tuckwell.

—— and Morris, R. J. (forthcoming). 'Civil Society, Governance and Nation: Scotland,

1830–1914', in R. Houston and W. Knox (eds), *Penguin History of Scotland*. Harmondsworth: Penguin.

Moser, C. (1998). 'The Asset Vulnerability Framework: Reassessing Urban Poverty Reduction Strategies'. *World Development*, 26/1: 1–19.

Mouqué, D. (1999). *Sixth Periodic Report on the Social and Economic Situation and Development of the Regions of the European Union*. Brussels: European Commission.

Mundo, P. A. (1992). *Interest Groups: Cases and Characteristics*. Chicago: Nelson Hall.

Munn, P. (1999a). 'The Darker Side of Pupil Culture', in J. Prosser (ed.), *School Culture*. London: Paul Chapman, 111–21.

—— (ed.) (1999b). *Promoting Positive Discipline in Scottish Schools*. Edinburgh: Faculty of Education, University of Edinburgh.

—— Cullen, M. A., Johnstone, M., and Lloyd, G. (1997). *Exclusions from School and In-School Alternatives*. Edinburgh: Scottish Office (Interchange No. 47).

—— Lloyd, G., and Cullen, M. A. (2000). *Alternatives to Exclusion from School*. London: Sage.

Muntaner, C. and Lynch, J. (1999). 'Income Inequality, Social Cohesion and Class Relations: A Critique of Wilkinson's Neo-Durkheimian Research Program'. *International Journal of Health Services*, 29/1: 59–81.

Murnane, R. and Levy, F. (1999). *Teaching the New Basic Skills*. New York: Free Press.

Nairn, T. (1977). *The Break-Up of Britain*. London: Verso.

—— (1997). *Faces of Nationalism*. London: Verso.

Naphapiet, J. and Ghoshal, S. (1997). *Social Capital, Intellectual Capital and Organizational Advantage* (Management Research Papers 97/6). Oxford: Oxford Centre for Management Studies.

Narayan, D. (1997). *Voices of the Poor: Poverty and Social Capital in Tanzania*, Environmentally and Socially Sustainable Development Studies and Monographs Series 20. Washington, DC: World Bank.

—— (1999). *Bonds and Bridges: Social Capital and Poverty* (Policy Research Working Paper 2167). Washington: World Bank.

—— and Pritchett, L. (1997). *Cents and Sociability: Household Income and Social Capital in Rural Tanzania* (Social Development Policy Research Working Paper No. 1796). Washington, DC: World Bank.

Nauck, B. (2000). 'Social Capital and Intergenerational Transmission of Cultural Capital Within a Regional Context', in J. Bynner and R. K. Silbersen (eds), *Adversity and Challenge in Life in the New Germany and in England*. London: Macmillan, 212–38.

Neal, D. (1997). 'The Effects of Catholic Secondary Schooling on Educational Achievement'. *Journal of Labor Economics*, 15/1, i: 98–123.

Newton, K (1976). *Second City Politics*. Oxford: Oxford University Press.

—— (1997). 'Social Capital and Democracy'. *American Behavioral Scientist*, 40/5: 575–86 (Special Edition: 'Social Capital, Civil Society and Contemporary Democracy').

Nielsen, K. and Pedersen, O. K. (1988). 'The Negotiated Economy. Ideal and History'. *Scandinavian Political Studies*, 2/11: 79–101.

Norris, P. (1996). 'Does Television Erode Social Capital? A Reply to Putnam'. *Political Science and Politics*, 29: 474–79.

Nye, J. S. (1997). 'In Government We Don't Trust'. *Foreign Policy*, 108/Fall: 99–111.

O'Neill B. J. (1987). *Social Inequality in a Portuguese Hamlet: Land, Late Marriage and Bastardy 1870–1978*. Cambridge: Cambridge University Press.

Organisation for Economic Co-operation and Development (OECD) (1998). *The Knowledge-Based Economy*. Paris: OECD.

Organisation for Economic Co-operation and Development (OECD) (1999). *Managing National Innovation Systems*. Paris: OECD.

Ofsted (1995). *Pupil Referral Units: The First Twelve Inspections*. London: Ofsted.

Ogbu, J. U. (1991). 'Immigrant and Involuntary Minorities in Comparative Perspective', in M. A. Gibson and J.U. Ogbu (eds), *Minority Status and Schooling: A Comparative Study of Immigrant and Involuntary Minorities*. New York: Garland, 3–36.

Olson, M. (1982). *The Rise and Decline of Nations: Economic Growth, Stagflation and Social Rigidities*. New Haven: Yale University Press.

Onyx, J. and Bullen, P. (1997). *Measuring Social Capital in Five Communities in New South Wales: An Analysis* (Working Paper 41). Sydney: Centre for Australian Community Organisations and Management, University of Technology, Sydney.

Orphanides, A. and Zervos, D. (1998). 'Myopia and Addictive Behaviour'. *The Economic Journal*, 108/446: 75–91.

Osler, A. and Hill, J. (1999). 'Exclusion from School and Racial Equality: An Examination of Government Proposals in the Light of Recent Research Evidence'. *Cambridge Journal of Education*, 29/1: 33–62.

Ostrom, E. (2000), 'Social Capital: A Fad or a Fundamental Concept?', in P. Dasgupta and I. Serageldin (eds), *Social Capital: A Multifaceted Perspective*. Washington, DC: World Bank, 172–214.

Pahl, R. and Spencer, L. (1997). 'The Politics of Friendship'. *Renewal*, 5/3/4: 100–7.

Parcel, T. L. and Menaghan, E.G. (1994). 'Early Parental Work, Family Social Capital and Early Childhood Outcomes'. *American Journal of Sociology*, 99/4: 972–1009.

Park, R. (1928). 'Human Migration and the Marginal Man'. *American Journal of Sociology*, 33: 881–93. Reprinted in Turner, R. H. (1967). *Robert E. Park: On Social Control and Collective Behavior*. Chicago: University of Chicago Press.

Parker, M. (1990). *Creating Shared Vision*. Illinois: Dialog International Ltd.

Parry, G., Moyser, G. and Day, N. (1992). *Political Participation and Democracy in Britain*. Cambridge: Cambridge University Press.

Parsons, C. (1996). 'Permanent Exclusions from School in England: Trends, Causes and Responses'. *Children and Society*, 10: 177–86.

—— (1999). *Education, Exclusion and Citizenship*. London: Routledge.

Parsons, T. (1959). 'The School Class as a Social System: Some of its Functions in American Society'. *Harvard Educational Review*, 29: 297–318.

Pateman, C. (1989). *The Disorder of Women: Democracy, Feminism and Political Theory*. Cambridge: Polity Press.

Paterson, L. (1994). *The Autonomy of Modern Scotland*. Edinburgh: Edinburgh University Press

—— and Wyn Jones, R. (1999). 'Does Civil Society Drive Constitutional Change? The Cases of Wales and Scotland', in B. Taylor and K. Thomson (eds), *Wales and Scotland: Nations Again?* Cardiff: University of Wales Press, 169–97.

Pattie, S. P. (1997). *Faith in History: Armenians Rebuilding Community*. Washington and London: Smithsonian Institution Press.

Pentzopoulos, D. (1962). *The Balkan Exchange of Minorities*. The Hague: Mouton.

Perkin, H. (1969). *The Origins of Modern English Society 1780–1880*. London: Routledge and Kegan Paul.

Phelps Brown, H. (1988). *Egalitarianism and the Generation of Inequality*. Oxford: Clarendon Press.

Phillipson, N. (1969). 'Nationalism and Ideology', in J. N. Wolfe (ed.), *Government and Nationalism in Scotland*. Edinburgh: Edinburgh University Press, 167–88.

—— (1983). 'The Pursuit of Virtue in Scottish University Education', in N. Phillipson (ed.), *Universities, Society and the Future*. Edinburgh: Edinburgh University Press, 87–109.

Piachaud, D. (1999). 'Progress on Poverty: Will Blair Deliver on Eliminating Child Poverty?'. *New Economy*, 6/3: 154–60.

Pierson, C. (1991). *Beyond the Welfare State?* Cambridge: Polity Press.

Platt, S. and Treneman, A. (1997). *The Feel Good Factor: A Citizens' Handbook for Improving your Quality of Life*. London: Channel 4 Television.

Politics and Society (1996). Special section of critical assessments of *Making Democracy Work*, with articles by Ellis Goldberg, Filippo Sabetti, Margaret Levi and Daniela Gobetti. *Politics and Society*, 24/1: 3–82.

Portes, A. (1987). 'The Social Origins of the Cuban Enclave Economy of Miami'. *Sociological Perspectives*, 30: 340–72.

—— (1995). 'Economic Sociology and the Sociology of Immigration: A Conceptual Overview', in A. Portes (ed.), *The Economic Sociology of Immigration*. New York: Russell Sage Foundation, 1–41.

—— (1998). 'Social Capital: Its Origins and Applications in Modern Sociology'. *Annual Review of Sociology*, 24: 1–24.

—— and Landolt, P. (1996). 'The Downside of Social Capital'. *The American Prospect*, 26: 18–21.

—— and MacLeod, D. (1996). 'Educational Progress of Children of Immigrants: The Roles of Class, Ethnicity, and School Context'. *Sociology of Education*, 69: 255–75.

Prahalad, C. K. and Hamel, G. (1990). 'The Core Competence of the Corporation'. *Harvard Business Review*, 3: 79–91.

Putnam, R. D. (1993a). *Making Democracy Work: Civic Traditions in Modern Italy*. Princeton: Princeton University Press.

—— (1993b). 'The Prosperous Community: Social Capital and Public Life'. *The American Prospect*, 4/13: 11–18.

—— (1995a). 'Bowling Alone: America's Declining Social Capital'. *Journal of Democracy*, 61: 65–78.

—— (1995b). 'Tuning In, Tuning Out: The Strange Disappearance of Social Capital in America'. *PS: Political Science and Politics*, 28/4: 664–83.

—— (1996). 'Who Killed Civic America?' *Prospect*, March: 66–72.

—— (1998a). 'The Distribution of Social Capital in Contemporary America'. Plenary Address to Michigan State University International Conference on Social Capital, 20–2 April.

—— (1998b), 'Foreword'. *Housing Policy Debate*, 9: i–viii.

—— (2000). *Bowling Alone: The Collapse and Revival of American Community*. New York: Simon Schuster.

Putzell, J. (1997). 'Accounting for the "Dark Side" of Social Capital: Reading Robert Putnam on Democracy'. *Journal of International Development*, 9/7: 939–49 (Special Issue on the Concept of Social Capital).

Ranson, S. (1993). 'Markets or Democracy for Education'. *British Journal of Educational Studies*, 41/4: 333–52.

—— and Stewart, J. (1994). *Management for the Public Domain*. London: Macmillan.

Read, D. (1961). *Press and People 1790–1850*. London: Arnold.

Reed, R. and DeFillippi, R. J. (1990). 'Causal Ambiguity, Barriers to Imitation and Sustainable Competitive Advantage'. *Academy of Management Review*, 1/15: 88–102.

Rees, G. (1997). 'Making a Learning Society: Education and Work in Industrial South Wales'. *Welsh Journal of Education*, 6/2: 4–16.

—— Fielder, S., and Rees, T. (1992). 'Employees' Access to Training Opportunities: Shaping the Social Structure of Labour Markets'. Paper to Seminar on Training and Recruitment, Royal Society of Arts, London.

—— Williamson, H., and Istance, D. (1996). ' "Status Zero": A Study of Jobless School-Leavers in South Wales'. *Research Papers in Education*, 11/2: 219–35.

—— Fevre, R., Furlong, J., and Gorard, S. (1997). 'History, Place and the Learning Society'. *Journal of Education Policy*, 12/6: 485–97.

Reich, R. (1991). *The Work of Nations*. London: Simon and Schuster.

Reid, T. (1969) [1785]. *Essays on the Intellectual Powers of Man*. Cambridge, MA: MIT Press.

Rhodes, R. A. W. (1996). 'The New Governance: Governing Without Government'. *Political Studies*, 44/4: 652–67.

Richardson, G..B. (1953). 'Imperfect Knowledge and Economic Efficiency'. *Oxford Economic Papers*, 5/2: 136–56.

—— (1972). 'The Organisation of Industry'. *Economic Journal*, 82: 883–96.

Riddell, S. (1997). 'The Concept of a Learning Society for Adults with Learning Difficulties'. Professorial Lecture, Napier University, Edinburgh, June.

—— Baron, S., and Wilson, A. (1999a). 'Captured Customers: People with Learning Difficulties in the Social Market'. *British Educational Research Journal*, 25/4: 445–61.

—— —— —— (1999b). 'Supported Employment in Scotland: Theory and Practice'. *Journal of Vocational Rehabilitation*, 12/3: 181–95.

—— —— —— (2000). 'The Meaning of the Learning Society for Adults with Learning Difficulties: Bold Rhetoric and Limited Opportunities', in F. Coffield (ed.), *Differing Visions of the Learning Society: Research Findings*, ii. Bristol: Policy Press.

Rifkin, J. (1996). *The End of Work*. New York: Tarcher/Putnam.

Rissel, C. (1994). 'Empowerment: The Holy Grail of Health Promotion?' *Health Promotion International*, 9/1: 39–45.

Robertson, J. (1990). 'The Legacy of Adam Smith: Government and Economic Development in the *Wealth of Nations*', in R. Bellamy (ed.), *Victorian Liberalism*. London: Routledge, 15–41.

Romer, P. M. (1987). 'Growth Based on Increasing Returns Due to Specialization'. *Papers of the American Economic Association*, 2/77: 56–62.

Rosenberg, N. (1972). *Technology and American Economic Growth*. White Plains, NY: Sharpe.

Rothstein, B. (forthcoming). 'Sweden—The Rise and Decline of Organized Social Capital', in R. D. Putnam (ed.), *A Decline of Social Capital? Political Culture as a Precondition for Democracy*. Gütersloh: Bertelsmann Verlag.

Rowthorn, B. (1992). 'Government Spending and Taxation in the Thatcher era', in J. Michie (ed.), *The Economic Legacy 1979–92*. London: Academic Press, 261–95.

Rubinstein, W. D. (1986), *Wealth and Inequality in Britain*. London: Faber and Faber.

Rule, J. (1992). *The Vital Century. England's Developing Economy 1715–1814*. Harlow: Longman.

Rumbaut, R. G. (1995). 'The New Californians: Comparative Research Findings on the Educational Progress of Immigrant Children', in R. G. Rumbaut and W. A. Cornelius (eds), *California's Immigrant Children: Theory, Research and Implications for Educational Policy*. San Diego: Center for U.S.-Mexican Studies, University of California.

—— (1997a). *Passages to Adulthood: The Adaptation of Children of Immigrants in Southern*

California. Report to the Russell Sage Foundation Board of Trustees from the project 'Children of Immigrants: The Adaptation Process of the Second Generation'. Project Site: San Diego, California.

—— (1997*b*). 'Assimilation and its Discontents: Between Rhetoric and Reality'. *International Migration Review*, 31/4: 923–60.

Runciman, W. G. (1998). *The Social Animal*. London: Harper Collins.

Rutter, M., Maugham, B., Mortimore, P. and Ouston, J. (1979). *Fifteen Thousand Hours: Secondary Schools and Their Effects on Children*. London: Paul Chapman.

Ryan, A. (1995). *John Dewey and the High Tide of American Liberalism*. New York: Norton.

Sabel, C. (1982). *Work and Politics*. Cambridge: Cambridge University Press.

Sabetti, F. (1996). 'Path Dependency and Civic Culture: Some Lessons from Italy about Interpreting Social Experiments'. *Politics and Society*, 24/1: 19–44.

Salamone, S. (1987). *In the Shadow of the Holy Mountain: The Genesis of a Rural Greek Community and its Refugee Heritage*. Boulder, CO: East European Monographs.

—— and Stanton, J. B. (1986). 'Introducing the Nikokyra: Ideality and Reality in Social Process', in J. Dubisch (ed.), *Gender and Power in Rural Greece*. Princeton: Princeton University Press, 97–120.

Sammons, P., Thomas, S., and Mortimore, P. (1997). *Forging Links: Effective Schools and Effective Departments*. London: Paul Chapman.

Sampson, R., Raudenbush, S., and Earls, F. (1997). 'Neighbourhoods and Violent Crime: A Multilevel Study of Collective Efficacy'. *Science*, 277: 918–24.

Sandefur, R. and Laumann, E. (1998). 'A Paradigm for Social Capital'. *Rationality and Society*, 10/4: 481–501.

Sanderson, M. (1972). 'Literacy and Social Mobility in the Industrial Revolution in England'. *Past and Present*, 56: 75–104.

Sassoon, D. (1996). *One Hundred Years of Socialism*. London: I. B. Tauris.

Saxenian, A. (1994). *Regional Advantage: Culture and Competition in Silicon Valley and Route 128*. Cambridge, MA: Harvard University Press.

Schiff, M. (1992). 'Social Capital, Labour Mobility, and Welfare: The Impact of Uniting States'. *Rationality and Society*, 4/2: 157–75.

Schofield, R. S. (1972). 'Crisis Mortality'. *Local Population Studies*, 9: 9–22.

—— (1981). 'Dimensions of Illiteracy in England 1750–1850', in H. J. Graff (ed.), *Literacy and Social Development in the West: A Reader*. Cambridge: Cambridge University Press, 201–13.

Schudson, M, (1996). 'What If Civic Life Didn't Die?' *The American Prospect*, 25/March–April: 17–20.

Schuller, T. (1997). 'Building Social Capital: Steps Towards a Learning Society'. *Scottish Affairs*, 19/Spring: 77–91.

—— (2000). 'Human and Social Capital: The Search for Appropriate Techno-methodology'. *Policy Studies*, 21/1: 25–35.

—— and Bamford, C. (2000). 'A Social Capital Approach to the Analysis of Continuing Education: Evidence from the UK Learning Society Research Programme'. *Oxford Review of Education*, 26/1: 5–20.

—— and J. Field (1998). 'Social Capital, Human Capital and the Learning Society'. *International Journal of Lifelong Education*, 17/4: 226–35.

—— —— (1999). 'Is There Divergence between Initial and Continuing Education in Scotland and Northern Ireland?' *Scottish Journal of Adult and Continuing Education*, 5/2: 61–76.

Schultz, A. (1995). 'Empowerment as a Multi-Level Construct: Perceived Control at the

Individual, Organisational and Community Levels'. *Health Educational Research: Theory and Practice*, 10/3: 309–27.

Schulz, T. W. (1961*a*). 'Investment in Human Capital'. *American Economic Review*, 51: 1–17.

—— (ed.) (1961*b*). *Investment in Human Beings*. Chicago: Chicago University Press.

Schumpeter, J. (1934). *The Theory of Economic Development*. Cambridge, MA: Harvard University Press.

Schutz, A. (1967). *The Phenomenology of the Social World*. London: Heinemann.

Scott, H. and Bolzman, C. (1999). 'Age in Exile: Europe's Older Refugees and Exiles', in A. Bloch and C. Levy (eds), *Refugees, Citizenship and Social Policy in Europe*. New York: St. Martin's Press, 168–86.

Scott, J. (1991). *Social Network Analysis: A Handbook*. Thousand Oaks: Sage.

Scott, P. H. (1989). *Cultural Independence*. Edinburgh: Scottish Centre for Economic and Social Research.

Scottish Consultative Committee on the Curriculum (SCCC) (1999). *Guidelines for the Curriculum of Secondary Schools*. Dundee: SCCC.

Scottish Office (1998). *Guidance on Issues Concerning Exclusion from School*, Circular No. 2/98. Edinburgh: Scottish Office.

—— (n.d.). *Social Inclusion: Opening the Door to a Better Scotland*. Edinburgh: Scottish Office.

Sehr, D. T. (1997). *Education for Public Democracy*. New York: State University of New York Press.

Seligman, A. B. (1992). *The Idea of Civil Society*. New York: The Free Press.

Senghaas, D. (1982). *Von Europa lernen*, Frankfurt am Main: Suhrkamp. Translated by K. H. Kimmig (1985) as *The European Experience: A Historical Critique of Development Theory*. Leamington Spa and Dover: Berg Publishers.

Sennett, R. (1998). *The Corrosion of Character: The Personal Consequences of Work in the New Capitalism*. New York: Norton.

—— and Cobb, J. (1977). *The Hidden Injuries of Class*. Cambridge: Cambridge University Press.

Shearmur, J. and Klein, D. B. (1997). 'Good Conduct in the Great Society: Adam Smith and the Role of Reputation', in: D. B. Klein (ed.), *Reputation: Studies in the Voluntary Elicitation of Good Conduct*. Ann Arbor: University of Michigan Press, 29–45.

Sher, R. B. (1985). *Church and University in the Scottish Enlightenment*. Edinburgh: Edinburgh University Press.

Shiell, A. and Hawe, P. (1996). 'Health Promotion Community Development and the Tyranny of Individualism'. *Health Economics*, 5: 241–7.

Similä, M. (1994). 'Andra generationens innvandrare i den svenska skolan', in R. Erikson and J. O. Jonsson (eds), *Sorteringen i skolan*. Stockholm: Carlssons.

Skocpol, T. (1996). 'Unravelling From Above'. *The American Prospect*, 25/March-April: 20–5.

—— (1997) 'America's Voluntary Groups Thrive in a National Network'. *The Brookings Review*, 15/4: 16–19.

Slack, P. (1988). *Poverty and Policy in Tudor and Stuart England*. Harlow: Addison Wesley Longman.

Sloan, D. (1971). *The Scottish Enlightenment and the American College Ideal*. New York: Teachers College Press.

Smith, A. (1976) [1776]. *An Enquiry into the Nature and Causes of the Wealth of Nations*, i, ed. R. Campbell and W. Todd. Oxford: Clarendon Press.

—— (1984) [1759]. *The Theory of Moral Sentiments*, ed. D. D. Raphael and A. L. Macfie. Indianapolis: Liberty Fund.

Smith, G. (1998). 'A Very Social Capital: Measuring the Vital Signs of Community Life in Newham', in B. Knight *et al.* (eds), *Building Civil Society: Current Initiatives in Voluntary Action.* West Malling: Charities Aid Foundation, 51–73.

Smith P., Morita Y., Junger-Tas J., Olweus D., Catalanot E., and Slee P. (eds) (1999). *The Nature of School Bullying: A Cross Cultural Perspective.* London: Routledge.

Social Exclusion Unit (1998). *Truancy and School Exclusion Report.* London: Stationery Office, cm 3957.

—— (1999). *Social Exclusion Unit: What It's All About?* www.cabinet-office.gov.uk/seu

Solomos, J. and Back, L. (1995). *Race, Politics and Social Change.* London: Routledge.

Solow, R. (2000). 'Notes on Social Capital and Economic Performance', in P. Dasgupta and I. Serageldin (eds), *Social Capital: A Multifaceted Perspective.* Washington, DC: World Bank, 6–10.

Somers, M. (1994). 'The Narrative Constitution of Identity: A Relational and Network Approach'. *Theory and Society*, 23: 605–49.

Spence, M. (1973). 'Job Market Signalling'. *Quarterly Journal of Economics*, 873: 355–74.

Spender, J. C. (1996). 'Making Knowledge the Basis of a Dynamic Theory of the Firm'. *Strategic Management Journal*, 17: 45–62.

Stalker, K., Baron, S., Riddell, S., and Wilkinson, H. (1999). 'Models of Disability: The Relationship between Theory and Practice in Non-Statutory Organisations'. *Critical Social Policy*, 19/1: 5–31.

Stanton-Salazar, R., and Dornbusch, S. (1995). 'Social Capital and the Reproduction of Inequality: Information Networks among Mexican-origin High School Students'. *Sociology of Education*, 68/2: 116–35.

Steinberg, L. (1997). *Beyond the Classroom.* New York: Simon and Schuster.

Sternberg, R., (1996). 'Myths, Countermyths, and Truths about Intelligence'. *Educational Research*, March: 11–16.

Stirling, M. (1992). 'How Many Pupils Are Being Excluded?' *British Journal of Special Education*, 19/4: 128–30.

Stockdale, J. (1995). 'The Self and Media Messages: Match or Mismatch?', in I. Markova and R. Farr (eds), *Representations of Health, Illness and Handicap.* London: Harwood, 31–48.

Stoker, G. (1997). 'Local Government Reform in Britain after Thatcher', in J. Lane (ed.), *Public Sector Reform.* London: Sage, 74–87.

—— (1998). 'Governance as Theory: Five Propositions'. *International Social Sciences Journal*, 155: 17–28.

—— and Young, S. (1993). *Cities in the 1990s.* Harlow: Longman.

Streeck, W. (1989). 'Skills and the Limits of Neo-Liberalism: The Enterprise of the Future as a Place of Learning'. *Work, Employment and Society*, 3/1: 89–104.

Sturgess, G. (1997). 'Taking Social Capital Seriously', in A. Norton, M. Latham, and S. G. Sturgess (eds), *Social Capital: The Individual, Civil Society and The State.* Sydney: Centre for Independent Studies, 49–83.

Suarez-Orozco, M. M. (1991). 'Immigrant Adaptation to Schooling: A Hispanic Case', in M. A. Gibson and J. U. Ogbu (eds), *Minority Status and Schooling: A Comparative Study of Immigrant and Involuntary Minorities.* New York: Garland, 37–62.

Swedberg, R. (ed.) (1990). *Economics and Sociology, Redefining Their Boundaries: Conversations with Economists and Sociologists,* Princeton: Princeton University Press.

Szreter, S. (1997a). 'Economic Growth, Disruption, Deprivation, Disease and Death: On the Importance of the Politics of Public Health'. *Population and Development Review*, 23: 693–728.

—— (1997*b*). 'British Economic Decline and Human Resources', in P. F. Clarke and R. C. Trebilcock (eds), *Understanding Decline: Perceptions and Realities of British Economic Performance*. Cambridge: Cambridge University Press, 73–102.

—— (1999). 'A New Political Economy for New Labour: The Importance of Social Capital'. *Renewal*, 7/1: 30–44.

—— and Mooney, G. (1998). 'Urbanisation, Mortality and the Standard of Living Debate: New Estimates of the Expectation of Life At Birth in Nineteenth-Century British Cities'. *Economic History Review*, 50: 84–112.

Tannen, D. (1990). *You Just Don't Understand: Women and Men In Conversation*. London: Virago.

Tarrow, S. (1996). 'Making Social Science Work Across Space and Time: A Critical Reflection on Robert Putnam's *Making Democracy Work*'. *American Political Science Review*, 90/2: 389–97.

Tawil, O., Verster, A. and O'Reilly, K. (1995). 'Enabling Approaches for HIV/AIDS Promotion: Can We Modify the Environment and Minimise the Risk?' *AIDS*, 9: 1299–306.

Tawney, R. (1982). *The Acquisitive Society*. Brighton: Wheatsheaf.

Taylor, M. (1997). *The Impact of Local Government Changes on the Voluntary and Community Sectors: New Perspectives on Local Government*. London: Joseph Rowntree Foundation.

Taylor, S. and Spencer, L. (1994). *Individuals Attitudes: Individual Commitment to Lifetime Learning: Report on Qualitative Phase*, Research Series No. 31. Sheffield: Employment Department.

Teachman, J., Paasch, K., and Carver, K. (1997). 'Social Capital and the Generation of Human Capital'. *Social Forces*, 75/4: 1343–59.

Temple, J. (1999). 'Initial Conditions, Social Capital, and Growth in Africa'. *Journal of African Economics*, 7/3: 309–47.

Terman, L. (1923). *Intelligence Tests and School Reorganisation*. New York: World Book Co.

Thane, P. (1982). *The Foundations of the Welfare State*. Harlow: Longman.

Thompson, E. P. (1967). 'Time, Work-Discipline and Industrial Capitalism'. *Past and Present*, 38: 56–97.

Tiryakin, E. (1998). 'Is There a Future for Sociology in the Global Age?'. Paper to British Association Conference, Cardiff University, September.

Titmuss, R.M. (1950). *Problems of Social Policy*. London: HMSO.

Tomer, J. (1987). *Organisational Capital: The Path to Higher Productivity and Well-Being*. Westport, CT: Praeger.

Tomlinson, S. (1991). 'Ethnicity and Educational Attainment in England: An Overview'. *Anthropology and Education Quarterly*, 22: 121–39.

Toumarkine, A. (1995). *Les Migrations des Populations Musulmanes Balkaniques en Anatolie (1876–1913)*. Istanboul: ISIS.

Tsouros, A. (ed.) (1990). *WHO Healthy Cities Project: A Project Becomes a Movement (Review of Progress 1987 to 1990)*. Copenhagen: WHO/FADL.

Urban Task Force (1999). *Towards an Urban Renaissance: Final Report of the Urban Task Force* (Lord Rogers of Riverside, Chair). London: Department of the Environment, Transport and the Regions.

Uphoff, N. (1996). *Learning from Gal Oya*. London: Intermediate Publications.

Vallet, L-A. and Caille, J. P. (1996). *Les Elèves Étrangers dans l'École et le Collège Français. Une Étude d'Ensemble*, Les Dossiers d'Éducations et Formations 67. Paris: INSEE.

van, Deth J. W. (1998). 'Introduction: Social Involvement and Democratic Politics', in J. W. van Deth (ed.), *Private Groups and Public Life: Social Participation, Voluntary Associations, and Political Involvement in Representative Democracies*. London: Routledge, 1–23.

—— and Kreuter, F. (1998). 'Membership of Voluntary Associations', in J. van Deth (ed.), *Comparative Politics: The Search for Equivalence in Comparative Politics*. London: Routledge, 135–55.

Verba, S. and Nie, N. (1972). *Participation in America: Political Democracy and Social Equality*. New York: Harper Row.

—— Schlozman, K. L., and Brady, H. (1995). *Voice and Equality: Civic Voluntarism in American Politics*. Cambridge, MA: Harvard University Press.

—— —— —— (1997). 'The Big Tilt: Participatory Inequality in America'. *The American Prospect*, 32/May–June: 74–80.

Vincent, C. and Tomlinson, S. (1997). 'Home-School Relationships: The Swarming of Disciplinary Mechanisms?' *British Educational Research Journal*, 23/3: 361–77.

Walker, J (1991). *Mobilizing Interest Groups in America: Patrons, Professions and Social Movements*. Ann Arbor: University of Michigan Press.

Warde, A., Martens, L., and Oben, W. (1999). 'Consumption and the Problem of Variety: Cultural Omnivorousness, Social Distinction and Dining Out'. *Sociology*, 33/1: 105–27.

Wayland, F. (1963) [1835]. *The Elements of Moral Science*, ed. J. L. Blau. Cambridge, MA: Harvard University Press.

Weil, S. W. (1986). 'Non-Traditional Learners within Traditional Higher Education Institutions: Discovery and Disappointment'. *Studies in Higher Education*, 11/3: 219–35.

Weisskopf, T. E. (1987). 'The Effect of Unemployment on Labor Productivity: An International Comparative Analysis'. *International Review of Applied Economics*, 1/1: 129–51.

Whetstone, A. E. (1981). *Scottish County Government in the Eighteenth and Nineteenth Centuries*. Edinburgh: John Donald.

Whitehead, A. (1996). *Exit Voice and Loyalty in City Communities*, Southampton Institute Professorial Lecture. Southampton: Southampton Institute.

Whiteley, P. (1999), 'The Origins of Social Capital', in J. van Deth, M. Maraffi, K. Newton and P. Whiteley (eds), *Social Capital and European Democracy*. London: Routledge, 3–24.

Whittington, K. E. (1998). 'Revisiting Tocqueville's America'. *American Behavioral Scientist*, 42/1: 21–32 (Special Edition: 'Beyond Tocqueville: Civil Society and Social Capital in Comparative Perspective').

Wilkinson, R. (1996). *Unhealthy Societies: The Affliction of Inequality*. London: Routledge.

—— (1999). 'Putting the Picture Together: Prosperity, Redistribution, Health, and Welfare', in M. Marmot and R. G. Wilkinson, *Social Determinants of Health*. Oxford: Oxford University Press, 256–74.

Williams, B., Campbell, C., and MacPhail, C. (1999). *Managing HIV/AIDS in South Africa: Lessons from Industrial Settings*. Johannesburg: CSIR.

Williamson, J. (1994). 'Coping with City Growth', in R. Floud and D. McCloskey (eds), *The Economic History of Britain Since 1700 (Vol. 1: 1700–1860)* (2nd edn). Cambridge: Cambridge University Press, 332–56.

Willis, P. (1977). *Learning to Labour*. Farnborough: Saxon House.

Wilson, W. J. (1987). *The Truly Disadvantaged: The Inner City, The Underclass and Public Policy*. Chicago: Chicago University Press.

Winter, S. G. (1987). 'Knowledge and Competence as Strategic Assets', in D. J. Teece (ed.), *The Competitive Challenge: Strategies for Industrial Innovation and Renewal.* Cambridge, MA: Ballinger, 159–83.

Withrington, D. J. (1988). ' "A Ferment of Change": Aspirations, Ideas and Ideals in Nineteenth-Century Scotland', in D. Gifford (ed.), *The History of Scottish Literature: Volume 3, Nineteenth Century.* Aberdeen: Aberdeen University Press, 43–63.

Woolcock, M. (1998). 'Social Capital and Economic Development: Toward a Theoretical Synthesis and Policy Framework'. *Theory and Society*, 27/1: 151–208.

—— (2000). *Using Social Capital: Getting the Social Relations Right in the Theory and Practice of Economic Development.* Princeton: Princeton University Press.

World Bank (1997). *Expanding the Measure of Wealth: Indicators of Environmentally Sustainable Development.* Washington, DC: World Bank.

—— (2000). *World Development Report.* Washington, DC: World Bank.

Wrigley, E. A. (1987). *People, Cities and Wealth: The Transformation of Traditional Society.* Blackwell: Oxford.

—— (1988). *Continuity, Chance and Change: The Character of the Industrial Revolution in England.* Cambridge: Cambridge University Press.

Yap, J. Y.-C. (1986). 'Refugee Trauma and Coping: A Study of a Group of Vietnamese Refugee Children Attending School in Southern England', unpublished Ph.D. thesis. London: Institute of Education, University of London.

Zhou, M. and Bankston, C. L. III (1994). 'Social Capital and the Adaptation of the Second Generation: The Case of Vietnamese Youth in New Orleans'. *International Migration Review*, 23/4: 821–45.

Zuboff, S. (1988). *In the Age of the Smart Machine.* New York: Basic Books.

INDEX

Note: **emboldened** page references indicate chapters.